T0408448

Cases on Global Innovative Practices for Reforming Education

Sriya Chakravarti
Higher Colleges of Technology, UAE

Bistra Boukareva
Higher Colleges of Technology, UAE

A volume in the Advances
in Educational Marketing,
Administration, and Leadership
(AEMAL) Book Series

Published in the United States of America by
    IGI Global
    Information Science Reference (an imprint of IGI Global)
    701 E. Chocolate Avenue
    Hershey PA, USA 17033
    Tel: 717-533-8845
    Fax: 717-533-8661
    E-mail: cust@igi-global.com
    Web site: http://www.igi-global.com

Library of Congress Cataloging-in-Publication Data

Title: Cases on global innovative practices for reforming education / Sriya
   Chakravarti and Bistra Boukareva, editors.
Description: Hershey, PA : Information Science Reference, 2022. | Includes
   bibliographical references and index. | Summary: "For contemporary
   educators affected by technological disruptions, looming pandemic,
   global financial woes and changing higher education structure and needs,
   this book is a snapshot of time capturing this transition towards
   delivering innovative and sustainable education worldwide"-- Provided by
   publisher.
Identifiers: LCCN 2021031874 (print) | LCCN 2021031875 (ebook) | ISBN
   9781799883104 (hardcover) | ISBN 9781799883111 (paperback) | ISBN
   9781799883128 (ebook)
Subjects: LCSH: Educational change--Cross-cultural studies. | Educational
   innovations--Cross-cultural studies. | Education and
   globalization--Cross-cultural studies.
Classification: LCC LB2806 .C317 2022 (print) | LCC LB2806 (ebook) | DDC
   370--dc23
LC record available at https://lccn.loc.gov/2021031874
LC ebook record available at https://lccn.loc.gov/2021031875

This book is published in the IGI Global book series Advances in Educational Marketing, Administration, and Leadership (AEMAL) (ISSN: 2326-9022; eISSN: 2326-9030)

British Cataloguing in Publication Data
A Cataloguing in Publication record for this book is available from the British Library.

For electronic access to this publication, please contact: eresources@igi-global.com.

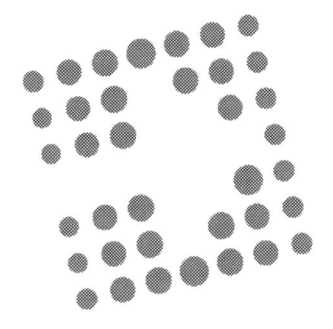

Advances in Educational Marketing, Administration, and Leadership (AEMAL) Book Series

ISSN:2326-9022
EISSN:2326-9030

Editor-in-Chief: Siran Mukerji IGNOU, India Purnendu Tripathi IGNOU, India

MISSION

With more educational institutions entering into public, higher, and professional education, the educational environment has grown increasingly competitive. With this increase in competitiveness has come the need for a greater focus on leadership within the institutions, on administrative handling of educational matters, and on the marketing of the services offered.

The **Advances in Educational Marketing, Administration, & Leadership (AEMAL) Book Series** strives to provide publications that address all these areas and present trending, current research to assist professionals, administrators, and others involved in the education sector in making their decisions.

COVERAGE

- Educational Finance
- Educational Leadership
- Consumer Behavior
- Students as Consumers
- Educational Marketing Campaigns
- Governance in P-12 and Higher Education
- Academic Administration
- Marketing Theories within Education
- Educational Management
- Technologies and Educational Marketing

IGI Global is currently accepting manuscripts for publication within this series. To submit a proposal for a volume in this series, please contact our Acquisition Editors at Acquisitions@igi-global.com or visit: http://www.igi-global.com/publish/.

Titles in this Series

For a list of additional titles in this series, please visit:
www.igi-global.com/book-series/advances-educational-marketing-administration-leadership/73677

Developing Entrepreneurial Ecosystems in Academia
Muhammad Nawaz Tunio (Greenwich University, Karachi, Pakistan & Alpen Adria University, Klagenfurt, Austria) Erum Shaikh (The University of Modern Sciences, Tando Muhammad Khan, Pakistan) Kiran Chaudhary (Shivaji College, University of Delhi, India) and Tiep Le Thanh (Ho Chi Minh City University of Economics and Finance, Vietnam)
Information Science Reference • © 2022 • 312pp • H/C (ISBN: 9781799885054) • US $195.00

Impact of School Shootings on Classroom Culture, Curriculum, and Learning
Gordon A. Crews (The University of Texas Rio Grande Valley, USA)
Information Science Reference • © 2022 • 355pp • H/C (ISBN: 9781799852001) • US $195.00

Policy and Practice Challenges for Equality in Education
Theresa Neimann (Oregon State University, USA) Jonathan J. Felix (RMIT University, Vietnam) Elena Shliakhovchuk (National Transport University, Ukraine) and Lynne L. Hindman (Oregon State University, USA)
Information Science Reference • © 2022 • 351pp • H/C (ISBN: 9781799873792) • US $195.00

Assessing University Governance and Policies in Relation to the COVID-19 Pandemic
Mansoor A. Alaali (Ahlia University, Bahrain)
Information Science Reference • © 2022 • 339pp • H/C (ISBN: 9781799882794) • US $195.00

Building Integrated Collaborative Relationships for Inclusive Learning Settings
Dena AuCoin (Purdue University Global, USA)
Information Science Reference • © 2021 • 316pp • H/C (ISBN: 9781799868163) • US $195.00

For an entire list of titles in this series, please visit:
www.igi-global.com/book-series/advances-educational-marketing-administration-leadership/73677

701 East Chocolate Avenue, Hershey, PA 17033, USA
Tel: 717-533-8845 x100 • Fax: 717-533-8661
E-Mail: cust@igi-global.com • www.igi-global.com

Table of Contents

Detailed Table of Contents

    Mahati Kopparla, University of Calgary, Canada
    Aditi Pathak, UNESCO Mahatma Gandhi Institute of Education for
        Peace and Sustainable Development, India

There is general recognition that 'Education has the power to transform the world' and equip young people to build a sustainable and peaceful world. As a step towards understanding the current state of education and collectively reimagining the future of education, a series of focus group discussions were conducted with students, teachers, and parents from all over the world. Eight prominent themes emerged from the participant discussion as follows: (1) education as a means to an end, (2) external influences on education system, (3) test centric system of education, (4) constrained curriculum and teaching practices, (5) education as a social and emotional activity, (6) school climate and power dynamics in the classroom, (7) educational infrastructure, and (8) technology and remote learning. Based on participant insights, the major issues in education, emerging innovative solutions, and recommendations for the future are discussed.

Chapter 2
    Tamar Davis Larsen, University of Colorado at Boulder, USA

College students and professors have experienced dramatic change in how they are able to attend and participate in classes, convey information, interact with one another, and teach in a meaningful, dynamic way. This chapter explores what worked and what did not work during this shift to online teaching as universities in the United States closed down for almost all in-person classes. Research includes narrative identity, with data derived from collecting stories of the lived experience during COVID-19. Topics explored are issues of how higher education relates to the traditional U.S. college experience, ethics, leadership, money, equitable technology, and mental health. Suggestions will be presented in terms of what can be learned from this particular crisis that can be enacted in framing better practices in higher education as future domestic and global crises emerge.

Martin Parsons, Hannan University, Japan
Mikel Garant, Beijing Institute of Technology, Zhuhai, China

The COVID-19 pandemic has thrown up many challenges to international cooperation, to the promotion of sustainable development, and indeed, to education. This chapter describes a telecollaborative project between university students in Japan and China. The students planned, wrote, recorded, and produced video podcasts on the theme of sustainable development, which were then exchanged via a password-protected, online, collaborative platform. On completion of the project, students wrote reflective essays, which are used here to gain insights into their impressions of topics such as sustainable development and telecollaboration. Results indicate that students improved their understanding of sustainability in addition to developing video editing and podcasting production skills. They also improved their pronunciation as well as other English skills. Overall, they were proud of their podcasts and enjoyed collaborating online with students from another country.

Sandra Gudino Paredes, Tecnologico de Monterrey, Mexico
Felipe J. Jasso Pena, Tecnologico de Monterrey, Mexico

In a global health pandemic context, a group 16 of education Master's students met voluntarily with their tutors in a virtual research support seminar, during the Saturday mornings of the first and second semester of 2020. This study aimed to know to what extent did mentoring and human tutoring characteristics emerge in a virtual research seminar experience. Through a qualitative research approach that included the analysis of the conversations and dialogues of the recorded sessions, insights showed that some of these characteristics emerged naturally along with the sessions, but as time passed, emotional and personal aspects were appearing more often than some others, showing that students felt more comfortable talking about themselves and supporting their classmates, as well as expressing their academic doubts and project thoughts freely because of humanistic tutoring approach. Most of them achieved the goal of finishing their project chapters on time. The humanistic and professional characteristics of teachers emerged as the main factors to develop this humanistic tutoring approach.

Chapter 5

    Emily Saavedra, Massey University, New Zealand
    Leonard Sanders, Massey University, New Zealand

Learning experiences and educational opportunities around the world have been disrupted due to the outbreak of COVID-19. This chapter outlines a case study involving foundation-level students enrolled at an urban university in Aotearoa New Zealand. The case study is designed to gain a deeper understanding of student experiences during this time of crisis. Student narratives are analysed to identify common experiences and gain a clearer understanding of the self-reported factors that students identified as affecting their success, allowing academic and support staff to improve the pre-degree experience for foundation students. Affordable access to connectivity, increased pastoral care, and a digitally responsive curriculum were identified as key considerations to addressing inequities present in a crisis context (COVID-19) within the educational context and wider community.

Chapter 6

    Rosalind Rice-Stevenson, Edinburgh Napier University, UK

Globalization and technology are two features of the modern world impacting all activity, and the resultant effect on education is causing much to be questioned about the teaching and learning paradigm. Ways in which the learning experience must change in response to changing global demands placed on societies and economies forms a large part of the current discourse around reforming education. This chapter puts forward a definition of globalization, 21st century skills, and the four main competencies known as the 4Cs, and then makes links between these phenomena as a way of understanding the digitization of education. The connections are possible through a process of gathering reflections and experiences from experienced educational practitioners.

The Bachelor of Science in physiotherapy is a four-year program that has been offered at The University of Jordan since 1999. Just like all other educational programs across the world, teaching pedagogy in this program underwent a major overhaul due to the COVID-19 pandemic. In this chapter, the changes implemented in this program due to the pandemic and a discussion of their different aspects are presented. First, an overview of traditional teaching model and all the changes it underwent during the first year of the pandemic are presented. After that, specific aspects of the changes are addressed in depth and discussed in light of evidence from the literature. These include changes made to clinical and practical education, modifications of assessment methods, and responses and adjustments of students and faculty members. The chapter concludes with recommendations for future implementation of online teaching in physiotherapy education.

Work-integrated learning (WIL) continues to be an essential topic of conversation among governments, educators, employers, and students. By various names and definitions, WIL attempts to inject the realism of workplace employment tasks into the post-secondary learning environment. The COVID-19 pandemic has forced stakeholders to innovate in the WIL space often using the advances in information and communications technologies (ICT) to build further bridges between learners and real work experiences. The chapter provides an overview of WIL followed by three specifics cases from marketing faculty at the Southern Alberta Institute of Technology (SAIT). In each of the three cases, faculty used different ICT to provide engaging learning environments linking business, industry, consumers, and the learners.

Online learning is accepted as an effective educational learning process that can respond to rapidly and constantly changing learner needs. Increasing the quality of online learning is an important point to be addressed. Within this context, motivation in online learning that affects what learners will learn, how they will learn, and when they will learn is one of the most important components because the motivation of learners has a very important place in terms of achieving desired goals in the learning and teaching process. It is not easy to continuously motivate learners in online learning process over a long period. Creating the motivation of everyone involved in the learning and teaching process is very important in terms of the efficiency and quality of the process. Within the context of a theoretical framework, "motivation," "motivation process," "types of motivation," "internal motivation," "extrinsic motivation," "the importance of motivation in education," and "motivation in online learning" were addressed in the present study.

This chapter describes an action research in which creative story writing was used to assess student understanding of graph construction. Students were encouraged to write stories involving motion and visually depict verbal descriptions of stories in the form of tables and line graphs. Student work revealed several misconceptions held by students vis-à-vis writing motion-based stories, tabulation of data, plotting of graphs, and establishing congruence between stories and graphs. This study suggests several feedback measures that can be used by teachers to rectify these misconceptions.

Preface

The contemporary education system is disrupted by the plethora of emerging technologies, the aftermath of the COVID-19 pandemic, global financial woes, and the ever-present shifting of higher education structuration and needs. There is a necessity for a marker to capture this transition in order to teach future generations how to recover educational losses in crisis situations.

Cases on Global Innovative Practices for Reforming Education broadens the perspective of global educators on innovative methodologies for ensuring the resilience of teaching and learning in the 21st century. Discussing teaching and learning cases from around the world, this research creates scholarship and documentation of various innovative practices in education, covering crisis contexts, green education, and education technologies. This book provides a valuable resource for educators, school administrators, K-university, educational researchers, educational software developers, textbook publishers, pre-service teachers, professors, academicians, organizations interested in funding educational initiatives, and national education policymakers.

The book comprises of nine chapters. Following is a brief summary on each:

Chapter 1 discusses the power of education and its ability to transform the world by equipping young people to build a sustainable and peaceful world. The authors of this chapter took a step towards understanding the current state of education and collectively reimagined the future of education through a series of focus group discussions with students, teachers, and parents from all over the world. Based on participant insights, the major issues in education, emerging innovative solutions and recommendations for the future are discussed in a detailed format in this chapter.

Chapter 2 debates reimagining education as response to the ongoing crises surrounding Covid 19 in the classrooms of United States. The author of the chapter delves and explores what worked and what did not work during this shift to online teaching as educational institutions closed down for almost all in-person classes. The chapter presents learnings and recommendations in terms of what can be learned from this particular crisis that can be enacted in framing better practices in higher education policies.

Chapter 3 presents an opportunity that presented itself during the pandemic. This chapter describes a tele collaborative project between university students in Japan and China. The students planned, wrote, recorded, and produced video podcasts on the theme of sustainable development. On completion of the project, students wrote reflective essays, to gain insights into their impressions of topics such as sustainable development and tele collaboration. Results indicate that students improved their understanding of sustainability in addition to developing video editing and podcasting production skills. They also improved their pronunciation as well as other English skills. Furthermore, they enjoyed collaborating online with students from another country.

Chapter 4 discusses humanistic tutoring approach that came about in virtual Mexico classes. A group of 16 education master students met voluntarily with their tutors in a virtual research support seminar. This study aimed to know: to what extent did mentoring and human tutoring characteristics emerge in a virtual research seminar experience? The research was qualitative in nature, and it included the analysis of the conversations and dialogues of the recorded sessions. Results indicated that students felt more comfortable talking about themselves and supporting their classmates, as well as expressing their academic doubts and project thoughts freely because of humanistic tutoring approach and most of them achieved the goal of finishing their project chapters on time. The study concluded that humanistic and professional characteristics of teachers emerged as the main factor to develop this humanistic tutoring approach.

Chapter 5 examines learning experiences of classes in New Zealand that felt disrupted by Covid 19. This chapter outlines a case study involving students enrolled at an urban university in Aotearoa New Zealand. The case study presents an understanding of student experiences during this time of crisis. Student narratives identified common experiences that affected their success, allowing academic and support staff to improve the educational experience for students. Affordable access to connectivity, increased pastoral care and a digitally responsive curriculum were identified as key considerations to addressing inequities present in a crisis context of the pandemic within the educational context and wider community.

Chapter 6 brings the element of globalization and technology in modern education. This chapter focusses on the digitization of education and reveals a unique perspective on the ways in which globalization is influencing education. Focusing on the integration of 21st century skills into a digitized learning environment from the perspective of experienced educational practitioners allows a view of their experiences as they strive to re-imagine education. The chapter aims to contribute to the views held by educators globally on innovative methodologies for ensuring the resilience of teaching and learning in the 21st century.

Chapter 7 presents the Jordan education disruption due to the pandemic. Bachelor of Science in physiotherapy is a four-year program at The University of Jordan since 1999. Just like all other educational programs across the world, teaching pedagogy in this program underwent a major overhaul due to Covid 19. The study presents changes implemented in this program due to the pandemic and concludes with recommendations for future implementation of online teaching in physiotherapy education.

Chapter 8 voices the approach of Canadian class programs during the pandemic. Work-Integrated Learning (WIL) continues to be an essential topic of conversation among governments, educators, employers, and students. By various names and definitions, WIL attempts to inject the realism of workplace employment tasks into the post-secondary learning environment. The Covid 19 pandemic forced stakeholders to innovate in the WIL space often using the advances in information and communications technologies (ICT) to build further bridges between learners and real work experiences. The chapter provides an overview of WIL followed by three specifics cases from marketing faculty at the Southern Alberta Institute of Technology (SAIT). In each of the three cases, faculty used different technologies to provide engaging learning environments linking business, industry, consumers, and the learners.

Chapter 9 focusses on the importance of motivation in online education, especially in light of the effect of pandemic on education. Creating the motivation of everyone involved in the learning and teaching process is very important in terms of the efficiency and quality of the process. Within the context of a theoretical framework, "Motivation", "Motivation Process", "Types of Motivation", "Internal Motivation", "Extrinsic Motivation", "The Importance of Motivation in Education", and "Motivation in online learning" were addressed in the study.

Chapter 10 discusses an action research in which creative story writing was used to impart 21st century skills and in due process assess student understanding of graph construction. Students were encouraged to write stories involving motion and visually depict verbal descriptions of stories in the form of tables and line graphs. The work revealed several misconceptions held by students vis-a-vis writing motion-based stories, tabulation of data, plotting of graphs, and establishing congruence between stories and graphs. The study suggested several feedback measures that can be used by teachers to rectify these misconceptions.

Each chapter of the book reflects an important aspect of meeting the book objectives. This manuscript is a valuable resource for educators, school administrators, K-university, educational researchers, educational software developers, textbook publishers, pre-service teachers, professors, academicians, organizations interested in funding educational initiatives, and national education policymakers.

The lessons learned in education via teaching in pandemic times through the use innovative digital tools; pedagogies, methodologies, humanistic mentoring, creative story writing etc. must lead educators to reflect on how education can be transformed now and in the future, so that it not only prepares students for the job market but also develops the full potential of students. Further research is needed on the topic of reforming education, as the pandemic eases and the world adjusts to the new normal. A deeper reflection and analysis of the pandemic education goals and policies will shed light on understanding the needs and wants of the post pandemic world.

Sriya Chakravarti
Higher Colleges of Technology, UAE

Acknowledgment

I have to start by thanking Shri Shyam Sundar, Ma *, my parents (Maj. Ashok Chakravarti and Mrs. Ruma Chakravarti for always believing in me. A special thanks to my brother Mr. Agrim Chakravarti for keeping my spirits high, all the contributors and reviewers from around the world and the elite educational community who supported this book project to reach its creative zenith.

Thank you so much, everyone!

Very gratefully,

Sriya Chakravarti
Higher Colleges of Technology, UAE

Chapter 1

Reimagining Education:
Perspectives From Students, Teachers, and Parents

Mahati Kopparla
University of Calgary, Canada

Aditi Pathak
UNESCO Mahatma Gandhi Institute of Education for Peace and Sustainable Development, India

EXECUTIVE SUMMARY

There is general recognition that 'Education has the power to transform the world' and equip young people to build a sustainable and peaceful world. As a step towards understanding the current state of education and collectively reimagining the future of education, a series of focus group discussions were conducted with students, teachers, and parents from all over the world. Eight prominent themes emerged from the participant discussion as follows: (1) education as a means to an end, (2) external influences on education system, (3) test centric system of education, (4) constrained curriculum and teaching practices, (5) education as a social and emotional activity, (6) school climate and power dynamics in the classroom, (7) educational infrastructure, and (8) technology and remote learning. Based on participant insights, the major issues in education, emerging innovative solutions, and recommendations for the future are discussed.

DOI: 10.4018/978-1-7998-8310-4.ch001

PROBLEM STATEMENT

Human societies have been marred with several issues of social and economic inequalities and continue to face newer challenges such as climate change and global pandemics. As much needs to be done to address global problems that we face individually, and collectively, there is general recognition that education has the power to transform the world and equip young people to build a sustainable and peaceful world (UNESCO, 2015). Thus, education is identified as a key factor in ensuring human flourishing in the generations to come.

By April 2020, the COVID-19 health crisis had affected more than 1.5 billion school students (UNESCO, 2020). There was disruption in the 'normal' way of being. Interventions such as social distancing impacted education systems with students affected the most. Nearly 90% of learners were unable to attend school with uncertainty on when effective schooling will resume. This statistic along with other global debates on education have renewed impetus to rethinking and reimagining education systems for the future.

While several questions about education today and for the future are worth contemplating, these questions cannot be answered in isolation and require participation and collaboration with the key stakeholders i.e., the students, teachers and the parents. As a step towards understanding and reimagining education, a series of focus group discussions were conducted with key stakeholders in education, i.e., the students, teachers and parents from all over the world. Through a thematic analysis of these focus group discussions, the major issues in education and emerging innovative solutions were identified.

EDUCATION SYSTEMS AND REFORMS

While education systems were present in civilizations around the world from 2000 BC, systems of modern mass education originated in 16th century Europe, and since then have been adapted in various forms world over (Bowen, 2018). During the 19th and 20th century, compulsory education gradually came to be mandated by most governments across the world. In 1948, education was recognized as a basic human right in the Universal Declaration of Human Rights (UDHR) by the United Nations General Assembly. Adapting and morphing with local and global changes through the years, the current education system is intricately situated within the existing socio-cultural, economic and political systems (Ghaffarzadegan, Larson & Hawley, 2017).

With constantly evolving societal needs, the purpose and expectations of receiving an education are often debated (Mayfield, 2019). This process of negotiating the ideals of education and restructuring the different components of the education system to achieve the ideal is broadly referred to as *education reform*. While most education reforms take a top-down approach driven by government policies, some are driven by non-governmental or international organizations, and a few others take a bottom-up approach driven by teachers or parents (Arnove, 2005). However, given the complexity of education systems, reforms face unique challenges during wider implementation (Honig, 2004; Shaked & Schechter, 2019). Based on observations from global educational reforms, Cummings (2010) explained the challenges of implementation:

Even after a seemingly dramatic educational reform, the memory of past ideals and practices will persist to exert influence on the new and even possibly at some later date to replace the new. Thus, educational reform, in its particulars, tends to turn inward reproducing and creating indigenous patterns, rather than outward, converging on internationally celebrated patterns (p.20).

Thus, the implications of reforms are often unfavorable, unforeseen or unintended, with the original vision of educational reform remaining unrealized (Murphy, 2017). While intentional educational reform is usually unsuccessful, changes in the society such as "changes in demographics, in social morals, in labor markets, in views of human rights and capacities, in legal codes, in gender roles – these over times do produce important and lasting changes in what schools do" (Levin, 2004, p.195).

Following decades of partially successful educational reforms, there is general sentiment that modern education systems are failing (Cabrera, 2016). Global education systems are converging towards "increased standardization, a narrowing of the curriculum to focus on core subjects/knowledge, the growth of high stakes accountability and the use of corporate management practices" (Fuller & Stevenson, 2019, p.1). A lack of agency and growing discontentment among educators is leading them to mechanically deliver curriculum while emotionally withdrawing from the education system (Goodson, 2007). Even though the pivotal role of teachers and societal factors in triggering educational change is unmistakable (Priestley & Drew, 2016), the voice of students, teachers, and parents remain unheard in developing educational policies and government reforms (Rentner, Kober, Frizzell & Ferguson, 2016). Education reform can greatly benefit by including the voices of teachers, students and parents that represent the views, opinions, and needs of the ever-changing society.

As a step towards understanding the complex education system and aiding meaningful change, this chapter presents traditionally unheard voices within the education system. Through engagement with students, teachers, and parents across the world, this chapter will systematically synthesize the discussions with stakeholders to:

1. Critically examine the existing education system
2. Collectively reimagine a functional and sustainable education system for the future
3. Make recommendations to educators and policy makers to move towards better systems of education.

METHODS

The research study began with an identification of the major themes, based on which the focus group protocol was developed. A series of focus group discussions were conducted with groups of students, teachers, and parents from the five UNESCO regions of the world. The discussions were transcribed and thematically analyzed.

Identification of themes

Under the overarching idea of Reimagining Education, four major themes were identified for the discussion with the stakeholders in line with UNESCO's Futures of Education initiative. Based on the four major themes identified, the research team iteratively prepared a semi-structured discussion protocol. The themes were as follow:

1. **Purpose of Education:** Purpose is defined here as the broader aim, meaning, reason and the end goal of education. This theme focuses on the "why" of education. Participants were encouraged to think about why people go to school or get an education.
2. **Overall experience of learning:** Experience includes any interaction, content, curriculum, pedagogies, knowledge, learning assessments and teaching methodologies that enable the process of learning. This theme focuses on the "what" and "how" of education. Under this theme, participants were given an opportunity to discuss some examples of things they like and dislike about teaching and learning, assessments and use of technology in education.
3. **Spaces of learning:** Spaces of learning could be the classroom, home, the street, the playground, online, or any other place where we learn. This theme focuses on the "where" in education. Under this theme, participants were encouraged to describe the important components of an ideal learning space and talk about what they liked or disliked about their current learning spaces.
4. **Education and Environment:** Environment refers to the natural, social, economic and political setting/surrounding where we live and where education takes place. This theme focuses on the external factors influencing education. Under this theme, participants discussed the relationship between the things learned in school and the environment or society around them.

Focus group discussions

The focus group discussions (FGD) were conducted in the 5 UNESCO regions (Africa, Arab States, Asia and the Pacific, Europe and North America, Latin America and the Caribbean) with 2 discussions in each region for each stakeholder group. Participants were selected through an open call and were required to submit a short write up to be able to participate in the discussion. The write up was evaluated by the project team and then invited for the discussion. Special attention was given to ensure gender balance and geographical distribution. Participants completed the informed consent and assent process prior to the FGD, informing them of the format of the FDG but not the specific questions. Each discussion consisted of 3-7 participants from the same stakeholder group and lasted for about 1.5 to 2 hours. In total, 32 FGDs were conducted in five regions with about a total of 170 participants (see Table 1). In some cases, discussions had to be cancelled at the last minute due to technical issues, no show, or other unforeseen circumstances. Even though efforts were made to compensate, there was an uneven distribution of groups. The data was collected between August and November 2020. Focus group discussions were transcribed by professionals who adhere to strict policies regarding confidentiality and anonymity.

Table 1. Details of participants included in the focus group discussions

Region	Number of participants		List of Countries
	By group	Total	
North America and Europe	Teachers: 11 Parents: 11 Students: 12	35	Canada, France, Germany, Great Britain, Greece, Mexico, Netherlands, Ukraine, United States of America (9 countries)
Asia and the Pacific	Teachers: 10 Parents: 12 Students: 12	34	Afghanistan, Australia, Bangladesh, Bhutan, India, Indonesia, Japan, Kyrgyzstan, Malaysia, Maldives, Philippines, South Korean, Sri Lanka (13 countries)
Africa	Teachers: 8 Parents: 14 Students: 12	34	Botswana, Congo, Ethiopia, Ghana, Kenya, Liberia, Nigeria, South Africa, Tanzania, Uganda, Zambia, Zimbabwe (12 countries)
Latin America and Caribbean	Teachers: 10 Parents: 12 Students: 12	34	Argentina, Belize, Brazil, Chile, Columbia, Jamaica, Venezuela (8 countries)
Middle East	Teachers: 9 Parents: 12 Students:12	33	Iran, Iraq, Saudi Arabia, Qatar, United Arab Emirates (6 countries)
Total		170	48 countries

Analysis

The data analysis was conducted with a combination of manual coding and machine learning algorithm. Initially, 10 transcripts were coded manually by a team of 3 coders. To establish inter-coder reliability, the first transcript was coded by all 3 coders in the team. Differences in codes were resolved through discussions. The initial set of 10 transcripts was broken down into excerpts and manually coded for inductive and deductive codes. Deductive codes were those that the research team identified ahead of time based on the four major themes - purpose, experience, learning spaces, and environment. Inductive codes were those that emerged from the data transcending the deductive codes such as "need for stakeholder agency", "connecting with real-life experience", and "social and emotional experiences". A machine learning model was trained on the data obtained from these 10 transcripts and was used to make predictions on the next 6 transcripts. These predictions were manually checked for new inductive codes and any coding errors by the machine learning model were rectified. The updated model was then used to code the rest of the transcripts.

Limitations

Education systems are large and complex with millions of students, teachers, administrators, and policy makers. This study composed of 170 participants was a humble effort to understand some global trends in education. While the researchers broadly compare the views and opinions of students, teachers and parents from different regions, the nuances in historical, social and political context of the individuals and associated education system were beyond the scope of this research.

FINDINGS

During the focus group discussion, the participants expressed their opinions on a wide range of issues in education. Through a thematic analysis, eight major themes were identified and each of the themes is discussed in detail along with key insights:

1. Education as a means to an end
2. External influences on education system
3. Test centric system of education
4. Constrained curriculum and teaching practices
5. Education as a social and emotional activity
6. School climate and power dynamics in the classroom

7. Educational infrastructure
8. Technology and remote learning.

Education as Means to an End

Attending school or receiving an education was the norm in societies around the world, often enforced by government laws and policies. The stakeholders had a clear vision of what education could do for them and viewed education as a means to an end.

Key insights

- Education is largely viewed as a system that produces individuals who can fit into the society, become employable and eventually live independently.
- There were regional differences in defining the purpose of education among teachers. While education was viewed as a source of empowerment in Asia, Middle East and Africa, it was viewed as a means of social and environmental change in North America, Europe, Latin America and Caribbean. These differences contributed to regional variances in the teaching-learning practices.
- There was potential for conflicting definitions of the purpose of education by the stakeholders and the government policy makers. In such cases, stakeholders expressed discontentment in the system and a need to redefine the purpose of education to ensure holistic development of individuals.

Participant voices

Students echoed the notion that education was important for a "secure", "bright", and "successful" future and schools helped them develop skills like literacy and knowledge about the world. Almost 40% of the students said that going to school 'gave them power', made them feel 'empowered' and provided them with tools that helped them to 'think for themselves'. Alisha, a 15-year-old girl from United States of America explained:

I would say at first, I went to school because I had to but now, I go to school because I just believe in general that Education gives you a lot of power. It helps you know what's real and what's fake and I think it's a really important skill in the world to be successful. You know I think the most successful people have a good background, a good education and are just able to think for themselves. I don't think a lot of people are able to think for themselves and you know other people are able to mess with that so I think it's important to have a good education for that reason.

Even though most parents viewed sending children to school as a customary practice, they recognized the numerous benefits and iterated the need for education. Overall, parents hoped that schooling would "lay a foundation" to help children to live independently and "fit into the society". Most parents largely viewed education as an "empowering tool" that not only "taps into the qualities and strengths of individuals" but also connects people from all over the world and opens up opportunities for collective evolution.

Parents were concerned that they would not be able to cater to all the needs of their children without schools. Carrie, mother of a child with learning disabilities from the Philippines, hoped that school will support her son to have "good living conditions in the future even though [she] may not always be there". Several parents from Asia-pacific and Africa explained that schooling bridges the gap between the limited skill set of parents and the unlimited opportunities present in the world:

All children do not have educated parents... the world is changing so fast and the way children need to be handled is changing so fast, but parents are the same one who are uneducated, they do not have the skills that are necessary to deal with the children as per their own needs. There is a conflict between [parents and children] ... Parents do not understand the psychological need of the children in this present generation (Naima, Bhutan).

About a tenth of the teachers used a historical perspective to point out that education was vital for the development of human civilization. Currently, education has become an inherent part of society and people without education "become almost like an outsider or outcast". Even though almost all teachers agreed that the purpose of education was to help students "fit in the society" and "lead meaningful lives", there were stark regional differences in teacher priorities while explaining the purpose of education.

Teachers from Africa strongly agreed that education provided them empowerment. Several participants from Asia-Pacific, Africa, Middle East and LAC mentioned that education provided them an opportunity to learn different languages and communicate their ideas with the world. They cited the example of being a part of the focus group discussions as an outcome of "being educated". A teacher, Manny, from the Middle East claimed that "formal education is the single greatest predictor of social mobility and economic empowerment". Several teachers from Asia-pacific agreed that the primary goal of education was to prepare students to ensure financial stability in the future. However, two teachers from Japan and Malaysia, believed that "the purpose of education is really to have fun" and to "create a society where people learn with inspiration and fun as opposed to just having second hand material and knowledge". Teachers from North America and Europe predominantly spoke about the need to prepare students to communicate and cooperate with others, while the teachers from Latin America and Caribbean emphasized the need for education to contribute towards better societies and environmental sustainability.

Both the parents and teachers felt that learners are sent to the schools to fit into the societal norms. Most of them agreed that the implicit reason for going to school was to ensure financial security. Schooling was equated with getting good grades and getting a good job. Nora from the UK explained that from a government perspective, the "purpose of education is economic purpose. It's to make sure that there is a work force in the future and so I think sometimes we lose the true purpose of education". To truly fit in the society, parents hoped that education should not only concentrate on academic knowledge and employability, but also equip students with key social and emotional skills such as decision making, problem solving, communication, relationship skills and critical thinking.

Several teachers were concerned that schooling is a very automated process "we all meet in the same paradigm break- school, work, life and somewhere in this, school is just kind of the first step in this path" (Maria, Ukraine). However, all stakeholders were confident that schools had great potential to contribute positively to the lives of students. Specifically, in the context of schooling, teachers saw a need to reexamine the purpose and consider alternative ways of educating students. Simon, a male educator from Sri Lanka who was aiming to build an alternate school system explained:

[going to school is] what everybody else is doing, so, it's sort of taken for granted that this is what you have to do. And in some cases, it is also forced by legislation that you have to go to school and parents could be fined if they don't let their children go to school. So, there's just a lot of inertia around it… that sort of question … 'is this the best way for a young person to spend thirteen years of their life' doesn't get probed well enough.

External Influences on Education

All participants recognized that there is an inseparable relationship between schools and society. However, a majority of the participants noted a dysfunctional relationship between schools and society. Ezra, a parent and teacher from Mexico explained metaphorically that schools and society have got "a divorce and they need to go to therapy" to recover their relationship.

Key insights

- Societal dynamics related to political affiliations, economic ideologies and social stereotypes are replicated in schools and constantly affect student experiences and education.
- Even though government policies play a pivotal role in driving educational change, societal factors such as public opinions and stereotypes can have a strong influence on the way policies are implemented.
- In recent times, students and youth have been claiming their power to drive social change. Schools and educators have the responsibility to expose students to contemporary social and political issues and provide spaces for dialogue.

Participant voices

Participants had recognized that a primary purpose of education was to fit in the society. So, they observed a strong relationship between societal dynamics and schooling. As students, parents and teachers are inherently a part of the society, schools are heavily influenced by societal values and norms. Several problems in society like discrimination, bias and inequality have constantly infiltrated education and controlled the dynamics within the education system. Several parents, students, and teachers were concerned that education was being treated as a commodity and that commercialization was denying quality education access to less privileged children:

school can be very discriminatory ...in a sense that if you didn't have money you would not be doing as great as if you did have money... if you don't have the money you don't have the resources, then school is not that great because a lot of students don't do that great in school and then they can't necessary move forward or go to the college that they want to go to, get their Degrees that want, get the jobs they want to go to all because of the background they come from (Shannon, a female student from the United states of America)

The political and social climate, government decisions about funding and policies have a significant impact on education. Parents from all regions recognized that educational materials were influenced by local governments and politics, sometimes overlooking the interests of the society. Teachers explained that they strived to cater according to the expectations of the society and policies even if it "conflicts with [their] personal philosophy of education".

Sometimes government policies made for equality and inclusion cannot be implemented effectively due to societal sentiments. For example, Poonam, a teacher from India explained that a government initiative to integrate economically disadvantaged children into private schools was unsuccessful due to opposition from affluent families. As a result, several teachers noticed that their schools were composed of homogenous populations of students who had a biased understanding of the dynamics and problems in the society. Few parents reported specifically choosing more diverse schools to educate their children not only academically, but also to become more conscious and learn "to navigate the society".

Even though society contributed to several problems within the education system, the role of societal factors on students' upbringing and education was indispensable. Quoting the popular saying, "it takes a village to raise a child", teachers and parents urged that everyone should take responsibility in developing the next generation of responsible adults:

the value that society places on education actually affects quality that has been delivered back to society...you have less budgeting given into the education sector you have demoralization of teachers and all that would come together to affect the quality of the education that the society would receive...[for] example, you have people who have done so well academically ... and [society] turns the other way and you have somebody who does something not exactly on the academic life but maybe something on the social aspect and then you reward him you make him an ambassador for youth and all that, you are sending a message to the society that education is not equally important. So, the younger ones will feel if I don't have to go through this process to be recognized. To be applauded I can cut corners and all that and make society applaud me. This shows how much a society values education that society would draw from (Ophelia, a mother from Nigeria).

A majority of participants believed in the potential of education and schooling to positively impact society with phrases such as "schools are agents of social change", "the real goal, or the mission of the school is social reform", and education empowers people "to seek a better life". Participants highlighted the need for schools and educators to take a more active role in recognizing and contributing to societal issues to bridge the gap between schools and society.

With students being at the forefront of the climate change movement and other recent political movements, parents and teachers noted the merits of exposing students to the realities of the society from a very young age to build empathy and tolerance. Some teachers suggested a "community service learning" approach to support student agency "especially for adolescents... because they want to do it, they have the right to do it and they have the tools".

Echoing the general sentiment of education policy makers, Vance, a father from the USA noted that "everyone thinks that they're an expert [in education] because they all went through it". However, the participants hoped for more agency for students, teachers and parents in educational matters to voice their opinions and collectively be a part of the solution. Finally, recognizing the existing clash between schooling and local cultures, teachers and parents urged for mutual respect between the two:

if we harness [education] correctly, it can bring values to all societies. but it must be done in a culturally [responsive] and sustainable way where we respect the society that you are trying to bring education to without kind of saying that education that you have is kind of subpar and all the skills that your learning has come down from generation like the mother tongue you learn from your generation is now not really what society out there needs (Thea from South Africa)

Test Centric System of Education

Education around the world is tending towards a system driven by tests and assessments. In line with quote "one can, albeit with difficulty, defy the effects of bad teaching but escaping the impact of bad assessments is onerous indeed" (Wattal & Singh, 2021, para. 2), the stakeholders highlighted the impacts of being a part of a test centric system of education.

Key insights

- Teachers noted that the education systems were currently test-centric as students' scores were used to evaluate teachers, schools and countries at large. The general competition at the global level was trickling down to students.
- Students considered the societal norm of judging them based on their test scores as unfair. Parents acknowledge that assessments cause a lot of stress and anxiety around assessments due to labeling of students and other discriminatory behavior. Teachers and parents should play a key role in identifying and supporting student's interests that are not assessed on traditional assessments by embracing a 'whole child assessment' framework.
- Parents and teachers acknowledged that the assessment centric systems were deeply rooted in the education system; but the extreme stress associated with these assessments can be reduced by consciously changing the narrative around test scores.

Participant voices

Teachers from all regions viewed assessments as "an essential part of school because we have to know where we are ... so that [we] know how to move forward" (Angie,

USA). However, many teachers were unhappy that the education system had become test-centric. While some parents like Hani from Malaysia noted that 'exams are bothersome' and the 'standards set by the government were very high', about a tenth of the teachers spoke about the inherent flaws in the idea behind large scale testing. They were not only a mechanism to evaluate students, but also to evaluate teachers. Miles, 33-year-old male teacher working in Brazil explained:

We are under a lot of pressure to show that the students are progressing and that pressure comes from the government ... Students must be making X amount of progress and if you cannot prove this you will be put under special measures.

Teachers were disappointed by the "lack of trust" in them and noted that the governments used "these formal examinations to try and create some sort of assurance to people outside that the education system" is functioning well (Nora, UK). Teachers were concerned that the global rankings and competition between countries is ultimately trickling down to create stress, pressure and anxiety for students and teachers.

Students described tests and exams as "stressful" events or "nightmares". They were under a lot of pressure to avoid performing poorly in exams as scores were "the only way the people [were] going to judge" them and treat them in prejudiced ways (Asher, Sri Lanka). Tests and exams were primarily used to create an atmosphere of competition. After facing the nervousness and anxiety, being able to perform better than their peers was enjoyable for some students. While some students from different regions felt pressured to write what the teachers 'want' or 'expect' instead of their own views and opinions, some other students tend to forget everything they have learnt and underperform in exams due to stress. Irrespective of their ability to perform, students felt that the current assessments were "too crude" to judge their ability to succeed in the future, or accurately evaluate their learning.

In agreement with students, most parents felt that the labelling was often discriminatory and would leave students "believing for life that they are worth nothing". Olfa, mother of a teenage boy from South Africa shared her concerns:

[students] cannot learn when they are driven by fear and anxiety that creates a society where every child is on anti-anxiety or antidepressant or a calmative or focusing pill. So, we are dealing with a society of young children who have to be medicated in order to learn, it doesn't make any sense to me.

Dismissing the idea of "dull children" parents hoped that assessments focused on students' strengths, making education more fun for them and pushing them in the right direction. Most parents and students across the regions agreed that 'assessments should aid learning'. Students hoped for assessments to move away from memorization and evaluate their ability to apply their knowledge to solve real world problems. Parents preferred formative assessments and more comprehensive evaluations that are not limited to academic grading only. Many parents suggested alternate tools of assessments for all K to 12 students such as observing students in their natural environment, how they interact with each other, how they observe and learn.

While most parents advocated for the reforms in the assessment system, with more active involvement of the students, a few parents from middle east and Asia pacific regions were satisfied with the current assessment systems and felt that "we turned out to be ok" and the status quo should work fine for their children as well.

Teachers collectively identified a need for reforms in the existing assessment system. However, as assessments were an important part of the educational experience, they cannot be changed independently from the rest of the educational experience. Some teachers from Asia-pacific region reported that they were unable to move away from the traditional way of testing and assigning grades as they had too many students to manage. However, several teachers suggested using "creativity and imagination" to adopt a "escape the test approach" (Maria, Ukraine). Few teachers from Africa and North America suggested using Project based or game-based assessments. Some teachers from Latin America and the Middle East suggested ways of using students' mistakes as opportunities for learning. Jacob, 46-year-old male teacher from Belize gave an example of a student who unknowingly recorded herself while explaining her confusion to her mother. When Jacob decided to grade her mistake, "she felt confident in what she was doing" and was "so happy!". Similarly, Yuri, a 54-year-old male teacher from Qatar had observed that students were more confident when they were allowed to self-assess, as students "feel trust [when] they give themselves the feedback and learn something."

In spite of their vision of ideal assessment systems, parents and teachers recognized the existing constraints of the education system. Parents particularly felt that rhetoric around assessments should change and parents need to take ownership of the 'pressure' it puts students under. In words of Lina, a mother from Kyrgyzstan:

assessment is standardized in each country. Honestly, I don't think it's easy to change. Since there is a standard setting which they have to keep in mind. I think it's more important how parents perceive assessment. I think as parents we need to change our attitude and even schools should change their attitude like if a student is getting grade F.

Constrained Curriculum and Teaching Practices

The students, teachers and parents felt that even after spending a considerable amount of time in school, most learners don't feel prepared to face life after school. Based on their experiences, stakeholders discussed some desirable changes in the education system.

Key insights

- All stakeholders recognized a lack of student agency in the learning process. While the school curricula are predefined, teachers realized a need to take into account students' learning interests and find ways to accommodate them into their classes.
- Students want to learn beyond the basic literacy and numeracy skills. They demanded discussions and exposure to topics such as sexuality, global political movements, and inter-cultural issues.
- Most parents felt that the primary objective of education systems was to aid students to obtain jobs, however this goal was often unmet by the current curriculum.

Participant voices

Successful schooling was globally equated with "more materialistic things, … getting good grades, … getting into good universities, … building a career". Parents were concerned that the current education system valued academic knowledge and degree certifications to "build a workforce" rather than develop informed and free thinkers. Anna, a mother of two teenage girls from Germany noted that children will "face even bigger problems" and unforeseen global challenges in the future, so, they have to learn "to think and innovate". Ironically, the outdated syllabus in schools were not preparing students for the real world:

you get the message again both as a parent and as an educator that 'oh, we're putting this focus on writing and math and reading because that's what they need in the job market'. But we know when we hear from CEOs that what they need in the job market is just the opposite and seeing people who can think critically and creatively and we're not producing that we're not encouraging children to do that in school (Emmette, a father from the US).

Similarly, students strongly agreed that "we have totally outlived" the utility of the education system, referring to the current state of the curriculum. Almost all the students who participated in the focused group discussions stressed on the importance of gaining "practical knowledge" over "theoretical concepts". Students demanded that education should prepare them for life by addressing concerns like exploring career options, "how to get a job", "how to rent an apartment", how to plan finances, and "how to pay taxes". They wanted to learn more about "real world issues" and more about "other cultures and countries".

Ultimately, students suggested education should "start going towards development of individuals" and teach them "to be a good human being". Most students felt that the schools in the current form were not 'inclusive' 'safe spaces' for discussions about a variety of topics such as sexuality and sexual preferences, as educators were hesitant to discuss taboo topics. Frustrated by the slow changes in the education system, a student from Sri Lanka voiced his lack of hope:

[these problems] of education system have been prevalent from very long time... it's also a bit disappointing that you know after all this education system and all these policies have been changed to a better one that we won't be able to benefit from that, during our school life

In agreement with parents and students, teachers recognized the general challenges with the education systems. Manny, a female teacher who works in North America and the Middle East explained:

Education in general is coming under this criticism as the world is stuck in fairly archaic models of what knowledge is required for success in life. We are treating subjects and disciplines as fairly arbitrary and not necessarily integrative into most people's practical life experiences

Teachers from all regions recognized that students lacked agency in the learning process. Even though education should equip students to survive independently in the world, teachers recognized that "a lot of the education system doesn't really nurture that agency" (Ivan, Bangladesh), describing it as a "prescription for failure" (Raylee, USA). Elementary school teachers identified that young children were "curious about a lot of things" (Isiri, India), but high school teachers observed that their students did not exhibit this curiosity anymore. Kiara, 53-year-old female teacher from USA elaborated:

to answer the question of what our students want to learn, they have no idea. They have no idea what they want to learn. They've been told, they've been tracked, they've been put into classes because somebody somewhere the guidance counsellor or somebody said that you know, you need to take this class in order to be successful.

As a step towards promoting student agency, there is a need for dialogue within the classroom instead of a "monologue from the teacher to students" (Maria, Ukraine).

Education as a Social and Emotional Activity

Most parents, students and teachers acknowledged that the role of education should not be limited to instill academic knowledge. The stakeholders viewed education as a social and emotional activity and demanded that schools should ensure 'Social and Emotional' well-being of the learners while equipping the learners with necessary SE skills.

Key insights

- An important aspect of education for students is to navigate social situations and understand personal strengths and weaknesses.
- Learning is not only limited to intellectual activities, but strongly influenced by the social and emotional experiences during learning.
- In conjunction with academics, supporting mental health and social and emotional well-being of the learners should be a primary objective of the education system. In other words, Social and emotional learning needs to be mainstreamed in education systems.

Participant voices

Most students said that apart from "gaining knowledge and skills", school plays a very important role in helping them acquire social skills as it provides an opportunity to meet and engage with their peers. Students also stressed on the importance of 'interaction' with their peers and teachers as they feel that the engagement gains them skills such as "problem solving", "self-management" and "ability to work together with different people".

Almost all teachers recognized that the learning at school is not only academic knowledge from books but also from their social and emotional experiences. A teacher Rylee from the USA reiterated, "we know that the learning is social and it's emotional so we have to create these rich learning experiences in innovative ways". Some other teachers from Europe, North America, Latin America and Caribbean noticed that students want to discover more about themselves and how to fit into the world. Kora, a 39-year-old female Montessori teacher from Columbia explained:

The whole motivation of students is discovery, not just discovering at an intellectual way but also discovering how I can get this person to like me or how can I be his friend or be his girlfriend or stuff like that. discovering ways of getting stuff done and learning about yourself.

Teachers were often concerned that important aspects of student development were getting lost in the complex education systems. While young children have the opportunity for a balance between their academic and social life, school interferes with organic development of children in higher grades. Mugo from Kenya explained that students sometimes are not able to even interact with their parents and siblings, "because it is homework, homework, one teacher after another one". Several teachers like Denise, a female teacher from Qatar, noted that students' needs were often unmet by schools:

There is no other species on this planet that needs to learn how to survive or live or exist. They do it, but we have complicated the process because we are not in touch with our true self. And to find that true self, we need to be more connected to our immediate surroundings, family, values, and what schooling has done is take out all that from us.

Since the participants identified "a mismatch between [the current education] system designed for efficiency and the human need to find your space or place in the world", teachers and parents considered it of utmost importance to "consider [students] have a life as children and they should have a more meaningful life as children as well". Thus, the responsibility of schools was not only to equip students with degrees for the future, but provide them with meaningful life experiences in school itself.

Similarly, most students stressed on the importance of mental health and echoed the notion that schools are not doing enough for the social and emotional well being of the students. Students stressed on the importance of "caring more for the mental health of the students" and providing tools to the students to "manage relationships, stress and emotions". A young female student from the United States shared,

I just hope that relationships and school could change so that schools may care more about mental health and more about the person outside of school, and they also care about education but also about what people have going on outside of school because that can impact the person a lot. So, I just hope to see like a change in everything that teachers care about

Even when teachers saw a need for supporting some additional competencies such as social and emotional skills, they were constrained by the slow changes in the education systems:

We have this gap where we are still learning hard skills without asking any questions. Why are we not putting the course on emotional intelligence, for example meditation, consciousness or how to make decisions, how to become, how to use your personal time, how to sit well ... [there is] around may be 50 years of positive research on it specially on social learning, social emotional learning and we still not putting inside of our academic programs ... because it's very difficult to move and change system (Alesia, Ukraine)

School Climate and Power Dynamics in the Classroom

Several participants identified the need for the school climate to be a 'safe space' for students. Components of a safe space included an environment where students could express themselves freely, learn from their experiences and mistakes, and become "lifelong learners to continue to learn and grow in their development as human beings". Peers and teachers were the major factors contributing to the school climate.

Key insights

- Students feel a sense of belonging in learning spaces when they establish strong, respectful and inclusive relationships with their peers and teachers.
- Role of the teachers is critical not only in influencing the learning experience, but also in the overall development of children. Biases or negative comments from the teachers can scar students for life and have devastating effects on them.
- Teachers have the responsibility to acknowledge an unequal power dynamic within the classroom and act cautiously.

Participant voices

Most students agreed that relationships with peers was critical in developing a sense of belonging at school. Some students like Alexie from UAE described their motivation for going to school was to "meet friends" and "have a fun time" as friendships were "the best" part of life at school. Some other students like Max from Mexico noted that through interactions with their friends, they learn to respect people, take care of them and be better people. For several students like Sri from India, their peers were a strong support group, "because they are still there for [them], through everything". However, in rare cases, peers negatively contributed to students' experiences due to instances of bullying.

All stakeholders noted the pivotal role of teachers who "orchestrate everything in the classroom". As students constantly observe their teachers, everything about a teacher's behavior including their smile impacts the students. Parents were concerned about the impact of unconscious bias and stereotypes held by the teachers on their children and their future career paths. Highlighting the trend of categorizing students based on their academic abilities, Thomas, father from the US shared:

There are teachers and there are systems of Education that along the way make us feel lesser than we are, make us feel dumb. Making someone feel a certain way. Like those feelings get deep rooted into our beings into our minds and our hearts and we live with this this belief, this self-view that can deeply limit who we are

Several students from all regions provided instances of biased treatment. Some students reported that a gender bias was restricting female students' from using school resources and choosing specific sports, while some others noted biased grading. For example, Karina, a student from Germany noted that she received a better grade than her friend who "wrote down similar things" in a test because of teacher favoritism and wished that teachers would actually grade the work and "not just who you are". Students often associate a teacher with an "open mind", who could relate to them in terms of real-life experiences, as a better teacher rather than a teacher who knows the subject very well. Broadly classifying teachers and describing an ideal teacher, Rajesh from Bangladesh explained:

The teachers in our school are in two opposite directions, [teachers] in center, balanced out are very rare. So, one side is evil, egoistic and angry all the time and very strict teachers. What I mean by egoistic is that if you point out their mistake, they will take us out of the class, scold us. The other side is the teachers who do not say anything to students, those teachers are the teachers who are taken advantage of and my school people bully those types of teachers...So, it's very rare to find teachers in our schools who are friends to you, only at times like when it's necessary admitting their mistakes and helping the students out. And those are the teachers that all would like.

Some teachers like Jordan from Columbia suggested that teachers have the responsibility to build better relationships with their students by becoming aware of their own values:

adolescents have ways to communicate and sometimes when we are not prepared [or] don't know ourselves and our fears or weaknesses we just shout at them and ask them to sit down... so that is where the problem remains ... because as soon as some voices began to raise up in their ways, it's easier to shut them down. so, it is important to understand ourselves better and know yourself better and the characteristics of every stage of development of students.

Further, by changing the norms of the traditional classroom and encouraging "two-way conversation", teachers can motivate their students and indicate that students are "important enough", "significant enough" and their "opinions and questions matter".

Educational infrastructure

Key insights

- Participants from all regions indicated that physical learning space was an important factor in their overall educational experience.
- Several schools in Asia-pacific and Africa regions had inadequate infrastructure in terms of school building, furniture and basic educational resources.
- Allowing flexible use of resources available inside and outside the classroom could benefit the teaching - learning experience in all regions of the world.

Participant voices

All participants felt that learning spaces are critical to student's learning and attention to the physical environment is necessary to create a conducive environment for learning. Teachers from all regions noted that ensuring a safe physical space for students was their primary concern as educators. Teachers especially from Africa and Asia-pacific mentioned existing challenges with infrastructure. Aurora, a 34-year-old educator from Nigeria explained that commercialization of education had led to establishment of private schools that educated students from "just three-bedroom apartments" with several partitions for classrooms. These types of arrangements were very restrictive and difficult for students to learn in. Several participants noticed that the elements within the learning spaces and their arrangement could shape the overall classroom dynamics. Simon, an educational entrepreneur from Sri Lanka elaborated:

In the typical classroom setup, children [are seated] in rows and teacher [is] in front of the blackboard ... There is a power dynamic that comes when someone is standing in front [and] you are seated and facing the person, and you essentially need permission to talk to somebody else or get up to go to the toilet, that kind of thing.

In an effort to move away from the typical teacher-led classrooms and promote "engagement and social interaction between the teachers and the students", parents and students suggested flexible seating arrangements such as sitting in groups or in a circle. Highlighting the limitations of rigid classroom arrangements, Elizabeth, mother of a teenage boy from Canada explained:

Some of [the students] adapt easily to sitting in a chair for long hours and then others, if we restrict kids from moving, then they're going to not be able to concentrate anymore. Because that's just how they learn, a lot of kids learn by doing. And if we just make them sit and listen, they're not going to succeed in their going to be labeled as the failure.

Students, teachers and parents collectively identified some key components of a classroom that was ideal for learning activities:

- Ample natural light or good lighting
- Well ventilated classrooms with comfortable temperature
- Not crowded and congested with a reasonable student-teacher ratio
- Comfortable and flexible seating for the students
- Colorful walls in the classroom and display of paintings, artworks from the children
- Access to green space or inclusion of indoor plants in the classroom

A few students and parents mentioned that having subject wise classrooms helps students learn better as students "associate learning with the learning space" and the subject related things present there. Further, participants emphasized the idea that learning spaces need to be more than a physical arrangement of objects:

This place should inspire, motivate to learn, to search, to study, to create and I need to give this opportunity starting from the classroom... walls with stickers, posters, some kind of quotes... it's always changing. It's like moving, you can feel the life inside of this ... For me it's not the class, it's not just a box, it's not just a room, it's a space and we need to fill this space with a lot of opportunities for kids (Maria, teacher from Ukraine).

Teachers and parents noted that there were global trends in designing classrooms and learning environments. Along with "taking children away from nature and putting them more and more into four walls of concrete", school systems looked to adapt classroom structures used in other successful education systems. Participants noted that these trends are far from effective and called for more initiates to draw on local culture and resources to design their learning spaces.

Teachers shared examples of using flexible classroom arrangements in low resource scenarios such as replacing old uncomfortable chairs with a carpet (Pardaj, a teacher from Afghanistan), and using nature and outdoors to ensure an enjoyable learning space:

some of the schools in rural Uganda where there wasn't electricity, there were very great classes ... for example, the teacher had made a giant compass in the compound where the children were moving around the compass in different ways giving each other challenges... [there was another] science lesson, which was built around the whole story [on] ...how could you separate the sugar and the dirt and they did this practically (Lia, Scottish teacher working in Uganda).

While more than 70% of the children reported to enjoy learning in an outdoor environment or green space, teachers noted that school management and leadership were often hesitant to approve or allow non-traditional classroom structures.

Educational Technology and Remote Learning

Using online modes of teaching was the new norm due to the COVID-19 Pandemic. As the focus group discussions were conducted between August and November of 2020, the experiences of the stakeholders with educational technology were influenced by the use of remote learning during the pandemic.

Key insights

- Use of educational technology such as the internet challenges the traditional notion of "teacher as a gatekeeper of knowledge" and promotes student agency in learning.
- Technology enhances the teaching-learning processes in innovative ways. However, digital tools and resources should be used cautiously to supplement traditional teaching, but not as a replacement.
- Along with technology literacy, students should be informed of the health risks associated with technology use and trained to use devices responsibly.

Participant voices

All participants observed the ubiquitous role of technology in the world and viewed technology literacy as a necessary component of education. While all students were using technology for remote education, most students from Africa and few students from the middle east reported a lack of technology use at school prior to the COVID-19 pandemic. The stakeholders collectively identified the prominent constraints for educational use of technology such as (a) limited access to devices and internet, (b) restrictive school policies, and (c) gaps in teachers' technology literacy.

Most teachers from Asia-pacific, North America, Europe and LAC expressed enthusiasm about the possibilities of technology in revolutionizing teaching and learning practices. Parents and teachers were excited by the possibilities of multimodal digital learning that can effectively cater to learners with different abilities and learning preferences. In contrast to other rigid educational policies imposed by the government, teachers viewed that emergency online teaching during the pandemic could provide them with opportunities for educational innovations from bottom up. More than 60% of the students reported that technology supported their learning experience by providing them new opportunities to gain knowledge and more agency to choose the 'what', 'when' and 'how' to learn. However, teachers advised caution in choosing digital tools for education, as some common applications such as YouTube "designed to become aggressively more extreme" might lead students to incorrect or biased information when used without guidance.

Completely online classes presented unique challenges for teachers in different regions. Several teachers from Africa and the Middle East and few teachers from Asia-pacific emphasized the need to continue traditional face-to-face teaching with physical educational materials given the embedded socioeconomic inequalities within the society. Particularly in households with several children, parents struggled to ensure access and a suitable learning environment for all learners. Teachers from all regions expressed concerns over virtually occupying students' personal space. Teachers from North America and the Middle East were concerned that data privacy laws prevented them from seeing the students and their body language, thus interfering with their communication and teaching.

Due to mandatory remote classrooms, most students went from almost "zero screen time during the school week and limited on the weekends, to full screen time". While an overwhelming majority of the parents were concerned about the health risks of prolonged device use, several students reported a fatigue of digital interactions. Students felt that some remote schooling practices kept them under constant surveillance, but lack of personal connection with teachers and peers leading to a feeling of social isolation.

In the midst of rapid technological advancements and automation, the question of whether technology will radically shape our education system has been constantly examined (Selwyn, 2019). While all participants recognized the role of digital technology in education for the future, less than 1% of the participants described a future education system without traditional school buildings and teachers. In this futuristic view, there is an extreme reliance on devices and the internet for educational activities (Elayyan, 2021). However, an overwhelming majority of the participants did not view this as a desirable direction for education. Instead, participants hoped for a hybrid of technologically innovative and traditional ways of teaching. Further, two teachers, Ezra from Mexico and Mugo from Kenya expressed a need to redefine technology for education. By going beyond "technology related to computers" they suggest imagining creative technology to close access gaps (such as assistive technology for physically challenged students), rather than amplify the existing gaps.

CONCLUSION

Education was primarily viewed as a means to ensure financial stability and independence by preparing children for real life. Students, teachers and parents from different regions of the world unanimously agreed that education, in its current form, was overly focusing on academic knowledge and standardized tests while ignoring important aspects of children's overall development. Due to the test centric nature of the education system, teachers often felt overburdened and micromanaged, while their agency to contribute towards educational change was severely limited. Similarly, students appreciated the opportunity to receive education, but felt limited by the rigidity of the system.

DISCUSSION

Globalization has provided opportunities for countries to share knowledge and educational practices, but also created an atmosphere of comparison and competition between nations. Competitive international assessments such as Trends in International Mathematics and Science Study (TIMSS) and Programme for International Student Assessment (PISA) are increasingly used by several countries to evaluate their education system and drive policy changes (Kijima & Lipscy, 2020). The convergence of education systems around the world towards a globalized ideal education system has created tensions between standardizing education and promoting quality education according to student needs (Sahlberg, 2006). These tensions were very apparent in the stakeholder discussions when students, teachers, and parents expressed their concerns with the current education system. Stakeholders from all regions were concerned that the test centric approach to education limits the focus to performance on standardized tests in few subjects. The curriculum overly focused on academic knowledge and skills that improve test performance and ignored social and emotional wellbeing, real-life events, practical skills and applications of knowledge. At the policy level, there is a strong need to reevaluate the role of assessments and adverse effects of standardized testing.

The crucial role of education and educated citizenry in improving the economic competency of nations is widely accepted. However, an emerging body of literature is challenging this view by positioning education towards human flourishing instead of economic dominance (Bang, M., & Vossoughi, 2016; Gutiérrez & Jurow, 2016; Takeuchi, Sengupta, Shanahan, Adams & Hachem, 2020). Participants echoed this sentiment. Students came to school from unique social, political and historical backgrounds. However, students all over the world were restricted to similar subject content at school that often ignored their rich lived experiences. As a result, participants questioned if the education system in its current form was adequate to support the achievement of their individual life goals. In order to fill the gap between national curriculum objectives and local student needs, education systems should support the agency of students, teachers and schools in locally altering curriculum requirements and teaching practices.

In a world that is increasingly focusing on quantification, ranking, efficiency and optimization, there is a need to approach education and educational reform in a more nuanced way. We recommend that education systems around the world shift their focus away from global comparison and refocus on meeting local needs. Ensuring the well-being and personal growth of students and teachers must be an educational priority rather than mass production of "educated" citizens. Finally, the key stakeholders in education must be afforded opportunities to contribute to educational change in various capacities.

ACKNOWLEDGMENT

This research was supported by the UNESCO Mahatma Gandhi Institute of Education for Peace and Sustainability (MGIEP). The views, thoughts, and opinions expressed in this article belong solely to the authors and do not reflect the views of UNESCO MGIEP.

REFERENCES

Arnove, R. F. (2005). To what ends: Educational reform around the world. *Indiana Journal of Global Legal Studies, 12*(1), 79–95. doi:10.2979/gls.2005.12.1.79

Bang, M., & Vossoughi, S. (2016). *Participatory design research and educational justice: Studying learning and relations within social change making.* Academic Press.

Bowen, J. (2018). *A History of Western Education: The Ancient World: Orient and Mediterranean 2000 BC–AD 1054*. Routledge. doi:10.4324/9781315016221

Cabrera, J. (2016). *Factors of Failure in National Education Systems Reforms*. https://www.academia.edu/27118771/Factors_of_Failure_in_National_Education_Systems_Reforms_2nd_Draft_

Cummings, W. K. (2010). How Educational Systems Form and Reform. In J. Zajda & M.A. Geo-JaJa (Eds.), The politics of education reforms (pp. 19-39). Springer. doi:10.1007/978-90-481-3218-8_2

Elayyan, S. (2021). The future of education according to the fourth industrial revolution. *Journal of Educational Technology and Online Learning*, *4*(1), 23–30.

Fuller, K., & Stevenson, H. (2019). Global education reform: Understanding the movement. *Educational Review*, *71*(1), 1–4. doi:10.1080/00131911.2019.1532718

Ghaffarzadegan, N., Larson, R., & Hawley, J. (2017). Education as a complex system. *Systems Research and Behavioral Science*, *34*(3), 211–215. doi:10.1002res.2405 PMID:28522920

Goodson, I. (2007). All the lonely people: The struggle for private meaning and public purpose in education. *Critical Studies in Education*, *48*(1), 131–148. doi:10.1080/17508480601120954

Gutiérrez, K. D., & Jurow, A. S. (2016). Social design experiments: Toward equity by design. *Journal of the Learning Sciences*, *25*(4), 565–598. doi:10.1080/10508406.2016.1204548

Honig, M. I. (2004). Where's the "up" in bottom-up reform? *Educational Policy*, *18*(4), 527–561. doi:10.1177/0895904804266640

Kijima, R., & Lipscy, P. Y. (2020). International assessments and education policy: Evidence from an elite survey. In J. Kelley & B. Simmons (Eds.), *The Power of global performance indicators* (pp. 174–202). Cambridge University Press. doi:10.1017/9781108763493.007

Levin, B. (2004). *Reforming education: From origins to outcomes*. Routledge. doi:10.4324/9780203482193

Mayfield, B. (2019). *The purpose of education: a talk on teaching our students how to think* [Unpublished thesis]. Ball State University, Muncie, IN, United States.

Murphy, B. G. (2017). *Inside our schools: Teachers on the failure and future of education reform*. Harvard Education Press.

Priestley, M., & Drew, V. (2016, September). *Teachers as agents of curriculum change: closing the gap between purpose and practice* [Paper Presentation]. *The European Conference for Educational Research*, Dublin, Ireland.

Rentner, D., Kober, N., & Frizzell, M. (2016). *Listen to us: Teacher views and voices*. Retrieved from Centre on Education Policy website: http://www.cepc.org/displayDocument.cfm?DocumentID=1456

Sahlberg, P. (2006). Education reform for raising economic competitiveness. *Journal of Educational Change*, 7(4), 259–287. doi:10.100710833-005-4884-6

Selwyn, N. (2019). *Should robots replace teachers? AI and the future of education*. John Wiley & Sons.

Shaked, H., & Schechter, C. (2019). School middle leaders' sense making of a generally outlined education reform. *Leadership and Policy in Schools*, 18(3), 412–432. doi:10.1080/15700763.2018.1450513

Takeuchi, M. A., Sengupta, P., Shanahan, M. C., Adams, J. D., & Hachem, M. (2020). Transdisciplinarity in STEM education: A critical review. *Studies in Science Education*, 56(2), 213–253. doi:10.1080/03057267.2020.1755802

UNESCO. (2015). *Education 2030 Framework for Action: Towards inclusive and equitable quality education and lifelong learning for all*. http://www.unesco.org/new/fileadmin/MULTIMEDIA/HQ/ED/ED_new/pdf/FFA-ENG-27Oct15.pdf

UNESCO. (2020). *Education: From disruption to recovery*. https://en.unesco.org/covid19/educationresponse

Wattal, A. M., & Singh, C. (2021, June 8). An era of new-age school assessments. *Hindustan Times*. https://www.hindustantimes.com/analysis/an-era-of-new-age-school-assessments-101622990312580.html

Chapter 2

Reimagining Higher Education as Response to Ongoing Crises:
Lived and Learned Experiences by College Students and Professors Surrounding COVID-19

Tamar Davis Larsen
University of Colorado at Boulder, USA

EXECUTIVE SUMMARY

College students and professors have experienced dramatic change in how they are able to attend and participate in classes, convey information, interact with one another, and teach in a meaningful, dynamic way. This chapter explores what worked and what did not work during this shift to online teaching as universities in the United States closed down for almost all in-person classes. Research includes narrative identity, with data derived from collecting stories of the lived experience during COVID-19. Topics explored are issues of how higher education relates to the traditional U.S. college experience, ethics, leadership, money, equitable technology, and mental health. Suggestions will be presented in terms of what can be learned from this particular crisis that can be enacted in framing better practices in higher education as future domestic and global crises emerge.

DOI: 10.4018/978-1-7998-8310-4.ch002

INTRODUCTION

As the Covid-19 pandemic erases and disrupts traditional educational experiences, how can global educators become more adept at teaching during times of crisis? While acknowledging the limitations and advantages technology plays in this shift, there is space to explore the intangible additional elements of academic wonder, rigor in learning and creative exchange of ideas in the classroom. These are the topics which will be explored in this chapter, including perspectives that frame this question that come from fields including critical hermeneutics, cultural anthropology, the lived college experience, and the current shifting state of higher education in the U.S.

Educators must be able to pivot as never before- and not just as a response to this specific Covid-19 pandemic. While this specific pandemic is being experienced around the world in ways that profoundly disrupt lives and interrupt learning, there have been (and will continue to be) dramatic events that interfere with higher education. In learning techniques that aid in adapting to crises in general, this can be applied to ongoing issues that will disrupt higher education in future- disrupting events related to climate change (such as lack of air conditioning to facilitate safe learning when temperatures are too high), related to disruption of internet access (addressing here issues connected to money, class and allocated educational resources), relating to adjusting expectations to facilitate some learning over optimal learning. By exploring these issues, educators can better understand how much learning will need to change in response to crises, how to do it effectively, and when it's appropriate to do so.

BACKGROUND

Weaving together critical theory, participatory narratives of professors in the field trying to teach during crisis, and responses from college students in the U.S. struggling to learn, there will be an exploration of how to change as reaction to crisis. And how to do so in a way that has meaning, facilitates effective learning and creates a sense of joy and wonder in the context of the college learning experience. In looking at theory from critical hermeneutics there is room to recontextualize the role of culture in framing educational experiences, expectations and demands. In this way, the role of narrative identity allows for greater understanding of how teachers and students react best to these changing expectations of how to teach, when to teach, and what modality to use to teach. Constantly emerging technology provides additional virtual modalities of teaching, but also leads to inequities: inequities in the space, privacy and availability that students each have (relating to issues of poverty, financial struggle of some students- to be further addressed in this chapter) as well as to the fact that some professors are far more adept at utilizing this new technology than others. And this range by professors regarding ability, fluency and comfort (with such tools that Zoom provides, such as: virtual whiteboard, breakout rooms, sharing screens to show/discuss/read together articles, film clips and provide guest speakers) affects the overall experience that students have. While a charismatic professor is a wonderful way to make a traditional in-person lecture engaging and memorable to students, a professor that struggles to use the online technology (by accidentally "hanging up" on students during Zoom session or by not knowing how to utilize the breakout rooms in a way that creates meaningful conversations) creates frustration and dis-engagement. This brings up the issue of tradition vs. change. Weaving in issues around technology and ethics into the realm of culture and tradition can provide a deepening of understanding here. In this vein, Paul Ricoeur's theory of Mimesis can be used, as well as his framework for using field work to reveal truths. When Ricoeur writes, "to interpret is to follow the path of thought opened up by the text, to place oneself *en route* towards the *orient* of the text" (Ricoeur,1982, p.112), there is a pathway for using narrative identity of educators and learners to better frame understanding of changing education in times of crisis. In this way, the text devised from the narrative identities can provide the truths about what needs to change and why. It is only by truly hearing what has been tried, what did not work, what is craved by students and by teachers, that there can be insights gained that can provide new frameworks for lasting and authentic educational responses during dramatic upheaval. Using Ricoeur's theory of narrative identity, the text has meaning. Thus, shared desires and missed opportunities in higher education as universities, students and teachers respond to crisis can be noted, and used to do better in the future.

As hermeneutic-based field research suggests, guidelines offer a way towards revealing central truths as experienced by participants. This means the researcher is a part of the story, as the researcher chooses how to reveal the data, the stories, and the noted outcomes. In this way, the researcher must take an ethical and moral position on an issue (Herda,1999, p.9). This reinforces the idea that to have useful and meaningful outcomes presented in this chapter, the researcher has to accommodate not only what has occurred regarding educational failure during crisis, but acknowledge why this is, and how it can be improved upon.

When the main focus of higher education is acknowledged to be "to become full of wisdom", there is a sense of wanting to bring wisdom into the world. The Hebrew word "tikkun" comes to mind (meaning, to repair the world), as wisdom in its truest form seeks to bring knowledge to communities, to people. The critical pedagogist Peter McLaren writes that "tikkun" is in line with the ethical direction that good education must take (McLaren, 1989, p.160). It is with this lens of how to make education both more ethical as well as morally present, that students and educators need help adjusting to learning during crisis. While McLaren admits the focus of so many in higher education has been on producing students who will go out and earn great salaries, so is it imperative to examine this focus on "capitalists and conquerors", as McLaren calls them (McLaren, 2005). There is a moral imperative to create great thinkers; and yet- during a crisis when the learning is curtailed and the stress levels of students prohibit much learning, how can this be done?

Hans Georg Gadamer reminds us that we react to situations around us, and in doing so, affect change. He writes, "communication… is a living process in which a community of life is lived out" (1988, p.404). This urges the researcher to examine the truth that even the "sacrosanct" areas of traditional higher education must be reimagined to more truly reflect crisis unfolding. How can this done while maintaining that which is worthy about tradition? How much of tradition should be sacrificed to embrace modern and effective ways to teach and to learn in the college setting? Should traditional essays and timed exams still be used to calibrate grades? What is the role of conversation in learning today, and can the Socratic tradition be a valuable learning tool if crisis make students learn off-campus and physically distant from one another? It is important to examine the role that the teacher must now take on as more and more classes become taught via Zoom, or other online platforms in response to Covid. By removing the in-person human contact element, is there something precious that is sacrificed in the educational experience? How important is the in-class, traditional, human-filled conversational aspect of college? By framing these questions in hermeneutic philosophy and cultural anthropology, the researcher will better provide a framework for global educators of how better to teach during crisis.

Gadamer writes "to reach an understanding….is not just a transformation but a communion, in which we do not remain what we were" (1988, p. 341). This reminds the researcher that in facing the crisis of Covid (and further unfolding global crises that will surely come), educators need a real framework for responding to educational challenges that authentically reflect what is happening in our communities, and in our world. Crises affect the ability of teachers to teach well, and of students to learn fully. But by admitting where and how educational practices can better at addressing learning needs, can there be authentic beneficial shifts in higher education practices.

MAIN FOCUS OF THE CHAPTER

Issues, controversies, problems

The current Covid-19 pandemic has affected lives of college students and professors psychologically, emotionally and financially. In Maslow's Hierarchy of Needs, there are five levels of needs that humans must have in order to be optimally functional:

Self-Actualization, Esteem, Love and Belonging, Safety, Physiological. These five elements are imagined in a pyramid, with the elements of Physiological and Safety at the bottom (and at the widest part of the pyramid) and Esteem and Self-Actualization at the smallest areas at the top of the pyramid. The bottom levels on this hierarchy are focused on more basic physical needs, while the upper levels address the more intangible emotional and psychological needs. While all range of these needs are universally accepted as valuable, it is the physical needs of home, money, safety that are most urgent. Covid-19 has challenged many students and professors in meeting these basic needs. And future crises will do so as well.

In Simply Psychology Journal, Dr. Saul MacLeod writes, "once an individual's physiological needs are satisfied, the needs for security and safety become salient. People want to experience order, predictability and control in their lives. These needs can be fulfilled by the family and society (e.g. police, schools, business and medical care)" (MacLeod, 2020). He is referring to the Safety Needs here. The university for students provides a framework that includes social life, on-campus classes, interaction in person with professors and fellow students, study groups, chance meetings to find others on campus with the same interests, potential friendships and romantic interests… campus in person traditionally has provided a microcosm of a world to students. In the U.S. college system, even the town surrounding a large university provides support and caters to the college student crowd. There are often cafes, entertainment such as movie theaters, bowling alleys, dance and music clubs, cheap food, optometrists, hair salons, laundromats, shops and bookstores. It is a world designed to tend to and nurture the college student community. Keeping students physically close to campus (as many do not have cars), and often woven into the larger community by providing concerts, lectures and events open to the entire town. This student community was rocked off its predictable, comfortable existence with Covid-19. And while the community-at-large was traumatized by lockdowns as well, for college students the lockdown limitations were even more un-mooring. As the tether for college students was severed- and trying to provide this link via solely a virtual experience did not really work. The pandemic eliminated opportunities to interact socially as events on campus as well as classes on campus were shut down. It restricted students' ability to socialize together and State and City laws limited social interaction-at-large. And because students live often away from their families, this created a sense of isolation. At the same time, students were expected to continue their studies. There is a dissonance occurring here: with everything as students have known closing down, there was an expectation of continued academic rigor. And no meaningful acknowledgment of the issues of depression from the isolation once all social interactions, classes, gathering on campus and off campus were restricted. In conversations with 50 students, there were recurring themes of depression, loneliness, frustration at the online education experiences, and an overall longing for the predictability of order and control in their lives. This correlates directly with Maslow's identification of physical safety and physiological needs of stability being the precursors to a fulfilling, productive and happy life. The very issue of continuing higher education studies while these needs were not met is problematic. This begs the question: should colleges even have been teaching during the pandemic?

There is a connection between colleges in the U.S., the towns they are a part of, and the role that this interconnected community plays in the experience of the college student. Colleges and the immediate surrounding towns function as a sort of "finishing school" to aid and support in college students gaining the skills to navigate life as young adults, this too becomes a missing link once the campus and town shut down during Covid. In a recent study around mental health and college students, Larkin McReynolds, assistant professor of psychiatry at Columbia University's College of Physicians and Surgeons says, "Society has empowered colleges and universities to not only educate our youth but to serve as *locus parentis*. These institutions are, in part, responsible for facilitating the final phase of student development into adulthood, ushering the next generation through this transformative milestone. They are entrusted with the responsibility of providing the nation with a well-educated and skilled workforce, as well as future leaders. Unfortunately, the current crisis has untethered students from these institutions" (Hoven, McReynolds, Amsel, 2020). This is why so many international students opt to attend college in the U.S.- it is not just the education that U.S. colleges provide, but the "entire experience" they provide: clubs and towns built around facilitating young adults, a sense of joi de vivre that traditional college towns have (Krislov, 2019).

Should the pandemic have been addressed even more concretely in terms of stating: education needs to be paused so that the safety and physiological needs of students can be fully met? Meaning, students return home to their families, campus life completely shut down (as it was in some of the smaller colleges), and a generous spirit of educational forgiveness enacted. Instead, most large U.S. colleges (after an initial pause of varying amounts) continued education- and just moved it to online platforms. The research suggests this was because colleges in the US are primarily now businesses, and making money is the overarching concern. If the absolute focus was student well-being, classes would all have been paused during the crisis. While this would have interrupted the condition of studies (and in its own way, contributed towards missing out on predictability of routine schedule and planned expectations to graduate within a preconceived amount of time), it might have been the more authentic and care-focused path. In this vein, the discussion of money vs. student well-being must be examined. This includes the issues of trauma and resilience with regards to college students. These two issues are being currently researched, and it will be interesting to discover what the outcomes are once published (Hoven,

McReynolds, Amsel, 2020). Medicine and current studies are referring to this as an intersection of behavior economics and mental health. Illustrating how economics, U.S. colleges and students have an interdependency that is quantifiable as well as intangible. While the economics of the college can be measured (as can the profits of businesses in college towns), the more amorphous experiences of fun, events, community, excitement, engagement- all cannot be measured in the same way. Neither can the effect this current crisis has had on students' mental health in terms of a quantifying study. These will more fully emerge in the coming months and provide a deepening of understanding regarding mental health, college students and crisis.

Dr. Christina Hoven says, "From the perspective of college students, COVID-19 has caught them at a most pivotal moment in their personal, interpersonal, educational, and pre-professional development". Hoven continues, "For most, it has disrupted the well-worn and expected trajectories from adolescence to adulthood, from dependence to social responsibility and leadership. Therefore, it is critically important to understand the impact and consequences of the pandemic on U.S. college students, because the pandemic's impacts will not only affect the students personally but the future of our nation" (Hoven, McReynolds, Amsel, 2020).

What has emerged in conversations with 50 college students at the University of Colorado at Boulder is the overarching theme of mental health in conjunction with the Covid-19 crisis. These conversations were recorded, transcribed and became text (some might use the term data). From this data, commonalities came forth. Specifically, how students have experienced a surge in depression during the Covid-19 pandemic and the ensuing closure of social life, campus experiences, all in-person classes. Coupled with fear of the virus's unknown detrimental health factors, this led students to become frustrated, lonely and depressed. Substance abuse became increasingly present around the campus, an alcohol-fueled riot adjacent to campus emerged (Deakins, 2021). While riots are far and few between, the pent-up frustration and "pandemic fatigue" are clearly present in the undergraduate population. The conversations revealed a range of experiences in terms of discontentment. These were greatly affected by each student's immediate sense of community/family as well as by income status.

The issue of economic disparity needs to be addressed in terms of how poverty/ wealth affect the experience students have during a crisis. This is true as well with professors, but for students is more obvious. Students with more money have the ability to live in a building with fast, working internet. They also have their own bedroom, which provides privacy and a quiet place to participate in their online studies. In an expensive college town like Boulder, Colorado (location of the flagship campus of the University of Colorado system), this disparity is a glaring factor. Rooms regularly rent monthly for over $1,200 per month per student. When costs of tuition, food and utilities are added to this rent amount, it is an expensive undertaking large to live and study here. Because of these high costs, students often move further away from campus, in other cities and towns. In an article in Atlantic Magazine, Professor Michael D. Smith from Heinz College suggested that the "relative stability of higher education and its place in the economic feedback loop created an industry plagued by overconfidence, overpricing and an overreliance on business models tailored to a physical world" (Smith, 2020). While it is no secret that colleges and universities are businesses and strive to make money, these businesses seem now to prize financial profits far more than intellectual learning. What is striking is that these universities no longer even pretend to value the storied traditions of on-campus discourse, lively intellectual arguments, and of furthering artistic endeavors. This is partially in reaction to the rise of litigation in US society, where professors can lose their jobs for saying the "wrong" things. There is a real danger of higher education in the US verging so much towards the online experience (it's cheaper to provide, and makes the university more money per student), and thus create a loss of what a real education means. Smith asks the question in the title of his Atlantic Magazine article, "Are Universities going the Way of CDs and Cable TV?" (Smith, 2020). Meaning, are universities in the U.S. going to become obsolete in both what they provide and how they are valued? Smith continues, "like the entertainment industry, colleges will need to embrace digital services in order to survive" (Smith, 2020). There is an acknowledgment that once tried, the virtual serving of higher education to students will not easily be withdrawn. Both students and professors learned how to do it, and now there is an expectation such virtual classes will continue to be on offer. This brings up another question, which is, are online classes as valuable as in-person ones? And should they cost the same amount?

In Frontiers in Psychology Journal, the authors of a recent study note that "To ensure an equitable student experience in this new scenario, universities must guarantee that students from less privileged socioeconomic backgrounds are not disadvantaged" (Garcia-Morales, Garrido-Moreno, Martin-Rojas, 2021). While this sounds wonderful, it has yet to happen at the University of Colorado. Smaller, very wealthy, private colleges have strived actively more towards this goal. Ensuring access to a quiet space to participate in online learning, fast internet, and a good, working computer are all necessary ingredients towards creating an equitable student learning experience during times of crisis. Usually, the universities in the U.S. provide some of these things: free, quiet spaces to study and vibrant student union centers in which to gather in groups and brainstorm projects. These same spaces provided free, fast, reliable internet. By moving all academic life online there is no longer access to these free university spaces. This creates a keen lack of the necessary tools for participating virtually in a meaningful way in classes online. This further creates a chasm between the wealthy students at U.S. colleges and students that struggle financially. Those that struggle often lack access to fast internet, lack new computers that can handle the online content and latest software necessary to participate in classes via video, etc.

For professors in this same learning community, the issue of economic disparity is more hidden. This is partially due to the element of embarrassment and shame US adults experience in receiving regarding social welfare assistance. This sense of shame prevents professors from openly admitting a need for help paying rent, help paying for food, help paying for medical treatment. This is in contrast with the Nordic countries (indeed, with Europe as a whole), where all adults receive some sort of social welfare assistance- thus de-stigmatizing welfare (Larsen, 2008). Another factor is that highly educated adults in this wealthy Boulder, Colorado community understand how to advocate for themselves and participate in social welfare services. The university has provided free laptop computers during the Covid-19 crisis to professors (but not to students). This is where there is an intersection of economics and ethics (or, ethical responsibility). A telling feature of the very present need for professors (as well as with the student community) at the University of Colorado at Boulder was how the pandemic pop-up food bank on campus ran out of food in 15 minutes. The University severely underestimated the need of both professors and students in the community, and thought a pop up food bank would merely be a welcome addition to food needs. The University did not realize that this food bank was not going to merely supply "supplemental" groceries: but all the groceries that week. The line for free food boxes on campus (limited to university affiliates) went around the block. Clearly illustrating a financial need for basic human goods, like groceries. When examined in light of the earlier mentioned Maslow's Hierarchy of Needs, this shows the lack of the strongest human need: Safety. Without food, there is not safety of health nor any kind of authentic well-being.

This brings the researcher to another element of ethical well-being: the importance of feeling loved, heard and valued during crisis. And the ensuing affect this has on a student's ability to learn, as well as a professor's ability to teach. There are many studies addressing links between health and increased educational ability (Taras, 2006). During the Covid-19 crisis, a painful element was the issue of isolation. As this particular crisis necessitated people isolate from one another. Online platforms became the only way for many students and professors to connect socially as well as to teach. Zoom because the primary teaching platform of the University of Colorado, but it also became a way to remain in connection with one another- a way to have coffee dates, "happy hours", conversations as well as a way to instruct courses and hold office hours. The human need for connection, physical contact, hugs, being physically and fully present with one another- were all severely limited. This limitation is one that will certainly reverberate in ways not yet determined not fully understood.

The physiological need to feel loved and a part of a community are intangible, but nonetheless pivotal elements of human well-being. Maslow refers to these needs as the third tier in his hierarchy: Belongingness and Love Needs. This specific tier addresses how the psychological relationships in life provide grounding that is necessary for happiness and health. Dr. Saul MacLeod says that "Belongingness, refers to a human emotional need for interpersonal relationships, affiliating, connectedness, and being part of a group", and that without this, there is a deficiency (MacLeod, 2020). For both students and professors, the university is often the pivotal anker in life- for social life, for income, for creating relationships. It is the physical place that both these groups gather regularly- whether it is for the job professors have at the university, or the classes that students attend. That is one of the reasons U.S. college campuses spend tremendous resources designing and building these campus gathering places. They are a kind of community within a community; they function as a microcosm of the town-at-large. This is especially true of college campuses that embody the "traditional" kind of college campus, the kind that have student dormitories, large grassy fields both for sporting events and for hanging out, Saturday football games, weekly concerts and performances. It is in this way that these kinds of campuses function as a "community within a community." This is the case for the University of Colorado at Boulder, where the researcher held conversations with professors and undergraduate students to explore their experiences and reactions to how Covid-19 changed (and for the most part limited) teaching access.

What emerged from students were two primary reactions from this experience. The first reaction from the majority of students was the sense of loss they were experiencing while in college. They felt cut-off from anything fun. They missed the social aspect of attending a class, such as meeting new fellow classmates, and being in the presence of their professors. Because this generation of college students has so much of their life often online (with the copious use by many of social media), they viewed attending classes in person, on a beautiful college campus a respite from the overwhelming social media construct that floods much of their time. Moving all classes online, which college did in the U.S. as a response to Covid, meant that students no longer had the ability to turn off their phones and computers to focus on learning, focus on meaningful in-person discussions. The ability to judge timbre of voice, expressions, body language- all this is somewhat limited by moving all interaction to online formats. Discussions become necessarily stilted and more formal, as Zoom limited speaking to one person at a time. Zoom break-out rooms provided a slightly more "intimate" space for students to brainstorm in smaller groups. But as the format even in break-out rooms is limited to monologues only (meaning one person only speaking at a time for the platform's software to recognize the speaker's microphone), there is little ability for dynamic, interactive experience. No students thought that pre-taped lectures that professor posted counted as "dynamic, interactive experience". Classes with a primary content of pre-recorded lectures were the least valued educational experience from the students the researcher spoke with. Freshman students had a more challenging time than seniors. This seemed partially due to the fact that most lived in the campus dormitories (unless they had returned home), and thus shared a bedroom with a roommate- making talking out loud in classes online challenging in a shared space. Seniors (as well as non-traditional students) expressed being more content with learning via online platforms. This could be because these students have more maturity, increased amounts of resilience through experience, and because they had the bulk of their social life already formed before Covid. They had existing social circles and support from peers- they did not need to somehow create this structure during the crisis itself. This could also be because the seniors and non-traditional students had other life focuses beyond the university. Many are envisioning imminent jobs, moves, changes that they actively are seeking out. These students have a goal that transcends the immediate crisis. They are imagining future aspirations and in process of creating these. So, in a sense, they are actively looking beyond the college experience even while in it. They are completing classes and academic requirements, but also focused on what is coming next. For freshman and younger students, this element is not present. Thus, the lack of being able to imagine the future in any immediately light in a different way is just not happening. Because of this, the younger students feel a more exhausting sense of limitation in life during Covid. They are more overwhelmed and discontent by the lack of in-person classes and opportunities to socialize. Students had the most valuable experience in online classes in the smaller, seminar-type classes in which discussion was the bulk of the class time, and where break-out rooms were facilitated by professors. When break-out rooms were not facilitated actively by professors (meaning, where professors visited each break-out room and presented additional prompts and questions), these spaces were not valued.

Which leads to an important topic: teaching styles and methods used by professors, and the value that students found in these variations. What students most valued during this crisis from professors was flexibility. Flexibility in assignment deadlines, in the ability to make-up tests and quizzes missed, etc.... They also greatly valued flexibility in terms of something less tangible- the empathy professors offered. Empathy is described here as "flexible" as it not only varies from professor to professor, but within the same person depending on their personality and the life stressors that influence them. During this time of crisis, students found that empathy provided by professors during their classes was deeply helpful. Professors that wove real-life themes surrounding Covid (especially in a way that connected to course topics) was appreciated and useful. The students then felt heard, valued, understood. And this allowed students to persevere in coursework during times they might otherwise have given up. In the Chronicle of Higher Education, Beth McMurtrie writes, "[f] lexibility and leniency have historically been problematic words in higher education, raising the suspicion that faculty members are "going easy" on students. Yes, many professors did scale back their requirements during the pandemic. But several readers told us that they realized that being flexible, such as with deadlines, is not the same as giving students a pass. Rather, it's a sign of trust that students want to do their best but can't always meet a particular schedule" (McMurtrie, 2021). What emerged was that students were grateful for this kind of flexibility, and instead of it resulting in late assignments it contributed towards an overall feeling of community. In a time when real in-person community has been lacking. The rules needed to change in some way, both as a reaction to the pandemic but also as a reaction to the lack of human connection students and professors experienced. Flexibility is a catch-all word that encompasses some ways in which rules, policies, expectations were allowed to bend in a manner that felt an appropriate response to this crisis.

McMurtrie says that enacting empathy in higher education during time of crisis is valuable. She believes "[t]reating students with respect and care builds trust, this serves as the foundation for learning. It also allows me to focus on the 'big' issues, and not the nitpicky issues. I mean, really, if I am not going to grade at the strike of midnight, why does it matter if their work is a bit late?" (McMurtrie, 2021). This is an example of how the flexibility that professors provided during this crisis, and the way it was experienced by students created a dual benefit. Both groups felt it was helpful. Clay Shirky, Vice Provost for Educational Technologies at New York University, believes that professors must demonstrate extra levels of compassion and concern for students during a crisis, which can be done with increasing care regarding engagement. He thinks that "greater concern for student engagement, check-ins before and at the end of class, and greater awareness of the vagaries of students' outside lives" are very important strategies (McMurtrie, 2021). This is very in line with what many professors at University of Colorado at Boulder believe. Professors in Boulder tried various ways to weave such "check-ins" as a weekly or daily part of their online class experience. This was easier to do for smaller classes of less than 30 students. By doing this, professors felt they were honoring the very human part of this crisis, and allowing a moment of class time for sharing, communing together in compassions.

The concept developed by Jon Kabat-Zinn of Mindfulness-Based Stress Reduction (MBSR) comes to mind with the need expressed by students for greater compassion during times of crisis. Kabat-Zinn is Professor of Medicine Emeritus at the University of Massachusetts Medical School, where he founded its world-renowned Mindfulness-Based Stress Reduction Clinic (in 1979), and the Center for Mindfulness in Medicine, Health Care, and Society (in 1995). Kabat-Zinn espouses that Professors would clearly benefit from this same compassion too. When thinking about MBSR with regards to expressed empathy in higher education, one can think of this compassionate flexibility manifesting outwardly from students towards professors. There are many ways this can happen, but professors during this crisis most valued how it was expressed by students in the form of patience and kindness. Professors struggled to become fluent in the Zoom and other online teaching platforms (and the accompanying break-out rooms, white boards, sharing screens, etc…), as well as more deeply utilizing the Canvas online teaching platform. As the University of Colorado shifted to online teaching only during Covid-19, this university-wide platform become more important than ever. It became the way professors communicated syllabi changes in real time, made announcements, posted and facilitated "Discussion Threads", posted additional material for classes such as videos, music, film and literature clips. Learning to use these online teaching modalities with increasing fluency was a challenge for many professors. This led to some professors choosing not to use them much, sticking with pre-recorded lectures made in previous years (which students found lazy), or just using as little as possible of the new technology. Other professors embraced this challenge and learned as much as they could as quickly as they could. The more comfortable professors became with the online teaching tools, the better and more engaging the experience was for the students.

A repeated theme that emerged from conversations with students is that when they felt valued and heard by their professors during this crisis, they felt better about life and about attending their classes virtually. Einstein wrote, "A human being is a part of the whole, called by us "Universe," a part limited in time and space" (Sullivan, 1972). These words are a reminder of how important it is for everyone during crises to feel as if they are connected, that they belong to something of value. For student and professors, this place of value is the university. When students felt valued and heard by professors, they responded with increased respectfulness when interacting with professors. This shift to more respectful and less demanding behavior was shown during online zoom classes and in emails to professors. Thus, there was a kind of reciprocation of care in the experience had by both professors and students during this pandemic. The more professors actively acknowledged and gave space for students to share their truths during this crisis, the more students adjusted their approach when interacting with professors. During the pandemic, professors greatly appreciated when students were kind and less demanding. The oft-present competitive academic spirit students display in classes took a back seat during this crisis to focus on a more inclusive communal energy (in smaller classes). In larger classes, this communal spirit, or sense of care and community, was more challenging to enact for both students and professors. Shirky says, "[a]s we start teaching online, the need to think harder about ways of getting the students talking, not just listening, is one of the first things that became apparent in digital instruction" (McMurtrie, 2021). This is one way that professors can show authentic care. When professors invite students to speak, it creates an opening for a sense of community. This becomes very important during a time of crisis. In Mindful Journal Magazine, Jon Kabat-Zinn says, "[f]ormal loving-kindness practice can function to soften one's relationship to overwhelmingly afflictive mind states, so that we can avoid succumbing completely to their energies. It makes them more approachable and it makes them less intractable" (Kabat-Zinn, 2021). This illustrates why students and professors need and crave more flexibility during this pandemic (and will during future times of crisis). This flexibility in higher education includes kindness, increased options for when to turn in assignments without penalty, greater awareness of what is happening outside the class, and a chance to let all in the class speak about what is happening in their life during class time. In short, it requires a kind of acknowledgement of the crisis-as-trauma and a space (online or in person) to speak to this truth in the classroom. When trauma and crisis are acknowledged, it creates a cognitive cohesiveness. It also contributes towards what McLaren calls "tikkun" or loving kindness (McLaren, 1989). By creating space in the classroom to commune, share, and voice personal needs as well as intellectual thoughts, there is place made for the deepest kind of learning.

There were a few things that the University of Colorado (and many other colleges in the U.S.) did during this pandemic that made sense and helped students and professors. The university brought Covid testing mobile units (vans) to the neighborhood near campus most popular for students to live. Bringing this tool to the students where they live was smart, and helped students get tested with ease and greater frequency. This also helped professors because they were allowed to access these mobile testing units, though professors do not live in this neighborhood in high numbers. The university allowed both students and professors to bring a guest to be tested (with no charge) as well, which was helpful. Another thing the university did was something specifically for professors- they set up a free computer program for any professor who needed one. And it was done discreetly as to not embarrass any professor who needed help getting one. Students were not given this option. Another thing that helped professors (though this depended on the specific department head) was allowing them to choose the modality of the online classes they would teach. Meaning, letting professors choose whether their classes would be asynchronous or synchronous or a blend of both. This provided a kind of freedom for professors academically and personally. It allowed professors the ability to work in a way that honored what their own capabilities were during this crisis. For admittedly, a crisis limits ability- it creates stress, affecting physical and psychological well-being. By allowing professors this flexibility and autonomy, department heads displayed a kind of respect. The university also set up a "Covid Emergency Fund" for students. This fund allowed for up to $200 to be given to any student who demonstrated a need relating to Covid for extra help. This was useful to many students, though figures have not been released as to how many participated. The "Food Bank" set up on campus was also a brilliant and popular idea. The problem with this particular weekly event was that the need for food was dramatically underestimated. Meaning that food boxes could only be distributed to a small amount of the people who showed up. But it clearly addressed a need in a way that made sense (in distributing food, and doing it on campus), just not on a scale that worked. This event was enacted and staffed by a local Boulder, Colorado food pantry and allowed by the university to be on campus.

SOLUTIONS AND RECOMMENDATIONS

This researcher has a few recommendations. Firstly, that the crisis at hand take full center stage- and that academic work come after students' and professors' well-being. This did not happen at the University of Colorado at Boulder during Covid-19. While it would cost the university lost income, pausing a semester would have allowed for authentic acknowledgment of what was occurring, and allowed for human needs to be met first. Secondly, professors should have been given extra assistance in teaching and learning online modalities in the form of "facilitators". This was done only at the very end of the pandemic teaching year (in the Spring 2021 semester) but would be very helpful if done as soon as a crisis is recognized. Thirdly, students should have been refunded their tuition for any semester interrupted, and professors should have been given teaching stipends to develop new skills regarding online teaching modalities. This would pay for professors' effort and time as syllabi had to be re-created to move entirely online, and some students had leave university studies to feel safe. In a capitalist economy, money shows how things are valued; this would have shown authentic care from the university towards the students and professors. Fourthly, students should be given new working computers and private learning spaces with fast-working internet. Without these two things, students cannot participate actively or meaningfully in online classes. The economic disparity among university students showed up here blatantly and could be addressed in a solution-based way by doing this. Fifthly, the university should use resources to provide students and professors with a most basic element showing care: food. There was a weekly food pantry distribution location on campus initially created by a local organization, but it did not have enough resources to serve the number of students, faculty and staff that showed up needing food. By having the university itself oversee and pay for this, it would be a more powerful and effective tool to help the university population. By delivering groceries to students and professors during any lock-down during times of major crisis, basic care and meaningful action would be demonstrated.

CONCLUSION

There will undoubtedly be numerous articles, studies and data soon published on how Covid-19 has affected college students. There will also be data that comes forth regarding how the lives of professors were upended and challenged. Both of these will factor into how higher education responds to future crises. The most important element that can frame understanding of the current pandemic and provide useful framework for future crises (in terms of how they affect students and professors in higher education) is for the university to show that it is not a business first, but an ethical community of academic pursuits first and foremost. Shifting behavior guidelines in terms of what is expected from students and professors to a more humane one that fully acknowledges that crises disrupts regular learning would create space for productivity, increased happiness and ability to learn. This shift in how universities in the U.S. can respond to future crises depends on accepting what did NOT work as higher education institutions responded to this pandemic. Global warming and political strive have the potential to cause great disruptions- such as hurricanes, earthquakes, depleted energy resources, water shortages, and even war- affecting the lives of students and professors, and thus requiring a change in learning and teaching. As universities begin to more fully understand and acknowledge the mental health issues experienced by students that are exacerbated during this pandemic, they can more adequately respond ethically to this pervasive need. There needs to be a framework of emergency guidelines to use during future crises gleaned from what was experienced during Covid-19. Previous emergency guidelines are no longer sufficient. Times have changed. This needs to be acknowledged so that teaching can continue during future crises, but continue in ways that honors the students' experiences, and the professor's challenges too. Without this, higher education will remain in a state of patchwork pieces. Universities need to put greater resources towards supporting students and professors. By doing this, they would authentically look after physical and emotional well-being of the campus communities that propel future generations of great thinkers into the world.

This research received no specific grant from any funding agency in the public, commercial, or not-for-profit sectors.

REFERENCES

Barsotti, S. (2020). The Transformation of Higher Education After the COVID Disruption: Emerging Challenges in an Online Learning Scenario. *Carnegie Mellon University News*. www.cmu.edu/news/stories/archives/2020/september/higher-education-covid-disruption.html

Deakins, J. (2021, Mar. 9). The Riot at the University of Colorado Was Driven by Pandemic Fatigue and Pent-up Emotion. *Denver Post.*

Gadamer, H.-G. (1988). *Truth and Method.* Sheed and Ward.

García-Morales, V. J. (2021, February). The Transformation of Higher Education After the COVID Disruption: Emerging Challenges in an Online Learning Scenario. *Frontiers in Psychology, 11.* www.frontiersin.org/articles/10.3389/fpsyg.2021.616059/full

Herda, E. A. (1999). *Research Conversations and Narrative: a Critical Hermeneutic Orientation in Participatory Inquiry.* Praeger.

Hoven, C. (2020). National College COVID-19 Study. In *Will U.S. College Students' Lives Be Forever Transformed by COVID-19?* Columbia University Press. dc.alumni.columbia.edu/covidcollegestudy

Kabat-Zinn, J. (2021). This Loving-Kindness Meditation Is a Radical Act of Love. *Mindful: Healthy Mind, Healthy Life.* www.mindful.org/this-loving-kindness-meditation-is-a-radical-act-of-love/

Kristof, N. (2021). If You Would Go Out on a Limb for Us, It Might Just Save Our Lives. *New York Times.* www.nytimes.com/2021/05/29/opinion/sunday/covid-impact-us.html

Larsen, T. S. D. (2008). *Surviving the Arctic; Narrative Identity of Foreign Women in Norway.* University of San Francisco Press.

McLeod, S. (2020). Maslow's Hierarchy of Needs. *Simply Psychology.* www.simplypsychology.org/maslow.html

McMurtrie, B. (2021, April). Teaching: After the Pandemic, What Innovations Are Worth Keeping? *The Chronicle of Higher Education, 1.* www.chronicle.com/newsletter/teaching/2021-04-01

Ricoeur, P. (1981). *Hermeneutics and the Human Sciences.* Cambridge University Press. doi:10.1017/CBO9781316534984

Smith, M. D. (2020, July). Are Universities Going the Way of CDs and Cable TV? *Atlantic, 22.* www.theatlantic.com/ideas/archive/2020/06/university-like-cd-streaming-age/613291/

Sullivan, W. (1972, Mar. 29). The Einstein Papers. A Man of Many Parts. *New York Times.*

Taras, H. (2006). *How Health Affects a Child's School Performance*. University of San Diego Press. health.ucsd.edu/news/2006/Pages/04_07_Taras.aspx

Chapter 3

Student Voices on the Use of International Telecollaboration and Sustainability During the COVID-19 Pandemic

Martin Parsons
Hannan University, Japan

Mikel Garant
Beijing Institute of Technology, Zhuhai, China

EXECUTIVE SUMMARY

The COVID-19 pandemic has thrown up many challenges to international cooperation, to the promotion of sustainable development, and indeed, to education. This chapter describes a telecollaborative project between university students in Japan and China. The students planned, wrote, recorded, and produced video podcasts on the theme of sustainable development, which were then exchanged via a password-protected, online, collaborative platform. On completion of the project, students wrote reflective essays, which are used here to gain insights into their impressions of topics such as sustainable development and telecollaboration. Results indicate that students improved their understanding of sustainability in addition to developing video editing and podcasting production skills. They also improved their pronunciation as well as other English skills. Overall, they were proud of their podcasts and enjoyed collaborating online with students from another country.

DOI: 10.4018/978-1-7998-8310-4.ch003

INTRODUCTION

In recent decades, the importance of developing sustainable systems across all areas of human activity has become clear. Human intellectual and technological advancements have led to outstanding achievements, such as sending humans to the moon and returning them safely to Earth, the deployment of systems of satellites which have provided us with a huge range of scientific insights and benefits, the advent of the internet which has provided millions around the world with new possibilities, the development of beneficial medical treatments and drugs, the eradication of health scourges such as polio and smallpox, and much more. At the same time, human economic activity has caused or exacerbated many deleterious phenomena, such as deforestation, loss of habitats leading to mass extinctions, industrial pollution of air and waterways, and climatic changes which threaten the very existence of humans.

While the word "sustainability" simply means to maintain something or to enable it to continue into the future at some given level, the positive and negative effects of human activity such as these are, of course, the antithesis of simply "maintaining" the world's ecosystems and allowing them to continue into the future at a given level. The term "sustainable development", however, is a much deeper and more nuanced concept. It implies the necessity of finding a balance between continued economic growth which may bring improved opportunities for all, and at the same time maintaining ethical standards in development which allow for the dignity of all people and respect for the natural world. The United Nations offers this, originally proposed by the Brutland Commission: "Sustainable development has been defined as development that meets the needs of the present without compromising the ability of future generations to meet their own needs" (UN, n.d.), which has come to find expression in the UN's Sustainable Development Goals (2015).

Turning that aspiration into reality cannot be achieved merely on a local, or even national level. As has become starkly obvious during the COVID-19 pandemic, international cooperation and collaboration are required to deal with global issues. Promoting awareness of issues and problems and possible solutions is now a global concern requiring the attention of all citizens, not merely of those working in governmental institutions or international corporations and the like. Further, it is now an issue which transcends fields and specialities, demanding a holistic approach to problem analysis and problem solving (Fisher, 2015). This makes it a responsibility for all levels and areas of education, including language education. In fact, education is hard wired into the UN's vision for enhancing equality and sustainable development as Goal 4 of the Sustainable Development Goals. Language education may be especially well suited to engaging with these kinds of issues, due to its very nature of promoting communication across borders and between different cultural milieu.

However, in some East Asian nations such as Japan and China, language education is often seen more as a gatekeeper for access to higher levels of education through competitive entrance examinations, rather than as a way of promoting communicative ability or developing intercultural awareness and understanding (Kikuchi & Sakai 2009, Yeung, 2017). An important aspect in the learning of a second language is motivation (Dörnyei, 1998; Gardner, 1985). While entrance examinations do offer some form of motivation to some learners, the overall focus on test taking as a goal often leads to the adoption of traditional, outmoded approaches to teaching language which lack the communicative input and output necessary to stimulate deeper motivation (Muñoz, 2007), an issue which has long been of concern in Japan and China where traditional, teacher-centred language teaching methodologies are still in common usage (Kimura, Nakata & Okumura, 2001, Yueng 2017).

Another feature of language learning in EFL environments like Japan and China is the dearth of opportunities to use English outside the classroom. There are very few reasons, if any, for pupils and students to use a language other than their mother tongue in their daily lives, reinforcing the perception of English as merely a subject to study for testing purposes, rather than as a tool or means of communication, something which could assist in learning more about cultural diversity. Frisk and Larson (2011) argue that collaboration is an important tool in developing an understanding of different ways of thinking and understanding the world, a crucial element in creating successful education for sustainability. This chapter describes an initial attempt to encourage university students from two different nations and cultural backgrounds, Japan and China, to develop awareness of cultural differences through a collaborative project in English. The students planned, wrote, recorded and produced video podcasts on the theme of sustainable development, which were then exchanged via a password-protected, online, collaborative platform.

Results from earlier projects of a similar nature (Parsons, et. al., in press) have indicated improved student attitudes towards the other country. In this chapter, we investigate the impressions of students as described in their own words, via reflective essays written after completing the project.

INTERCULTURALITY

The notion of culture is a fluid one, encompassing many different viewpoints which may change in place and over time. As such, a clear and universally accepted definition is difficult to formulate, though in broad-brush terms, culture can be thought of as the values, practices and beliefs of a particular group of people. As a consequence, as Moeller and Nugent (2010) note, any definition of intercultural understanding or competence must also come with a large degree of ambiguity. Deardorff (2006) defines it as the "ability to communicate effectively and appropriately in intercultural situations", while Sharifian (2018) suggests that "generally, intercultural competence is defined as knowledge and skills that enable speakers to communicate effectively and appropriately with speakers of other cultural backgrounds", both of which can be considered useful, general descriptions.

In a globalising world, where people from different cultural settings are increasingly coming into contact with one another, whether through increasing trade, tourism or virtual interactions, "intercultural situations" are now probably more commonplace than at any other time in history. As a consequence, foreign language education has come to take on a role in helping learners to not only develop language skills, but also in developing their abilities to interact appropriately with others from different backgrounds (Byram & Wagner, 2018; Kramsch & Aden, 2012). This will be essential if collaborative approaches to sustainable development are to succeed.

How this plays out in the language classroom is not clear-cut. Is it simply providing information, such as facts and data about a country or place where the target language is spoken, or is it a case of introducing learners to certain mores or customs of a particular place? Or is it something different again? And if it is more than simply the teaching and learning of empirical facts and figures, how is this to be effectively done? And perhaps more importantly, how is it to be evaluated? At what point can someone be said to have a "competence" in interculturality, particularly for learners who may never have set foot in a place where the target language is spoken? In fact, Zotzmann (2015) suggests that the concept of competency is not one which is easily applicable to the area of intercultural learning, and that attempting to assess or measure intercultural learning or understanding is essentially not a practical exercise.

Developing intercultural understanding, competency, or communication in an EFL setting becomes all the more difficult in the present day when English has become something of a lingua franca. L2 speakers of English might nowadays be realistically expected to interact with many different mother-tongue speakers of English and/or ESL/EFL speakers of English from almost anywhere on the globe, many of whom may have profoundly different, or even conflicting, notions of culture and attitudes to what constitutes appropriate forms of communication. Conceptions of intercultural understanding or competence which may exist between two people with differing cultural backgrounds is by no means guaranteed to ensure that the same understanding will necessarily extend to other people with different cultural backgrounds from the original two.

This is not to suggest that helping learners to develop deeper or better understandings of others is doomed to failure, simply that it is a difficult endeavour, the parameters of which are not easily defined. However, as Nikitina and Furuoka (2019) point out, people do build mental images of others, and the language classroom can be of help in creating or revising these images in a positive way. Danovitz and Tuitt

(2011) suggest that "diversifying the curriculum assists students" in this cultural development.

This may infer the need for a bespoke approach towards intercultural education relevant to the cultural context(s) involved. In the project described here, we are dealing with students from two nations with an extremely long and profound history of cultural interchange. Japanese cultural borrowing from China has been vast and diverse, including such influences as the writing system, religion and ethics, art, and even something as deeply embedded in everyday life as tea. Unfortunately, the situation has changed greatly over the course of the last 125 years. A brief war was fought in in 1894-5, and then a much longer and more cruel conflict between 1933-45 has caused long lasting enmity between the two nations. Today, that enmity can manifest over seemingly trivial disputes such as a territorial squabble over a small group of uninhabited islands, known as the Diaoyu Islands in China and the Senkaku Islands in Japan (e.g., Smith, 2012; Bosak, 2019).

TELECOLLABORATION

A further complication in the current environment is the global pandemic caused by COVID-19. Any possibility of foreign travel and the opportunity to engage with people from other cultural backgrounds has been curtailed. The affordances of the internet and the development associated technologies in recent years have opened up new possibilities in education, such as audio or video podcasting and telecollaboration, and in a time of reduced movement this is invaluable. The use of podcasting, one relatively new technology, in education is growing around the world, offering a flexible approach to engage with students in deliver academic content. A podcast itself is an audio or video file which is available to be downloaded from the internet and consumed on end-user devices such as smart telephones, computers, tablets, mp3 players, etc. In this respect, podcasts are similar to traditional radio or television broadcasts, though more flexible for the consumer, given that once downloaded they can subsequently be consumed at any time regardless of Internet connection. Recent years have witnessed a boom in the production and consumption of podcasts. Edison Research estimates that 28% of the population of the USA alone listen a podcast weekly, and over 40% listen to podcasts monthly (Edison Research, 2021). Simply using the technological capabilities of the internet, however, is no guarantee of success. As Chun et. el. note, "the use of technology should not be seen as a panacea, or a goal in and of itself, but rather as one means to support specific learning goals" (Chun, Kern & Smith, 2016: 77).

Podcasts have been shown to have positive benefits for students in such areas as reviewing lectures or catching up on missed classes, preparing for assessment and for note taking (Copely, 2007; Scutter, et. al., 2010). Two recent reviews of the literature on podcasts, by Kay (2012) in general on education and Hasan and Hoon (2013) in language learning, found that most studies reported positive results. Indeed, Hasan and Hoon cited studies which "claim that the integration of podcasts in learning can improve academic performance, enhance motivation, and promote learning".

In foreign language settings a number of studies have reported promising outcomes. Lord (2008) found peer-feedback using podcasts to be beneficial for improving pronunciation and attitudes towards an L2. A project conducted by Perez, et. al. (2011) aimed at promoting listening comprehension through the use of podcasts and online interaction resulted in active student participation and satisfaction. Al Qasim and Al Fadda (2013) claim that using podcasts led to improved listening skills and motivation among university students. Bamanger and Alhassan (2015) also found that students were motivated by podcasts, which led to improved ESL writing performance. Parsons (2021) found podcasting technology has the potential to provide opportunities for Japanese students to engage in an innovative approach to English language learning while developing digital literacy skills.

A potentially useful aspect of podcasting technology is the opportunity it provides to students to have control of what, when and how they listen to English. Being able to listen to language learning materials in a non-threatening atmosphere, as Kavaliauskiene and Anusiene (2009) explain, may alleviate the stress or sense of intimidation students often feel when expected to produce answers to listening activities on the spot in a classroom. This same aspect of control can also open up possibilities for greater creativity in educational practice. Middleton (2009), concluded that audio podcasts have the potential to provide educators with the means to move their practice towards more learner-centred approaches, and that they "demonstrated a capacity to facilitate authentic engagement, allowing students to connect in various ways to the outside world, both as listeners and publishers." Student-produced audio and video podcasts also allow for the transmission of cultural concepts in a unique way. In comparison to other modes of interaction, such as textbooks, newspapers, official documents, TV, commercial audio and video, etc., podcasts allow for a direct personal and emotional connection between students. These studies suggest that the use of podcasts in an EFL environment such as that found in China and Japan may well have the potential to aid students in a variety of areas related to learning English, but also including understanding or appreciating viewpoints different from their own.

In fact, researchers, such as O'Dowd (2012) and Chun (2011), have noted the positive possibilities of telecollaboration for developing intercultural communication. Ware and O'Dowd (2008) and Hung (2016) have found that peer-feedback is valued by students. Hung believes feedback via video can "promote more interaction but also foster more personalized learning and attentive engagement" (Hung, 2016: 98).

As such, a telecollaborative project utilising video podcasts was devised with the aim of promoting intercultural understanding, sustainable development, English language skills and digital literacy.

THE PROJECT

The project involved 17 Chinese university student participants and 32 Japanese university student participants. The Chinese students were first-year students at a private tertiary institution in China. They were aged between 18 and 19 and all had studied English for at least 10 years. The Japanese students were second-year students at a regional university, aged between 19 and 20 and all had studied English for a minimum of six years prior to entering university. Their English level was approximately B1 to B2.

The organization of the project is as follows:

1. Students were divided into groups or pairs and were asked to select a topic based on one of the UN's Sustainable Development Goals (2015). Students then wrote a short script in English on the topic, which was lightly edited by their English teacher for general issues relating to intelligibility.
2. After being given instruction on the basics of copyright, students then either took or acquired photographs and images to create a visual representation of their written script. The issue of copyright was referred several times throughout the project, as it appeared to be a concept only hazily understood by many students.
3. Students then edited their scripts in order to create greater cohesion between the written word and the images they had acquired.
4. Students were provided with a number of examples of video editing software packages and applications with directions to online tutorials in their use. Students chose the application that best suited their needs.
5. In pairs or groups students then worked to create a first draft of a video podcast, which included video clips, photographs and other images, an audio recording of the script they had written, and background music or sound effects.
6. Feedback from teachers was provided at this point on a number of factors, including English pronunciation, quality control in video and auditing and relevance of images to the story they were attempting to convey.
7. The nascent podcasts were then distributed among domestic peers, who evaluated them and provided written and oral feedback. Once the first draft of the podcasts were complete, all podcasts were uploaded to a dedicated, password protected online notice board called Padlet to facilitate exchange

with international peers. The podcasts were also exchanged between teachers by other means as a back option if Internet issues were experienced.

8. At this point, the students in the other country watched the video podcasts sent to them and gave feedback according to a prepared rubric.

9. This feedback was then returned to the original production team who used it to edit and improve their work, re-record their script for a final time, taking into account the new feedback they had received and produce a final version of their podcast for grading.

10. Finally, students reviewed and evaluated their own recorded work by comparing their final podcast with their original podcast.

In order to ensure that the learners understood the rubrics, they were translated into Japanese and Chinese and L1 templates were provided for reference, although the actual rubrics used were in English.

After completing the project, students were asked to write essays reflecting on the project, addressing the following questions:

What did you learn about video podcasting during the course?
What effect did this project have on your spoken English?
How did you feel about working with other people to make your video podcast?
What did you think about the podcasts from the other countries (e.g. Did anything surprise you? Did anything inspire you?)?
Would you like to do this kind of exchange with students in other countries again?
If yes, what topics would you be interested in exploring?

RESULTS

Excerpts from the essays addressing the specific questions, and their thoughts on sustainability more generally, have been selected to show the impressions students from both countries had of the project and are presented in this section. The excerpts from the student writing are representative of the overall comments in all of the essays that were examined.

Comments by Chinese students are preceded by the acronym CS, and those of Japanese student are preceded by JS. The comments are taken directly from the students' writing so they express the students' ideas in their own words.

Sustainability

CS1: The podcast we produced should be able to express the significance of the goal set by the United Nations, the method of implementation, and to popularize the knowledge related to the goal. Our group chose topics related to environmental pollution and clean energy. I chose this topic because the environmental problem is more and more serious, and it has been around me for a long time. The haze in my hometown made me feel like I was in the fog all day. Breathing these tiny particles of air at home will cause problems in our lungs and respiratory system. So we chose this topic to help you understand the importance of clean energy.

CS2: We have made a video about garbage sorting this semester. In order to make this video more and more perfect, we searched a lot of resources and improve skills. We have some new knowledge about garbage sorting, and we can sort garbage correctly in our daily life. Garbage sorting is needed to be implement immediately.

We had to tell about the SDGs, but for me, the main thing is to complete the video rather than telling the content.

JS1: I also learned some effective expressions from the videos created by Chinese students. For example, in one of the videos, students said, "Goodbye, raw garbage. Goodbye, recyclables. Goodbye, ~." to explain how to separate garbage.

JS2: In addition, it was a good opportunity to think deeply about the topic we chose (gender equality.) Even though I had heard of the Sustainable Development Goals, it was my first time to do a research on SDGs, discuss with my partner what we can do to achieve the goals, and communicate the ideas to other students as a video. This is the part where I was motivated and where I am most proud of.

The Chinese students wrote about the kinds of aspects of sustainability which they learnt in the course. One of the students talked about the fog in his hometown and why clean energy is important. Another discussed the sorting of garbage for recycling, which is rarely done in China. Another student mentioned vegetarianism which is also uncommon in China. The topic of sustainability enabled them to become acquainted with many new ideas and expanded their understanding as well as their vocabulary.

Overall, the Japanese students wrote less in their essays about the idea of sustainability. They tended to focus more on the practical aspects of the project, such as podcast production and their English skills. The first comment here expresses that explicitly by explaining the way the student learnt new English expressions. In Japan, garbage sorting has been the norm for decades, so it appears it is not the act of sorting garbage that is of interest, but the way of describing it in English. Another Japanese comment shows how the very act of discussing the project was a motivation to do the project well. This appears to be a significant indication of satisfaction with the project and its aims.

Skills in Making Video Podcasts

CS1: In this course, I learned about the access and production of video podcasts. What I am most proud of is my learning process of this video podcast production. I participated in the video editing and content introduction of the theme of this video production, which made me grow up a lot and helped me a lot in the future

CS2: According to this class's study. I have learned a lot. The first thing I learned was roughly how to shoot and edit a video, how to shoot and edit some videos, how to choose the shooting angle and place, what points of the video should be edited, and of course, some common division of labor among the team, and then there's my proudest point. I learned how to pull a shot, to make it more beautiful, to increase the animation and vividness of the video. That's what I'm most proud of, and that's what I learned the most.

CS3: This is our first contact with video podcasting. At the beginning, we are very strange to video podcasting, but in the continuous learning, we realize that video podcasting is very novel and interesting. The production process of a video podcast includes data collection, document arrangement, audio recording, video editing and feedback evaluation. My proudest part is feedback and evaluation.

JS1: Through this podcasting project, I work hard and enjoyed for making video of which I was in charge interesting and easy for viewer to watch. I think I made good video, and this project was very valuable project for me, and I'm proud of having completed enjoyable video to learn the theme.

JS2: What I learned most from this project is the difficulty of making videos and the awe of the people who make videos. The reason is that I usually watch YouTube and thought that it would be nice to get money even though they were just making videos. I thought it would be quite easy because I had never made a video. Also, I thought they should fix mistakes if they made them in their video. However, when I made a video this time, I realized that making videos were very difficult.

Many of the Chinese students expressed pride in their videos. They made note of the fact that knowing how to edit videos would help them in the future. They also talked about the mechanics of producing a video podcast: data collection, audio recording, shooting and editing videos, and dividing labor with their partners as something that made them proud. The Japanese students tended to write more about skills in making their podcasts. Unlike the Chinese students who wrote in more detail, they also tended to write in more general terms about things like making videos and fixing mistakes. It is interesting to note that JS2 has discovered that there is more to what happens behind the scenes of a YouTube video that they had imagined.

What Effect Did This Project Have on Your Spoken English?

CS1: Then this project also improved my oral English ability a lot, from the beginning of the stumbling, through this exercise, I can basically finish reading an English article fluently.

CS2: In this project, my spoken English has improved and my pronunciation is clearer than before.

CS3: My English level has been greatly improved. I not only learned a lot of words, but also learned a lot of knowledge. Like the vegan. After the professor explained vegetarians, I learned that there are many kinds of vegetarians.

CS4: This is a great progress for my oral English. Now I may not speak very fluently, but I believe I can do better in the future.

JS1: Firstly, this video project gave me a chance to improve my writing and speaking skills of English. In order to make our video more organized and more attractive, I discussed a lot with my partner what expressions or words to use and the order of the contents.

JS2: After that I practiced reading the script many times, listened carefully to my recording, and improved my speaking. I especially paid attention to the intonation, which is said to be difficult for Japanese people. I decided which words to emphasize and practiced reading to make it sound naturally.

JS3: I also think that we were able to work on clarifying speaking speed and pronunciation. I put a lot of emphasis on that because it was not only something that people would hear, but also something that they would hear in conjunction with visual materials. If I speak too fast, people's mind cannot keep up with organizing the information. On the other hand, if I talk too slow, people will get bored while listening. Speaking at just the right speed and with just the right pauses was something I was conscious of.

Students from both countries mentioned improvements in their spoken English, although Japanese students tended to write more about the improvement of their English skills than Chinese students. Students wrote about how the project improved their oral English and pronunciation, and JS1 also mentions improvements in writing proficiency. Improvements in English language skills was one of the goals of the project. Again, there seems to be an appreciation on the part of the students that the project has been valuable to them.

How Did You Feel About Working with Other People to Make Your Video Podcast?

CS1: I like working together to make video podcasts. In the process of group cooperation, we will put forward our own opinions. It's very exciting when we come to a consensus through collective discussion. In group cooperation, we need to have a clear division of labor, understand tolerance, inspire inspiration, and make the greatest contribution to a better video podcast.

CS2: There's good and there's bad, during the course of this semester's video division of labor, I had some unnecessary disputes and some disagreements with my team members. There will always be conflicts and disagreements in interpersonal relations, but fortunately, we finally resolved them. Everyone was at fault, there should be mutual tolerance and tolerance.

CS3: I think the most proud thing is that in the process of making the video, everyone in our group put in 100% of their efforts and worked together to make the video well. We have a clear division of labor, each perform its own duties, and make the video to the degree that we think is satisfactory. Through this video, I learned that only by unconditionally giving, don't care about personal tasks, can the team's strength be maximized. Each of us is a part of this group. Only by working together can we accomplish the task well. This may be the strength of the team.

JS1: Although making video with my partner went smoothly this time, I'm really feel regret for not support my partner well, because of a trouble of my computer. I left the most of editing task to her. When I work on similar project, I will do my best for reducing my partner's burden.

JS2: On the contrary, what I was not satisfied with was that I could not cooperate much. It was a pair work in an online environment in very busy days, so when I tried to tell my partner what I wanted her to do briefly, I almost needed doing it by myself. For example, when I tried to record through after adding music, I had to record by myself even though it was a video of two people. I really regret not having the opportunity for my partner to record English speaking even though there was the opportunity to receive feedback from Chinese students. The next time I do pair work, I think it is necessary to separate what I do and what the partner does.

JS3: Due to the epidemic of the new coronavirus infection, we were not able to have face-to-face classes, and we were not able to collaborate with our video production partner as we had hoped, so there were many difficulties.

Among the goals of this project was to promote collaboration among classmates, as well across borders. The Chinese students often made note of divisions of labor and working together, and also about disagreements with their team members. They also tended to reflect upon what they had learnt from working as a team. There were more positive experiences than negative experiences. The Japanese students tended to write more about the problems they encountered in doing pair work. One of the reasons for this is likely that their classes were conducted online because of the COVID-19 pandemic, making working together more complex and more difficult. The Chinese students, on the other hand, were in regular classes so could work on their podcasts face-to-face. The Chinese students are expected to engage in numerous group projects in their courses at university. The structure of their specialized English emersion study program trains them for studying overseas, meaning they are more used group work than the Japanese students might be. This may explain the tendency among the Japanese students to mention more problems with teamwork than the Chinese.

What Did You Think About the Podcasts from the Other Countries (e.g. Did Anything Surprise You? Did Anything Inspire You?)?

CS1: After we made podcast, we saw the works of Japanese college students, who are also about sustainable development goals. Their works are quite capable, from which we can learn about Japan's approach to sustainable development. Their English pronunciation is different from ours. And their podcast give examples of one point, which is easier to understand.

CS2: Some podcasts from other countries, such as podcasts from Japan, surprise me with a video called life on land, because the theme of my video is also life on land. This deeply inspired me, let me feel my own shortcomings, let me constantly motivate myself to change, for example, my spoken English has a certain accent, which is what I need to make changes.

CS3: After watching videos made by classmates from other countries, I think especially the videos made by Japanese classmates, in terms of dubbing, their spoken language is not very good, maybe because of the differences in language and culture, their pronunciation is not too authentic.

JS1: I got an impression that Chinese student did not use subtitles in their videos so much. I think they succeeded to let viewers concentrate their attention to the narration, It is also the good way and every videos were well-done needless to say, but I still prefer adding subtitles.

JS2: It was my first experience to communicate in English with foreign students whose native language is not English, so it was very refreshing. I felt that the evaluations from Chinese people were more credible without compliments than the evaluations from my university friends, which helped me to make my own videos and improve my English pronunciation skills. Chinese English was very easy to hear. If possible, I felt that I could more improve my skills of speaking and cooperating by pairing with Chinese students and making videos.

JS3: I wondered what editing softs (software) Chinese students used so much. Some my classmates also said that their videos are different from us. In addition to this, I noticed that Chinese students are better at pronouncing English than Japanese students.

JS4: I felt that the evaluations from Chinese people were more credible without compliments than the evaluations from my university friends, which helped me to make my own videos and improve my English pronunciation skills. Chinese English was very easy to hear. If possible, I felt that I could more improve my skills of speaking and cooperating by pairing with Chinese students and making videos.

Working with students from other counties through telecollaboration was seen as positive by all students. Some of the Chinese students mentioned that the pronunciation of the Japanese students was difficult to understand, while some Japanese students felt that the Chinese students were easier to understand. Interestingly, JS4 felt that the feedback from Chinese students was more useful than what was received from classmates in Japan. As a general rule in Japanese society, criticism is avoided wherever possible. This can have the effect of brushing over things that need improvement. Being exposed to other varieties of English was a feature of the project for students, and it seems this also inspired them to improve their own English pronunciation. The first passage addresses subtitling and says that the student prefers to use subtitling. The most interesting aspect of these comments is that the some of the Chinese students criticized the Japanese students' pronunciation while some of the Japanese students praised the Chinese pronunciation.

Would You Like to Do This Kind of Exchange with Students in Other Countries Again? If Yes, What Topics Would You Be Interested in Exploring? Do You Have Anything Else that You Would Like to Say About the Podcasting Project?

CS1: If there is any chance, I hope I can communicate with students from other countries in this way. This way breaks the embarrassment of face-to-face communication. At the same time, it can also understand the methods of a certain policy or a certain goal of other countries. Next time I want to know about the culture of other countries. Culture is the historical precipitation of a country. This topic should be very interesting.

JS1: Finally, I would like to do exchange with foreign students like this project, and I think it will be better not only writing text feedback, but also recording it and send that sound file to tell our opinion, I want to speak English until the end of the project.

Lastly, of course I want to interact with many countries' students and talk to them! But, to be honest, I don't want to make a video one more time. It was so hard work for me... But anyway, this video project was a really good and valuable experience for me!

JS2: I thought it would be more fun to be able to interact with various students and give advice from the creation stage. The themes we worked on were common throughout all over the world, so it was fun to hear various opinions. This time, we interacted with Chinese students, in the same Asian region as Japan, but I thought it would be fun to interact with students from English-speaking countries such as the United States and Europe. I would like to have this kind of exchange again if I have the opportunity.

There were few comments about ideas for the future in the Chinese students' essays. One response suggested culture or history as topics for future podcasts. They also expressed a preference for using podcasts instead of video chat because it is less embarrassing. The Japanese students wrote more suggestions for future podcasting projects than the Chinese students. Like the Chinese students, they enjoyed working with students from other countries, although one student said that they did not like making the video podcast because of the degree of difficulty. None of the Chinese students expressed a sentiment like this. Another student said that they wanted to work with students from English speaking countries such as the United States or Europe. This is a tantalising idea, although perhaps there would be problems if native speakers EFL speakers attempted a project like this, due to a disparity in language proficiency.

CONCLUSION

This study integrated language and technology by means of a supra-national, collaborative project to facilitate interaction between students through podcasts on sustainability. Bringing people from two different geographical locations, in this case tertiary students, together for personal meetings is a difficult task for various reasons, not least financial and temporal. Designing and executing such a project required a great deal of cooperation between the teachers in the planning stages as well as during the actual teaching and in the post course analysis stage. The researchers saw this as useful and a way to develop their teaching as well as a way to generate interest among the participating students.

In response to the question about what they learned about podcasting during the course, the students from both countries wrote about sustainable development goals and producing the actual work through editing, adding background music and other aspects. The Chinese students tended to use more details when they wrote about sustainability. One of the Japanese students wrote about how the Chinese students used their English skills when they said the Chinese said *"Goodbye, raw garbage. Goodbye, recyclables. Goodbye, ~."* to explain how to separate garbage. The comments about producing the podcasts tended to be similar with all the students. They were overwhelmingly positive and lead into the next question about what are you most proud of or least happy with. The students tended to say they were proud of their podcast. A few students in both countries mentioned difficulties doing teamwork as something that they were least proud of.

Most of the students in both countries mentioned that the projects improved their spoken English as well as other facets of their English skills. None said that it made their English skills worse. The following question addressed teamwork. When the students addressed this in their essay, they tended to be positive or even extremely positive. The Japanese students met online because of COVID 19 so they discussed cooperation with their team in their essays more than the Chinese. Some had problems with their team members. The Chinese met face to face in the classroom, so this theme does not appear commonly in their essays. Some of the Chinese essays said that they initially had some problems with their teammates but worked them out.

Working with students from other countries was seen as overwhelmingly positive. Some of the students mentioned the ease or difficulty in understanding the students from the other country. The final question asked if they liked interacting online with students from another country as well as suggestions for future topics and other suggestions. The students were positive about working with students from another country. Some suggested more sustainability as other topics while others talked about culture and history. Some students suggested making projects between 3 countries. One student from Japan specifically mentioned the US.

Overall, the responses of the students were very positive. Students enjoyed telecollaboration between Japan and China as well as learning about sustainability. Despite the COVID-19 pandemic, they used the project to deepen their knowledge on sustainability as well and improve their English and learn about the other country.

REFERENCES

Al Qasim, N., & Al Fadda, H. (2013). From CALL to MALL: The effectiveness of podcast on EFL higher education students' listening comprehension. *English Language Teaching*, 6(9). Advance online publication. doi:10.5539/elt.v6n9p30

Bamanger, E. M., & Alhassan, R. (2015). Exploring Podcasting in English as a Foreign Language Learners' Writing Performance. *Journal of Education and Practice*.

Bosak, M. M. (2019). China's Senkaku Islands ambition. *The Japan Times*. Retrieved from: https://www.japantimes.co.jp/opinion/2019/06/12/commentary/japan-commentary/chinas-senkaku-islands-ambition/#.XaoXlegzY2w

Byram, M., & Wagner, M. (2018). Language Teaching for Intercultural and International Dialogue. *Foreign Language Annals*, 51(1), 140–151. doi:10.1111/flan.12319

Chun, D., Kern, R., & Smith, B. (2016). Technology in Language Use, Language Teaching, and Language Learning. *Modern Language Journal*, 100(S1), 64–80. doi:10.1111/modl.12302

Chun, D. M. (2011). Developing Intercultural Communicative Competence through Online Exchanges. *CALICO Journal*, 28(2), 392–419. doi:10.11139/cj.28.2.392-419

Copely, J. (2007). Audio and Video Podcasts of Lectures for Campus-based students: Production and Evaluation of Student Use. *Innovations in Education and Teaching International, 44*(4), 387–399. doi:10.1080/14703290701602805

Danowitz, M. A., & Tuitt, F. (2011). Enacting inclusivity through engaged pedagogy: A higher education perspective. *Equity & Excellence in Education, 44*(1), 40–56. Advance online publication. doi:10.1080/10665684.2011.539474

Deardorff, D. (2006). The Identification and Assessment of Intercultural Competence as a Student Outcome of Internationalization at Institutions of Higher Education in the United States. *Journal of Studies in International Education, 10*(3), 241–166. doi:10.1177/1028315306287002

Dörnyei, Z. (1998). Motivation in second and foreign language learning. *Language Teaching, 31*(3), 117–135. doi:10.1017/S026144480001315X

Edison Research. (2021). *The Infinite Dial, 2021*. https://www.edisonresearch.com/the-infinite-dial-2021-2/

Fisher, P. B., & McAdams, E. (2015). Gaps in sustainability education. *International Journal of Sustainability in Higher Education, 16*(4), 407–423. doi:10.1108/IJSHE-08-2013-0106

Frisk, E., & Larson, K. (2011). Educating for Sustainability: Competencies & Practices for Transformative Action. *Journal of Sustainability Education, 2*. http://www.jsedimensions.org/wordpress/wp-content/uploads/2011/03/FriskLarson2011.pdf

Gardner, R. C. (1985). *Social Psychology and Second Language Learning: The Role of Attitudes and Motivation*. Edward Arnold.

Hasan, M., & Hoon, T. (2013). Podcast Applications in Language Learning: A Review of Recent Studies. *English Language Teaching, 6*(2), 128–135.

Hung, A. (2016). Enhancing Feedback Provision through Multimodal Video Technology. *Computers & Education, 98*, 90–101. doi:10.1016/j.compedu.2016.03.009

Kavaliauskiene, G., & Anusiene, L. (2009). English for Specific Purposes: Podcasts for Listening Skills. *Filologija. Edukologija, 17*(2), 28–37. doi:10.3846/1822-430X.2009.17.2.28-37

Kay, R. H. (2012). Exploring the use of video podcasts in education: A comprehensive review of the literature. *Computers in Human Behavior, 28*(3), 820–831. doi:10.1016/j.chb.2012.01.011

Kikuchi, K., & Sakai, H. (2009). Japanese learners' demotivation to study English: A survey study. *JALT Journal*, *31*(2), 183–204.

Kimura, Y., Nakata, Y., & Okumura, T. (2001). Language Learning Motivation of EFL Learners in Japan—A Cross-Sectional Analysis of Various Learning Milieus. *JALT Journal*, *23*(1), 47–68. doi:10.37546/JALTJJ23.1-3

Kramsch, C., & Aden, J. (2012). *ELT and intercultural/transcultural learning* [Approche culturelle en didactique des langues: hommage à Albane Cain]. Retrieved from https://www.academia.edu/4280731/ELT_AND_INTERCULTURAL_TRANSCULTURAL_LEARNING

Lord, G. (2008). Podcasting communities and second language pronunciation. *Foreign Language Annals*, *41*(2), 364–379. Advance online publication. doi:10.1111/j.1944-9720.2008.tb03297.x

Middleton, A. (2009). Beyond podcasting: Creative approaches to designing educational audio. *ALT-J Research in Learning Technology*, *17*(2), 143–155. doi:10.1080/09687760903033082

Moeller, A. J., & Nugent, K. (2014). Building intercultural competence in the language classroom. In S. Dhonau (Ed.), *2014 report of the Central States Conference on the Teaching of Foreign Languages* (pp. 1–18). Richmond, VA: Robert M. Terry.

Muñoz, C. (2007). CLIL: Some Thoughts on its Psycholinguistic Principles. *Revista Española de Lingüística Aplicada*, *1*, 17-26. Retrieved from https://dialnet.unirioja.es/servlet/articulo?codigo=2575488

Nikitina, L., & Furuoka, F. (2019). Language learners' mental images of Korea: Insights for the teaching of culture in the language classroom. *Journal of Multilingual and Multicultural Development*, *40*(9), 774–786. Advance online publication. doi:10.1080/01434632.2018.1561704

O'Dowd, R. (2012). Intercultural communicative competence through telecollaboration. In J. Jackson (Ed.), The Routledge Handbook of Language and Intercultural Communication (pp. 340–356). Academic Press.

Parsons, M. (2021). Podcasting Technology for Student Engagement and English Language Learning in the Japanese Context. In D. Ktoridou, E. Doukanari, & N. Eteokleous (Eds.), *Fostering Meaningful Learning Experiences Through Student Engagement* (pp. 245–265). IGI Global. doi:10.4018/978-1-7998-4658-1.ch013

Parsons, M., Garant, M., & Shikova, E. (in press). Video-Exchange Telecollaboration: Towards Developing Interculturality in EFL Environments. In S. M. Hilliker (Ed.), *Second Language Teaching and Learning through Virtual Exchange*. De Gruyter Mouton.

Pérez, B.C., Vigil, M.G., Georgíeva, D., Níkleva, Jiménez, Á.J., MaríaTeresa, L., Molina, Ó., Morales, F.F. & Rodríguez, L. S. (2011). The Esepod Project: Improving Listening Skills Through Mobile Learning. *Proceedings of the 4th International ICT for Language Learning*. https://www.researchgate.net/publication/259009828_The_Esepod_Project_Improving_Listening_Skills_Through_Mobile_Learning

Scutter, S., Stupans, I., Sawyer, T., & King, S. (2010). How do students use podcasts to support learning? *Australasian Journal of Educational Technology, 26*(2). Advance online publication. doi:10.14742/ajet.1089

Sharifian, F. (208). Learning Intercultural Competence. In A. In Burns & J. C. Richards (Eds.), The Cambridge Guide to Learning English as a Second Language. Academic Press.

Smith, S. (2012). Why Japan, South Korea, and China Are So Riled Up Over a Few Tiny Islands. *The Atlantic*. Retrieved from: https://www.theatlantic.com/international/archive/2012/08/why-japan-south-korea-and-china-are-so-riled-up-over-a-few-tiny-islands/261224/

UN. (n.d.). *The Sustainable Development Agenda*. https://www.un.org/sustainabledevelopment/development-agenda/

United Nations. (2015). *Resolution adopted by the General Assembly on 25 September 2015: Transforming our world: The 2030 Agenda for Sustainable Development A/RES/70/1*. Retrieved from https://www.un.org/ga/search/view_doc.asp?symbol=A/RES/70/1&Lang=E

Ware, P., & O'Dowd, R. (2008). Peer Feedback on Language Form in Telecollaboration. *Language Learning & Technology, 12*(1), 43–63.

Yeung, P. (2017). Why can't Chinese graduates speak good English? Blame the teaching methods. *South China Morning Post*. Retrieved from: https://www.scmp.com/comment/insight-opinion/article/2110113/why-cant-chinese-graduates-speak-good-english-blame-teaching

Zotzmann, K. (2015). The Impossibility of Defining and Measuring Intercultural Competencies. In D. J. Rivers (Ed.), *Resistance to the Known*. Palgrave Macmillan. doi:10.1057/9781137345196_8

Chapter 4
Humanistic Mentoring in Graduate Education:
An Urgent Innovation in Uncertain Times

Sandra Gudino Paredes
Tecnologico de Monterrey, Mexico

Felipe J. Jasso Pena
Tecnologico de Monterrey, Mexico

EXECUTIVE SUMMARY

In a global health pandemic context, a group 16 of education Master's students met voluntarily with their tutors in a virtual research support seminar, during the Saturday mornings of the first and second semester of 2020. This study aimed to know to what extent did mentoring and human tutoring characteristics emerge in a virtual research seminar experience. Through a qualitative research approach that included the analysis of the conversations and dialogues of the recorded sessions, insights showed that some of these characteristics emerged naturally along with the sessions, but as time passed, emotional and personal aspects were appearing more often than some others, showing that students felt more comfortable talking about themselves and supporting their classmates, as well as expressing their academic doubts and project thoughts freely because of humanistic tutoring approach. Most of them achieved the goal of finishing their project chapters on time. The humanistic and professional characteristics of teachers emerged as the main factors to develop this humanistic tutoring approach.

DOI: 10.4018/978-1-7998-8310-4.ch004

INTRODUCTION

Educational Innovation in Times of COVID-19

It seems that world is currently facing a learning culture change in which the number and scores of standardized tests go up, but the understanding and commitment of the student decreases (Ramsay, 2020). As a result of surveys of world business leaders, in 2008, Wagner compiled what he called the seven survival skills that should be developed in the university of the future:

- Critical thinking and problem solving
- Collaboration
- Agility and adaptability
- Initiative and entrepreneurship
- Communication
- Information analysis
- Curiosity and imagination

Other studies support the above mentioned by referring to the need of nurturing human potential inside of universities that enhances individual learning results and at the same time complains about facing, what they call, a crisis in human resources and entrepreneurship (Robinson, 2014 and Fayolle et al. 2020). Characteristics such as flexibility, inclusion, collaboration, authenticity, relevance and the extension of influence of the university will be those that distinguish higher education in institutions of the third millennium according to various authors such as Feliz, 2005, Jonker et al., 2020 or Toraman et al. 2020 to name just a few. While ideal educational objectives should remain lifelong learning, global interaction and metacognition. The importance of interaction in the learning process is further strengthened, since it has been consistently shown that students learn more when they interact with the material, when they interact with each other and when they interact with teachers (Friedman, 2005; Dede and Richards, 2020).

Studies carried out on commitment, interaction and participation of students with their own learning in higher education (learning engagement) proposed that they should be involved in practical situations where they can apply their theoretical knowledge by interacting with teachers and with their classmates. The challenge then prevails to promote knowledge capable of addressing global and fundamental problems in order to register partial and local knowledge according to Arocena and Sutz, 2001 or Nursalam, 2020. It seems - say Flynn and Vredevoogd (2010) - that the new generation of University students prefer an educational model based on activity and interaction that does not align with the one currently prevalent in several of the universities. It the same line, Prensky, who coined the term "Digital Natives" in 2001, agrees that today's students are not interested in taking classes in large lecture rooms and prefer, instead, discussion in small groups, often led to carried out on digital platforms, as an ideal means to understand the contents of your study plan. This author also states that students prefer to use search engines to find information and frown on library research methods (as cited in Sanchiz et al., 2020).

The social nature of digital natives, as well as their desire for experiential learning, sends a message to educators about the importance of incorporating interaction and action into the curriculum, say authors such as Philip and Zakkariya (2020). Recently, the relationship between the faculty and the student is changing and the study plans should be transformed in order to give rise to a co-designed course in which the student participates in establishing the learning outcomes and in deciding the experience that they will live; While the faculty seems to be in charge of monitoring, evaluating and certifying their progress, some others are seeking to collaborate and work with colleagues in order to make a challenging, rich and diverse curriculum stated Pérez et al., (2011) and Harrison (2019).

The educational needs of a particular human community, arises as a result of the search for the preservation and cultural projection of the said society in time (values, context, beliefs, history, traditions, etc.) (Jaeger, 2019). However, due to the current large amount of information to be transmitted, the generation of new knowledge and the power, submission or democratic relations between nations, this process naturally had increased in complexity (Abbagnano and Visalberghi, 2019).

The above implied the adaptation or innovation of the teaching and learning processes; That is, to elucidate the best way of "how" to teach and "how" to learn, exclusive purposes of didactics, from the Greek "didasco", which means to teach and instruct, but also refers to clearly demonstrate and expose (López, 2016). This abbreviated review of the historical development of education in the world and the need to innovate according to the circumstances that prevail in each era, is again fulfilled with the outbreak of the COVID 19 pandemic, notified for the first time in Wuhan, China on 31 December 2019, all of 2020 and prevailing to date (WHO, 2021). Of course, with all this number of events, it was no longer possible to continue with the regular educational processes as all face-to-face education was transferred to virtual, as part of the international efforts to avoid and contain contagions, with their usual social and technical and economic complications (Cicha, Rizun, Rutecka and Strzelecki, 2021). In this way, nowadays, teaching strategies (now more than ever) should be oriented towards the promotion of the student´s active participation on the object of knowledge and an innovative teacher intervention by providing appropriate study materials, organizing the materials in accordance with learning objectives and accompanying and advising in his activities (Zawacki, 2021). This includes providing a demonstration and examples with new material, guided and systematic practice through dialogue and reasoning; Promotion of self-instruction, self-management of learning to obtain, as a consequence, an autonomous, creative and analytical work of the student with new material the teacher's help (Syahrin, Dawud, Suwignyo & Priyatni, 2019).

RESEARCH AND CRITICAL THINKING DEVELOPMENT

For centuries, developing this kind of competences, besides a scientific thinking approach, has not being easy. When the study of science begins in any of its areas, concretely in graduate education, students do not have enough research experience in order develop a research study of any phenomenon, by themselves (Meza, et. al., 2020). In fact, some of their knowledge regarding these subjects is unspecialized; It means, empirical; since it is the product of their first impression obtained from the phenomena they are facing (Pasek, 2018). Of course, this type of knowledge has always been part of human life. The big difference is that it has been obtained without a research methodology, in a circumstantial and informal way or transmitted by cultural tradition or by ideological issues, such as the so-called "Covid-idiots" (Haoran, Shupei, Sixiao and 2013) or religious (Perry, Baker and Grubbs, 2021). Another current example is the beliefs of social media users about the veracity of their shared messages (Tae, Duhachek, Briñol & Petty, 2020). The opposite occurs with scientific knowledge where it seeks to establish laws, theories and principles that govern natural phenomena and that is characterized by being objective, verifiable, fallible, systematic, cumulative, general and factual (Copi and Cohen, 2011; Reddy, 2021). Thus, the methodology of scientific research can be considered as a discipline in charge of the principles and procedures, techniques and instruments of knowledge to discover the truth (Jain, 2019). Relying on the search for solutions to the approaches that researchers generate on the light of any phenomenon of their interest (Gravetter and Forzano, 2019).

In order for a student to develop his scientific thinking in research, it will be necessary to promote skills that include something beyond observing, describing, explaining and proposing a conclusion (Asmoro, Suciati and Prayitno, 2021). Because such kind of thinking involves the ability to elaborate questions, define problems, seek evidence and make decisions based on them, consider the scope effects of said decisions and review their effects (Ekicia and Erdemb, 2020; Hendrich, Licklider, Thompson et al., 2018). Nevertheless, it will also require solid foundations to critical thinking, this means, being scientifically creative (Qiang, et. al; 2018). In that way, teachers must be aware to the student's research abilities that go beyond the spectrum of scientific education, such as:

- Individual capacity for deep learning (Arvidsson and Kuhn, 2021; Manalo, 2019)
- Motivation levels (willingness to learn) (Pasek, 2018)
- Self-esteem to solve different problems and believing in their judgments and solution proposals (Demirdag, 2019)
- Curiosity level of about the studied phenomena (Jirout, 2020)

DIALOGIC APPROACH AND LEARNING PROCESS

Deep learning, such as the required from any graduate student, is a process that requires specific skills regarding problem solving, creativity, innovation, and self-direction (Hava, 2021), in addition, the willingness and ability to interact with their peers and teachers in order to extend their range in the reflective acquisition of knowledge (Yaacob, Mohd Asraf, Hussain and 2021). Another important aspect to consider in educational field are the attitudinal and confrontational aspects of emotions, since from these it will be possible to understand the reactions that individuals take as a consequence of their emergence and of the performance of activities related to the academic field, such as scientific research (Merkel, 2020). On the other hand, when the student lacks experience in carrying out scientific work and exchanging ideas between teachers and classmates, they will most likely make cognitive behavioral efforts to handle these new specific demands (Olave, Moni & Renshaw, 2020). They can also be seen as a burden or exceed your available resources to cope with an adverse phenomenon; or, being unable to have personal control over them (Holdsworth, Turner & Scott, 2018; Wright, 2006).

Because learning is socially constructed, learners do not depend on themselves for the acquisition of knowledge (Brockbank and McHill, 2007). In that way, dialogue, as a rational discourse and epistemic instrument, is necessary (Gadamer, 2007), placing itself in the field of training in higher education as a means to know how to carry out (generally for the first time), the exercise of relating and adapting to the scientific method (Nind, Holmes, Insenga et al., 2020). Paradoxically, although communication is a natural part of human existence, not every exchange of messages between people (sender and receiver) through a language that can be decoded by them (Beristáin, 2010; Gómez, 2018), can be called dialogue.

Nevertheless, a very significant characteristic for the dialogue in order to be useful to expose and contrast ideas, ideological positions, argumentative resources and knowledge is reflection (McAndrews and Hansberry, 2018), whose benefits, when fostered among students, extend beyond their formal studies to their professional life (Roessger, 2020). Conducting a reflective dialogue requires that both parties (teachers and students) to be capable of observing and engaging in a critical dialogue with themselves and subsequently with each other in the educational process, thus reinforcing their reflective practice (Choy, Dinham, Yim et al., 2020; Teo, 2020).

HUMANISTIC TUTORING AND MENTORING APPROACH

In Pedagogy of the Oppressed, Freire (1970) stated, "Concern for humanization leads at once to the recognition of dehumanization" (43). Humanization refers to the integral processes of formation where two persons look at each other with dignity and respect in all their dimensions: intellectual, affective, social and cultural. It is to recover the individuality that makes every human being unique (Lozada et al. 2013, Saida and Yusubovna, 2020). In the same line, the process of providing humanistic approach feedback, in educational fields, allows the teacher and the student to have an interpersonal communication that is not linear, but circular (Ren, 2020), in this way, the educator becomes a facilitator and a dialogue partner (Umar, 2020). The bond that exists between the two parties in a virtual environment is strengthened through an adequate regulated feedback processes so that virtual tutoring fulfills the goals of a true educational process, because it on it that the student creates and have confidence in himself, generate reflection, feed his self-esteem, motivates, reinforces and increases his learning. Hence

Humanistic tutoring, especially in times of uncertainty, emerges as a pedagogical strategy that encourages closeness in virtual environments. If the teacher or tutor figure is recognized as the architect of the student's development in normal educational situations would be much greater during unexpected events of international scope, such as the COVID 19 pandemic (Youde, 2020, Walpola and Lucas, 2021).

Regarding the "mentoring" concept, it has been used in many fields, for so many years, in The Odyssey, Odysseus, the Greek king and warrior. when he knew he would be away from home for so long, he chose a trusted friend, a mentor, to educate, tutor, protect, and guide his son (Doherty, 2009) Since the 1970, several definitions of mentoring or mentors have emerged in the literature (Blackwell, 1989), these definitions are extremely diverse, hence, there is no professional consensus on any "acceptable" definition as Wrightsman (1981) stated " "There is a false sense of consensus, because at a superficial level everyone "knows" what mentoring is. But closer examination indicates a wide variation in operational definitions, leading to conclusions that are limited to the use of particular procedures." (p 3–4). Even though formal and informal mentoring programs have been popping up in colleges and universities nationwide, especially in medical schools there only a few books had described a guideline for developing such programs, one example is Johns Hopkins University School of Nursing whom undertook the task to define the construct of "mentorship" and to develop new generic instruments in order to measure the effectiveness of a faculty mentoring relationship (Berk, et. al. 2015).

According to Jacobi (1991) mentoring relationship involves five basic characteristics: (1) focuses on achievement or acquisition of knowledge; (2) consists of three components: emotional and psychological support, direct assistance with career and professional development, and role modeling; (3) is reciprocal, where both mentor and mentee derive emotional or tangible benefits; (4) is personal, involving direct interaction; and (5) emphasizes the mentor's greater experience, influence, and achievement within a particular organization. Having a space where student feels free to express themselves and reflect on her experiences with research, on how they have been affected by her personal and professional experiences (due to forced sanitary confinement) with their teachers and classmates can help to developing their professional identity through the reaffirmation of their self-esteem, self-image, motivation for work and vision for the future (Engelbertink, Colomer, Woudt et al., 2021). During COVID 19 scenery, dropout as a consequence of school failure or the manifest difficulty of students at the time of acquiring knowledge and investigative skills, was latent (Xavier and Meneses, 2020).

METHOD

This study took place in a Mexican private university during the first and second semester of the 2020 year; pandemic was just arriving to the country and all schools closed their doors and changed their regular teaching format from face to face into online. Even though, the master in education program used to be an online program since its foundation, students enrolled in *Research Project* course one and two. Research project one course, involves the development of three first chapters and research project two course cover intervention itself and the last two chapters. All this work is performed by the student within a tutor companion, usually one tutor is in charge of five students. Students are enrolled into in a virtual program but their projects supposed to be developed face to face in a normal context, unfortunately this generation had to change their original face to face educational interventions plans in to online format suddenly.

The aim of these courses is making students able to build an intervention project inside their professional context in order to apply all the knowledge gained during their education master. These projects should emerge from a real educational context and in order to address a real problem and they are not private of formal scholar context but non-formal educational context, professional context and any other that involves learning and teaching aspects. Students should build their projects in several defined steps:

1. Problem establishment: the objective of this chapter is to share the problem background detected based on the information collected with an initial diagnosis.
2. Theoretical framework: the objective of this chapter is to provide information that allows readers to understanding the basic concepts that make up the development of this intervention project according to the subject.
3. Intervention project design: this chapter aims to detail resources of any kind to be used during implementation, it also includes instruments developed to measure intervention impact.
4. Results interpretation and analysis.
5. Conclusions: the objective of this chapter is to present the intervention project findings or conclusions, as well as some recommendations derived from them in order to support future decision making.

Framed into a grounded theory paradigm (Creswell, 2007) which unit of analysis frequently involves human interactions, this study analyzed 18 virtual mentoring sessions that took place every Saturday from 10:00 AM to 11:00 AM. For this chapter we will focus only in six of those, three from first semester (Research Project 1) (RP1) and three from second semester (Research Project 2) (RP2). Students enrolled in research project courses were invited to freely attend. Sixteen graduate students were invited but ten of them where connected constantly in every saturday session.

Analysis categories involved five basic characteristics of a mentoring relationship according to Jacobi (1991), which were codified as follows (Characteristic of a Mentoring Relationship number)

1. Focuses on achievement or acquisition of knowledge. (CMR1)
2. Emotional and psychological support: direct assistance with career and professional development, and role modeling. (CMR2)
3. Reciprocity: where both mentor and mentee derive emotional or tangible benefits. (CMR3)
4. Personal: involving direct interaction. (CMR4)
5. Mentor's greater experience: influence, and achievement within a particular organization. (CMR5)

And the four humanistic tutoring dimensions from Saida and Yusubovna (2020), which were codified as follows (Humanistic Tutoring Dimension number)

1. Intellectual aspect (HTD1): when conversation involves academic aspects.
2. Affective aspect (HTD2): when conversation touches personal or emotional aspects from participants.

3. Social aspect (HTD3): when conversation involves several aspects regarding social subjects that not necessarily are about academic aspects.
4. Cultural aspect (HTD4): involves subjects regarding cultural elements from the students or the tutors, those aspects emerge usually during the process and impacts also work construction.

The study research question was: to what extend mentoring relationship characteristics (Jacobi,1991) and tutoring dimensions (Saida and Yusubovna, 2020) were found in a virtual mentoring sessions experience during COVID-19 pandemic context?

The study also aimed to know the level of frequency which characteristics involved emotional and affective aspects were found along the year sessions and to know how many participants were able to achieved their goal of reaching their results chapter of their projects. It is important to mention that students' participations voices extracts were labeled according to their professional role in order to anonymized their identity. Three mentors (tutors) were participating in every session, all of them experts in education and one of them (tutor one) was also psychologist, specialist in developing and applying user training programs in face-to-face and electronic formats with a marked interest in the design of teaching, learning and evaluation strategies of Meta-Skills in Information (metaliteracy).

RESULTS

Regarding main research question: to what extend mentoring relationship characteristics (Jacobi,1991) and tutoring dimensions (Saida and Yusubovna (2020) were found in a graduate virtual mentoring sessions experience during COVID-19 pandemic context?

Sessions analysis were performed after the transcriptions of these Zoom sessions recordings were made, in order to extract fragments where these categories were found. Transcriptions were made with Dictation.io tool, which work with google https://dictation.io/

It is important to mention that most of the sessions time was dedicated to intellectual aspect (HTD1) and focused on achievement or acquisition of knowledge (CMR1), nevertheless and according to the time that sessions occurred several dialogues regarding affective (HTD2), cultural (HTD4) and social (HTD3) aspects emerged, as well as emotional and psychological support (CMR2), reciprocity (CMR3) and personal (CMR4). Mentor one appeared as a main figure, above the other two tutors, along the sessions, regarding his psychologist profile that emerged as important characteristic to make students felt comfortable.

Table 1. Categorization of phrases and dialogues recovered from mentoring sessions

Number and topic of each session	Characteristics of a mentoring relationship according to Jacobi (1991) and four humanistic tutoring dimensions from Saida and Yusubovna (2020)
Session 1 (RP1) Topic: this session was focused in establishing research problem question.	• *"One of my great concerns for the project is that my children be motivated to learn. I teach English in primary"* (Student English teacher) (CMR1, HTD1) • *"If we work with school-age students, it is very important to know the characteristics of the students' development, we must have developmental psychology books at hand"* (Mentor 1) (CMR1, HTD1, CMR4, CMR5) • *I am a doctor and I have a specialty in rehabilitation but for personal reasons I changed my state. I have been a full professor and I realized that students lack critical thinking. As we are in an extraordinary situation, the students have not had class and now they are entering the COVID area without having the necessary tools.* (Student Medical specialist in rehab) (CMR1, HTD1, CMR4, CMR5, HTD3) • *"Please please reflect on all this we had saw here, do not drop the question and we will keep working on the question. What interests me is that the reflective process is very clear to you".* (Mentor 1) (CMR1, HTD1, CMR5, CMR4)
Session 2 (RP1) Topic: this session was focused in instrument construction to diagnose the problems that students will address with their projects. In this section, for the first time, one of the students shared an emotional thought about feeling confused at this stage.	• *"M asked me in an email if at this stage it was normal to feel confused, the answer is yes; and it happens to all of us: those who are doing doctorates, those with masters and those with undergraduate degrees".* (Mentor 1) (HTD3, CMR4, CMR2, CMR3) • *"I would like to know if a virtual classroom can impact the learning of medical students".* (Student medical specialist physiotherapist) (HTD1, CMR1) • *"Why when I search in academic google the result places some texts on the top and others on the bottom? Ah well, because the ones that Google places above are the ones that have the keywords that I placed in the search engine repeated more times".* ((Mentor 1) (CMR1, HTD1, CMR4)
Session 3 (RP1): this session was focused in theoretical frame work development and how to search for academic sources in our databases and outside of them. In this session more, emotional dialogues were found while students share their doubts.	• *"You just gave me the answer to what I was going to ask you about how to define my problem, but I don't know if I also have to support that with literature?".* (STEM teacher) (CMR1, HTD1, HTD2, CMR4, HTD4) • *"Sometimes to read I use the kindle reader. Is there one recommended or better?"* (Rural teacher) (CMR1, HTD1, CMR4) • *"I'm going to answer you in library slang. Which one is the best? The one that allows you to read it and that's it".* (Mentor 1) (CMR4) • *"Remember, write, write and write, let go writing and trust yourselves, my fellow teachers and I are looking for you to find your inner writer, the writer of academic papers".* (Mentor 1) (HTD2, HTD3, CMR4, CMR2, CMR3) • *"I think everything is clear doctor; we just have to let ourselves go."* (Music teacher) (HTD2, HTD3, CMR4, CMR2, CMR3)
Session 1 (RP2) this session was focused in methodological aspects and intervention description. In this session emotional dialogues were found more frequently.	• *"Let's see… what was the goal? This was. Was it achieved or not? Well, yes or no. One of the biggest researcher's fear is: what if what I wanted or predicted doesn't happen? Well, nothing happens! because they will be also insights! Please don't be afraid".* (Mentor 2) (CMR1, HTD1, HTD2, HTD3, CMR4, CMR2, CMR3) • *Before we go please remember to write as much as you can, as much as you can.* (CMR1, HTD1) • *Play your favorite music jajaja* (STEM teacher) (CMR4) • *This is because then some of you send us just a small paragraph to receive feedback, for us it is better to have a lot of writing to give feedback and corrections than only a paragraph.* (Mentor 1) (CMR1, HTD1)
Session 2 (RP2) this session was focused in results aspects and intervention performance. In this session emotional dialogues were found more frequently, pandemic effects emerged impacting all the students.	• *"This situation that I have to deal with colleagues that supposed to teach musical instrument, most likely, they will not be working next semester unless it was face to face but probably this will not happen and they might be fired, so I do not know what to do; if I have to think of another alternative this is so stressful"* (Music teacher) (CMR4, CMR2, CMR3). • *"Do not stress, you can start thinking of a plan b in which you can carry out the intervention yourself, the main thing is to be calm".* (CMR4, CMR2, CMR3) • *"In education one tenth up or one tenth down in terms of performance or achievement, is a finding and it is perfectly valid. It is a reality in all interventions, pandemic currently affects and it is something that is affecting us all and all studies around the world at this time. If you think that your study does not work, wait! You will see… something is going to move, maybe not to the extent you expected but there will. The educational phenomenon is not an app educational phenomenon is always influenced by context".* (Mentor 1) (CMR1, HTD1, HTD2) • *So, does this mean that the results without a pandemic could have been different?* (Music teacher) (CMR1, HTD1, HTD2) • *We will never know that, because we are doing it right now, but if you could compare it with a similar study carried out outside the pandemic context.* (Mentor 1) (CMR1, HTD1, HTD2)
Session 3 (RP2) this session was focused in results aspects and intervention performance. In this session emotional dialogues were found more frequently among knowledge and intellectual content but in terms of proportion, it was clear that a personal connection had been stablished among the members of this community.	• *"At this time teachers and students, we are all exposed to the conditions around us. For example, Stephany that became a mother during this course. What can I tell her? Stephany don't worry, being a mother is very easy, no. Right Stephany?* (Mentor 1) (HTD2, HTD3, CMR4, CMR2, CMR3) • *On the contrary, professor, I really appreciate your support in the last emotional crisis I had towards the end of last semester due to my pregnancy and labor, everything is fine now* (Elementary teacher) (HTD2, HTD3, CMR4, CMR2, CMR3) • *From this moment on, nobody can tell you what could happen to you by doing research, nobody is going to tell to something new, because you have already lived it during this year, the research is life itself.* (Mentor 1) (HTD2, HTD3, CMR4, CMR2, CMR3) • *I once saw a child who was taken to school at 7 in the morning and picked up at 7 at night, during this time he was in several classes and his family did not see him at all. I am not saying learning is bad or studying is bad, but overexposure to something can have an adverse effect. Hence the importance of resting and changing the stimulus every so often.* (Mentor 1) (HTD2, HTD3, CMR4, CMR2, CMR3)

Source: self-elaborated

Figure 1. level of frequency
Source: Self- elaborated

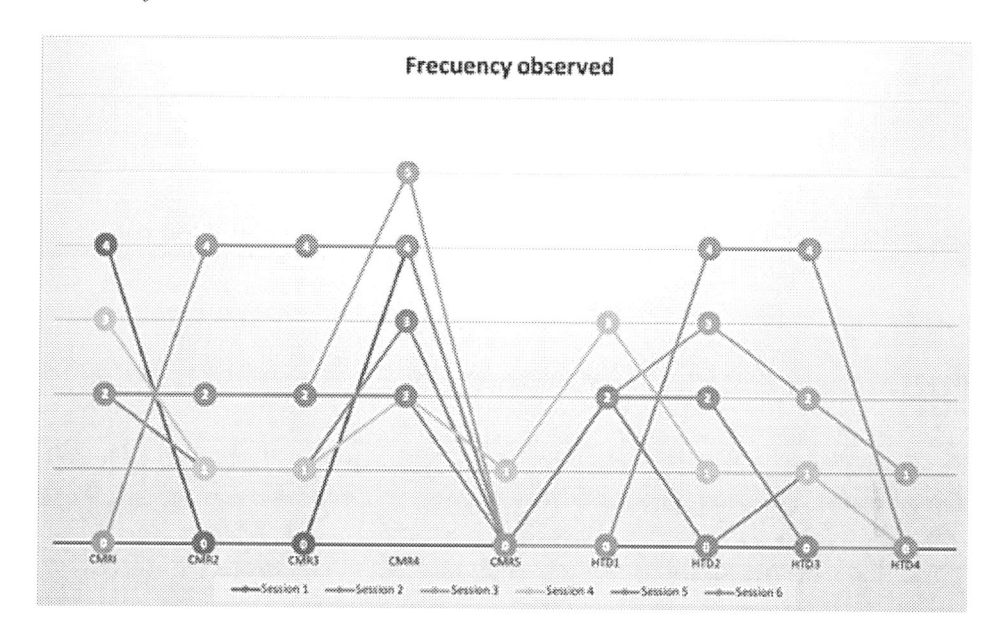

The level of frequency which characteristics involved emotional and affective aspects were found along the year within sessions occurred, different factors that hindered their personal and emotional context came to light and it was noticed by the frequency of emotional categories emerged gradually trough the sessions as it can be observed in figure one, were session 6 showed a higher frequency level of categories like: Emotional and psychological support (CMR2), reciprocity (CMR3), personal interaction (CMR4), affective (HTD2) and Social aspects (HTD3), compared with first sessions that showed more categories like: achievement or acquisition of knowledge(CMR1) and Intellectual aspect (HTD1).

There was one category that only emerged once, the cultural aspect of human tutoring direction (HTD4), it might had been because most of the students were living in the same country and shared a common cultural background.

Regarding how many students from the group achieved their goal of accomplished their interventions and projects, it can be said that majority of them did. At the beginning, students were nervous about how to solve the problem of not being able to do their projects face to face as they thought during first semester, when most of them thought that pandemic will be gone by their application semester; however, virtual tutoring group seemed to helped them to achieve their purposes and came up with several ideas for online projects instead of face to face projects. Most of them conducted their projects successfully. Some of the student´s projects titles were:

- Emotional education for secondary school teachers and the impact on your stress levels.
- Gamification as motivator in learning a second language.
- Development of emotional intelligence in resident doctors, through mobile learning.
- The impact of learning a musical instrument on logical-mathematical thinking in 5th grade students.
- Intervention on the development of emotional intelligence for the impact on the learning of children in preschool.

FUTURE RESEARCH DIRECTIONS

Resent educational global context and emerging trends had shown that mentoring and humanistic tutoring functions become high valuated, as well as the dialogical approach over traditional format classes. It seems important to point that educational innovations not always deal with new technologies incorporation but with a different relationship approach among students and tutors, a trustful and closer relationship that allows them to be able to develop self-direction, critical thinking and metacognition. As Zawacki (2021) stated, teaching strategies nowadays are oriented towards the promotion of the student´s active participation on the object of knowledge and an innovative teacher intervention that includes accompanying and advising student´s activities in a closer way in a virtual or face to face context.

CONCLUSION

A viability of a paradigm emerged regarding mentoring and humanistic tutoring approaches, as well as dialogue innovative practices for reforming actual educational context. As the seminars sessions interventions and dialogues were analyzed within a year, this study shows how a confidence relationship emerged among teachers and students resulting in deeper dialogues that implied emotional and personal subjects combined with intellectual ones. As Hava (2021) and Yaacob, et. al (2021) stayed, deep learning, is a process that requires specific skills such as problem solving, creativity, innovation, and self-direction as well as the ability to interact with peers and teachers in order to extend their range of reflective and social acquisition of knowledge. Reflection can only take place inside a reflective dialogue and this was observed among the graduate students whom participated in the Saturday meetings during the development of their research project. Not only to review their progress according the established protocol, but also to reflect on all the events that were

Figure 2. Humanistic tutoring/mentoring model for graduate students
Source: Self- elaborated

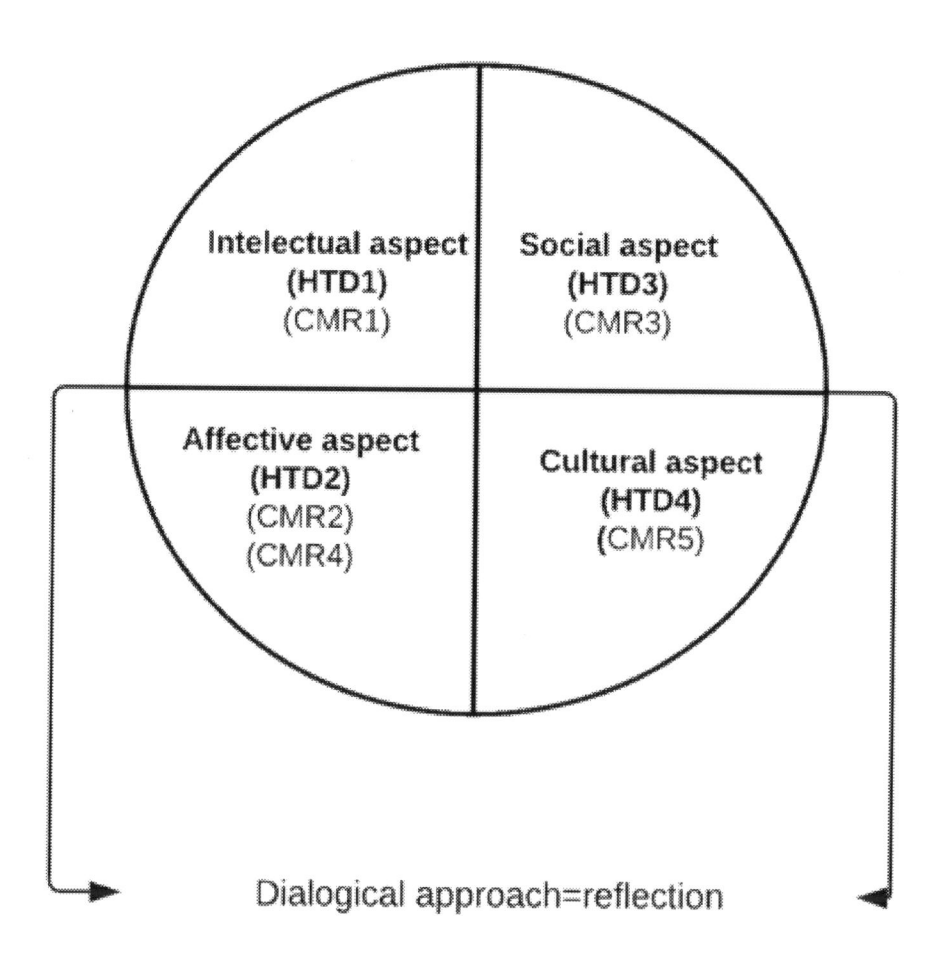

happening (personal and professional) at the same time that they were approaching the study of the chosen phenomenon (Botelho, 2021). As graduate students' teachers we proposed to develop a mentor concept as the close relationship that emerged between mentee and mentor that goes beyond academical aspects into human aspects. In this way, a proposal model emerged, involving Jacobi (1991) mentoring relationship characteristics and including them in to the four humanistic tutoring dimensions proposed by Saida and Yusubovna (2020), all these within a dialogical approach that promotes reflection. Our proposal can be seen in figure 2, where the four dimensions of humanistic mentoring within these sessions encompass the main characteristics of a mentoring relationship, all in a continuum that remains in motion and framed in a dialogical approach that entails reflection.

This research received no specific grant from any funding agency in the public, commercial, or not-for-profit sectors.

REFERENCES

Abbagnano, N., & Visalberghi, A. (2019). History of pedagogy. Economic Culture Fund (FCE).

Arvidsson, T. S., & Kuhn, D. (2021). Realizing the full potential of individualizing learning. *Contemporary Educational Psychology*, *65*, 101960. Advance online publication. doi:10.1016/j.cedpsych.2021.101960

Asmoro, S. P., Suciati, S., & Prayitno, B. A. (2021). Empowering scientific thinking skills of students with different scientific activity types through guided inquiry. *International Journal of Instruction*, *14*(1), 947–962. doi:10.29333/iji.2021.14156a

Arocena, R., & Sutz, J. (2001). *The Latin-American university of the future*. UDUAL.

Blackwell, J. E. (1989). Mentoring: An action strategy for increasing minority faculty. *Academe*, *75*(5), 8–14. doi:10.2307/40249734

Beristáin, H. (2010). *Rhetoric and Poetic dictionary*. Editorial Porrúa.

Berk, A., Berg, M.S., Mortimer, M.S., Walton, B., & Yeo, P. (2005). Measuring the Effectiveness of Faculty Mentoring Relationships. *Academic Medicine*, *80*(1), 66-71.

Brockbank, A., & McGill, I. (2007). *Aprendizaje reflexivo en la educación superior*. Morata.

Botelho, N. (2021). Reflection in motion: An embodied approach to reflection on practice. *Reflective Practice*, *22*(2), 147–158. doi:10.1080/14623943.2020.1860926

Cicha, K., Rizun, M., Rutecka, P., & Strzelecki, A. (2021). COVID-19 and Higher Education: First-Year Students' Expectations toward Distance Learning. *Sustainability*, *13*(4), 1–19. doi:10.3390u13041889

Choy, S. Ch., Dinham, J., Yim, J., & Williams, P. (2020). Comparing reflective practices of pre-service teachers in Malaysia and Australia: A mixed-methods approach. *Issues in Educational Research*, *30*(4), 1264–1285.

Creswell, J. W. (2007). *Qualitative inquiry and research design: Choosing among five traditions* (2nd ed.). Sage.

Copi, I. M., & Cohen, C. (2011). *Introduction to logic*. LIMUSA.

Dede, C. J., & Richards, J. (Eds.). (2020). *The 60-Year Curriculum: New Models for Lifelong Learning in the Digital Economy*. Routledge. doi:10.4324/9781003013617

Demirdag, S. (2019). Critical thinking as a predictor of self- esteem of university students. *The Alberta Journal of Educational Research*, *65*(4), 305–319. https://journalhosting.ucalgary.ca/index.php/ajer/article/view/56587

Doherty, L. E. (Ed.). (2009). *Homer's Odyssey*. Oxford University Press.

Engelbertink, M., Colomer, J., Woudt- Mittendorff, K. M., Alsina, Á., Kelders, S. M., Ayllón, S., & Westerhof, G. J. (2021). The reflection leveland the construction of professional identity of university students. *Reflective Practice*, *22*(1), 73–85. doi:10.1080/14623943.2020.1835632

Ekicia, M., & Erdemb, M. (2020). Developing Science Process Skills through Mobile Scientific Inquiry. *Thinking Skills and Creativity*, *36*, 100658. Advance online publication. doi:10.1016/j.tsc.2020.100658

Fayolle, A., Lamine, W., Mian, S., & Phan, P. (2020). Effective models of science, technology and engineering entrepreneurship education: Current and future research. *The Journal of Technology Transfer*, 1–11.

Feliz, U. (2005). E-learning pedagogy in the third millennium: The need for combining social and cognitive constructivist approaches. ReCALL: The Journal of Eurocall, 17(1), 85-100.

Flynn, W. J., & Vredevoogd, J. (2010). The future of learning: 12 views on emerging trends in higher education. *Planning for Higher Education*, *38*(2), 5.

Freire, P. (1970). *Pedagogy of the Oppressed*. Continuum.

Friedman, T. L. (2005). *The World is Flat: A Brief History of the Twenty-First Century*. Farrar, Straus and Giroux.

Gadamer, H.G. (2007). *Truth and method*. Follow Me Editions.

Gómez Flores, A. M. (2018). *Expression and communication*. IC Editorial.

Gravetter, F. J., & Forzano, L. B. (2019). *Research Methods for the Behavioral Sciences*. Cengage Learning.

Harrison, N., & Luckett, K. (2019). Experts, knowledge and criticality in the age of 'alternative facts': Re-examining the contribution of higher education. *Teaching in Higher Education*, *24*(3), 259–271. doi:10.1080/13562517.2019.1578577

Hava, K. (2021). The effects of the flipped classroom on deep learning strategies and engagement at the undergraduate level. *Participatory Educational Research, 8*(1), 379–394. doi:10.17275/per.21.22.8.1

Haoran, C., Shupei, Y., & Sixiao, L. (2021). Call them COVIDiots: Exploring the effects of aggressive communication style and psychological distance in the communication of COVID-19. *Public Understanding of Science (Bristol, England), 30*(3), 240–257. doi:10.1177/0963662521989191 PMID:33517854

Hendrich, S., Licklider, B., Thompson, K., Thompson, J., Haynes, C., & Wiersema, J. (2018). Development of scientific thinking facilitated by reflective self-assessment in a communication-intensive food science and human nutrition course. *Journal of Food Science Education, 17*(1), 8–13. doi:10.1111/1541-4329.12127

Holdsworth, S., Turner, M., & Scott Young, C. M. (2018). Not drowning, waving. Resilience and university: A student perspective. *Studies in Higher Education, 43*(11), 1837–1853. doi:10.1080/03075079.2017.1284193

Jacobi, M. (1991). Mentoring and undergraduate academic success: A literature review. *Review of Educational Research, 61*(4), 505–532. doi:10.3102/00346543061004505

Jaeger, W. (2019). Paideia: The ideals of Greek culture. Economic Culture Fund (FCE).

Jain, S. (2019). *Research methodology in arts, science and humanities.* Society Publishing.

Jirout, J. J. (2020). Supporting early scientific thinking through curiosity. *Frontiers in Psychology, 11*, 1717. Advance online publication. doi:10.3389/fpsyg.2020.01717 PMID:32849029

Jonker, H., März, V., & Voogt, J. (2020). Curriculum flexibility in a blended curriculum. *Australasian Journal of Educational Technology.*

Lozada, O. P., Beltrán, O. M., Vargas, F. A., Martin, D. A., Hincapié, B. S., Herrera, M., & Pérez, B. A. (2013). *Humanization of university teaching practice.* doi:10.14742/ajet.4926

Saida, R., & Yusubovna, K. G. (2020). Humanization of education as the basis of pedagogical communication. *European Journal of Research and Reflection in Educational Sciences, 8*(2).

Sanchiz, M., Amadieu, F., & Chevalier, A. (2020). An evolving perspective to capture individual differences related to fluid and crystallized abilities in information searching with a search engine. In *Understanding and Improving Information Search* (pp. 71–96). Springer. doi:10.1007/978-3-030-38825-6_5

Teo, P. (2020). Teaching for the 21st century: A case for dialogic pedagogy. *Learning, Culture and Social Interaction, 21*, 170–178. doi:10.1016/j.lcsi.2019.03.009

Toraman, Ç., Özdemir, H. F., Koşan, A. M. A., & Orakcı, Ş. (2020). Relationships between Cognitive Flexibility, Perceived Quality of Faculty Life, Learning Approaches, and Academic Achievement. *International Journal of Instruction, 13*(1).

López Gómez, E. (Coord.). (2016). General didactics and teacher training. International University of La Rioja, S.A.

McAndrews, C., & Hansberry, J. (2018). Facilitation and dialogue as methods of reflective practice in professional education. *Planning Practice and Research, 33*(1), 86–95. doi:10.1080/02697459.2017.1419653

Manalo, E. (Ed.). (2019). *Deeper learning, dialogic learning, and critical thinking: Research-based strategies for the classroom* (1st ed.). Routledge. doi:10.4324/9780429323058

Merkel, W. (2020). "What I Mean Is…": The role of dialogic interactions in developing a statement of teaching philosophy. *Journal of Second Language Writing, 48*, 100702. Advance online publication. doi:10.1016/j.jslw.2019.100702

Meza Salcedo, G., Rubio Rodríguez, G., Mesa, L., & Blandón, A. (2020). Formative and pedagogical nature of the literature review in research. *Technological Information, 31*(5), 153-162. doi:10.4067/S0718-07642020000500153

Nind, M., Holmes, M., Insenga, M., Lewthwaite, S., & Sutton, C. (2020). Student perspectives on learning research methods in the social sciences. *Teaching in Higher Education, 25*(7), 797–811. doi:10.1080/13562517.2019.1592150

Nursalam, N. (2020). Glocal Vision to Deconstruct Internationalization in Indonesian Higher Education. *Journal of Social Studies Education Research, 11*(1), 137–152.

Olave Encina, K., Moni, K., & Renshaw, P. (2020). Exploring the emotions of international students about their feedback experiences. *Higher Education Research & Development, 39*(2), 200–2014. doi:10.1080/07294360.2020.1786020

Pasek, J. (2018). It's not my consensus: Motivated reasoning and the sources of scientific illiteracy. *Public Understanding of Science (Bristol, England), 27*(7), 787–806. doi:10.1177/0963662517733681 PMID:28942728

Pérez, S., Saritas, O., Pook, K., & Warden, C. (2011). Ready for the future? Universities' capabilities to strategically manage their intellectual capital. *Foresight, 13*(2), 31–48. doi:10.1108/14636681111126238

Perry, S. L., Baker, J. O., & Grubbs, J. B. (2021). Ignorance or culture war? Christian nationalism and scientific illiteracy. *Public Understanding of Science (Bristol, England), 30*(8), 1–17. doi:10.1177/09636625211006271 PMID:33855921

Philip, A. V., & Zakkariya, K. A. (2020). Effective Engagement of Digital Natives in the Ever-Transforming Digital World. In Digital Transformation in Business and Society (pp. 113-125). Palgrave Macmillan. doi:10.1007/978-3-030-08277-2_7

Qiang, R., Han, Q., Guo, Y., Bai, J., & Karwowski, M. (2018). Critical thinking disposition and scientific creativity: The mediating role of creative self-efficacy. *The Journal of Creative Behavior, 54*(1), 90–99. doi:10.1002/jocb.347

Ramsay-Jordan, N. (2020). Preparation and The Real World of Education: How Prospective Teachers Grapple with Using Culturally Responsive Teaching Practices in the Age of Standardized Testing. *International Journal of Educational Reform, 29*(1), 3–24. doi:10.1177/1056787919877142

Ren, J. (2020). Cultivation of Humanistic Qualities in the Blended Teaching Model of College English. *In International Conference on Education Studies: Experience and Innovation* (pp. 602-604). Atlantis Press. 10.2991/assehr.k.201128.112

Roessger, K. M. (2020). Assessment strategies for reflective learning in the workplace. A pragmatic approach. *Adult Learning, 31*(4), 175–184. Advance online publication. doi:10.1177/1045159520941947

Robinson, K., & Aronica, L. (2014). *The element: how finding your passion changes everything*. Penguin Books. http://rbdigital.oneclickdigital.com

Saida, R., & Yusubovna, K. G. (2020). Humanization of education as the basis of pedagogical communication. *European Journal of Research and Reflection in Educational Sciences, 8*(2).

Syahrin, A., Dawud, Suwignyo, H., & Priyatni, E. T. (2019). Creative Thinking Patterns In Student's Scientific Works. *Eurasian Journal of Educational Research, 19*(81), 21–36. doi:10.14689/ejer.2019.81.2

Tae Woo, K., Duhachek, A., Briñol, P., & Petty, R. (2020). How posting online reviews can influence the poster's evaluations. *Personality and Social Psychology Bulletin*, 1–13. doi:10.1177/0146167220976449 PMID:33267745

Umar, M. (2020). Humanistic Approaches in Learning Processes Package C Equity Program (Case Study of the Setia Mandiri Community Learning Center). In *1st International Conference on Lifelong Learning and Education for Sustainability* (pp. 206-211). Atlantis Press.

Walpola, R., & Lucas, Ch. (2021). Reflective practice: The essential competency for health systems and healthcare practitioners during the COVID-19 pandemic. *Reflective Practice, 22*(2), 143–146. doi:10.1080/14623943.2020.1860925

World Health Organization. (2021). *Coronavirus disease (COVID-19) outbreak.* Retrieved from https://www.who.int/es/emergencies/diseases/novel-coronavirus-2019

Wrightsman, L. (1981). *Research methodologies for Assessing mentoring.* Paper presented at the Conference of the American Psychological Association, Los Angeles, CA.

Xavier, M., & Meneses, J. (2020). *Dropout in Online Higher Education: A scoping review from 2014 to 2018.* eLearn Center, Universitat Oberta de Catalunya.

Yaacob, A., Mohd Asraf, R., Hussain, R. M. R., & Ismail, S. N. (2021). Empowering Learners' Reflective Thinking through Collaborative Reflective Learning. *International Journal of Instruction, 14*(1), 709–726. doi:10.29333/iji.2021.14143a

Youde, A. (2020). I don't need peer support: Effective tutoring in blended learning environments for part-time, adult learners. *Higher Education Research & Development, 39*(5), 1040–1054. doi:10.1080/07294360.2019.1704692

Zawacki Richter, O. (2021). The current state and impact of Covid-19 on digital higher education in Germany. *Human Behavior and Emerging Technologies, 3*(1), 218–226. doi:10.1002/hbe2.238 PMID:33363276

KEY TERMS AND DEFINITIONS

Educational Innovation: To elucidate the best way of "how" to teach and "how" to learn.

Humanistic Mentoring Model for Graduate Education: A model that includes social, intellectual, cultural, and affective aspects.

Humanistic Tutoring: Humanization tutoring refers an integral educational process, where two persons look at each other with dignity and respect in all their human dimensions: intellectual, affective, social, and cultural.

Mentoring: The close relationship that emerged between mentee and mentor that goes beyond academical aspects into human aspects.

Reflection: A very significant characteristic for the dialogue whose benefits, when fostered among students, extend beyond their formal studies to their professional life.

Reflective Dialogue in Learning Process: Conducting a reflective dialogue requires that both parties (teachers and students) to be capable of observing and engaging in a critical dialogue with themselves and subsequently with each other in the educational process.

Teaching Strategies: Are procedures or resources (organizers of knowledge) used by the teacher in order to promote meaningful learning.

Chapter 5
Identifying Common Student Experiences That Affect Success in a Crisis Context (COVID–19):
A Case Study from Aotearoa New Zealand

Emily Saavedra

(iD) https://orcid.org/0000-0001-7840-5161
Massey University, New Zealand

Leonard Sanders
Massey University, New Zealand

EXECUTIVE SUMMARY

Learning experiences and educational opportunities around the world have been disrupted due to the outbreak of COVID-19. This chapter outlines a case study involving foundation-level students enrolled at an urban university in Aotearoa New Zealand. The case study is designed to gain a deeper understanding of student experiences during this time of crisis. Student narratives are analysed to identify common experiences and gain a clearer understanding of the self-reported factors that students identified as affecting their success, allowing academic and support staff to improve the pre-degree experience for foundation students. Affordable access to connectivity, increased pastoral care, and a digitally responsive curriculum were identified as key considerations to addressing inequities present in a crisis context (COVID-19) within the educational context and wider community.

DOI: 10.4018/978-1-7998-8310-4.ch005

INTRODUCTION

Educational practices and student experiences have been profoundly affected by the most recent epidemic. First reported at the end of 2019, COVID-19 (the name of the disease caused by a new coronavirus called SARS-CoV-2) was subsequently declared a global pandemic in March 2020, placing education in a situation of crisis. What quickly followed were radical and far-reaching changes to education systems at all levels. This chapter presents a case study of a tertiary foundation program delivered at an Aotearoa New Zealand university in the context of the COVID-19 crisis. The program is available for both international and domestic students and is delivered using a blended pedagogical approach that supports students with the transition into university studies.

Research by the authors conducted prior to the outbreak of COVID-19 showed common trends and variations across pre-degree programmes at a tertiary institution in Aotearoa New Zealand, which resulted in a clearer understanding of the factors that affect foundation student success. Moreover, necessary and relevant support systems for students in foundation programs could then be promoted, ensuring academic and support staff collaborated to improve the pre-degree experience for foundation students.

This chapter builds on what has already been learned to discuss commonalities identified from self-reported student experiences of the COVID-19 crisis. The data collected in this case study has been useful to ascertain what additional factors need to be considered, as well as to re-evaluate areas of practice and support currently available to students and teachers within the institution and the wider community.

It is important to understand (tertiary) education in the context of the global COVID-19 context, and more specifically in Aotearoa New Zealand (NZ). This chapter considers the framework of the United Nations Educational Scientific and Cultural Organisation (UNESCO) Sustainable Development Goals (SDGs) and how they apply to foundation education in NZ. A brief overview of NZ's Tertiary Education Strategy (TES) is then presented, focusing on key priorities with direct relevance to foundation education. This is followed by the findings obtained from a case study conducted at a NZ university during the COVID-19 crisis, and recommendations that reaffirm the need for ongoing digital transformation within NZ's tertiary education sector.

BACKGROUND

Education in the Context of COVID-19

According to UNESCO, the recent pandemic has brought unprecedented disruption to education; more than 1.5 billion students and youth across the planet are or have been affected by school and university closures in 178 countries at the end of April, 2020 due to the COVID-19 pandemic (UNESCO, 2020a).

Many students in New Zealand were affected by the pandemic (COVID-19) especially when they were locked-down as a result of measures to contain the spread of the pandemic. This occurred on 25 March 2020: a state of emergency was declared, and the country went into a four-week Alert Level 4 lockdown. This put into effect the plan announced on 21 March 2020, the establishment of a four-stage 'alert' level system: Level 1 (Prepare), Level 2 (Reduce), Level 3 (Restrict); and Level 4 (Eliminate), deemed the highest risk. For New Zealanders, this meant that the Ministry of Health had deemed the risk of widespread outbreaks and the possibility of sustained community transmission to be extremely high. Under Level 4 lockdown procedures, all public venues and businesses were closed, except for those providing essential services (such as supermarkets, petrol stations, and hospitals). Everyone was instructed to stay at home and remain inside their 'bubble'. The metaphor of a bubble was used to describe one's "immediate and usual family or household" (Henrickson, 2020, p. 123) and was referred to during public briefings from the Government and Ministry of Health. Under Level 4, movement outside one's immediate bubble was restricted to personal exercise within local areas, travel between home and essential services (such as supermarkets), and essential workers travelling between home and work. When outside your home, physical distancing of two metres from anyone not in your immediate bubble was enforced, face covering was advised, and inter-bubble interaction was strongly discouraged. It was under Level 4 lockdown protocols that all educational facilities and institutions were closed.

During this time, the educational community was forced into an instant adaptation (Burgos et al., 2020) and, as the COVID-19 pandemic has continued to escalate, educators around the world have been encouraged to move to online and distance learning modalities (Ossiannilsson, 2020, p. 99). In response to the virus, educational institutions were forced to shift their practices to emergency remote teaching as they pivoted all provisions of physical classroom-based lessons to an online context. In many cases, this pivot incorporated e-learning solutions that could be embedded in available educational platforms. This sudden digital transformation presented several challenges for students, teachers, and institutions around the world. In particular, when students did not have access to personal devices, the NZ government provided laptops which were distributed to primary and secondary school students, but this initiative was not extended to tertiary level students. A lack of accessibility to appropriate devices coupled with the closing of public spaces that enabled access to the internet, such as libraries and educational institutions with computers available onsite, meant that not all students were able to access classes.

While COVID-19 has disrupted education for millions across the globe, "many in the education community treat COVID-19 as an opportunity to build back better – to re-imagine and re-design education for the future" (Iyengar, 2020). Research is appearing on the issues, challenges, and advantages of using online e-learning systems during emergency periods such as COVID-19. Accessibility (internet connectivity, using compatible smartphones and laptops) has been identified as one of the most important challenges students face in an online learning situation such as COVID-19 (Aboagye et al., 2020). Although previous research identified cost and access to the internet as less important barriers to online learning (Muilenberg & Berg, 2005), accessibility is an important challenge to online learning and in the era of COVID-19 "this can be attributed to different geographical locations" (Aboagye et al., 2020, p. 6).

Due to the response – moving online and the emergence of virtual learning communities – it is expected that many learners will struggle with issues of access, affordability, motivation, and self-management. Constraints to digital justice (which in principle advocates that all members of communities have equal access, common ownership, and prioritizes the participation of people who may have been excluded) have previously been observed during regular classroom interactions; many students have limited access, and in some cases no access, to online or blended learning because they do not have appropriate digital devices or do not have adequate access to stable wi-fi connections off campus. A shortage in digital literacy also prevents full engagement in the online environment for some learners. The lockdowns, restrictions on movement and disruption of routines, as well as limitations on social interactions, and deprivation of traditional learning methods have led to "increased stress, anxiety, and mental health concerns for learners worldwide" (Holzer et al., 2021, p. 1).

The pandemic has further emphasized the importance for educators to reflect on the existing education system, what it means to design for transition (Green et al., 2020) during an emergency, how tools, social arrangements and tasks can be orchestrated to support learning activity in emergency remote education, and specifically how best to meet the individual needs of students (Ossiannilsson, 2020). This, at least in part, can be addressed using a heutagogic approach to learning and teaching which provides a more learner-centred, holistic approach to academic studies (Blaschke & Hase, 2016). In a well-designed, online environment, learners are enabled to direct their own learning path and to be more active in deciding what that learning path will look like. An online learning environment can be more responsive and adaptable, serving diverse needs simultaneously, than a traditional didactic context. One suggested approach has been to utilise end-user data to support the provision of more learner-centric education by accessing data "to personalize the learning support and to provide the right feedback and guidance to every group in the educational community" (Burgos et al., 2020, p. 9) which are available in most educational platforms and learning management systems (LMS).

Foundation Education in Aotearoa New Zealand

The tertiary education sector in NZ consists of universities, institutes of technology and polytechnics (ITPs), wānanga (publicly owned tertiary institutes situated in a Māori cultural context), private training establishments (PTEs) and industry training organisations (ITOs). One area, within the tertiary education sector, is foundation education, which is the focus of this chapter.

In NZ, foundation education provides support for students to gain the academic and study skills necessary for sustained success in their university studies. Foundation education programmes aim to embed multiple literacies (including but not limited to, digital, information, attention, and critical literacies) alongside content knowledge and foster independence. Foundation education programmes are situated in the tertiary education sector and serve as a post-secondary educational opportunity. Some programmes offer a pathway into degree level study for students who have not gained university admission and also for students who are returning to academic study after an extended gap in their formal study (Saavedra, 2018).

Students discussed in this chapter were enrolled full time in foundation courses on an urban campus in NZ. Classes are taught using a blended learning approach whereby technology is used alongside more traditional face-to-face methods. Each week, full-time students are expected to attend 16-20 hours of synchronous classes on campus and to spend up to 20 additional hours working autonomously on course content and assignments. Students are encouraged to spend some of the autonomous time in small groups, but it is not a requirement. All courses are delivered using a LMS that is accessible online.

Framework: UNESCO's Sustainable Development Goals (SDG) 4 (specifically SDG 4.3,4.5) and SDG3 (specifically 3.4)

UNESCO member countries adopted the 2030 Agenda for Sustainable Development in September 2015 envisaging "a world with equitable and universal access to quality education at all levels, to health care and social protection, where physical, mental and social well-being are assured" (United Nations, 2015). The rational for implementing the sustainable development projects focused on equipping key

Table 1. Significance of UNESCO SDG targets (4.3 and 4.5) for foundation education

UNESCO SDG Targets	Significance for Foundation Education in NZ
Target 4.3: Quality technical and vocational education and training (TVET) and tertiary education By 2030, ensure equal access for all women and men to affordable and quality technical, vocational, and tertiary education, including university.	Foundation education offers opportunities to support students to enter tertiary education. This includes students who may not have otherwise considered university level studies. It also offers opportunities, particularly for women, to return to education after starting a family or having had a hiatus in their formal education.
Target 4.5: Equal access to all levels of education and training for the vulnerable By 2030, eliminate gender disparities in education and ensure equal access to all levels of education and vocational training for the vulnerable, including persons with disabilities, indigenous peoples and children in vulnerable situations.	Foundation education aims to scaffold and facilitate students' transition into university. Foundation education aims to provide opportunities for students to have safe access to education. This includes students who are neurodiverse or who have faced challenges in the education system in its current form.

Source: (UNESCO, 2019)

areas of educational facilities and learning environments with the contemporary technologies. Education projects focused on providing access to modern learning technologies and support, financial or otherwise, for students' safe access to education opportunities (UNESCO, 2016).

This historic global crisis (COVID-19) has underlined the need to adapt educational systems to increase the flexibility of learning, to which UNESCO's Sustainable Development Goals (SDGs) have long been committed. Foundation education in NZ is well-placed to address a number of relevant key targets identified in the SDGs. Central to the global endeavour is Sustainable Development Goal 4 (SDG 4) which aims to integrate sustainable development into formal education at all levels, as well as through informal and non-formal education opportunities. SDG4 ensures inclusive and equitable education and promotes life-long opportunities.

Recently discussion regarding the growth in the role of digital technology, how to address learning needs for vulnerable students, and designing a curriculum for the future has been the focus for education innovators and leaders around the world (UNESCO, 2020b). The targets in UNESCO SDG 4 address diverse levels of education and institutions. The context for this chapter is that of tertiary education and, therefore, targets 4.3 and 4.5 are the most pertinent (see Table 1).

Another key Sustainable Development Goal that is particularly relevant to Foundation Education is SDG 3, to ensure healthy lives and promote well-being for all at all ages. SDG 3 is applicable within the foundation education context as it includes involving and supporting students online, as each one has individual needs, may also now require an empathetic approach which is not so much about how to successfully teach educational content but about how learners relate to this crisis (Ossiannilsson, 2020).

The learning objectives, topics and activities for SDG 3 are designed to be relevant for all learners worldwide and to be applied in all sorts of learning settings (UNESCO, 2017); implementation should be adapted to the national or local context, and educators and curriculum developers must define the level to be achieved by their learners (from "basic" in primary education to "expertise" in tertiary education). Key concerns, as identified in target 3.4, are the importance of mental health, what behaviours impact on mental health and well-being, strategies to foster positive physical and mental health and well-being (see Table 2).

Table 2. Significance of UNESCO SDG targets (3.4) for Foundation Education

UNESCO SDG Targets	Significance for Foundation Education in New Zealand
Target 3.4: Promote mental health By 2030, ... promote mental health and well-being.	Foundation educators are aware that mental health is a significant factor impacting young people. For young people, mental wellness needs to be promoted. Ensuring an environment where mental wellness is just as important as physical wellness.

Source: (UNESCO, 2017)

In the wake of COVID-19, university students have experienced fundamental changes of their learning and their lives as a whole. The "lockdowns, school closures, physical distancing and loss of familiar environments ... has led to increased pressure, stress and anxiety for young people, their families and communities" (UNESCO, 2020c). Research has identified psychosocial characteristics associated with students' well-being in this situation (Holzer et al., 2021). The report by UNESCO further highlights the importance of undertaking "careful needs assessment to contextualise interventions, adapt curriculum and teaching and learning methods to the situation of school closure and home isolation" (UNESCO, 2020c). It also emphasises the need to amend content so that it addresses issues that emerge and change rapidly. Gender and social inclusion must be kept in focus to remove discrimination, which is often exacerbated in emergency situations.

New Zealand Tertiary Education Strategy (TES)

The NZ Tertiary Education Commission *Te Amorangi Mātauranga Matua* (TEC) is the administrative authority responsible for the shape, direction and funding of the tertiary education sector in NZ. The TEC provides career services from education to employment, leadership and strategic direction. One of the primary functions of the TEC is to provide leadership within the tertiary education sector. One such initiative is the Tertiary Education Strategy, (TEC, 2020) which sets out the government's current priorities, and long-term strategic direction for tertiary education. The Tertiary Education Strategy (TES) is intended to address economic, social, and environmental goals, and the development aspirations of Māori and other population groups. The TES priorities build on the Education and Training Act 2020, and increased investment in trades training and student well-being. Foundation education is fundamental to providing a context within which to address a number of the key priorities identified in the current NZ Tertiary Education Strategy.

The TES recognises that learners change and grow as they move through their education and that the education system "needs to listen to them, adapt to their needs, and empower them to achieve their aspirations, whatever their age or stage of learning" (TEC, 2020, para. 1). The priorities identified in the TES are important for learners/*ākonga* and their family/*whānau* (Māori terms are used to acknowledge the importance of indigenous values and concepts). Those priorities particularly relevant to foundation education are referenced in Table 3, but the TES recognises that the current education system is not delivering on this for everyone.

It has been reported that Māori and Pacific peoples are especially vulnerable not only to public health crises more generally, but also the economic effects of the pandemic, such as COVID-19-associated unemployment (Henrickson, 2020). The TES counsels that now more than ever it is important that the education system "sharpens its focus on equity" (Ministry of Education, 2021): Māori and Pacific learners/*ākonga* are likely to be disproportionately affected by the impacts of COVID-19, so it is critical that the education system supports their success.

In NZ, the unsuccessful completion of courses is disproportionally higher for Māori students and students from the Pacific Islands as many of these students experience inequalities in the predominantly white-dominated education space of mainstream institutions (Milne, 2017). One role of foundation education is to link students with culturally appropriate support and advice integrated within the wider institutional support infrastructure.

Moreover, there will be a lasting impact on Māori and Pacific young people. Accordingly, existing factors are likely to be exacerbated by COVID-19. While some young people/*rangatahi* may recover relatively quickly from lockdown, others may struggle or experience ongoing distress, such as dealing with ongoing family/*whānau* financial insecurity and mental health ("Youth plan", 2020). The Youth Plan sets out actions that the government will take to mitigate the impacts of COVID-19. Thus, the well-being of young people/*rangatahi*, their family/*whānau*, and their communities is supported and strengthened.

In terms of implementation of the TES priorities within the sector, there are a number of actions that tertiary education organisations can take by way of response. In the context of foundation education, the following are particularly applicable:

Table 3. Significance of Tertiary Education Commission (TEC) priorities for Foundation Education

TEC Priorities	Significance for Foundation Education in Aotearoa New Zealand
Priority 1: Ensure places of learning are safe, and inclusive	Foundation education offers a pathway into tertiary education for students who have not gained university admission and for students who are returning to academic study after an extended gap in their formal study. Foundation education endeavours to provide pastoral support and culturally appropriate responses to student's diverse learning needs.
Priority 2: Have high aspirations for every learner/ *akonga,* and support the design and delivery of education that responds to their needs	Foundation education aims to motivate students by providing opportunities to succeed in areas they may not have experienced success previously. Foundation education builds skills in content knowledge areas as well as transferable skills such as time management and self-confidence by having high expectations for student success.
Priority 3: Reduce barriers to education	Foundation education provides a pathway to tertiary education for students who have had a break in formal education or who have not gained university entrance from secondary education. For students who face financial barriers or access to technologies, foundation education is one space where inequalities are encountered.
Priority 4: Ensure every learner/*akonga,* gains sound foundation skills, including language, literacy, and numeracy.	Foundation education programmes are designed to promote content knowledge, academic skills, and foster independence. More recently, as access to technology increases, digital literacies are also addressed as curriculums reflect a digital transformation.

Source: (Tertiary Education Commission, 2020)

Digital Transformation in Aotearoa New Zealand's Tertiary Education Sector

In NZ, being digitally capable has been defined as New Zealanders having the necessary skills to live and work in a digital economy. Skill areas that are essential for digital literacy include "managing information, communicating, transacting, problem solving and creating" ("Digital literacy," 2018). In addition, the need to develop competencies that include the upskilling in several areas of literacies including connection-based literacies, critical literacies, and attention literacies among other digital literacies (Hockly, 2012) is essential in any response to crisis such as the COVID-19 pandemic.

The report on digital New Zealanders indicated digital inequality exists between levels of digital literacies within different communities. Some key contributing factors that have been identified as affecting who is or is not digitally literate include household income, age, geographic location – especially those living in rural areas, and ethnicity. Of particular concern, it has been noted that, Māori and Pacific Island people are less likely to have access to the internet at home than other ethnic groups in New Zealand. Also, Māori and Pacific families are likely to have extended families living within the same bubble. This means, even in houses with internet connections, more devices may be trying to access the service at the same time. It was also noted that an inability to access and use digital technologies not only impacts accessibility to education, but it can also affect wellness, well-being, and opportunity, as well as other forms of disadvantage.

Despite these discrepancies, provision of digital education in NZ has increased. The number of tertiary institutes that offer online courses prior to COVID-19 has increased as a result of the pandemic. It is, however, important to highlight that emergency remote teaching differs from quality online learning. The former is a short-term response to an emergency event whereas quality online learning is the considered, conscious planning of online delivery that is grounded on sound pedagogical principles.

CASE STUDY FROM AOTEAROA NEW ZEALAND

Within the framework of the issues addressed by the TES priorities (and SDG 3.4, 4.3 and 4.5) the research project (case study) presented in this chapter seeks to gain a deeper understanding of the experiences and educational background of students entering foundation courses, to hear from learners/*ākonga* about their experiences during the time of the COVID-19 pandemic global crisis.

This chapter describes the second phase of a longitudinal study conducted at an established tertiary institution in NZ. The findings of the first phase of the project (Saavedra & Sanders, 2016) identified common themes and experiences across foundation students. The second phase of the research presented here not only explores how students have experienced education (specifically in a crisis context) but also aims to inform necessary support mechanisms for students and teachers in similar foundation programmes and to explore whether factors that students perceived to have an effect on their success change when in a crisis context.

Identifying Common Student Experiences in a Non-Crisis Context (pre-COVID-19)

The first phase of our research utilised a diagnostic task implemented as part of the beginning of semester activities. Students self-report in the form of written narratives on their prior personal experiences, challenges, and educational background.

Respondents were asked to identify factors that they perceived had affected their success. The responses from students enrolled in foundation courses were collected (according to full ethics approval) and grouped into themes. Thematic analysis, which is a method of identifying, analysing, and reporting patterns (themes) within data, was chosen because it allowed the researchers to compare (and contrast) the emergent themes. It was supported by NVivo 11 Software, and a contextualist approach (Braun & Clarke, 2006). Iterative analysis was undertaken to establish thematic networks, which allow themes within analysis to be identified by either an inductive and/or deductive approach (Fereday & Muir-Cochrane, 2006; Rasmussen et al., 2012).

For the data collected, five core themes emerged (see Figure 1). The theme that was most prevalent in the narratives indicated individual factors were most likely to affect success, followed by social factors, then physical and economic factors. One theme that appeared to cross all of these aspects was time (Saavedra & Sanders, 2016).

Figure 1. Identified Themes
Source: Saavedra & Sanders, 2016

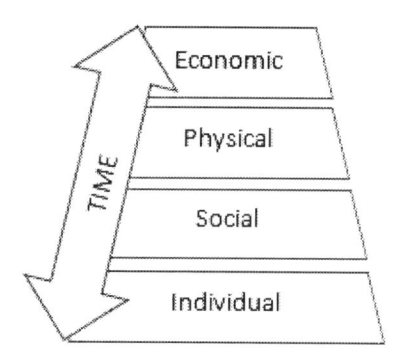

Understanding what students self-reported to be factors most likely to affect their success, academic and pastoral support teams were able to collaborate with students to ensure positive educational experiences for foundation students. Through the evaluation of support currently available to students and teachers, it is possible to identify areas and opportunities for development and growth within our institution and wider community. In particular, it makes it possible to identify factors and early indicators that necessitate additional areas of support to ensure future improved accessibility, flexibility, and equity within and across foundation programmes. One specific outcome of the first phase of the study was as follows:

The process of orientation and enculturation should also not be considered to cease once the semester has commenced. Foundation courses need to consider how to work on reassuring students, by instilling confidence, improving motivation, and supporting individual, social, physical, and economic factors, as well as designing study strategies which explicitly emphasize time issues. (Saavedra & Sanders, 2016, p. 14)

Since 2016, and the completion of the first phase of the study, the authors have continued to collect narratives from students as one mechanism for identifying early intervention needs and opportunities. The data reported in the following sections refer specifically to data collected for the second phase, between February and June of 2021, which has been the first semester since the initial outbreak of the global COVID-19 pandemic to not include a lockdown period for tertiary students in NZ.

Identifying Common Student Experiences in a Crisis Context (COVID-19)

For the second phase of research that is the focus of this chapter, the researchers expanded on the diagnostic task implemented as part of the beginning of semester activities, whereby students self-report in the form of written narratives on their prior personal experiences, challenges, and educational background. The narratives were read and analysed in order to distinguish any specific challenges that students have faced that can be directly (or indirectly) linked to their experience with COVID-19.

In order to gain further insights, the researchers conducted interviews with the participants. Given the diverse cultural backgrounds of some students, participants were offered the opportunity to expand on what they had written, through semi-structured interviews (Wilson, 2014). These discussions afford the opportunity for students to further elaborate on how they have experienced challenges and success within the context of COVID-19 to let students voice their experiences, feelings, and thoughts. Working within a framework that ensures students respond to a set of central questions, it also gave the researchers the opportunity to ask follow up questions to help students offer fully developed answers and to gather contextually rich, detailed data (Cartwright, 2020).

Figure 2. Identified themes in a crisis context

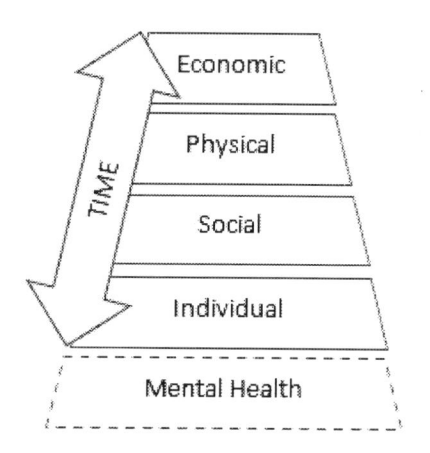

Comparisons with themes identified in the first study show that many of the factors identified as affecting student success remain with time continuing to feature across the factors identified. However, an additional theme emerged from the data collected for the second phase of the study, in 2021 (5 years later). The theme of mental health emerged as a theme that was mentioned more often than time, economic, physical, social, or individual factors (see Figure 2).

Crisis context data was collected from 43 students. From the themes that emerged, the economic factors that were noted to have changed when comparing data, was that more students were balancing work with studies in the 2021 cohort. Approximately one in five were working and studying simultaneously, which contrasts with one in ten in the 2016 cohort.

The physical factors mentioned were different. Only one student mentioned transport as being a factor that would affect success. This contrasted with other cohorts where transport was more regularly noted as a factor that might affect success. Ongoing physical health challenges were the most likely factor to affect success in this theme.

Social factors such as having difficulties with communicating or articulating themselves were considered factors that had affected student's success in the past. Other social factors mentioned involved commitments to different social groups such as church, sports teams, and special interest groups. Also, one in every ten students reported having children.

Individual factors such as lack of motivation, learning disabilities, overthinking, and lack of self-organisation skills were self-reported as factors anticipated to affect success. Almost one in four students mentioned a lack of motivation to studies which is double the number of students who reportedly felt the same in 2016. Neurodiversity and learning challenges, such as ADHD and dyslexia, were mentioned as being known factors that had affected students' academic studies in the past and may likely affect success in their upcoming studies. These factors were not openly identified in the previous study.

Time featured prominently across all themes. 44% of students specifically mentioned time management being a key skill required to be successful. 33% of students, up from 18% in the previous study, mentioned having issues with procrastination and another 10 (23%) students described dealing with distraction was likely to affect their success.

However, one substantial change that has emerged from the data collected in 2021 is the identification of mental health, and often mental illness, as a factor noted to negatively affect success. In the first phase of the study (Saavedra & Sanders, 2016), mental health was classified as a physical factor due to the physical manifestations but very few students disclosed mental health challenges. This was noticeably different in the narratives collected in the crisis context. In the data collected in the second phase of the study, in 2021, approximately 44% of students mentioned mental health as an anticipated factor that would affect success. Approximately one in five students self-reported challenges with anxiety and one in seven reported depression as a challenge they had faced. An additional one in five reported feeling anxious in social situations which meant some prior schooling experiences had been difficult.

Findings from Focus Groups

A thematic analysis method was also adopted to analyze the commonalities that arose during focus group discussions. Analysis of students' comments indicated that not all challenges were perceived as inherently negative phenomena. Students also embraced some challenges as opportunities to gain different skills. From the data three categories emerged: (i) characterizations of challenges deemed to be negative; (ii) characterizations of challenges deemed to be positive; and (iii) characterizations of what has been learned through the COVID-19 experience.

Stressful challenges

Forty percent of the students explicitly mentioned an increase in personal, and family, mental health issues and concerns during the pandemic. Anxiety and depression were issues that were mentioned most frequently. An increase in the self-reporting of mental health concerns is consistent with findings in Europe (Holzer, et al., 2021). In the context of this study in NZ the researchers note, over the last few years of collecting narratives from students, mental health concerns are increasingly more commonly disclosed.

Financial challenges were prevalent throughout. One student described occasions when family members did not receive their salary despite having worked which meant the family were unable to pay rent on time. Students faced challenges keeping jobs during the pandemic and, in the case of front-line workers, their concern about bringing COVID-19 back into the home after a shift. These financial challenges and uncertainties had a negative impact on students' ability to concentrate on their studies. For some students this manifested in continual absences from classes as they took additional shifts in lieu of attending online classes.

Some students commented on issues with connectivity. Not all homes had access to the internet when NZ went into lockdown and this impacted on student's ability to keep up with classes. When the connection dropped out it was difficult to pay attention when reconnecting to the lesson which acted as a deterrent for students. Even in cases where there was an internet connection, the Level 4 lockdown put unprecedented strain on the network. Under normal circumstances, domestic internet connection would be under high demand in the evenings or peak times, such as weekends. However, with work and study now being completed from home throughout the day, telecommunication connections were in high demand on a daily basis and were not always stable.

Isolation was also identified as a key challenge. Students felt the absence of classmates and found maintaining relationships with tutors was made more difficult online during the pandemic. In addition to missing classmates, students missed connecting with their community social support groups such as church.

In some circumstances, particularly in the case of Pacific Island families, students were quarantined in bubbles that consisted of multi-generational, extended family. This brought increased opportunities to spend time together, which was described as a positive outcome of the lockdown, but it also brought increased pressures. Students reported having additional family responsibilities and family members to look after. They also reported needing to support other members in their bubbles with mental health issues.

The pivot to emergency remote teaching meant changing the regular delivery of classes. Students found the change in routine to be challenging. When attending classes on-campus, students had to organize themselves to be in a particular place at a particular time. Although being on time was still a requirement for synchronous online classes, students often avoided logging in. This phenomenon is not readily explained by the issues identified above (connectivity and access) or even procrastination and lack of motivation, so it is definitely a subject to be explored further.

Positive challenges

One of the positive challenges of living with other people is learning to live with those people day in and day out. During the lockdown, students reported learning more about people they lived with. One student mentioned it was during the lockdown that she spent time sitting with family and discussing personal issues that led her to return to studies. Other students reported that the slowing down from rushing out to work, study, and other social commitments meant that they spent time with family and other bubble members. For many, this enhanced their social bond. It must be acknowledged that, although narratives collected in this research did not describe any intensively difficult situations, not all bubble experiences were positive ones.

Students commented that although moving to emergency remote teaching was challenging, they found the experience to be positive when tutors kept in touch. So accessibility to teaching staff is an important aspect of a positive transition during crisis. This is an area that can be further capitalized on in non-crisis contexts. Students found connecting synchronously with others became more challenging due to competing needs for attention. However, they reported that when they did connect with others that the connection was more meaningful and sustained.

The lockdown provided enhanced engagement opportunities for students who were more introverted as they found there were fewer social pressures with online classes. For some students who were apprehensive about coming into classrooms and physical social settings, the online space eased that level of apprehension as they were physically in a familiar setting (i.e., their home). The pandemic offered opportunities for 'more time to relax and have fun' and gave students opportunities to connect to nature '[B]eing confined to the house, I grew a love for walks, and I felt connected to nature, and began feeling this profound sense of gratitude.' For example, time that had previously been used to commute to campus was now more available for relaxation or leisure activities such as walking.

Another positive challenge that students recognized was the value of learning new skills during this time. Software such as Microsoft and Zoom were given as examples of software packages and applications that students identified as upskilling in.

Hindsight: Student Reflections on the COVID-19 Experience

Recognition that everyone's experiences were different was referred to on multiple occasions. Students noticed that different generations have reacted differently to the pandemic. The pandemic has given students the opportunity to be patient and reflect on how others experience a situation.

Mental health issues were prominent when students reflected on what they felt they had learnt from the COVID-19 experience. One student in particular wrote of anxiety, worry, isolation, depression, and a breakup that led them to self-medicate with alcohol which also contributed to unusual, excessive weight gain. The first two weeks of Level 4 lockdown had left them feeling lost and empty. However, they turned the experience around and '[W]orked on my mental health and how to be kind to [myself].' This student considered the pandemic as 'an awakening chapter' that has made them more cautious and conscious.

Having restrictions placed on students' movements and social interactions was identified as a key factor that adversely impacted students' mental wellness and physical health. Increased bouts of depression, anxiety and feeling overwhelmed were highlighted by students. Actively working on keeping themselves intrigued and paying attention eventually took its toll on their level of engagement and on their sense of fulfilment.

Students demonstrated empathy in some of their reflective comments. A sense of gratitude for having a job that meant they could continue to have a revenue stream during the pandemic featured in a few students' narratives. This sense of gratitude, however, was also tempered with a concern of potentially bringing the COVID-19 virus into the home.

RECOMMENDATIONS

Many of our current foundation tertiary level students were in their final year of secondary schooling when the pandemic was at its peak in NZ. Whilst students had commented on the compassion and empathy demonstrated by their teachers, they also indicated that having a supportive teacher, who was easily accessible online, was not always what they felt they needed. Some students reported feeling that expectations were lowered when they were in lockdown. Although that was what they wanted at the time, they also acknowledge that they were more likely to give into procrastination and were lazier about completing work during the lockdown period than they would have otherwise been.

As lockdown was unprecedented, many students were not prepared to study from home. Due to the restrictive limitations on space under lockdown, many students did not have dedicated study spaces where they could concentrate uninterrupted on their study and having a safe study place is an important contributor to student success. In addition, during this crisis context, not all students had reliable access to a stable internet connection. This caused disruption to education. By supporting students to solve connectivity issues and set up a space that reduces barriers to access is vital for ensuring student success.

The cost of connectivity is another factor to be considered. Many students in this study identified challenges balancing work and study commitments. It is acknowledged that financial constraints mean that many students are required to work while studying and it is important that programmes are designed to enable flexibility in delivery to maximise opportunities for engagement.

To improve the likelihood of success for students the authors propose some key recommendations in the following areas: (i) access and affordability; (ii) pastoral care; (iii) motivation; and (iv) curriculum and digital transformation.

- **Assess access (connectivity) and affordability (financial constraints):** Future strategic plans will need to consider digital justice as a principle, recognising that students who do not have computers or share computers with other family members who also work online have the right to continue their learning. This is considered a major barrier to digital justice around the world, and each institution should find their own way to solve this problem. Foundation education is well-placed to achieve this, by reflecting on existing pedagogy in order to enhance students' skills, and promoting digital literacy as a goal.
- **Integrate pastoral care:** For learners who are not self-sufficient and may rely on support services (and this was exacerbated during COVID-19), pastoral care is especially important. Due to the complexity of the student cohort, pastoral care should be an integral part of any academic programme. Teaching and learning should move towards a caring pedagogy, that integrates an empathetic approach not just a didactic approach. Cultural obligations need to be factored into emergency situations, highlighting the need for culturally appropriate support. This is particularly important for learners whose study may be disrupted, if, for example, they need to stop study to support family, especially financially. Student needs are diverse and having multiple support systems is vital to ensure students experience sustained success throughout their academic journey. Having a more inclusive, empathetic, caring approach extends participation and promotes social justice and equality.
- **Comprehend student motivation:** Providing a context for success and understanding students' diverse motivations for engaging in foundation education is important for providing meaningful learning opportunities. For educators to support and encourage active participation, they must first understand students' motivations. This can be achieved by getting to know students through the gathering of student narratives to enable educators to develop a greater awareness of the holistic student. Through understanding a student's motivation, educators can support students to gain the necessary self-management tools to avoid procrastination and improve time management skills.

- **Engage in curriculum and digital transformation:** As the use of technology increases rapidly, it is apparent that the digital transformation in education is a global phenomenon. Curriculum transformation that supports students to gain appropriate digital literacies is vital for them to be successful in their future studies or workplaces. Access to and the use of digital tools for academic purposes differs across demographics and geographical locations. Technology can be used to support access to information outside the physical constraints of classrooms and can be used to promote changes in attitudes, ethics, and values.

These recommendations can be mapped alongside the global context encompassed in the UNESCO SDGs (2015) and the local TEC priorities (2020) to address some of the inequities encountered by learners. Furthermore, it has become evident that SDG10 is particularly pertinent to the recommendations stemming from this research (see Table 4).

Table 4. Overview of SDGs, TEC Priorities and Recommendations

UNESCO SDG	TEC Priorities	Recommendations
SDG3: Ensure healthy lives and promote well-being for all at all ages		Integrate pastoral care: Learning and teaching to be underpinned by a caring pedagogy to include integrated pastoral care.
SDG4: Ensure inclusive and equitable quality education and promote lifelong learning opportunities for all	TES 1: Ensure places of learning are safe, and inclusive. TES 4: Ensure every learner/ *ākonga,* gains sound foundation skills, including language, literacy, and numeracy	Comprehend student motivation: Understanding student's motivations can ensure meaningful, engaging learning opportunities are optimised. Engage in curriculum and digital transformation: Curriculums can be transformed through the appropriate, considered integration of digital tools and literacies.
SDG10: Reduce inequality within and among countries	TES 2: Have high aspirations for every learner/*ākonga,* and support the design and delivery of education that responds to their needs TES 3: Reduce barriers to education	Assess access and affordability: Improved access and affordability to address digital injustices is integral to enable supportive integration of digital literacies so students can access educational opportunities outside physical and timebound class restrictions.

Source: (United Nations, 2015; Tertiary Education Commission, 2020)

FUTURE RESEARCH DIRECTIONS

The focus of this chapter has been on foundation student experiences of the COVID-19 crisis at an Aotearoa New Zealand university. The research presented has shown the additional factors that need to be considered, as well as those areas of practice and support that may require a re-evaluation. There are emerging trends evident from the research that point to future directions and opportunities for further research which may benefit students and teachers within the institution as well as the wider community.

Digital inequities

The COVID-19 pandemic has further revealed the digital inequities that exist between students. As the tertiary education sector will increasingly rely on (emergency) remote education for course delivery of programmes and learning experiences, it is evident that those who already struggle to gain access to even the basic devices and network necessities will continue to do so. Limited access, and in some cases no access, prevents full engagement in the online or blended learning environment for some learners, and results in a shortage in digital literacy.

Re-focusing of programmes

The skills and capabilities shown to be especially important at the time of the COVID-19 pandemic has led to a rethinking of teaching practice and delivery. A renewed focus on engaging, blended learning is needed so that the strategic priority afforded to online learning at every tertiary institution can be realised.

Innovations in education, supported by integrated technology and a strong pedagogical design, will provide sustainable, supportive, and contextualised support to enable educators with appropriate tools to cater for diverse needs within student populations.

By focusing on providing safe spaces within a well-being framework, alongside academic skill development, educators will be able to support students to gain the necessary skills for an enhanced sustainable education. This will enable more emphasis to be placed on the development of critical thinking, collaborative, adaptable skills that support wellness and resilience.

Mental health

Mental health issues have been exacerbated by recent disruptions and changes brought about by the COVID-19 pandemic. This has presented tertiary institutions with additional challenges in order to ensure the well-being and safety of students. There is an opportunity here to build back better on an education ecosystem by not only providing quality development in terms of online delivery but also, by taking a holistic approach, to transform current student support models to better address mental health challenges.

CONCLUSION

A clearer understanding of the self-reported factors that students identified as affecting their success, allows academic and support staff to improve the pre-degree experience for foundation students. The additional data collected in a crisis context (COVID-19) can help us evaluate areas of practice and support currently available to students and teachers within our institution and wider community and ascertain what other factors need to be considered.

Based on the previous research conducted by the authors prior to the COVID-19 crisis, it was expected the challenges that foundation students experienced would have been exacerbated in the context of crisis (COVID-19). Although, this was true to an extent, what the new research also showed was an increase in the disclosure of mental health factors that students identified as having an impact on their studies. The crisis context data also highlighted the resilience of young people/*rangatahi* as students identified positive challenges emerged during the COVID-19 pandemic.

Thus, within the broader framework of the UNESCO SDG goals, notably SDG 3, 4 and 10, the research underscores the key targets in relation to access and well-being. The NZ TES priorities further highlight the importance of an education system that sharpens its focus on equity. As the TES clearly states, Māori and Pacific learners/ *ākonga*, those from diverse ethnic communities, already experience or risk poorer education and employment outcomes and are likely to be disproportionately affected by the labour market impacts of COVID-19.

This focus on equality aligns with the UNESCO SDG10 to reduce inequalities. Moreover, quality education is crucial to achieving this goal; it raises awareness about existing inequities and contributes to the empowerment and inclusion of all. It is, therefore, critical that educators reflect on learning and teaching practices and experiences to continually innovate and reform contemporary education that supports an education system that enables equitable successes.

REFERENCES

Aboagye, E., Yawson, J. A., & Appiah, K. N. (2020). COVID-19 and e-learning: The challenges of students in tertiary institutions. *Social Education Research*, *2*(1), 1–8. doi:10.37256er.122020422

Blaschke, L. M., & Hase, S. (2016). Heutagogy: A holistic framework for creating twenty-first-century self-determined learners. In The future of ubiquitous learning: Learning designs for emerging pedagogies (pp.25-40). Springer. doi:10.1007/978-3-662-47724-3_2

Braun, V., & Clarke, V. (2006). Using thematic analysis in psychology. *Qualitative Research in Psychology*, *3*(2), 77–101. doi:10.1191/1478088706qp063oa

Burgos, D., Tlili, A., & Tabacco, A. (2020). Education in a crisis context: Summary, insights and future. In Radical solutions for education in a crisis context: COVID-19 as an opportunity for global learning (pp. 3-9). Springer.

Cartwright, L. (2020). Using thematic analysis in social work research. *Sage (Atlanta, Ga.)*.

Digital literacy and young people: Key findings and implications. (2018). Department of Internal Affairs.

Fereday, J., & Muir-Cochrane, E. (2006). Demonstrating rigor using thematic analysis: A hybrid approach of inductive and deductive coding and theme development. *International Journal of Qualitative Methods*, *5*(1), 80–92. doi:10.1177/160940690600500107

Green, J. K., Burrow, M. S., & Carvalho, L. (2020). Designing for transition: Supporting teachers and students cope with emergency remote education. *Postdigital Science and Education*, *2*(3), 906–922. doi:10.100742438-020-00185-6

Henrickson, M. (2020). Kiwis and COVID-19: The Aotearoa New Zealand response to the global pandemic. *The International Journal of Community and Social Development*, *2*(2), 121–133. doi:10.1177/2516602620932558

Hockly, N. (2012). Digital literacies. *ELT Journal*, *66*(1), 108–112. doi:10.1093/elt/ccr077

Holzer, J., Lüftenegger, M., Korlat, S., Pelikan, E., Salmela-Aro, K., Spiel, C., & Schober, B. (2021). Higher education in times of COVID-19: University students' basic need satisfaction, self-regulated learning, and well-being. *AERA Open*, *7*(1), 1–13. doi:10.1177/23328584211003164 PMID:34192126

Iyengar, R. (2020). Education as the path to a sustainable recovery from COVID-19. *Prospects: Comparative Journal of Curriculum, Learning, and Assessment, 49*(1–2), 77–80. doi:10.100711125-020-09488-9 PMID:32836429

Milne, A. (2017). *Colouring in the white spaces: Reclaiming cultural identity in whitestream schools*. Peter Lang. doi:10.3726/b10459

Ministry of Education. (2021). *The Statement of National Education and Learning Priorities (NELP) and the Tertiary Education Strategy (TES)*. Retrieved from https://education.govt.nz/our-work/overall-strategies-and-policies/the-statement-of-national-education-and-learning-priorities-nelp-and-the-tertiary-education-strategy-tes

Muilenburg, L. Y., & Berge, Z. L. (2005). Student barriers to online learning: A factor analytic study. *Distance Education, 26*(1), 29–48. doi:10.1080/01587910500081269

Ossiannilsson, E. (2020). Some challenges for universities in a post crisis, as COVID-19. In Radical solutions for education in a crisis context: COVID-19 as an opportunity for global learning (pp. 99-112). Springer.

Rasmussen, P., Muir-Cochrane, E., & Henderson, A. (2012). Document analysis using an aggregate and iterative process. *International Journal of Evidence-Based Healthcare, 10*(2), 142–145. doi:10.1111/j.1744-1609.2012.00262.x PMID:22672603

Saavedra, E. (2018). *The effects of mobile devices on student learning in a New Zealand- based university preparation course: A case study* (Doctoral thesis). University of Southern Queensland, Australia.

Saavedra, E., & Sanders, L. (2016). Building on identifiable common student experiences to enable success. *FABENZ: Accessibility, flexibility, equity*. Retrieved from http://fabenz.org.nz/wp-content/uploads/2016/12/Saavedra-and-Sanders.pdf

Tertiary Education Commission. (2020). *The Tertiary Education Strategy*. Retrieved from https://www.tec.govt.nz/focus/our-focus/tes/

UNESCO. (2016). *Education for people and planet: Creating sustainable futures for all*. https://en.unesco.org/gem-report/report/2016/education-people-and-planet-creating-sustainable-futures-all

UNESCO. (2017). *Education for Sustainable Development Goals: Learning objectives*. https://unesdoc.unesco.org/ark:/48223/pf0000247444.page=21

UNESCO. (2020a). *COVID-19 education response*. https://en.unesco.org/covid19/educationresponse

UNESCO. (2020b). *Nine ideas for public action—New publication from the International Commission on the Futures of Education*. Paris: UNESCO. https://en.unesco.org/futuresofeducation/news/nine-ideas-for-public-action

UNESCO. (2020c). *Nurturing the social and emotional wellbeing of children and young people during crises. UNESCO COVID-19 education response.* https://unesdoc.unesco.org/ark:/48223/pf0000373271

UNESCO. (2019). *Meeting commitments: Are countries on track to achieve the SDG4?* http://uis.unesco.org/sites/default/files/documents/meeting-commitments-are-countries-on-track-achieve-sdg4.pdf

United Nations. (2015). *Transforming Our World: The 2030 Agenda for Sustainable Development*. United Nations.

Wilson, C. (2014). Semi-structured interviews. *Interview techniques for UX Practitioners*: A *user-centred design method*, 23-41.

Youth plan 2020-2022. (2020). *Turning voice into action: Rebuilding and recovering*. Ministry of Youth Development. https://www.myd.govt.nz/young-people/youth-plan/youth-plan.html

ADDITIONAL READING

Akuhata-Huntington, Z. (2020). *Impacts of the COVID-19 Lockdown on Māori University Students*. Te Mana Ākonga.

Bozkurt, A., & Sharma, R. C. (2020). Emergency remote teaching in a time of global crisis due to coronavirus pandemic. *Asian Journal of Distance Education*, *15*(1), i–vi. doi:10.5281/zenodo.3778083

Brown, M., McCormack, M., Reeves, J., Brooks, D., & Grajek, S. (2020). *Horizon Report: Teaching and learning edition*. Educause.

Chundur, S. (2020). Digital justice: Reflections on a community-based research project. *The Journal of Community Informatics*, *16*, 118–140. doi:10.15353/joci.v16i0.3485

Digital Inclusion Research Group. (2017). *Digital New Zealanders: The pulse of our nation*. https://www.mbie.govt.nz/dmsdocument/3228-digital-new-zealanders-the-pulse-of-our-nation-pdf

Every-Palmer, S., Jenkins, M., Gendall, P., Hoek, J., Beaglehole, B., Bell, C., Williman, J., Rapsey, C., & Stanley, J. (2020). Psychological distress, anxiety, family violence, suicidality, and wellbeing in New Zealand during the COVID-19 lockdown: A cross-sectional study. *PLoS One*, *15*(11), e0241658. Advance online publication. doi:10.1371/journal.pone.0241658 PMID:33147259

Murgatroyd, S. (2021) Insight: A cancelled future. What's next for universities and colleges? In Radical solutions for education in a crisis context (pp. 307-323). Springer. doi:10.1007/978-981-15-7869-4_22

Naqvi, S. (2020, April 20). Is e-Learning the inevitable future? *News International.* https://www.thenews.com.pk/magazine/you/647186-is-e-learning-the-inevitable-future

Pelletier, K., Brown, M., Brooks, D., McCormack, M., Reeves, J., & Arbino, N. (2021). *Horizon Report: Teaching and learning edition.* Educause.

Reddy, P., Sharma, B., & Chaudhary, K. (2021). Digital literacy: A review in the South Pacific. *Journal of Computing in Higher Education: Research & Integration of Instructional Technology*, 1-26. doi:10.1007/s12528-021-09280-4

KEY TERMS AND DEFINITIONS

Aotearoa New Zealand: Aotearoa comes from the Māori language and is used when referring to New Zealand to acknowledge the importance of the indigenous Māori culture.

Bubble: Metaphor used to describe a person's immediate family or household

Foundation Education: Post-secondary, pre-degree study that support students to gain literacy, numeracy, and independent study skills for university admission. Sometimes referred to as 'enabling' or 'bridging' education.

Foundation Programme: A programme of study that results in a pre-degree qualification.

Level 4: A four level system was devised by the NZ government to contain the spread of the COVID-19 virus. Level 4 is the most extreme level of social isolation.

Māori: The indigenous peoples and language of Aotearoa New Zealand. Many Māori words are used in everyday language.

Chapter 6

Integrating 21st Century Competencies Into a Digital Teaching and Learning Model:
Globalization of the Teaching and Learning Paradigm

Rosalind Rice-Stevenson
Edinburgh Napier University, UK

EXECUTIVE SUMMARY

Globalization and technology are two features of the modern world impacting all activity, and the resultant effect on education is causing much to be questioned about the teaching and learning paradigm. Ways in which the learning experience must change in response to changing global demands placed on societies and economies forms a large part of the current discourse around reforming education. This chapter puts forward a definition of globalization, 21st century skills, and the four main competencies known as the 4Cs, and then makes links between these phenomena as a way of understanding the digitization of education. The connections are possible through a process of gathering reflections and experiences from experienced educational practitioners.

INTRODUCTION

This chapter reveals a unique perspective on the ways in which globalization is impacting education. Focusing on the integration of 21st century skills into a digitized

DOI: 10.4018/978-1-7998-8310-4.ch006

learning environment from the perspective of experienced educational practitioners allows a view of their experiences as they strive to re-imagine education. The chapter aims to contribute to the views held by educators globally on innovative methodologies for ensuring the resilience of teaching and learning in the 21st century.

The study is qualitative in nature using a phenomenological study approach. The objective is the direct investigation of the issue under scrutiny with a description being given of the topic as experienced by individuals practicing within the higher education context. A carefully selected sample of six participants were interviewed representing various Higher Education institutions within the UK, all with widespread teaching experience in face-to-face and online teaching.

It is intended that the findings from this study will be useful to professionals and researchers working in the field of education leadership and administration. The outcomes could be useful to organizations interested in funding educational initiatives, also national education policy makers. Insights from this chapter may support and inform educators and administrators to improvise their current practices when working directly with students in the category - K-University. There may be value for other groups such as - educational researchers, educational software developers and textbook publishers.

Presented as a narrative, individual practitioner perspectives are drawn out from the data and presented as a way of sharing best teaching and learning practices. This approach allowed the researcher to explore perceptions of individuals through a series of qualitative interviews that were analysed and presented so as to inform the target audience. Yin (2003) advises that the topic of interest must be thoroughly investigated, only then the essence of the phenomenon is revealed. This provides a clear rationale for the chosen approach, thus allowing connections to be made between globalization of education and 21st century skills. Set against the context of digitized learning environments, the research explored the phenomenon through a variety of lenses allowing for multiple layers of understanding to be revealed.

It is envisioned that the recommendations will contribute to the global discourse around the future of education.

This research work is timely and relevant as the global education sector re-imagines a new reality post-pandemic.

RESEARCH QUESTIONS

This chapter explores the perceptions of professional practitioners by using their insights to address the following research questions:

- What is globalization of education?

- In what ways is globalization impacting the teaching and learning paradigm?
- In what ways is digitization of education impacting teaching and learning?
- Which instructional methods align with integrating 21st century skills?

OBJECTIVE

This chapter will present the issue of globalization and the impact this phenomenon has on the teaching and learning paradigm. Perceptions will be gathered from practitioners on their views of 21st Century skills and these insights will be explored so as to build an understanding of ways in which globalization is being interpreted.

The views of experienced educational practitioners are considered to be fundamental when exploring global influences on education as they are charged with the responsibility of reimagining education. Challenges will be highlighted and solutions presented in a way that is designed to inform professional educators and researchers working in the fields of - future of education, 21st century skills and globalization of education.

BACKGROUND

It is widely believed that globalization is when technology, information and communication come together and connect us in ways that previously would not have been considered (De Wit, 2011). Knowledge creation, education, technology and innovation are the foundations upon which the Sustainable Development Goals (SDGs) of the United Nations (UN) are built (Owens, 2017; The Sustainable Development Goals Report, 2017). Anderson (2020) tells us that economies and societies are being transformed by the applications of new technologies at a remarkable rate. An argument supported by Douse & Uys (2018) as they point out that a well-informed and well-prepared population and workforce is required to manage such changes. Globalization has been a transformative force according to Waller, Lemoine, Mense & Richardson (2019), as they discuss that if nations are to be sustainable in the global market place, there needs to be a change in the ways in which we shape our education systems. In fact these authors mention the "virtual mélange of educational models used in the global digital economy" (p185) as being a description of the current move from traditional to digital forms of education provision.

To understand the ways in which technology is impacting education, it is imperative that certain terminologies are explained Creswell (2014) and this next section is designed to inform the reader of the central concepts of this chapter.

Definitions

Globalization

As a concept *globalization* creates much controversy as definitions vary, although *interconnectedness* is a central principal mentioned whenever definitions are presented. Mixed views are to be found in the literature as to the impact of globalization on HE, however it is generally agreed that context is importance and as such influences the influence of this phenomenon. Globally, perceptions of globalization and its impact are influenced by history, culture, traditions and established practices (Green, Marmolejo, & Egron-Polak, 2012).

21st Century Skills

21st Century Skills provide a framework for effective learning whilst ensuring students are equipped to survive in a world where life-long learning and change are the new constants. The Four Cs (4Cs) of 21st Century Learning are: Critical Thinking, Communication, Collaboration, and Creativity.

Curriculum digitisation

As learning environments evolve, according to the Organisation for Economic Co-operation and Development, & PISA (2010), the global teaching and learning paradigm involves educators providing learners with a successful combination of many factors. The dilemma facing current educational practitioners and leaders is identifying what those factors. Russow, (2003) tells us that digitization of the curriculum will involve a paradigm shift to incorporate:

- integration of technology
- collaboration
- inquiry based approach to learning
- developing a problem-solving approach to learning
- providing authentic learning opportunities
- creating opportunities for creativity
- reflecting on learning
- learn by doing
- creating appropriate assessment instruments
- offering a variety of assessment opportunities

This was identified as being the list of factors impacting the curriculum almost two decades ago, more recently Douse, (2018) highlighted the need for educators to be aware of changes needed to the organization of teaching and learning environments – not just the introduction of technology.

Teacher education

Much of the discourse surrounding education is about preparing students for today's challenges. These challenges can be social, technological, personal, cultural, global and all are dynamic in nature, meaning that they as components of a modern-day life must be translated into the new paradigms for education. The consequence for educators and education systems is that education in the 21st Century must meet the demands for change by providing a holistic transformation, taking into consideration the complex relationship between:

- Curricular reform
- Assessment reform
- New teacher recruitment
- Teacher re-training
- Leadership development
- Technology integration

Providing systems that allow for the intricacy of these factors working effectively together is the new problem to be solved by educational leaderships.

United Nations Sustainable Development Goals

Globally, governments are increasingly being encouraged to shape their core business to fit within the SDGs of the UN. These Global Goals were established in 2015 by the UN as a concerted effort to encourage global leaders to commit to ending poverty, protect the planet and pledge that, by 2030, all people would benefit from a peaceful and prosperous life.

LITERATURE REVIEW

A wide exploration of literature was undertaken so that the research presented in this chapter would be informed by a variety of aspects of the evolving landscape of HE. The literature review was carried out to understand ways in which globalization is impacting education. As a central premise, the topic of 21st century skills was explored, revealing the connections to globalization and the integration of these skills into the digital teaching and learning paradigm.

As advised by Creswell (2007) and Crotty (1998) the aim of a solid literature review is to provide an understanding of the main areas of literature underpinning this research. The groupings are:

- Globalization
- 21st Century skills
- Curriculum digitization
- United Nations, Sustainable Development Goals

Bentz, & Shapiro (1998) and Blaxter, Hughes & Tight (2010) stress the importance of making connections between literature and outcomes of the research study, thus providing a meaningful contribution to knowledge. From this viewpoint, these areas of study were identified as establishing a solid basis upon which to place the arguments put forward in this chapter.

Globalization

One definition that gives a sense of the complexity of forces expected to work together in a globalised world is Marginson and van der Wende (2007), when they quote Held et al. (1999) when defining globalisation as: "The widening, deepening and speeding up of worldwide interconnectedness" (p. 4). The actions necessary to become 'interconnected' are not always defined or explained in the literature, but commonly the focus on 'interconnectedness' assumes that countries are discreet entities, culturally, socially and politically, and they *connect* rather than integrate. It can be argued that this is true, however Altbach, Reisberg & Rumbley (2009) in a report prepared for UNESCO, put forward an argument that - globalization as reflects a version of reality "shaped by an increasingly integrated world economy, new information and communications technology (ICT), the emergence of an international knowledge network, the role of the English language, and other forces beyond the control of academic institutions" (p. iv).

This research argues that globalization is a set of processes which represent social and national activities coming together and generating trans-national networks and processes. This was one of the themes coming from the narratives provided by the participants to the research as the reflected on the activities in their own experiences as educators.

21st Century Skills and Globalisation

21st Century Skills are categorised into – Communication, Collaboration, Creativity and Critical Thinking and impact the education landscape as the learning environment adopts different norms (Anderson, 2020). It can be argued that these skills have been taught for years, but now the view is that the ways in which they are being taught is changing and being redefined in ways that are impacting the learning experience of students (Douse & Uys, 2018; Kim, Raza & Seidman, 2019).

In order to understand the impact of these skills on the reforming of education, it is pertinent at this point to consider these skills in more detail. Table 1 gives a summary of the 4Cs and their rationales and poses questions to be addressed by educators and education leaders (Yang & McCall, 2014).

Curriculum digitisation

Attention is increasingly focussed on 21st century skills, evidenced in curricular reform and is being supported by global discussion of the changing needs of society in general and the workplace specifically. In response to the change required in existing practices, there is now much work being carried out to create innovative learning environments, integrating the 4Cs into the teaching and learning paradigm (Kim, Raza & Seidman, 2019; Waller, Lemoine, Mense & Richardson, 2019).

There is general agreement that a teacher-centric approach is not fit for purpose, cannot prepare learners for the global challenges facing societies and economies (Barber, Donnelly, Rizvi & Summers, 2013). Anderson (2020) takes this argument further when discussing the perceived situation post-pandemic, suggesting that it will be necessary to recognise the complexity of the world today. Incorporating the ability to provide learners with the skills to deal with problems of the future, Anderson argues, is essential when building new education paradigms.

Much of the literature on this topic point to the need for sustainable educational paradigms built for 21st century learners, must mean a holistic approach to the transformation of education. It has been suggested that a developing an all-inclusive plan Malik (2018) covering reform of both curriculum and assessment is essential to building a sustainable way forward. Other components of the paradigm include, according to Malik, recruitment of new educators and training strategies for existing practitioners would need to be given as much credence as the teaching and learning activities of curriculum and assessment. This research argues that Leadership development and the integration of digital technologies cannot be forgotten and must form the basis for any future reshaping of education. However globally, there are questions to be answered:

Table 1. 21st Century Skills - Rationale, examples and questions

21st Century Skills	Rationale	Examples	Questions for educators
Communication	Learners must become knowledgeable about and skilled in the various ways the world communicates.	Much of the business world communicates by: • Email • Linked in updates • Tweets	• How and when should these skills be taught? • How are these skills assessed? • Are these forms of communication being taught effectively and applied appropriately?
Collaboration	Relationships are built and teamwork takes place across times and places.	The business world now works in this way. Learners now collaborate with others globally.	• Does education offer sufficient opportunity for learners to collaborate across places and time?
Creativity	Learners could be creating output (artefacts etc) for a global audience, for people about whom they know little or nothing.	Learners should be aware of demands and expectations of global viewers of their work. Consideration must be given to language levels and cultural issues.	• Does education provide sufficient learning opportunities to allow students to develop these skills?
Critical Thinking	Not only problem solving, but identifying the problem that is to be solved. Creative problem solvers		• In what ways is education creating opportunities for learners to develop a critical mindset? • How is education allowing students to apply those skills?

- How can curricula be reformed to integrate new learning goals required to accommodate development of these 21st Century Skills?
- Have metrics been developed to measure different levels of competencies in these skills?

In an effort to answer these questions, this research considered the ways in which 21st century skills could be taught, all the while considering if these skills can be taught digitally. This complex question, needs to be considered from the point of view that, in a digital world, technology is an integral part of life and learning and as such requires to be integrated into curriculums at all levels.

This research argues that the teaching of the 4Cs can be taught, however education leaders must ensure that their systems are capable of developing characteristics of a sustainable teaching and learning paradigm. Too often the curriculum has features of a pre-digital age when attempting to add-on an online element to their provision (Douse & Uys, 2018). This results in the teaching of the 4Cs in a non-standardized way and often viewed as an extra task rather than an integrated component of the learning taking place.

It is not sufficient to discussion reform in education without addressing the issue of Assessment of learning. This topic is wide and much has been written about ways in which to evaluate students' learning, however it must be included and this next section now briefly outlines the place of assessment in this research.

Assessment

Assessment in education continues to be a hot topic of discussion, taking up a huge amount of time and energy as educators and the systems within which they operate strive to reshape and reform ways in which growth in a skill-set can be measured. There are constraints where, to a degree, certification and accreditation drive the criteria by which learning is measured. However, within frameworks set out by educational systems, there is space for development of a creative approach to assessing student learning. The tendency remains on summative assessments so there needs to be a concerted effort to continue with the trend to build concept-based assessments that measure students' competencies in the 4Cs.

Students must to be equipped with skills that will allow them to deal with the complexity of modern world problems. Education plays a key role in providing situations where learning takes place in a cohesive, holistic and authentic environment. Learners must know how to learn, and then to turn information into knowledge followed by reflecting on and analyzing their own learning. Changes to pedagogy, curriculum, assessment and policy all play a part in the transformation process. This research argues that assessment is a fundament element of any change to the teaching and learning paradigm. This claim is supported by the theme that emerged from the comments made by the participants to the research when giving their reflections on what could and should change in the evaluation of learning and setting metrics where quality of learning can be measured. How to do this effectively and in a sustainable way is the challenge facing education leaders and education systems.

The vision of the United Nations Sustainable Development Goals is that assessment of learning needs to be suitably targeted for, not only different levels of attainment, but also for differences in cultural contexts. Suitable assessment for all.

United Nations Sustainable Development Goals

As education is a human right it is considered central to sustainable development and peace globally. The goals of the UN 2030 Agenda demand that education leaders establish systems that will allow populations to be empowered with the knowledge, skills and values so that they may individually and collectively contribute in a meaningful way to society (United Nations, 2016; United Nations, 2017a). Education for Sustainable Development (ESD) is one of the central tenets of the SDGs outlined by the UN. Interpretations of this concept are context based, allowing nations to benefit from a global framework when planning their social, cultural and political responses to the expectations of the SDGs (UNESCO, 2016b).

The UN has defined the 2030 Agenda as a plan for "people, planet and prosperity", where education is a pivotal point within the strategy. The seventeen SDGs are set out as a way of directing governments globally on a common pathway to achieving these wider goals (The Sustainable Development Goals Report, 2017). Taking this understanding of the intentions of the UN a step further is the idea that at the core of ESD as a concept is the linking of education globally through technology and the ideology of lifelong learning (UNESCO, 2016a; UNESCO, 2018a; Wu & Shen, 2016).

Weitz, Carlsen, Nilsson & Skånberg, (2018) take the view that, while the UN in setting up the SDGs recognised that the reforms necessary involves complex actions from nations worldwide, many governments are moving forward. The rate of change is variable, largely due to these complexities with procedures and institutional limitations being mentioned as the main challenges.

MAIN FOCUS OF THE STUDY

Methodology

Data Collection and Analysis

Taking a qualitative approach to the study of the impact of globalization on teaching and learning and considering the ways in which 21st Century Skills could be incorporated into the digital learning environment, allowed the insights of educational practitioners to present their experiences. Six interviews were carried out of educators with proven experience in both face-to-face and digital forms of academic content delivery. There was a process of purposeful sampling thus ensuring reliability and rigour.

Scrutinizing and unpacking comments from interviewees, provided the narratives presented in this chapter. Central to the construction of new knowledge is the exploration of the components as understood and experienced by those practitioners taking part in the research (Denzin & Lincoln, 1998). To do this in a meaningful way required that a solid framework be build where understandings could emerge organically from the data – the experiences of the participants in this case.

A consent form was designed and created as a consistent method of obtaining informed consent from participants. Once informed agreement had been received from each of the participants individually, each participant in turn was asked to respond to the interview questions. Interviewees were informed in writing that there were no direct or known risks identified from participating in this research and that they could remove themselves from the data collection process at any point without penalty. Assurances were given that all personal details and/or identifying information would be removed.

Qualitative interviews

Drawing out the experiences of practitioners through a process of interviews was considered to be the most effective method of exploring their individual perceptions. So, from this standpoint, a carefully selected group of participants was identified. These participants were employed at a range of Further and Higher Education establishments across the United Kingdom (UK) all with at least 5 year's tenure. The process of data collection was carried out through online interviews with the interview questions having been previously sent to the interviewees. This ensured that participants had time to prepare themselves for the answers they would provide to the questions put to them. Other documentation was used as required to support this process of data collection.

This process was considered to be the most manageable due to restrictions placed on social interactions due to government imposed pandemic limitations. Ensuring rigour in this process is, as Creswell (2014) tell us important and was especially so in this research as the researcher strived to guarantee credibility in the ways in which data was collected for this study. Connecting literature to the experiences of participants meant that a process of verification was employed to provide a strong basis upon which to place the outcomes of the study. A focussed literature research was completed and themes were identified as they emerged from the data until a point of saturation was reached (Bentz & Shapiro, 1998; Blaxter, Hughes, & Tight, 2010).

Interview research questions

Semi-structured interviews formed the basis of the collection process. Questions were designed so that they may be asked of all participants to ensure standardization in the data collection process. Follow-up questions emerge organically from the process and were included in the analysis.

The following questions were asked of participants:

1. What is your name, specialist subject area and qualifications?
2. What experience do you have of both online and face-to-face teaching?
3. What is your understanding of globalization of education?

4. What impact has globalization had on education?
5. What is your understanding of the term 21st century skills?
6. In what ways do you integrate 21st century skills into your teaching?
7. Explain the difficulties of integrating 21st century skills into your teaching?
8. As an experienced educator, do you think that 21st century skills should be integrated or taught independently of content courses? Explain your answer.
9. What issues do you think should be addressed that we have not discussed during this interview?

Findings

In summarizing the findings, it is important to remember that although the digital revolution is global, adapting to the impacts of technology must be viewed as a contextual issue. National or regional responses will reflect differences in economic structures, social inclinations and be subject to commercial and governmental priorities. This study took place in the United Kingdom, and the research recognises that replication of this study will require to be adjusted to accommodate local (national, regional) setting.

When asked in questions 3 and 4 about awareness of globalization of education, participants felt that this concept is now understood as being a factor that underpins education activity. However, it was pointed out by all participants to the research that context is vital in the understanding of globalization. The impact of this global issue was not agreed upon. Two of the participants took the view that teaching methods are now more interrelated, in that more integration of skills takes place within one assessment activity. This leads, according to the participants a more prepared student going into the global workplace. Being more prepared for operating with a multi-national type organization was seen to be an advantage. Having a wider knowledge of global business and the ways in which these organizations operate and the behaviours and practices expected from those working in such organizations was also considered a benefit of globalized education.

Conversely, it was pointed out by three of the participants, there are downsides to the globalization of education. An example of this is the gap that exists in access to technology and of course to education that exists globally between developed and developing countries. There is a belief that this digital revolution will widen any such gaps.

In conclusion, globalization is a world-wide issue that is to be dealt with by global leaders in a way that recognises the issues mentioned above, the challenge is how does education adapt to a world that is constantly changing?

In response to Questions 5,6,7 and 8, there was a strong feeling that the study of creativity in terms of creative thinking and creative problem solving had not sufficiently been explored in terms of digital applications in the education (that is learning) setting. Further exploration (through follow-up questions) revealed that these skills are perceived to be 'discreet' elements of learning and are still taught independently of content information. Interestingly, it was felt by five of the six participants that there is a concerted effort to now measure problem-solving within 'integrated' projects where multiple elements of learning are measured in a single assessment activity. The same was not reported when the study delved deeper into the issue of creativity. Collaboration and communication, it was felt by all participants, were routinely assessed and measured in terms of student learning and from a pedagogy viewpoint, could now be considered to be a central part of all learning.

One outlier, mentioned by one participant argued that it is not only the 4Cs that are measured in unequal ways during the learning process, but also technology and technical skills. The participant put forward the issue of curriculum design and offered a solution, saying more consideration must be given to the overall teaching of content and 4Cs in a comprehensive and cohesive way. It was felt that too much importance was still being placed on the competency of content subjects rather than on the ways in which the 4Cs complement and support the application of content knowledge.

Four of the six interviewees to this research pointed out that, as 21st century skills have been identified as being the skills necessary for students to succeed in an information-driven, global society, a true understanding needs to be developed by educators. This was not voiced as a criticism but as a signal to educators to build a solid knowledge (within themselves individually and collectively) of the ways in which the 4Cs can be most effectively used to strengthen learners skill-set. Consistently providing students, it was suggested, with a set of learning outcomes against which demonstration of technical skills are measure together with transferable skills is the key to success for today's students.

SOLUTIONS AND RECOMMENDATIONS

In a fast changing and ever more interconnected world, information is readily available. Digitization and the application of technologies means that routine tasks will be carried out by computerization at all levels. Technology is now a fundamental in societies and economies, where business leaders and governments must devise policies and practices to exploit benefits and minimize short-term disruptions. Similarly, to be sustainable, the education sector (at all levels) must adapt to changes driven by advancements in technology. The teaching and learning paradigm must shift in response. Recommendations that emerge from this research are outlined below.

Education Systems in the Digital World

The impact of globalization has increased the challenges faced by education and educators. Add to this, the increasing impact of knowledge as a key driver of economic growth and the digital changes taking place exponentially, then the response required by education is imperative and obvious. Education leaders are required to confront challenges presented as the world moves to a more interconnected model.

Technology has made it possible to access subject experts from around the world and specialists in any and all subject matters from a diverse range of locations. Governments must find ways to harness this availability and use it to enrich the learning of our students. The real challenge is to identify the authenticity and value of the offerings to be found online and in doing so learners will be offered a learning experience that meets their needs. This will be successful and sustainable if education leaders adapt online provisions so that learning is meaningful in the context of the learners' situation.

Globally, societies are changing rapidly, due to the impact of technology (Andersen, 2020; Douse & Uys, 2018). However, it appears from the outcomes of this research that education systems are slow to respond, a view shared with Malik (2018), as established procedures and structures remain the preferred default. It is suggested in this research, that often skills taught are not required in a digital era. A common criticism, reported by the participants to this research, is that the use of computers to improve the out-dated systems is not sufficiently progressive to provide future generations with the skills of - critical thinking, creativity, communication and collaboration. This is where the 4Cs can be identified as being essential to future development of education systems Kim, Raza & Seidman (2019) and must be incorporated into all learning situations. Adopting an approach to teaching and learning where the 4Cs are discreet elements to learning is problematic according to Douse & Uys (2018) and lessens the impact on learners as they develop skills necessary to take them into the future as fully functioning members of a digital society.

The challenges for many developing countries are magnified as they struggle with weak infrastructures (Weitz, Carlsen, Nilsson & Skånberg, 2018; Wu & Shen, 2016). Countries in this category face additional challenges as they strive to reform pedagogical practices. Professionals are constrained by politico-social beliefs and lack of resources.

A 21st Century Workforce

This research proposes that a new workforce is required. It is imperative governments recognise this fact and help fund education systems so that education infrastructures are build where learners can be offered learning opportunities to develop skills using a range of electronic technologies. The workforce of the future must be made up of individuals who can access, evaluate, synthesize and apply information. People who are creative thinkers will be in high demand and being able to take a critical view of information and situation and be able to communicate effectively whilst collaborating with others will be fundamental to a sustainable career. It is not only job success career advancement that must be recognised as driving this shift, but the advancement of societies as technology demands new approaches to global solutions to global problems. Not to be forgotten will be the ability to operate in diverse and multicultural settings and to be aware of cultural sensitivities when dealing with individuals and systems globally.

Preparing global citizens with the ability to adopt an international perspective and have an understanding of cross-cultural issues, requires a change in the teaching and learning paradigm and a change in ideology in ways that were not previously required of education systems. Learners must have the multiplicity of skills that allows them to deal with the complexity of the global setting within which they will operate as part of the future workforce.

Transforming education

To allow for the development of a workforce that is sustainable and capable of adapting to new ways of working and connecting, education systems must give students the tools so that they can:

- be effective learners
- evaluate own learning
- change information into knowledge
- recognise the effectiveness of their own learning

Widening the term 21st century skills from the 4Cs to include knowledge manipulation, technical skills, work habits, and personal behaviours are all critically important for success in today's connected world and need to be part of all learning.

It is not sufficient to provide students with skills to survive in the workplace, but to offer them opportunities to develop skills so that they are global citizens, are culturally aware and be self-directed in their actions. Set against a backdrop of the growing need for an entrepreneurial mindset and the ability to solve problems the complexity of which we are not sure at the moment and the dilemma facing educators and governments becomes evident.

Governments that are successfully transforming their education systems have recognised the value of investing in producing citizens who are able to discover valid and reliable information, shape that information into knowledge and then apply that knowledge in a variety of contexts. There is a concern expressed by some employers that new recruits into the workforce struggle to demonstrate competence in the skills now required. This is the main challenge facing education at the moment – how and in what ways to transform. Education leaders and practitioners must find ways in which students can not only learn 21st century skills, but practice them so as to become proficient in those skills. The shift must be from teacher-centric to learner-centric models of learning. Whilst many nations are making this transition, progress is slow and from this perspective students are entering the workplace ill-equipped to deal with real world challenges, think critically and be capable of adapting to situations.

Globalization is strengthening its hold on societies and economies, and with this increased influence there is a demand that education moves from models of the past to new models capable of fulfilling the needs of individuals and communities. The new paradigm must be comprehensive in nature, covering pedagogy, curriculum, assessment, teaching education and leadership styles. Of course all this is set against the backdrop of ever-evolving technology. There is now a need for education establishments to work from a holistic perspective where innovation, collaboration, evaluation and ongoing- improvement are characteristics of the establishment's ethos.

FUTURE RESEARCH DIRECTIONS

The fundamental changes in society resulting from the dynamic nature of technology and its wide-ranging impact on all aspects of life and learning, calls for research into which particular aspects of learning require to be reformed. Creating new, informed, learning experiences will only be possible when a deeper understanding of which parts of the curriculum should be changed and in what ways. Of course, such a study would require to be set against a backdrop of globalization and the impact this phenomenon is having on education (Altbach, Reisberg & Rumbley, 2009).

There should be a further study into the ways in which learning occurs and how knowledge creation develops. This is especially pertinent as we propose the integration of the 4Cs into all learning situations. Andersen (2020) stresses the need to be mindful of all aspects of learning when considering the new type of learning and the new outcomes now expected of educational experiences.

Both of these issues will impact policy and inform policy makers with an understanding of possible futures for our education systems.

From a more learning activity-based approach it is suggested that research should take place into the most benefit tasks learners should be exposed to as they grapple with the integration of new skills into the learning experience. This would require research into authentic projects where students could practice working in multi-disciplinary teams, managing complex problems to find multi-dimensional solutions, all the while searching for reliable information and manipulating that information into knowledge. Blaxter, Hughes & Tight (2010) tell us that bringing together all aspects of a problem is the only effective way to research a topic. From this perspective it is suggested that having a goal of re-aligning curriculum with industry requirements would be a proposed framework for this type of research.

CONCLUSION

Globalization, education reform, digitization, 21st century skills are all terms that are used almost interchangeably as educators strive to find a way forward. Providing learners with learning opportunities that adequately prepare them to take their place in the workforce and/or make a meaningful contribution to society has always been a challenge. The dominant factor impacting all education activity is – technology. How do education leaders adapt their systems so that students gain most from their experiences whilst in education? This is the ongoing dilemma for educators, governments and global policy makers. The drive to set out a clear plan of action was one of the motivators for the United Nations to craft an initiative in 2015, where guidance was given to global leaders as to a sustainable way forward for all. Education is a central premise of the Sustainable Development Goals created by the United Nations where a set of goals was outlined for nations of the world to follow with the ultimate goal of providing solutions to political, economic and environment challenges world-wide.

REFERENCES

Altbach, P. G., Reisberg, L., & Rumbley, L. E. (2009). *Trends in global higher education: Tracking an academic revolution: A report prepared for the UNESCO 2009 World Conference on Higher Education.* Retrieved from https://unesdoc. unesco.org/images/0018/001832/183219e.pdf

Andersen, A. K. (2020). Educating free citizens for the 21st century. *IUL Research, 1*(1), 8–23.

Barber, M., Donnelly, K., Rizvi, S., & Summers, L. (2013). *An avalanche is coming: Higher education and the revolution ahead.* The Institute of Public Policy Research.

Bentz, V. M., & Shapiro, J. J. (1998). *Mindful inquiry in social research.* Sage.

Blaxter, L., Hughes, C., & Tight, M. (2010). Managing your project. In *How to research* (4th ed., pp. 134–154). Open University Press.

Creswell, J. W. (2007). *Qualitative inquiry and research design: Choosing among five approaches* (2nd ed.). Sage.

Creswell, J. W. (2014). *Research design: Qualitative, quantitative and mixed methods approaches* (4th ed.). Sage.

Crotty, M. (1998). *The foundations of social research: Meaning and perspective in the research process*. Sage.

Denzin, N. K., & Lincoln, Y. S. (1998). *Collecting and interpreting qualitative materials*. Sage.

De Wit, H. (2011). Globalisation and internationalisation of higher education. *Internationalisation of Universities in the Network Society, 8*(2), 241-325.

Douse, M., & Uys, P. (2018). Educational Planning in the Age of Digitisation. *Educational Planning, 25*(2), 7–23.

Green, M. F., Marmolejo, F., & Egron-Polak, E. (2012). The internationalization of higher education: Future prospects. In D. K. Deardorff, H. de Wit, J. D. Heyl, & T. Adams (Eds.), *The SAGE handbook of international higher education*. Sage. doi:10.4135/9781452218397.n24

Kim, S., Raza, M., & Seidman, E. (2019). Improving 21st-century teaching skills: The key to effective 21st-century learners. *Research in Comparative and International Education, 14*(1), 99–117.

Malik, R. S. (2018). Educational challenges in 21st century and sustainable development. *Journal of Sustainable Development Education and Research, 2*(1), 9–20.

Marginson, S., & van der Wende, M. (2007). *Globalisation and higher education* (OECD Education Working Papers No. 8). Retrieved from http://atoz.ebsco.com. ezproxy.liv.ac.uk/Customization/Tab/11404?tabId=8817

Organisation for Economic Co-operation and Development & PISA. (2010). *What Students Know and Can Do: Student Performance in Reading, Mathematics and Science*. OECD.

Owens, T. L. (2017). Higher education in the sustainable development goals framework. *European Journal of Education, 52*(4), 414–420. doi:10.1111/ejed.12237

Russow, L. C. (2003). Digitization of education: A panacea? *Journal of Teaching in International Business, 14*(2-3), 1–11. doi:10.1300/J066v14n02_01

The Sustainable Development Goals Report 2017. (2017). https://unstats.un. org/sdgs/files/report/2017/TheSustainableDevelopmentGoalsReport2017.pdf

UNESCO. (2016a). Education for people and planet: Creating sustainable futures for all (Global Education Monitoring Report 2016). Paris: Author.

UNESCO. (2016b). *Evaluation of UNESCO's regional conventions on the recognition of qualifications in higher education.* Author.

UNESCO. (2018a). *Policy brief, education for sustainable development and SDGs.* https://en.unesco.org/sites/default/files/gap_pn1_-_esd_ and_the_sdgs_policy_brief_6_page_version.pdf

United Nations. (2016). *The Sustainable Development Goals Report 2016.* http://www.un.org.lb/Library/Assets/The-Sustainable-Development-Goals-Report-2016-Global.pdf

United Nations. (2017a). *Statistical Commission. Report on the forty-eighth session.* https://unstats.un.org/unsd/statcom/48th-session/documents/Report-on-the-48th-Session-ofthe-Statistical-Commission-E.pdf

Waller, R. E., Lemoine, P. A., Mense, E. G., & Richardson, M. D. (2019). Higher education in search of competitive advantage: Globalization, technology and e-learning. *International Journal of Advanced Research and Publications, 3*(8), 184–190.

Weitz, N., Carlsen, H., Nilsson, M., & Skånberg, K. (2018). Towards systemic and contextual priority setting for implementing the 2030 Agenda. *Sustainability Science, 13*(2), 531–548.

Wu, Y.-C. J., & Shen, J.-P. (2016). Higher education for sustainable development: A systematic review. *International Journal of Sustainability in Higher Education, 17*(5), 633–651. doi:10.1108/IJSHE-01-2015-0004

Yang, L., & McCall, B. (2014). World education finance policies and higher education access: A statistical analysis of World Development Indicators for 86 countries. *International Journal of Educational Development, 35,* 25–36. doi:10.1016/j.ijedudev.2012.11.002

Yin, R. K. (2003). *Case study research: Design and methods* (3rd ed.). Sage.

Chapter 7
Physiotherapy Education During COVID–19:
A Jordanian Experience

Dania Qutishat
The University of Jordan, Jordan

Maha T. Mohammad
The University of Jordan, Jordan

EXECUTIVE SUMMARY

The Bachelor of Science in physiotherapy is a four-year program that has been offered at The University of Jordan since 1999. Just like all other educational programs across the world, teaching pedagogy in this program underwent a major overhaul due to the COVID-19 pandemic. In this chapter, the changes implemented in this program due to the pandemic and a discussion of their different aspects are presented. First, an overview of traditional teaching model and all the changes it underwent during the first year of the pandemic are presented. After that, specific aspects of the changes are addressed in depth and discussed in light of evidence from the literature. These include changes made to clinical and practical education, modifications of assessment methods, and responses and adjustments of students and faculty members. The chapter concludes with recommendations for future implementation of online teaching in physiotherapy education.

ORGANIZATION BACKGROUND

The University of Jordan, established in the year 1962 by a royal decree from

DOI: 10.4018/978-1-7998-8310-4.ch007

the belated King Hussein of Jordan, is the largest and oldest institute of higher education in Jordan. This public university is located in the capital city, Amman, in the heart of Jordan. The university includes 24 schools which offer around 250 different programs ranging from B.Sc., M.Sc., and Ph.D. in various specialties. In addition, the university includes various institutes (Institute of Archaeology, Social Work Institute, etc.), centers (Language Center, Stem Therapy Center, etc.), and a large hospital (University of Jordan Hospital). Programs offered by the university are generally classified under three streams; humanitarian (business, art, law, etc.), scientific (engineering, science, agriculture, etc.), and medical (medicine, dentistry, rehabilitation, etc.). Being the largest university in Jordan, more than 35,000 students are enrolled at the university. The more than 200,000 university alumni are among the top ranked graduates in the region with high employability rate.

The School of Rehabilitation Sciences at the university was established in 1999 and houses four departments; physiotherapy, occupational therapy, prosthetics and orthotics, and hearing and speech therapy. The Department of Physiotherapy offers two degrees; B.Sc. and M.Sc., the latter was started in 2019. In addition, the department started a new M.Sc. program in athletic therapy in 2021. The B.Sc. program has been granted Full Accreditation by World Physiotherapy (the international organization representing the profession of physiotherapy). Each year around 90 students are enrolled in the B.Sc. program. The twelve PhD-holding faculty members at the department (including the authors of this chapter) are graduates from the program who were granted scholarships by the university to complete their graduate studies at universities in the United States, Canada, and United Kingdom and have been teaching at the department since then. In addition, teaching assistant staff who hold M.Sc. and B.Sc. degree assist in the education of students during practical labs and clinical training.

SETTING THE STAGE

Physiotherapy practice and its education are rooted in manual contact and physical proximity especially during applied courses (World Physiotherapy, 2019). For decades, physiotherapy educators were used to teach, supervise, and assess the practical skills of their students in face-to-face format. Among the wide-scale changes caused by the COVID-19 pandemic, which include what appear to be long-lasting effects on every single aspect of human life, education, and that of physiotherapy in particular, are substantially impacted (Crawford et al., 2020). While at the very beginning of the COVID-19 pandemic, questions of whether the repercussions will be short-lived were raised, after one year since the start of the situation, all parties involved agree that they will not.

Large professional and accreditation bodies such as World Physiotherapy (WP), American Physical Therapy Association (APTA), and Chartered Society of Physiotherapy (CSP) emphasize the importance of delivering high quality online teaching that will preserve the fulfilment of intended learning outcomes (American Physical Therapy Association, 2021; Chartered Society of Physiotherapy, 2021; World Physiotherapy, 2020). However, clear guidelines regarding the design and delivery of practical courses were not available at the start of the pandemic. Educators had to be innovative in adopting new approaches to facilitate learning for practical skills (Suhail et al., 2020). Using online teaching in practical specialties is controversial; some skills cannot be taught and transferred to students without face-to-face learning. However, circumstances caused by the COVID-19 pandemic provided opportunities to stretch the boundaries of online learning in physiotherapy education and prepare institutions for future similar situations (Crawford et al., 2020).

In any educational environment, educators need to keep in mind effective theories of learning and teaching pedagogies that are best linked to their courses. It is difficult to claim that during the first few months of forced online learning the theories of learning were purposefully selected as faculty members were exploring possible ways to manage covering the content of courses. However, continued use of online education should be supported by underlying relevant learning theories (Unge et al., 2018). The switch from face-to-face mode of delivery into online learning does not only mean remote access to learning materials (Gagnon et al., 2020); it also involves systematic steps that start with the right choice of technology, appropriate design of synchronous and asynchronous learning activities that are based on sound learning theories, and the readiness of students to utilize the technology and engage in meaningful learning activities to fulfill intended learning outcomes (Unge et al., 2018). Learning theories that should be adopted as a framework while preparing online courses are based on andragogy and constructivism (Allen, 2016; Moore & Shemberger, 2019). Online education utilizes andragogy through increased learner engagement and responsibility (Gagnon et al., 2020). In its core, online education views students as active participants who are capable of self-regulation and taking lead of their own learning which is perfectly fitting with the theory of andragogy (Moore & Shemberger, 2019). Adopting the learning theory of andragogy encompasses the shift from an educator-oriented approach into a learner-centered one (Chan, 2010; Ozuah, 2005) as this theory is concerned with adults' education; learners are independent and practice reflecting on past experiences prior to the acquisition of new knowledge and skills (Chan, 2010; Ozuah, 2005). In addition to the theory of andragogy, most of the learning activities that were designed for online courses require interacting with the educator and peers, hence, fulfilling the principles of constructivism (Unge et al., 2018).

The Bachelor of Science physiotherapy program at The University of Jordan aims to educate professionals with knowledge and skills to apply evidence-based interventions that accomplish best results using a patient-centered approach. The intended learning outcomes for the program are listed in Table 1. In this case study, the experience of educators at the program is presented. The challenges faced by the authors in various aspects of the transition to online teaching process will be covered in this chapter. First, an overview of the traditional teaching model and the changes that unfolded since the start of the pandemic is presented, followed by a discussion of the various challenges, how they were dealt with, pitfalls, evidence from the literature, and possible areas for improvement.

CASE DESCRIPTION

Teaching Model at the University of Jordan

Phase 1: Pre-COVID-19

Prior to the pandemic, theoretical lectures covered the basis of the various techniques, introduction to different diseases and conditions that require physiotherapy; and broad concepts such as background frameworks, multidisciplinary team, and higher intellectual skills. During practical sessions, the educators introduced the different techniques and supervised the students during application of those techniques. Upon mastery of the basics of different techniques, more advanced skills such as clinical reasoning, problem-solving, and reflection were introduced. During clinical training, students' experience was graduated in two main stages; the first stage was done as part of the specialty courses in the curriculum (neuromuscular, musculoskeletal, cardiorespiratory, and pediatrics). During this stage, students were assigned to cases in groups of five to seven students. Competencies expected from the students were gradually progressed under the supervision of educators from focusing on assessment, to devising initial treatment plans, to setting short- and long-term goals, to finally being able to develop and apply a comprehensive treatment plan to the patients. During the second stage of the training, which represented the culmination of the educational experience at the program, students were assigned to various settings in which they independently applied all the skills they learnt in a holistic approach. By the end of the bachelor degree, students master competencies including rigorous approach to problem solving and decision making, effective communication with all parties involved in the rehabilitation process, demonstration of ethical conduct and professionalism, promotion of healthy lifestyle and physical activity, and integration

Table 1. Intended learning outcomes for the Bachelor of Science in physiotherapy program at The University of Jordan

Program ILO 1:	Recognize, critically analyze and apply the conceptual frameworks and theoretical models underpinning physiotherapy practice
Program ILO 2:	Demonstrate comprehension of background knowledge that informs sound physiotherapy practice
Program ILO 3:	Demonstrate the ability to use online resources and technologies in professional development
Program ILO 4:	Display a professional commitment to ethical practice by adhering to codes of conduct and moral frameworks that govern the practice of physiotherapy
Program ILO 5:	Evaluate the importance of and critically appraise research findings to inform evidence-based practice such that these skills could be utilized in continuing self-development
Program ILO 6:	Implement clinical reasoning, reflection, decision-making, and skilful application of physiotherapy techniques to deliver optimum physiotherapy management
Program ILO 7:	Adhere to the professional standards of physiotherapy practice in terms of assessment, management, outcome measurement, and documentation
Program ILO 8:	Display a willingness to promote healthy lifestyle and convey health messages to clients
Program ILO 9:	Value the willingness to exercise autonomy while appreciating the challenges associated with delivering physiotherapy services
Program ILO 10:	Display the ability to practice in a effective
Program ILO 11:	Demonstrate effective oral and written communication with clients carers

of evidence into practice. The teaching pedagogy relied on the conventional mode of face-to-face, teacher-centered approach.

As for the assessment, a plethora of methods were used to evaluate students' acquisition of the different competencies. These included written, theoretical exams; practical exams in which students applied on their peers; group or individualized assignments; and clinical evaluations which assessed the students coping mechanisms with their environment, dynamics with patient and family, professional attitude, in addition to development and execution of rehabilitation interventions.

Phase 2: Unexpected COVID-19 Lockdown

At the turn of the year 2020, news of the Coronavirus spread in China and various countries around the world started escalating. However, for a short while, things did not seem to be anywhere close at home, and education in the university proceeded as normal. It was in mid-March, which coincides with the middle of the Spring semester, when things came to a sudden halt when the government of Jordan announced an immediate, nation-wide lockdown, with education, just like all other sectors, being stopped. The uncertainty and unprecedence of the situation and the lack of clear plans on how to proceed created an unusual void for educators. A switch to online education seemed inevitable, but so many unanswered questions loomed in the horizon. First and foremost, for how long would this situation last? Was this switch to online education to be made for all aspects of teaching? What platforms were to be used for this switch? What were the possible compensatory approaches for practical and clinical education?

Due to the lack of any organizational guidelines or prior experience with such situations, each faculty member tried their best to deliver content to students in the best possible way. These attempts were largely individual or organized among few members at best. Teaching of theoretical lectures was made mostly using audio-over-PowerPoint. Similar methods were used for practical sessions, and the teaching was supplemented with videos from online resources. Those videos, while far from perfect, were the only available resource at this stage. Of all the teaching methods implemented in the department, clinical education suffered the most. No clear ways to compensate for the lost training at hospitals were attainable. The governmental lockdown was extended on biweekly basis, and each time there were promises of a near return. At this stage, very few live meetings were held with students. Few faculty members resorted to social media platforms to meet with students.

This hiatus period ended up lasting till the end of Spring semester. After the first few weeks, in which faculty members struggled to find ways to dealing with teaching, the focus moved to finding alternate assessment methods. For the first time in the history of the department, online exams were used to evaluate students' learning and replace traditional written exams. After solving the challenges associated with the technicalities of holding exams in this unconventional way, educators faced the challenge of finding optimal ways for monitoring students' performance and limiting cheating. As for practical exams, no possible alternatives were available at the time, so group projects were used.

Adding to the whole situation was the fact that faculty members at the department are mostly females with families of young children and lots of familial and household duties to care for. During the lockdown, day time was filled with teaching their young children, taking care of house chores, and caring for parents. Preparing online materials could only take place at night, with countless sleepless nights spent preparing those materials. Another important factor during this period was the psychological stress caused by the situation. All the stresses of this new, unprecedented situation at work and the heavy load of the many tasks the authors had at hand added up to the large-scale concerns of the pandemic itself. Many questions were left unanswered in the back of the minds of each faculty member; how serious is the disease? Will the country's healthcare system withstand the load? When will it hit at home? Faculty members had to suppress those questions and many others while trying to manage day-to-day life.

Phase 3: Return to Campus

By Fall of the new academic year (2020/2021), even though infection rates were high, things seemed to stabilize. A return to campus was granted for all health specialties only for practical sessions and hospital training. Theoretical lectures were still to be held online. However, this time measures for social distancing, minimal sharing of equipment, and sterilization were at place, therefore practical labs in which around 30 students attended the four-hour session were not possible. Even though the situation was novel, this time faculty members had the time to plan ahead. The idea adopted by most department members was to prepare video content of lab materials. Students studied the video content before coming to the practical sessions. Students in each session were divided to two groups; each group came for two hours and were guided on their acquisition of the skills taught. Fourth year students were allowed to go to clinical training at the available settings while abiding to the new infection control measures. In addition, online sessions were implemented for case discussions. A return to full online learning was expected at any moment, luckily, the semester ended and no such change was made.

Phase 4: Return to Online Teaching

By Spring semester, the same teaching methods that were used in the Fall semester were implemented. Only this time, less than three weeks into the semester the government announced the switch to full online teaching. This was due to the escalating situation as the country was hit with the second wave of the disease which caused a rise of infection rates; the emergence of new, highly infectious strains of the Coronavirus; and the increasing load on the healthcare system nationwide. This time, unlike the first period of complete online teaching, faculty members were better prepared for this change. The skills and technological knowledge of online teaching platforms had significantly improved and videos explaining and demonstrating lab material were already prepared. To ensure the students' acquisition of the skills taught in those labs, students were asked to turn on their cameras and demonstrate application of the techniques on their family members or themselves when possible. At the end of the semester, a return to campus was allowed for practical exams only.

Following this presentation of the teaching model, the next sections provide discussion of different aspects of teaching, assessment, and the impact on the two main players in the educational process; students and teachers.

Challenges Faced During Clinical Education

As mentioned earlier, clinical education was, and still is, among the most severely affected aspects of physiotherapy education by the pandemic. During the initial lockdown phase, educators resorted to using case studies built on real patients that students were managing before the lockdown.

During the return-to-campus phase, limited training sites were available to students. Therefore, a shifts-system was followed which meant that each student's share of on-site clinical training hours was reduced. At the time, recommendations by CSP emphasized the need to achieve around 1000 clinical training hours while still acknowledging that adjustments might be necessary based on the pandemic situation (Chartered Society of Physiotherapy, 2020). However, the experience of faculty members at the department proved that maintaining pre-COVID number of training hours was impossible.

In an educational system that has been focusing on developing students' competencies as can be seen in the program intended learning outcomes (Table 1), it has been a challenge to maintain the same expected levels of proficiency from students with regards to certain competencies related to clinical education. For example, the intended learning outcomes number 4, 6, 7, and 10 were most severely challenged. Taking the World Health Organization (WHO) rehabilitation competency framework into consideration, prior to the pandemic, the majority of students at the B.Sc. program were usually expected by the time of their graduation to fit around the intermediate level of proficiency (World Health Organization, 2020a). However, with the switch to online teaching, competencies such as correct application of interventions, managing workload, adjusting to environmental settings, and working as part of an inter-professional team were harder to develop and evaluate. Based on this framework, a five-phase model is proposed for curriculum development to support competency-based education for rehabilitation (World Health Organization, 2020b). This model was implemented when considering the modifications that were applied to accommodate the pandemic. In the Construction phase, the clinical competencies and their level of proficiency were revised. During the Assessment phase, new assessment methods for each learning outcome were set.

Challenges in clinical education were compensated for by holding several weekly online discussions with students. During these discussions, students were given the opportunity to present cases they worked with and direct questions they had to the clinical instructors. In addition, the educators led discussions on topics that advanced competencies such as evidence-based practice, clinical reasoning, and management of complex cases. Another innovative teaching method that was implemented during those meetings is the use of real patients' videos from an online website that the University made a subscription to. Students were also engaged in tele-rehabilitation sessions by participating in history taking, suggesting assessment methods, and prescribing exercises that patients could apply themselves or have family members assist with. This shift to tele-rehabilitation as a mode of physiotherapy service delivery imposed by the pandemic was applied at various settings globally, it ensured continued care for patients and even increased geographical coverage of services (Grundstein et al., 2021).

Assessment of clinical competencies during periods of online learning was one of the challenges faced by faculty members (Wilcha, 2020). Used assessments focused on case discussions and written reflections; during case discussions students discussed how they would have implemented comprehensive assessments and designed tailored, patient-centered management plans. On the reflection assignment, students elaborated on their experience of being physiotherapy students undergoing clinical training during the pandemic. In this assignment, students expressed their fears and lack of confidence in their clinical skills which might affect their employability prospects. Few students mentioned that they felt they had lost the clinical skills they had previously gained. Others mentioned that they lacked the ability to design effective interventions for patients or how to progress them. Similar findings were reported in a systematic review that examined the effectiveness of virtual education in medical schools (Wilcha, 2020). Due to the shifts-system, students had a reduced workload or follow up with patients. In general, fourth year students expressed widespread concerns in their skills as therapists and their readiness for graduation and working in the job market.

According to Miller's pyramid, which states that the four levels of assessment in clinical education are: knows, knows how, shows how, and does; the assessment methods adopted during the pandemic were mainly lacking in the fourth level of assessment (Miller, 1990). The ability to "do" a skill focuses on practice in the real setting and not in model, simulating environment.

In the future, if similar instances occur, physiotherapy programs should consider supporting alternative models of training for students. Even though many other places reverted to tele-rehabilitation (Tenforde et al., 2020), the applicability of such type of services in Jordan and other low- or middle-income countries remains limited. This can be due to multiple factors, such as limited adherence, limited knowledge of using technologies in rehabilitation, considerations of patient's safety, and application of hands-on techniques.

Modifications to Practical Teaching

The largest, and hopefully best, reform as a result of the pandemic involved practical teaching. Since the start of the pandemic, the most effective way for practical teaching adopted by the department was the hybrid mode; a combination of both online-based and campus-based delivery and supervision (Dziuban et al., 2018). Faculty members prepared a bank of videos for the practical courses. The department has now over 500 authentic videos that were purposely recorded to meet the requirements of the curricula. These videos are uploaded on YouTube channels for each faculty member; they are saved as public videos so anyone can access and benefit from them. The fact that students could access the learning materials at any time, watch, pause and repeat them as many times as they need was a major positive change that helped them improve their self-regulation, a skill that is emphasized in the andragogy theory which students were lacking at the time.

It is important to highlight that digital technologies alone may not substitute face-to-face encounter, as physiotherapy students still need to develop skills directly from their educators and they need to learn along with their peers in real time and place (Olivier et al., 2020). Some authors concluded that online courses should be exclusive to theoretical courses only in physiotherapy (Gencheva & Gencheva-Vassileva, 2020). However, it is the experience of the authors that online teaching provided a valuable asset that enabled delivery of practical content under the extreme circumstances of the pandemic. In this time in age, online teaching is here to stay. The American Council of Academic Physical Therapy (ACAPT) recommended that practical training via online platforms should be introduced to students as an effective alternative for face-to-face sessions (ACAPT, 2020). Students had a consistent belief that online practical courses have no value and could not be compared to traditional on-campus training. It is the responsibility of educators to persuade their students that this method is effective and offers new opportunities for self-development (ACAPT, 2020).

The department modified the practical sessions' schedule to allow for better adherence for contact reduction recommendations as issued by the ACAPT (ACAPT, 2020). The following measures were adopted to satisfy conditions for social distancing: students were divided into smaller groups, the number of students in each group ranged between 15-20 students occupying a 12X10 meter room. Few faculty members managed to pair students throughout the whole semester, but same partners were not necessarily the same across different courses. This might be very difficult given the large number of students and the large number of sections in each course. Table 2 shows the number of students enrolled in the department at the time of the pandemic and the number of different courses offered at the department by the twelve faculty members.

Even though this switch to online learning was imposed by the pandemic, faculty members see that it will continue after it. This adoption of digital technologies in education will help achieve the goals of accessibility, flexibility and sustainability which are listed by the Higher Education Sustainability Initiative, a part of the United Nations Sustainable Development Goals (United Nations, 2012). In addition,

Table 2. Number of students enrolled in the four years of the Bachelor of Science in physiotherapy program and the number of courses offered for each batch

Year	Number of students	Number of courses offered by the department		
		Theoretical	Practical	Clinical
First	100	1	0	0
Second	140	9	5	0
Third	88	7	6	3
Fourth	76	4	1	3

it enhances learners' engagement and learner-centered approach which form the foundation of andragogy theory (Gagnon et al., 2020).

A recent systematic review that aimed at comparing online versus face-to-face physiotherapy courses concluded that the outcomes of online courses were similar or better than those of traditional courses (Odegaard et al., 2021). It is important to highlight that the studies included in this systematic review were mostly during the pre-COVID-19 era which means those studies included only specific online courses, while post COVID-19 scenarios included changes at a program level, therefore, comparison is not necessarily valid.

Online learning in physiotherapy education is not new, in the last ten years different universities adopted online learning for a number of courses, these were planned and designed to be delivered as distant learning courses (Odegaard et al., 2021; Unge et al., 2018). However, the sudden and unplanned shift due to COVID-19 was totally different to all previous attempts because these courses were structured for conventional mode of delivery in the first place. The challenges faced during the first few months of forced online learning were not comparable to previous or following periods, two years into the COVID-19 situation, educators were better prepared. The acceleration in online physiotherapy education since the COVID-19 outbreak was tremendous, courses that were thought to be exclusive for face-to-face mode of delivery were transformed to be adequate for blended or hybrid learning. Scholars are referring to the reality of online learning as the "new normal" (Dziuban et al., 2018; Gagnon et al., 2020).

Modifications and Development of New Assessments

New, unconventional methods were used to compensate for the traditional methods of written or practical assessments. At first, the University did not have any guidelines as to the written exams and educators were left on their own to choose the platforms and set the rules for exams. Faculty members examined few platforms and resorted to one. Trial exams were held for students to familiarize them with those new interfaces.

Online exams presented new challenges and advantages. Being environment-friendly by saving paper is a top advantage. On average, each exam consumed no less than 700 sheets of paper. Multiplying that by the number of exams held for each course, the number of courses offered each semester, and the number of batches at the department shows that the savings in cost and at the environmental level are huge. Another advantage is the time saved as online platforms offered automatic grading.

However, on the down side, the unethical behavior of cheating was on the rise. There were reports of students cheating by referring to books, checking online resources, or working in groups to answer exams. On one of the courses a simple correlation between students' GPA prior to the pandemic and their scores on an online exam indicated that students were involved in cheating. A similar method of examining students' performance was used by Ikram et. al (Ikram & Rabbani, 2021) and indicated that academic dishonesty was evident with online exams. Cheating and inability to control it caused dissatisfaction mainly among high-performing students as their low-performing peers started competing with them on top grades. Another major challenge with online exams was the availability of access to reliable, high-speed internet. Several students lived in rural areas that did not have high-speed internet coverage, while others could not afford such a costly service. The internet issues not only affected students' performance during online exams, but also affected their studies in general raising serious concerns regarding the equity of online education (Akulwar-Tajane et al., 2020).

As the situation with online exams continued, the university introduced new measures and a set of legislations to help solve some of the issues. The university launched a website supported by its information technology department. The website had minimal loading demands which helped students in rural areas or areas with slow internet. In addition, the university sponsored internet bundles for students who could not afford the high-speed costly access. New legislations to limit cheating included restrictions on exams' durations, setting exam questions to appear at random order, and setting exams to be one-way. One-way exams meant that once answered, a question cannot be returned to. However, these legislations were not enough to control against all practices of academic dishonesty.

Even though exam strategies generally advise the balanced use of easy, moderate, and difficult questions, educators found themselves pressured to rely more on the latter two types of questions to limit the ability of students who attempted to cheat on exams. Educators started using questions that relied more on the students' advanced comprehension of the content. Later on, the use of cameras to provide real-time monitoring of students' during exams was introduced. This helped limit cheating, but it came with the cost of demanding high-speed internet. Other possible ways to

Table 3. Measures taken by the university and department to minimize cheating in online exams

Platform related measures	- Minimise the number of questions per page (1, 2, or 3 questions only). - Make the exam one way, questions were sequential and back feature was disabled. - Randomise the order of questions and answers in multiple choice questions.
Exam design related measures	- Avoid Google-based questions. - Include case study style questions as appropriate. - Increase the number of options in multiple choice questions. - Include questions that require higher thinking skills.
Students-related measures	- Talk with students about acceptable behaviour during exams. - Communicate explicitly the consequences of cheating and plagiarism according to the university's policies and regulations. - Include clear messages and instructions in the syllabi about academic dishonesty, cheating and plagiarism behaviours.
Staff-related measures	- Share technical tips that facilitate better control of exams. - Assign staff to be proctors during exams.
General measures related to remote assessment	- Open the web cameras during the exams.

limit academic dishonesty that could not be implemented at the university include advanced software that offer the ability to block students' access to websites other than the exam's one. However, the university did not show interest in investing in such software due to their high cost. Table 3 summarizes measures taken by the university to achieve transparent and fair online exams. The ACAPT published a guide on classroom and lab considerations and resources which included several valuable recommendations on setting online exams during the pandemic (ACAPT, 2020). Other methods of assessment other than online exams, also presented with their own set of challenges, for example; group projects involved other forms of academic dishonesty such as lack of accountability to the required tasks (Roe et al., 2019).

Students Attitude and Adjustment to Online Learning

Challenges and barriers faced during the pandemic not only included factors related to teaching, assessment, technology, and policies and regulations, but also extended to the human factors. The roles, responses, and wellbeing of students and faculty members were largely and differentially influenced by the pandemic.

Teaching and assessment pedagogy were not the only thing that faculty members had to change; their role as educators evolved especially the extent and nature of their relationship with their students. In a time when students were concerned that their learning might be compromised due to cancellation of face-to-face education, faculty members had a great responsibility to assure students that changes made to the courses' mode of delivery, practice, and assessment were effective. Faculty members constantly reminded students of their own responsibility and the change in their role to a more active one toward achieving the intended learning outcomes.

The discussion of students' attitude toward the dramatic changes in their learning environment should be done bearing in mind the extent of uncertainty involved in the changes that took place during the pandemic. Uncertainty is inherent in health-related professions and a number of approaches are suggested to better prepare undergraduate students to face the uncertainty in their professions (Moffett et al., 2021). The unprecedented uncertainty brought by the pandemic adds on the other existing reasons for uncertainty already faced by the students. Evidence suggests that uncertainty could be productive when students are supported by their educators and have role models to look up to (Moffett et al., 2021). However, this was not the case here, because faculty members were faced with uncertainty themselves and struggled to find effective coping and teaching methods. The uncertainty did not involve faculty members only; it dominated the scene from the highest level of administration down to the students. Simple questions asked by students like: "are we going back to campus?", "Will we have the opportunity to practice with our colleagues?", "Are there plans to resume clinical training in the hospitals?", "Will exams and assessments be held at the university?" These questions are examples of endless questions that were asked by students, and most of the time the answers they would get is either "actually we do not know" or "nothing has been announced yet". These answers were honest and real, but were not satisfactory for students and added more ambiguity to their feelings of uncertainty. Students were uncertain if they will meet the intended learning outcomes of their courses and whether they will be good enough to pass them. This left many students in despair and affected their performance negatively which was evident when many students failed their courses. Compared to the usual failure percentages in courses which ranged between 5 – 10%, the percentages rose to an unusual 15 or even 20% in the semesters during the pandemic.

Students' attitude towards online education was one of the main topics to be discussed by faculty members who were concerned that their students' performance during online sessions was poor when compared to face-to-face delivery. All agreed that students' participation was low, usually a small group were interested in the discussions and others remained inactive. This left the faculty members frustrated and worried about the wellbeing of their students. Some educators held lengthy informal online meetings with the students to discuss their concerns regarding online learning and what could be done to make their experience more rewarding. Students shared their fears regarding not meeting the intended learning outcomes, expressed how they missed being on campus, how they struggled with practice of skills, and they were frustrated from long hours of screen time. There is no doubt that the dramatic changes to the university lifestyle and education left the students vulnerable, uncertain and worried about their present and future (Quintiliani et al., 2021).

The changes to the teaching model and the uncertainties of the pandemic caused students to complain of several issues during the different phases of online education. Stress, anxiety, depression, reduced physical activity, and distorted sleep were among the most common complaints. These symptoms were similar to what other authors reported in the literature; either relevant to the general population (Stawicki et al., 2020) or undergraduate students in particular (Galle et al., 2020; Romero-Blanco et al., 2020a, 2020b). Students at the department reported an increase in their on-screen time. For example, third-year students reported an average of five hours spent in online classes during the weekdays. Similarly, a report of undergraduate students in Italy showed that they spent considerable time in sedentary positions and were not achieving the WHO recommended levels of physical activity (Galle et al., 2020). Their results also showed that students who were previously active were the ones most likely able to maintain better physical activity levels during lockdown (Galle et al., 2020). A study on nursing students in Spain reported worse sleeping patterns during the lockdown, particularly sleep latency and duration (Romero-Blanco et al., 2020b).

Stress and anxiety have negative impact on students' academic performance and mental wellbeing; therefore, appropriate coping and resilience strategies should be embraced to cope with the faced difficulties (Quintiliani et al., 2021). However, counseling services for students were not available at the university; individual efforts were made by some faculty members who dedicated part of their meetings with students to convey positive messages about how to cope with stress and anxiety. One of the learned lessons during this pandemic is the importance of including structured training for students about self-regulated learning and resilience strategies to avoid burnout (de la Fuente et al., 2021), and about self-efficacy to improve satisfaction with online learning (Aldhahi et al., 2021).

Another facet for students' attitude is their relationship with their educators. The use of new technologies shaped new boundaries between educators and their students (Cleland et al., 2020). Social media and other applications were widely used to communicate with students to facilitate accessibility. Before the pandemic, students were expected to communicate outside regular teaching hours via office visits or emails which were formal in nature. While during the pandemic, students opted to use the chat option available in different applications, which left the educators with round-the-clock online messages and enquiries. The use of these new technologies stretched the existing boundaries between the students and their educators. The impact of the used technology on the dynamics of educator-student communication is better understood in the light of sociomaterial approach which explains how the use of technologies affected the social aspects of the relationship between educators and their students (Cleland et al., 2020). It is important to stress that heterogeneous practices exist among different educators, while some were willing to engage in these new channels of communication, some were not. Educators acknowledged that while they were overwhelmed with their chores, extended working hours, and lacked support from their institution, at the same time, students needed every support possible to survive their academic duties. Students lacked skills of resilience, self-control, self-regulation and stress management. With all the uncertainty around, students had to deal with the different, multiple tasks, homework and exams. While many students performed well given the circumstances, the majority did not. Many reasons have contributed to the students' attitude toward changes brought by this pandemic, but with no doubt the major pitfall was not being ready to deal with uncertainty (Cleland et al., 2020; Moffett et al., 2021).

In addition to all factors mentioned above, the students' response to the changes caused by the pandemic is still multifold; students' screen time significantly increased, their physical activity levels dramatically dropped, their sleep followed unhealthy patterns, and they reported multiple bodily aches such as low back pain, shoulder pain, and dry eyes (Galle et al., 2020; Romero-Blanco et al., 2020b). With the increasing number of COVID-19 cases and deaths in Jordan, the pandemic also had its toll on the students' mental and emotional wellbeing as they had difficult times dealing with the illness or loss of loved ones. Frequent closures of the university facilities and the lack of first-hand social interactions with their friends and other people added to the whole situation. Findings of similar negative impacts on the general population, and students in particular, are widely reported in the literature (Romero-Blanco et al., 2020b).

In the semester when all education was held online and practical exams were held on campus, students were not confident to be assessed face-to-face because they felt they lacked the capability to successfully apply practical skills learned during online sessions. This reflected a major deficit in students' attitude towards practical online education. They had genuine hesitation about the transferability of what they learned during the online period to real practice. Faculty members realized that despite all the efforts, students still did not consider their performance good enough to be assessed. This response by the students was merely because most of their learning was held online while the exams were held on campus.

Reflecting back on the situation since the start of the pandemic, the authors realize that students had different expectations on how to meet their learning outcomes as compared to expectations set by educators, which led to dissatisfaction and exaggerated negative feelings for the whole online experiences. The ACAPT recommended that a group of educators should be available and ready to provide regular, structured, and assurance feedback on online learning benefits and gains (ACAPT, 2020). Despite the efforts to spread positivity regarding the effectiveness of the chosen teaching pedagogy within the limitation of the pandemic, students were struggling with their fears and were concerned that their education is being jeopardized.

The implementation of effective online education does not only depend on the content nor the design of courses, it requires active participation from students which is rooted in their actual readiness to use technological platforms. The readiness of educators and students is crucial, educators in physiotherapy went far in this matter and they were ready to engage in online education (Ranganathan et al., 2021). This is not true for students whose readiness is still questionable (Ibili, 2020); many factors contributed to this lack of readiness. This discussion might not seem logical for a generation best known for their advanced skills in technology (Ranganathan et al., 2021), although some scholars suggested that students might not be used to the use of technology for learning purposes (Ibili, 2020; Ranganathan et al., 2021), this is not a very convincing proposal and real causes for their lack of readiness might actually be found in some held beliefs, pre-assumptions, and prior expectations. Physiotherapy students share strong beliefs about physiotherapy education; one of them for example is: skills are best learnt face-to-face. Physiotherapy students might be ready in aspects related to the use of technology but not necessarily ready in terms of accepting change to traditional methods of learning especially those related to practical and clinical education. Hence, their responses toward online education appear to be more of resistance to change to their usual norm rather than lack of actual readiness. Therefore, one of the recommendations would be to provide pre-course orientation prior to online courses where expectations are discussed with students besides ensuring that they have pre-requisite cognitive and procedural skills to better accomplish the course and its objectives.

Students with disabilities faced extra struggles as available university guidelines to support them were inadequate for online learning, a situation similar to other institutions worldwide (Meleo-Erwin et al., 2021). At the time of the pandemic, two students with hearing disability and one student with mild visual disability were enrolled in the program. The biggest challenge was reported by students with hearing disability who, despite using hearing aids, were more dependent on reading lips while infection control measures mandated wearing face masks. Higher education should be inclusive and appropriate actions should be adopted to ensure equity among all students regardless of their needs (Meleo-Erwin et al., 2021). Dickinson et al. recommended that educators should reach out for students with disability, check on them regularly and voice out their concerns (Dickinson et al., 2020), therefore educators in the department made sure to dedicate extra teaching time for those students to answer their questions and explain content, a speaker was provided to one student to help him listen to material provided via videos, other faculty members tried putting on transparent face shield so the students can read lips. In addition to physical disabilities, there were two students who were struggling with mental health issues that deteriorated during lockdown. The head of the department discussed the case with the family and made arrangements with faculty members to ensure the wellbeing of the students.

At the time of the pandemic, the department of physiotherapy had several international students who could not return to their families and were alone during lockdown. Chen et. al. described international students during the pandemic as the overlooked minority (Chen et al., 2020); however educators were aware of the additional emotional stresses that were encountered by international students and their worries about their families and the pandemic status back in their country. Therefore, efforts were made by the educators to maintain extra communication with these students, provide them with the necessary support, and ensure that they were safe and able to manage their studies. ·

Faculty Members' Multiple Roles and Duties

While any educational process, and that of university education in particular, relies on the cooperative roles of multiple players across a wide range of specializations including, but not limited to, administrative, secretariat, and maintenance staff; no one can deny that the role of faculty members is the most central of all. This role extends from the planning of the process and setting competencies and intended learning outcomes; to the actual act of delivering content during theoretical lectures, labs, and clinical training; to performing assessment of students' acquisition of competencies and ability to progress to the next level. All of those steps are applied to the students' education during theoretical, practical, and clinical sessions. And all of those steps fall under one role of the multiple ones that any faculty member has to fulfill; education. Other roles that faculty members' play include being researchers in their fields of expertise, being part of different committees at the department and school such as curriculum and quality assurance committees, and participation and contribution to professional organizations of their specialties. And, of course, all of those roles fit under faculty members' "job." After all, faculty members have personal lives, hobbies, and other commitments.

Every single aspect of the multiple roles of faculty members was influenced by the COVID-19 pandemic. The educational process underwent a major overhaul as discussed in the previous sections. Faculty members showed a high level of resilience as they were replacing what they were used to do for years with new ways that were completely unfamiliar to them. They had to equip themselves with the knowledge and skills necessary to shift to online teaching, prepare and record educational content, and perform assessments using untraditional means. Digital competency is more important than ever as the switch to online education is the new reality (Akulwar-Tajane et al., 2020). Apart from those technical aspects of the changes implemented in the educational process, the authors cannot ignore the human-related aspects. Faculty members were consumed by the preparation of e-materials for the online education and then burned out in the process of execution. Despite all faculty members' efforts, students expressed negative views and lack of appreciation toward online teaching and were largely concerned about their acquisition of the practical skills and required competencies. In addition, educators were providing the much-needed support, motivation, and advice to students on how to cope during such hard times. New roles for educators emerged strongly during the pandemic, these involved intentional efforts to ensure that the e-learning environment is not socially isolating for students by encouraging them to be engaged and less prone to distraction or confusion (Akulwar-Tajane et al., 2020). While it has always been a well-known fact that faculty members' jobs never leave them when they leave office, the switch to online education further erased the already gray line between work and personal lives. And, just like their students, faculty members started complaining of bodily aches, were spending extensive number of hours sitting on their desks staring at computer screens, had severely-reduced physical activity levels, were sleep-deprived, felt dissatisfied with some of the decisions that were enforced on them by the administration, and were having mental and cognitive stresses. Two very common words that faculty members used to describe their status are burnout and exhaustion. A study from Jordan examining faculty members distress during the lockdown period revealed that 31% of faculty members had severe distress while 38% had mild to moderate distress (Akour et al., 2020). A study from Spain showed that while depression, anxiety, and stress scores were within the normal range, the scores were higher among females and administrative -as compared to teaching- staff (Salazar et al., 2021).

How then did faculty members manage this increased workload and vulnerability? It is the experience of the authors that working with colleagues, sharing experiences, and holding brainstorming sessions on how to solve the on-going challenges all helped manage this novel situation. Referral to the literature and guidelines published by international organizations such as WP, APTA, and CSP helped provide direction on how to proceed with the educational process. The value of social support networks cannot be emphasized enough. A good laugh with colleagues about some of the mistakes with the new technologies that faculty members were unfamiliar with helped resolve some of the distress. Being compassionate and in-love with one's profession and job gave momentum during hard times. Coping strategies also included creating boundaries between work and personal lives; at some point each person should realize that work will never end and one should stop working and attend to their own personal needs. Similar coping strategies are reported in the literature such as engagement with family, using social media platforms, and talking to friends (Akour et al., 2020). Another study reported use of active coping and emotion-focused strategies (Salazar et al., 2021).

To conclude, while no one can deny that this past period since the start of the pandemic has been a tough one, there were also many positive lessons learned. The reform that the teaching pedagogy and assessment methods underwent includes some aspects that faculty members will continue to implement even after the pandemic. At the same time, there were several difficulties and pitfalls that the educators need to have open discussions about to find ways to improve. However, most important of all is the fact that no matter how strong the influence of the pandemic or any situation might be, the teaching pedagogy can (and should) be modified in accordance with the circumstances so that the educational process is never interrupted.

SOLUTIONS AND RECOMMENDATIONS

Recommendations for future practice toward adopting online education for physiotherapy programs that emphasize the use of best technology practices:

- While traditional teaching pedagogy is teacher-centred, online education enhances andragogy which facilitates student engagement.
- Plan at a program level; this includes mapping all the courses and assessments within the program and making decisions at the department level.
- Involve all educators in the department in the process of online reform.
- Perform ongoing evaluation of the online experience from faculty members' and students' perspectives.
- Online exams present with a unique set of advantages and challenges that faculty members need to weigh-in to decide on their optimal use
- Provide orientation for students prior to the online courses ensuring their readiness to the chosen platform and methodology.
- Discuss expectations of learning and potential outcomes with students prior to the online courses to maximise effective engagement and avoid disappointment.

REFERENCES

ACAPT. (2020). *Classroom and Lab Considerations and Resources.* Version Two.

Akour, A., Al-Tammemi, A. B., Barakat, M., Kanj, R., Fakhouri, H. N., Malkawi, A., & Musleh, G. (2020). The Impact of the COVID-19 Pandemic and Emergency Distance Teaching on the Psychological Status of University Teachers: A Cross-Sectional Study in Jordan. *The American Journal of Tropical Medicine and Hygiene, 103*(6), 2391–2399. doi:10.4269/ajtmh.20-0877

Akulwar-Tajane, I., Parmar, K., Naik, P., & Shah, A. (2020). Rethinking Screen Time during COVID-19: Impact on Psychological Well-Being in Physiotherapy Students. *Int J Clin Exp Med Res, 4*(4), 201–216.

Aldhahi, M. I., Alqahtani, A. S., Baattaiah, B. A., & Al-Mohammed, H. I. (2021). Exploring the relationship between students' learning satisfaction and self-efficacy during the emergency transition to remote learning amid the coronavirus pandemic: A cross-sectional study. *Educ Inf Technol (Dordr)*, 1-18. http://www.ncbi.nlm.nih.gov/pubmed/34276239

Allen, S. (2016). Applying Adult Learning Principles to Online Course Design. *Dist Learn, 13*(3), 25–32.

American Physical Therapy Association. (2021). https://www.apta.org/

Chan, S. (2010). Applications of Andragogy in Multi-Disciplined Teaching and Learning. *Journal of Adult Education, 39*(2), 25–35.

Chartered Society of Physiotherapy. (2020). *COVID-19 Guidance for Higher Education Institutions (Updated Oct 2020).* https://www.csp.org.uk/system/files/documents/2020-10/COVID_19%20Guidance%20Oct%202020_0.pdf

Chartered Society of Physiotherapy. (2021). *Digital Physiotherapy.* https://www.csp.org.uk/professional-clinical/digital-physio

Chen, J. H., Li, Y., Wu, A. M. S., & Tong, K. K. (2020). The overlooked minority: Mental health of International students worldwide under the COVID-19 pandemic and beyond. *Asian Journal of Psychiatry, 54*, 102333. http://www.ncbi.nlm.nih.gov/pubmed/32795955

Cleland, J., Tan, E. C. P., Tham, K. Y., & Low-Beer, N. (2020). How Covid-19 opened up questions of sociomateriality in healthcare education. *Advances in Health Sciences Education: Theory and Practice, 25*(2), 479–482. http://www.ncbi.nlm.nih.gov/pubmed/32378152

Crawford, J., Butler-Henderson, K., Rudolph, J., Malkawi, B., Glowatz, M., Burton, R., Magni, P., & Lam, S. (2020). COVID-19: 20 Countries' Higher Education Intra-Period Digital Pedagogy Responses. *J of Appl Learn and Teach, 3*(1), 9–28. https://doi.org/https://doi.org/10.37074/jalt.2020.3.1.7

de la Fuente, J., Pachon-Basallo, M., Santos, F. H., Peralta-Sanchez, F. J., Gonzalez-Torres, M. C., Artuch-Garde, R., Paoloni, P. V., & Gaetha, M. L. (2021). How Has the COVID-19 Crisis Affected the Academic Stress of University Students? The Role of Teachers and Students. *Frontiers in Psychology, 12*, 626340. doi:10.3389/fpsyg.2021.626340

Dickinson, H., Smith, C., Yates, S., & Bertuol, M. (2020). *Not even remotely fair: Experiences of students with disability during COVID-19.* Report prepared for Children and Young People with Disability Australia (CYDA).

Dziuban, C., Graham, C., Moskal, P., Norberg, A., & Sicilia, N. (2018). Blended Learning: The New Normal and Emerging Technologies. *Int J Educ Tech High Educ, 15*(3). Advance online publication. doi:10.118641239-017-0087-5

Gagnon, K., Young, B., Bachman, T., Longbottom, T., Severin, R., & Walker, M. J. (2020). Doctor of Physical Therapy Education in a Hybrid Learning Environment: Reimagining the Possibilities and Navigating a "New Normal". *Physical Therapy, 100*(8), 1268–1277. http://www.ncbi.nlm.nih.gov/pubmed/32424417

Galle, F., Sabella, E. A., Ferracuti, S., De Giglio, O., Caggiano, G., Protano, C., Valeriani, F., Parisi, E. A., Valerio, G., Liguori, G., Montagna, M. T., Romano Spica, V., Da Molin, G., Orsi, G. B., & Napoli, C. (2020). Sedentary Behaviors and Physical Activity of Italian Undergraduate Students during Lockdown at the Time of CoViD-19 Pandemic. *International Journal of Environmental Research and Public Health, 17*(17). http://www.ncbi.nlm.nih.gov/pubmed/32854414

Gencheva, N., & Gencheva-Vassileva, A. (2020). A Study on Some Aspects of Distance Learning for Physiotherapy Students during a Pandemic. *Pedagogy, 92*(7s), 280–290.

Grundstein, M. J., Fisher, C., Titmuss, M., & Cioppa-Mosca, J. (2021). The Role of Virtual Physical Therapy in a Post-Pandemic World: Pearls, Pitfalls, Challenges, and Adaptations. *Physical Therapy, 101*(9). http://www.ncbi.nlm.nih.gov/pubmed/34106273

Ibili, E. (2020). Examination of Health Science University Students' Level of Readiness for E-Learning. *International Online Journal of Education & Teaching, 7*(3), 1010–1030.

Ikram, F., & Rabbani, M. A. (2021). Academic Integrity in Traditional Vs Online Undergraduate Medical Education Amidst COVID-19 Pandemic. *Cureus, 13*(3), e13911. doi:10.7759/cureus.13911

Meleo-Erwin, Z., Kollia, B., Fera, J., Jahren, A., & Basch, C. (2021). Online support information for students with disabilities in colleges and universities during the COVID-19 pandemic. *Disability and Health Journal, 14*(1), 101013. http://www.ncbi.nlm.nih.gov/pubmed/33082111

Miller, G. E. (1990). The assessment of clinical skills/competence/performance. *Academic Medicine, 65*(9, Suppl), S63–S67. doi:10.1097/00001888-199009000-00045

Moffett, J., Hammond, J., Murphy, P., & Pawlikowska, T. (2021). The ubiquity of uncertainty: A scoping review on how undergraduate health professions' students engage with uncertainty. *Advances in Health Sciences Education: Theory and Practice, 26*(3), 913–958. http://www.ncbi.nlm.nih.gov/pubmed/33646469

Moore, K., & Shemberger, M. (2019). Mass Communication Andragogy for Teaching Online Adult Learners. *Teach Journal Mass Commun, 9*(1), 35–40.

Odegaard, N. B., Myrhaug, H. T., Dahl-Michelsen, T., & Roe, Y. (2021). Digital learning designs in physiotherapy education: A systematic review and meta-analysis. *BMC Medical Education, 21*(1), 48. http://www.ncbi.nlm.nih.gov/pubmed/33441140

Olivier, B., Verdonck, M., & Caseleijn, D. (2020). Digital technologies in undergraduate and postgraduate education in occupational therapy and physiotherapy: a scoping review. *JBI Evid Synth, 18*(5), 863-892. http://www.ncbi.nlm.nih.gov/pubmed/32813350

Ozuah, P. (2005). First, There was Pedagogy and Then Came Andragogy. *The Einstein Journal of Biology and Medicine; EJBM, 21*, 83–87.

Quintiliani, L., Sisto, A., Vicinanza, F., Curcio, G., & Tambone, V. (2021). Resilience and psychological impact on Italian university students during COVID-19 pandemic. Distance learning and health. *Psychology Health and Medicine*, 1–12. doi:10.1080/13548506.2021.1891266

Ranganathan, H., Singh, D. K. A., Kumar, S., Sharma, S., Chua, S. K., Ahmad, N. B., & Harikrishnan, K. (2021). Readiness towards online learning among physiotherapy undergraduates. *BMC Medical Education, 21*(1), 376. http://www.ncbi.nlm.nih.gov/pubmed/34246264

Roe, Y., Rowe, M., Odegaard, N. B., Sylliaas, H., & Dahl-Michelsen, T. (2019). Learning with technology in physiotherapy education: Design, implementation and evaluation of a flipped classroom teaching approach. *BMC Medical Education*, *19*(1), 291. http://www.ncbi.nlm.nih.gov/pubmed/31366351

Romero-Blanco, C., Rodriguez-Almagro, J., Onieva-Zafra, M. D., Parra-Fernandez, M. L., Prado-Laguna, M. D. C., & Hernandez-Martinez, A. (2020a). Physical Activity and Sedentary Lifestyle in University Students: Changes during Confinement Due to the COVID-19 Pandemic. *International Journal of Environmental Research and Public Health*, *17*(18). http://www.ncbi.nlm.nih.gov/pubmed/32916972

Romero-Blanco, C., Rodriguez-Almagro, J., Onieva-Zafra, M. D., Parra-Fernandez, M. L., Prado-Laguna, M. D. C., & Hernandez-Martinez, A. (2020b). Sleep Pattern Changes in Nursing Students during the COVID-19 Lockdown. *International Journal of Environmental Research and Public Health*, *17*(14). http://www.ncbi.nlm.nih.gov/pubmed/32698343

Salazar, A., Palomo-Osuna, J., de Sola, H., Moral-Munoz, J. A., Duenas, M., & Failde, I. (2021). Psychological Impact of the Lockdown Due to the COVID-19 Pandemic in University Workers: Factors Related to Stress, Anxiety, and Depression. *International Journal of Environmental Research and Public Health*, *18*(8). http://www.ncbi.nlm.nih.gov/pubmed/33924133

Stawicki, S. P., Jeanmonod, R., Miller, A. C., Paladino, L., Gaieski, D. F., Yaffee, A. Q., De Wulf, A., Grover, J., Papadimos, T. J., Bloem, C., Galwankar, S. C., Chauhan, V., Firstenberg, M. S., Di Somma, S., Jeanmonod, D., Garg, S. M., Tucci, V., Anderson, H. L., Fatimah, L., ... Garg, M. (2020). The 2019-2020 Novel Coronavirus (Severe Acute Respiratory Syndrome Coronavirus 2) Pandemic: A Joint American College of Academic International Medicine-World Academic Council of Emergency Medicine Multidisciplinary COVID-19 Working Group Consensus Paper. *Journal of Global Infectious Diseases*, *12*(2), 47–93. http://www.ncbi.nlm.nih.gov/pubmed/32773996

Suhail, M., Sharath, C., & Mathew, A. (2020). Contemporary Learning or E-Learning in Physiotherapy, Pre and Post COVID-19: Short Communication. *J Nov Physiother Rehabil*, *4*(1), 9-10.

Tenforde, A. S., Borgstrom, H., Polich, G., Steere, H., Davis, I. S., Cotton, K., O'Donnell, M., & Silver, J. K. (2020). Outpatient Physical, Occupational, and Speech Therapy Synchronous Telemedicine: A Survey Study of Patient Satisfaction with Virtual Visits During the COVID-19 Pandemic. *American Journal of Physical Medicine & Rehabilitation*, *99*(11), 977–981. http://www.ncbi.nlm.nih.gov/pubmed/32804713

Unge, J., Lundh, P., Gummesson, C., & Amner, G. (2018). Learning Spaces for Health Sciences – What is the Role of e-Learning in Physiotherapy and Occupational Therapy Education? A Literature Review. *The Physical Therapy Review, 23*(1). Advance online publication. doi:10.1080/10833196.2018.1447423

United Nations. (2012). *Higher Education Sustainability Initiative.* Retrieved 20 October 2021 from https://sustainabledevelopment.un.org/sdinaction/hesi

Wilcha, R. J. (2020). Effectiveness of Virtual Medical Teaching During the COVID-19 Crisis: Systematic Review. *JMIR Medical Education, 6*(2), e20963. http://www.ncbi.nlm.nih.gov/pubmed/33106227

World Health Organization. (2020a). *Rehabilitation Competency Framework.* Geneva: World Health Organization. https://apps.who.int/iris/handle/10665/338782

World Health Organization. (2020b). *Using a Contextualized Competency Framework to Develop Rehabilitation Programmes and their Curricula: A Stepwise Guide for Programme and Curriculum Developers, Version for Field Testing.* World Health Organization. https://apps.who.int/iris/handle/10665/339205

World Physiotherapy. (2019). *Description of Physical Therapy: Policy Statement.* https://world.physio/policy/ps-descriptionPT

World Physiotherapy. (2020). *WCPT Response to COVID-19 Briefing Paper 1: Immediate Impact on the Higher Education Sector and Response to Delivering Physiotherapy Entry Level Education.* https://www.wcpt.org/sites/wcpt.org/files/files/wcptnews/images/Education-Briefing-1-HEI-A4.pdf

ADDITIONAL READING

Chartered Society of Physiotherapy. (2021). Digital Physiotherapy. https://www.csp.org.uk/professional-clinical/digital-physio

World Health Organization. (2020). Rehabilitation competency framework. World Health Organization. https://apps.who.int/iris/handle/10665/338782

World Physiotherapy. (2020). WCPT response to COVID-19 briefing paper 1: Immediate impact on the higher education sector and response to delivering physiotherapy entry level education. https://www.wcpt.org/sites/wcpt.org/files/files/wcptnews/images/Education-Briefing-1-HEI-A4.pdf

KEY TERMS AND DEFINITIONS

Andragogy: A learning approach that is student-centered and encourages self-regulation.

Clinical Training: The supervised direct provision of physiotherapy services to patients at clinical sites.

Defense Laws: National special laws activated in extreme circumstances such as wars, natural disasters, or health pandemics. These laws give the authority to designated personnel to undertake the necessary actions and measures to ensure the safety of citizens including the authority to suspend ordinary laws.

Faculty Member/Educator: An assistant or associate professor, holding a PhD in Physiotherapy who is responsible for the education of students at the university level.

Hybrid Mode: A teaching method that uses a combination of both online- and campus-based delivery and supervision.

Intended Learning Outcomes: A set of measurable objectives that are expected to be met by students by the end of specific courses or the whole program.

Practical Teaching/Practical Laboratory/Practical Session: The applied element of taught courses, that involves practicing skills and techniques through peer modeling and are usually held on campus.

Teaching Pedagogy: Approaches and methods used in teaching.

Chapter 8

Work–Integrated Learning:
Community and Student Engagement Through Informed Educational Technology Choices

Ross H. Humby
Southern Alberta Institute of Technology, Canada

Rob Eirich
Southern Alberta Institute of Technology, Canada

Julie Gathercole
Southern Alberta Institute of Technology, Canada

Dave Gaudet
Southern Alberta Institute of Technology, Canada

EXECUTIVE SUMMARY

Work-integrated learning (WIL) continues to be an essential topic of conversation among governments, educators, employers, and students. By various names and definitions, WIL attempts to inject the realism of workplace employment tasks into the post-secondary learning environment. The COVID-19 pandemic has forced stakeholders to innovate in the WIL space often using the advances in information and communications technologies (ICT) to build further bridges between learners and real work experiences. The chapter provides an overview of WIL followed by three specifics cases from marketing faculty at the Southern Alberta Institute of Technology (SAIT). In each of the three cases, faculty used different ICT to provide engaging learning environments linking business, industry, consumers, and the learners.

DOI: 10.4018/978-1-7998-8310-4.ch008

INTRODUCTION

The preparation of learners for careers through work experience and the advancement of educational technologies, including video conferencing, were well-established trends before the COVID-19 pandemic. However, the pandemic forced post-secondary educators to transition classroom-mediated learning into distance or online learning immediately. The change resulted in post-secondary learning transitioning without sufficient preparation, without the benefits of instructional design, regardless of the preferences of faculty and learners, and regardless of the subject matter. Further, the learning was now taking place in a world where social isolation, reduced social opportunities, and limited employment opportunities were impacting the environment for the learners. There have been innovative efforts to use information and communication technology (ICT) to expand the range and format of Work Integrated Learning (WIL) (Zeewaard & Rowe, 2019; BHER, 2016; Dean et al., 2020). Learning is a social activity enhanced with higher engagement and socialization. In this socially isolated environmental context, how can technological solutions facilitate faculty's efforts to continue to provide engaging, valued learning experiences for students? How can post-secondary educators continue to provide meaningful, relevant learning experiences that help prepare students for the world of work post-graduation? Through the case experiences of three Southern Alberta Institute of Technology (SAIT) marketing faculty, this chapter provides an overview of various technology-enhanced work-integrated learning and how course content, information and communications technologies, and faculty can provide enhanced WIL experience for the learners.

BACKGROUND

Within the Canadian landscape for WIL, provinces, who have the constitutional responsibility for education, are continuing to focus on WIL. For example, the Government of Alberta in the Alberta 2030: Building Skills for Jobs strategy summary set out a goal of becoming "the first province in Canada to offer every undergraduate student access to a work-integrated learning opportunity" (2021, p.2). As one of the long established post-secondary institutions in the province of Alberta, SAIT is enhancing the capacity for WIL with innovative experiences for learners.

In 1916, the Southern Alberta Institute of Technology (SAIT) doors opened in Calgary, Alberta, Canada with 11 students and a mandate to train veterans returning from the First World War. Over the years, SAIT matched community needs — as a hospital during the Spanish Flu pandemic and as a Royal Canadian Air Force Wireless Training School during the Second World War. Fast forward to today and

SAIT's action-based learning, solution-focused research and industry partnerships are helping to shape the next generation of inventors, entrepreneurs and pioneers. With more than 11,000 industry partners, SAIT blurs the lines between industry and education to strengthen the economy. WIL opportunities make up a large part of those connections.

There continues to be strong interest and conversation among students, educators, employers, and governments as to the importance of WIL because of the link between WIL in preparing learners for employment (Zeewaard & Rowe, 2019, p.324). There can be different understandings, interpretations, and definitions within these four stakeholder groups as to what constitutes WIL. Patrick et al. (2008) provide further details about the terminology used within the field. The top three identified terms were practicum used 35 times, professional practice 32 times, internship, workplace learning, and work integrated learning 31 times (Patrick et al., 2008). Additional terms often included in the vocabulary include co-op, directed field studies, field placement, applied research, apprenticeship, and work experience. Project-based learning can also be included as a WIL experience when those project activities tie into or involve the stakeholders employing post-secondary students and graduates. This in itself should not be surprising as each stakeholder group has a perspective on the role of post-secondary learning in preparing learners for careers. Given the inherently diverse nature of each stakeholder group, it is also not surprising that a diverse understanding of WIL within the stakeholder groups emerges across different sectors, different jurisdictions, different institutions, and different regulatory environments.

A Canadian federal government initiative, The Innovative Work-Integrated Learning Initiative, defines WIL for post-secondary activities, including short-term work placement, virtual internships, hackathons, business cases, and classroom projects to help the community (*The Innovative Work-Integrated Learning Initiative, 2020*). In addition, the Higher Education Quality Council of Ontario (HEQCO) (Stirling, et al., 2016) provided the information (Table 1) as a partial listing of structured work experiences.

Into this evolving WIL environment add the COVID-19 pandemic, and there was a rapid conversion to an alternative, virtual learning process, and work models. The pandemic also necessitated the re-thinking of alternative WIL experiences emerging, including virtual work experiences. A common theme has been the continued development and rapid accelerations into the delivery of technology-facilitated virtual experiences.

Another, though often less obvious, question is how to cut through the confusion and clutter of WIL terminology and communicate effectively with the stakeholders. In some of the data collected during learner exit or graduate surveys at SAIT School of Business (SAIT, 2020), student and graduate responses to the WIL questions

Table 1. Forms of Structured Work Experience

Term	Descriptor
Placement	Umbrella term describing all structured work experience. Learning emphasis is on career exploration and employability/professional skill development.
Practicum	Focus on developing professional capabilities and meeting professional registration requirements as defined by an accrediting body.
Internship	Work experience under the guidance of an experienced professional. Deep learning and realistic preview of the employment sector.
Co-op Education	Guided professional and employability skill development through alternating full-time study and full-time employment across an academic program.
Sandwich Course	A supervised work position in the practice of the student's future profession. Occurs during a period of time away from study.
Field Experience	Work experience linked to program content and designed for preparation of professional practice.
Field Work	Exposure to the work setting through participation in work activities, site visits, etc. Experience used to enhance the learning of academic content.
Work Study	Concurrent work experience not necessarily in the practice of a future profession. Often tied to general professional and/or personal development.

(Adapted from HEQCO 2016, p34, with permission based on O'Shea 2014)

indicate there is much work to be done on communicating WIL in a manner that is recognized, understood, and accepted by students.

The emerging 'new normal', post COVID-19, will include increased elements of technology-facilitated learning so further understanding of innovations in education, and in particular WIL, needs to be evaluated and considered in light of current practices available technologies.

For the balance of the chapter, WIL will be based on the definition of WIL as provided by the International Journal of Work-Integrated Learning:

An educational approach that uses relevant work-based experiences allows students to integrate theory with the meaningful practice of work as an intentional curriculum component. Defining this educational approach requires students to engage in authentic and meaningful work-related tasks and involve three stakeholders: the student, the university, and the workplace/community. (Wood et al., 2020)

The one clarification or addition to the International Journal of Work Integrated Learning's definition is the specific inclusion of entrepreneurial-related activities and experiences. While it can be assumed that the third stakeholder as defined, the workplace/community could include entrepreneurial effort, the need for an interest in the development of entrepreneurial skills where the learners interact directly with the community or customer base is an essential skill-building experience.

The balance of the chapter presents three faculty-led initiatives in the School of Business Marketing Major at SAIT. The faculty designed the activities to enhance WIL through technology-facilitated learning experiences. First, faculty provide a brief, practical orientation to the technologies and the fit with the course, followed by how those technologies were used in the virtual classroom. In the first case, faculty Rob Eirich integrates the QuirkLogic digital learning system 'Inkworks' into the learning and the culminating industrial sales presentation to a panel of industry professionals in the *Business Development and Customer Relationship Management* course. In the second case, faculty Julie Gathercole uses the Riipen WIL project platform to connect student project groups with industry partners around the corner and across the continent in the course *Integrated Marketing Communications*. In the third example, faculty David Gaudet, using an entrepreneurial approach, integrates the power of voice technologies and the Amazon 'Alexa' application into student projects that create digital content for 'Alexa' in the course *Innovation and Design*. These are three separate and unique sets of course activities, each with a different technology incorporated as part of the WIL linked classroom. Even with the common format, the experiences are expressed through the lived experiences of the individual faculty and as such there are differences in style and presentation as a natural consequence of the case stories.

CASE STUDY #1- AN INSTRUCTOR'S EXPERIENCE WITH REMOTE WHITEBOARD TECHNOLOGY AND THE IMPACT ON LEARNER PRESENTATION STYLE

Case background

In February 2020, SAIT's academic marketing program faculty was introduced to the Quilla® and Papyr® tablet teaching technologies developed by QuirkLogic® of Calgary, Alberta. The presentation focused mainly on delivering remote display of pdf (portal document format) content to learner devices in the classroom. The Quilla® is a multifunction touchscreen display that allows the synchronization of instructional content, either in predeveloped document format or in a whiteboard format, similar to the classroom, with a learner tablet (Papyr® or Ipad). The basic premise of the system was to place more instructional interaction into the learner's hands by allowing annotations to a live lecture or presentation. The main discussion revolved around how to deploy into a traditional classroom environment.

However, with the advent of restrictions placed upon classroom learning in March 2020, the Quilla® system presented a new opportunity in a remote setting. Academic leadership encouraged marketing instructors with experience and aptitude in learning technologies to experiment with the Quilla® in a remote classroom environment. Two sections of Business Development (MKTG 366/2366), one diploma and one degree cohort, were chosen for preliminary applied testing for the remainder of the semester. Even though only a few weeks remained in the semester, learner feedback was very positive and demonstrated that the Quilla®, delivered high learner engagement when paired with video. It was then decided to continue testing in the Fall 2020 semester, where classes would be offered remotely, albeit without the accompanying tablets for learners. A second-year diploma cohort in Business Development was chosen as the primary class for testing (based on previous exposure to remote learning in the closing days of their last semester in the winter). However, the same teaching approach was used with a first-year diploma cohort in the course Marketing Essentials. The first-year class was included mainly to gauge the level of adoption by new learners of the approach and monitor overall engagement.

Technology

QuirkLogic® is a Calgary-based company that develops remote collaboration solutions for business, healthcare, and education. The development work began with understanding the value of longhand performance (Mueller & Oppenheimer, 2014) and a single goal of making the digital learning experience as easy to use as 'paper and pen' (QuirkLogic, 2020). The Quilla® is the flagship product and provides organizations with the ability to collaborate in real-time while conducting remote meetings. The Quila is a 44-inch touch screen device that synchronizes with a web browser app for screen sharing and a proprietary tablet called a Papyr®. Both devices run on an Android backend, and a Chrome Browser is available on the tablet.

What is written on the Quilla® "whiteboard" or "flipchart", displays on tablets and associated apps in real-time. Other content can also be displayed and annotated (on a limited basis), such as pdf documents. One of the key benefits is the system's ability to display participant annotations to the live document, which is essential to collaboration. The Papyr® tablet, or app-enabled iPad, displays the host's content and allows meeting participants to interact by writing notes which are in turn displayed on the host's Quilla® display.

The Business Development Classroom

Course Content and Delivery Format

One of the Quilla® pilot implementation goals was to understand how the technology would contribute to an authentic workplace learning environment or WIL. Other goals were to examine the efficacy of the teaching and learning styles with the technology. For example, was this a technology that helped students learn? Would it help keep them engaged in the learning process? Was the technology useful to assist the delivery of the instructional material? What about adoption by instructional staff- would instructors want to use it?

As mentioned earlier, the course that was the pilot's focal point was Business Development (MKTG 366), a second-year business diploma requirement for the marketing major. The final assessment for the course has learners presenting a sales presentation to a buying panel of industry professionals in a remote selling environment. It is expected that close to 50% of the learners will find themselves in a sales role sometime in their career journey. Therefore, the class focuses on digital and in-person communication with business-to-business (B2B) customers and expectations for corporate meetings, especially sales presentations and negotiations.

This course is CPSA (Canadian Professional Sales Association) accredited and provides the learner with essential professional selling skills in an applied learning environment. The course (MKTG366/2366) and SAIT's Business Administration Diploma and Bachelor of Business Administration Degree received CPSA accreditation in March 2020. This allows graduates of the diploma and degree programs who have taken the Business Development and CRM course to sit for the Certified Sales Associate Designation (CSA) exam, providing another link to industry engagement.

The final remote sales presentation assessment is designed to achieve skill mastery in the following CPSA competency framework areas: 1) fostering client relationships; 2) developing client-focused solutions; 3) negotiating and closing; 4) sales process technology; 5) business acumen; and 6) professional sales conduct.

In March 2020, as a direct result of the Covid-19 pandemic, companies were forced to abandon traditional sales call approaches and conduct sales meetings remotely with video technology. This trend was emulated in the classroom by creating lectures that were more akin to short company sales meetings. Specifically, the lecture provided examples and motivation relating to the importance of the topic, but then the discussion revolved around learners sharing their personal experiences with sales topics, technology, and what the "new customer expectations" will be. This was partly achieved through the integration of MS TEAMS, not solely as an Learning Management System (LMS) platform, but rather as a sales team collaboration tool.

More importantly, the Quilla technology can be credited for keeping the environment more dynamic. Many learners specifically noted that their level of engagement increased as the lecturer was able to stand up and speak about the topics and write on the board. The faculty delivering the material also reported feeling more engaged in the teaching process standing and using the Quilla®, a situation more closely mirroring the face-to-face classroom and the use of the whiteboard system.

While this may have initially been viewed as a significant enhancement to the learning environment, vis-à-vis, emulating classroom activities, a new industry practice came to the class's attention- standing up for online sale presentations. One of the guest speakers involved with the class, Rob Eskens, is a vice president of a billion-dollar transportation carrier. In his class discussion, he explained how the organization he leads moved to stand up online sales presentations. As a result, he observed higher engagement from his sales force and customers with the new presentation format.

This insight allowed the lecturer to positively use the new skill and emulate effective styles while standing and presenting content. In addition, learners found this reinforcement useful and applicable for delivery in their final sales presentation assessment.

Outcomes

Key Contributions to Workplace Integrated Learning

1. **Group Collaboration**- Learners experienced the importance of using technologies to collaborate in a corporate team environment. This was achieved using MS TEAMS and regular exposure to the collaborative "flipchart" environment. By the end of the course, many learners remarked that they now understood the purpose, expectations, and importance of using these technologies in the workplace.

The presentation exercise in the Business Development course is a great way for students to wrap up the semester. They are allowed to display all their learning from previous classes in one final project. It also forces them out of their comfort zone by researching a subject they are generally unfamiliar with while presenting to industry professionals. The students can garner valuable feedback from industry professionals on their research and presentation skills before entering the job market. (Todd Latimer, Senior National Sales Manager at Nutrien, 2021)

2. **Corporate Remote Meeting Experience**- As much as possible, learners got a sense of attending a twice-weekly sales meeting in a company environment. This culminated for many learners at their final assessment. Learners remarked that the learning environment created with the Quilla® technology helped them understand the necessary behaviors (appearance, backgrounds, presentation slide delivery, comportment, troubleshooting) and etiquette required to present and close a major sales call.

Preparation for the presentation helps show students the work needed in the real world and creates tangible differentiation when viewed by the panel. The process gets students to think about the transition from the classroom to the boardroom. (Duncan Pottiger, MBA, Senior Director, AG Canada, Nutrien, 2021)

3. **Development of Sales Communication Skills in a Remote Selling Environment**- As mentioned earlier, the learners could get early exposure and acquire an emerging sales skill. Furthermore, as the lecturer was able to stand during presentations, ample observable examples were given to help learners develop an online presentation style.

SAIT's Business Development course features an important focus on presentation skills which is in direct alignment with our key selection criteria. We have complete confidence that the program's graduates will meet our needs when considering sales professionals for our organization. (Rob Eskens, CSL, Vice President Sales, Manitoulin Group of Companies, 2021)

Feedback

In all cohort trials, learner feedback has been overwhelmingly positive. Some of the comments received included:

It feels kinda like being back in the classroom. (student comment unattributed, 2021)

This is much more engaging than the instructor who sits on his couch and reads his PowerPoints to us. (student comment unattributed, 2021)

This class was a lot of fun. I learned so much and am really happy to know that I am going into the marketplace with up-to-date skills. (student comment unattributed, 2021)

The majority of the student feedback data was anecdotal and unsolicited. There were many other engagement factors in play that may have overwhelmed new learners, such as a first-time exposure to remote synchronous video classes, alternative learning platforms (MS Teams, BrightSpace and TopHat) and social presence issues. However, the feedback was generally positive, as many students felt more like they were in an actual face-to-face classroom.

Opportunities

The preparation of materials for the Quilla® format is time-consuming and should be carefully understood in the course preparation stages. The technology does require some training, especially troubleshooting syncing problems and menu navigation. However, given the file conversion process and synchronization timeouts, one of the key benefits to the instructor is standing up and engaging with the lecture, similar to the traditional classroom environment.

While the system was implemented on a limited basis (learners were not issued individual Papyr® tablets), visibility was also somewhat limited, especially if learners viewed a laptop screen or device with less screen "real estate". Many learners mentioned that they would have enjoyed the experience more if the display had been larger. For example, the Quirklogic® web portal provides the learning environment with a screen share of a browser page in portrait orientation, as that is the default orientation of the Quilla®. If a PowerPoint lecture slide is converted to the Quirklogic® pdf (*.qlw) format, the slide will display in landscape orientation. While this gives ample white space to annotate on the display side (instructor notes during lecture) or by a learner on a tablet, the size reduction means that a typical participant will view content at 1/6 of its intended size. The deployment of the Papyr tablet would go a long way to solve this issue for the learner.

CASE STUDY #2- AN INSTRUCTOR'S EXPERIENCE USING RIIPEN FOR REAL-WORLD EXPERIENTIAL LEARNING AND THE IMPACT ON LEARNER DEVELOPMENT

Case background

Over the past 100 years, SAIT has developed a reputation for hands-on classes and programs that produce job-ready graduates. That reputation has been built partially on the institution's connection to industry and its client-based and experiential learning projects.

A review of the literature shows clear benefits for students from experiential learning and client-based projects. For example, Baden and Parkes found that "the opportunity to work with social entrepreneurs and/or "responsible" business professionals provides the business students with inspirational role models and positive social learning opportunities" (2013). Additionally, a study in the Journal of Teaching in Travel & Tourism found that students cited many benefits from this practical learning including, "increased understanding of how organizations function, increased ability to take initiative, increased ability to adapt to change, and increased leadership skills" (Lee 2008).

With this in mind, the major project for Integrated Marketing Communications (MKTG 375 and 2375) was developed to allow students to work with real-world clients. Student groups were tasked with solving a client's promotional marketing challenge by developing an integrated marketing communications plan with at least ten fully developed tactics.

This client-based project provided many benefits similar to those outlined above. Some students secured employment from their projects. Others developed design skills. However, all students honed their strategic thinking and client-relations skills and developed a tangible project to include in their professional portfolios.

That said, client-based projects are not without their challenges. Each term, instructors must find appropriate clients to work with students. Riipen provided a solution to this challenge.

Technology

Riipen is a WIL platform based out of Toronto, Ontario. As North America's largest WIL marketplace, it connects educators, students, and organizations of all sizes from around the world. Their mission is to "enable all students from all backgrounds and geographies to access work-integrated experiential learning to support learners of all backgrounds to bridge the skills gap, gain career clarity, network with potential employers, and find jobs they love" (2020).

From an instructor's perspective, Riipen is a platform that expands your list of potential clients for project work exponentially. The team at Riipen works with instructors one-on-one to ensure project setup is seamless and that projects are built focusing on student and client success. Once instructors create projects, Riipen promotes the projects to the industry marketplace. However, instructors are not limited to only receiving requests from industry employers. They can also explore industry-posted projects through a recommendation engine to find potential matches.

Once a match is made, the platform provides avenues for management and communication. For example, in-app chat and file sharing make it possible to work directly with employers in one place and share additional project details. They also allow instructors to monitor student interaction with clients to help troubleshoot any potential project issues. Additionally, milestone tracking and reminders to update progress help keep students on track.

The Integrated Marketing Communications Classroom

Course Content and Delivery Format

As mentioned, Riipen was used to deliver the major project for Integrated Marketing Communications (MKTG 375), a second-year business diploma requirement for the marketing concentration. This course focuses on the promotions side of the marketing mix and ensuring all elements are unified across all digital and traditional channels. Working in teams, each student experiences the marketing communications planning process for a client. Knowing most students will work with social media, a large portion of the course focuses on integrating messages and promotions across social media. However, students are encouraged to develop ten creative tactics using all elements of marketing communications to solve their client's challenges.

During the semester, a company based in British Columbia was looking to launch their online business selling woman's martial arts and boxing apparel. The client's goal was to double sales by the end of 2021. After extensive consultation with the client, the students determined that the best approach would be to focus on social media, public relations, direct marketing, sales promotion, and events. The students developed a one-month content calendar for Instagram and Facebook and designed potential sponsored posts for each channel. They also identified influencers to target for collaborations and created a pitch for those influences. Knowing the client had an existing database, the students also developed an email marketing campaign and sweepstakes as part of the campaign to encourage fans to share with others. Finally, their campaign wrapped up with free online boxing lessons to encourage women to see the clothing in action.

In March 2020, much like the rest of the world, classes shifted to an online format. While this move to online learning presented several challenges, this shift provided benefits with client-related projects. In previous courses, in-person client meetings were prioritized, which required clients to be based in Calgary. The transition to online made it possible for students to work with clients worldwide, which exposed them to a broader range of clients for the projects. This year, students worked with a range, both geographically and industrially, businesses including a start-up out of New York, a yoga company out of California, a tourism company out of Ontario, and a non-profit from British Columbia. Without Riipen, this diversity of clients would not have been possible in the classroom.

Outcomes

1. **Client Relations Understanding** – Throughout the project, many students expressed that client-based projects are quite time-consuming. Some clients were difficult to reach or busy. While this was challenging, it did provide students insight into the realities of the workplace for marketers. In my experience, many marketing projects are driven by others where marketers are collaborating with internal or external clients. This can result in marketers having to flex to client work styles, which is what students learn during this process.

2. **Confidence in Skills** – Client projects help students gain confidence in their skills through their interactions with clients. While students receive positive feedback from instructors on their projects, in my experience, it is often more meaningful for the students to receive this positive feedback from the client. Riipen has a built-in mechanism that ensures clients provide comments on student work to make this feedback easier.

3. **Greater Diversity in Clients** – As one of the largest workplace learning platforms, Riipen provides greater diversity in clients than any instructors could access on their own. This ensures student groups can work with workplaces of different sizes and different structures and understand the differences. Small start-ups, large corporations, non-profits, government agencies are all on Riipen.

Feedback

In most classes, we just talk about what we can do. This project cool in that we got to do the stuff we talked about with actual businesses. (student comment unattributed, 2021)

Working with clients is hard. They have their ideas and their schedules that don't always line up with ours. But it makes me feel ready to do it in the real world. (student comment unattributed, 2021)

Hearing that our client is going to implement almost all of our suggestions was a huge boost. After years of learning about marketing, knowing that someone will use our marketing ideas is pretty cool. (student comment unattributed, 2021)

I never thought about starting my own marketing company after school. But working on this project made me realize I like solving problems for different companies. (student comment unattributed, 2021)

Opportunities

Successful client projects require effort from the instructor. From recruiting the clients to managing the relationship to ensuring the final projects are delivered, instructor oversight is needed every step of the way.

Riipen helps to make this work more manageable in several ways. In terms of recruiting clients, Riipen allows instructors to post their projects and easily search businesses looking for student support. This means there is a nearly endless source of clients available to work with students.

In terms of communication, Riipen helps by setting milestones for the clients and the students. This ensures communications take place on a regular basis, which is key for success. These milestones also include a project completion milestone, which helps ensure a successful project wrap-up.

Another way Riipen helps to make the client project process more effective is by providing instructors with the ability to supervise the relationship between the client and the student. By ensuring communications occur exclusively on the Rippen platform, instructors can monitor the students' relationship with the client and provide feedback.

Regardless of the platform used, meeting with the client before the course start date will help ensure success.

CASE STUDY #3: VOICE TECHNOLOGY AS A DESIGN THINKING PROJECT

Case background

Voice first makes for a compelling area of study in modern-day marketing. As Shaye Roseman wrote in the 2020 Harvard Business School Blog, "Why Voice is the Next Disruptive Platform Technology", "voice will precipitate a paradigm shift in how humans interact with technology, essentially creating a new kind of operating system. (Roseman, 2020) Bold predictions like these are playing out in the marketplace. Global revenue of smart speakers has gone from virtually zero to $12B in the last decade and is expected to reach $35B by 2025. (Statista, 2021)

Technology

The Amazon Developer Console is the central portal for the creation of Alexa Flash Briefings. This vast and diverse portal provides access to developers of all stripes, including voice technology. Early in the semester, all students can create an Alexa developer account by using the same Amazon ID and password to purchase something from the retailer's shopping platform. On rare occasions where students do not have an existing account, they are encouraged to obtain one to proceed to creating an Amazon Developer account. Note, never in three years since implementation has a student been identified who has not had an Amazon account nor resistance to creating a developer account.

Once signed up for an Amazon Developer account, learners are directed to the Alexa area of the site. There they obtain an Alexa Skills Kit, comprised of tutorials, write-ups, templates and, most importantly for these students of "Innovation and Design", the platform on which their Flash Briefing descriptions will be created, and linkages with a podcast host will be established. Importantly, the course can be structured as a standalone, Amazon Alexa audio product only. However, since the inception at SAIT, the audio content has been developed on a podcast hosting platform. It provides a codeless way of transmitting content from a personal computer to the Alexa platform and beyond if students opt to create a podcast with their creation.

The podcast hosting platform used for the course is Acast, a British audio-hosting platform that was chosen for its simplicity of use and frictionless interaction with Alexa. Once students have the audio content created, edited, and produced, it is easily uploaded to Acast, where it can be disseminated to myriad audio content players, including Alexa, Apple Podcasts, Spotify, Stitcher, and Soundcloud.

Aside from a personal computer, although technically all of this could be performed using a smartphone, the last remaining technology ingredient required is sound recording/editing software. For this, students are encouraged to use either a platform they are currently using, such as Garage Band, from Apple, or are directed to download a free app called Audacity. Finally, students are given a brief tutorial on how to record their own voices, how to record and layer additional audio tracks for music, sound effects, and so on.

The audio tech component of Innovation and Design is the most frequently accessed during the course. However, learners are tasked with developing visual branding elements to help identify and promote their flash briefings early in the process. At this point, student groups quickly identify one or more group members who have developed a skill set in graphic design. Those skill, paired with knowledge brought forward from previous courses (i.e. Brand Management), allow for brand elements such as logos to be designed. Additional graphic design work comes into play near the end of the course when students create an "innovation brief", describing the design-based journey which led them to the development of their Flash Briefing.

The Innovation and Design Classroom

Course Content and Delivery Format

The "Innovation and Design" course, is a third-year course for marketing majors. It is a project-based course where students work in groups to confront the fundamental goal of design thinking: solve people's problems through innovation. That's a pretty broad brush. When launched in fall 2016, learners worked with a local sporting goods and apparel retailer, which had its own portfolio of private label brands. Students had a mandate to introduce new products into these different brands. The subject area was of interest to the students, but in the end, their development of products remained entirely hypothetical. Year two saw an expansion of the central project concept, allowing groups to choose between two different product categories – athletic leisure apparel and gluten-free baking. Again, actual local small businesses representing these industries supported the course with regular consultation and evaluation of group presentations. Still, however, the notion of creating a finished product as an outcome of the course eluded. Business schools predominantly teach strategy, but rarely execution of that strategy where the end result is a consumer product.

The third year of the course's history changed that paradigm, by introducing a project concept that could see the development of a product from start to finish. This also would include execution of the marketing process at a high level (crucial for marketing majors), and entails working through the elements of design thinking. To do this, one of the world's biggest tech companies became an integral, albeit unbeknownst partner, providing the critical course infrastructure. The company was Amazon, and its Alexa/Echo voice-first ecosystem was fertile ground for identifying, analyzing, and ultimately solving problems, of varying degrees of seriousness, with the simple voice command, "Alexa, what's my flash briefing?" But what came out of an Echo speaker, upon provocation by those words, was the result of a term-long deep dive into sociology, psychology, demography, consumer behaviour, and, of course – technology. Importantly, in the true spirit of design thinking, however, students weren't only encouraged to think outside of the box, they were urged to remove it completely.

Today, the final project of the course is a 5 episode "Flash Briefing" series, focusing on a subject, researched by learner groups and are complete with all required digital elements of the Amazon Alexa framework, including branding materials, ethical criteria compliance, audience description and so on. But the "magic" happens when students seated arm's length from the speaker with their classmates, hear their audio productions come out of a smart device, and realize that their creation has the ability to penetrate hundreds of millions of homes. This non-credit reward for the project and course is often more valued by the students than the credit itself.

Outcomes

As has been discussed, the project outcome of Innovation and Design is a five-part Flash Briefing series. To be specific, these are five episodes of audio content connected to a central theme, which, when summoned by an Alexa user, provide information, education, entertainment, or some combination of these, to solve a problem. Class discussions in the early weeks of the semester go wide and deep into defining what constitutes a "problem". Fortunately, as marketing majors, Maslow's Hierarchy of Needs is never far from their minds. Therefore it is quickly established that these Flash Briefing series have a virtual limitlessness to problems they can solve. Referencing Maslow's theory, the problems could be based on human physical nature, such as a voice-guided workout activity. Or, on the other end of Maslow's classic pyramid, a Flash Briefing could be daily motivational quotes designed to assist in listeners' search of their purpose in life.

There are only two common denominators for each Flash Briefing series. First, they are designed to be delivered asynchronously, meaning that the Flash Briefings are played but never interacted with when voice-provoked by a user. This is a technical scope limitation simply due to the added teaching and learning complexity of producing synchronously based "skills" as they are known in the Alexa vernacular. Second, the audio outputs of Flash Briefings are labeled as such because they are intended to be "brief".

Amazon's prediction with Flash Briefings is that obtaining information through our ears will become more common than with our eyes. But, as opposed to consuming several minutes, or even hours, of content at a time through podcasts or audiobooks, the belief is that we'll evolve into relying on voice tech to "read" us our news, sports, stock information, weather, even tell us jokes, more and more over time. Thus, Flash Briefings are designed to be consumed in clustered sequences of personally chosen subject areas.

It is speculated that a typical Flash Briefing user would habitualize themselves by pre-scheduling their personalized audio program to roll out each day when summoned by the "Alexa, what's my flash briefing" command. Thus, a listener could have their choice of "daily news", followed by two different sports briefings, followed by weather, their zodiac reading, and then end with a "joke of the day". Strung together, these might amount to 10-20 total minutes of uninterrupted but diverse content, providing the Alexa user with information "needed" to go about their day.

For the Innovation and Design course, Flash Briefings are taught to be 1-2 minutes long, including a branded opening and closing, with meaningful content in the middle. Again, a minimum of five interconnected episodes must be produced and loaded so that they can be heard on an Echo speaker or through the Alexa app at the end of the semester.

It is important to note that there are no additional costs for the student. The Amazon Developer account is free, the recommended audio editing software is free, and the host platform offers free trials, sufficient to endure the length of a semester, although the latter agreement will need to be brokered between instructor and supplier.

Feedback

The Alexa project, now integrated into the Innovation and Design course elicits widely varying levels of support from past students. Some find the whole concept of design thinking a challenge, as it, by definition, attempts to remove the structure to stimulate creativity. Others find the freedom of this environment invigorating and take to it quite naturally, with little input from the instructor.

However, one consistent thing is that once completed, students more clearly see the design thinking model and feel a sense of satisfaction, having created a "product" to be distributed through Amazon.

While voice-first is the specific area of study for the term project, the infrastructure supporting the platform is, of course, reliant upon artificial intelligence, and thus giving students of this project valuable exposure to another technology shaping the future. As one student remarked in a term-ending essay:

I had more than one valuable takeaway as I thought this was a very current and informative class that could teach me potential skills I could use in marketing. Another aspect of this class that I was surprised to learn about was Artificial Intelligence. I had very little previous knowledge and learned a lot about how this is integrated in creating voice technologies like Alexa. Something that amazed me is how we use artificial intelligence, voice tech, and voice recognition, all very sophisticated innovations with something as simple as asking Siri what the weather is today (Kruger, 2020)

Another student viewed the course term project as a crucial connection for students between their post-secondary education, and the rapidly tech-evolving work-world:

This course has been a good example of how public and post-secondary "traditional" education programs can be altered to accommodate modern learning for today's society. It is a glimmer of hope that we will be able to "catch up" to the rest of the world after education (Moffatt, 2020)

There are over 100,000 Alexa skills (the broad category of voice apps in which flash briefings are a sub-category) currently available for consumption through the Amazon/Alexa/Echo smart speaker ecosystem (Kinsella, 2021). Large companies have introduced "voice" as a part of their digital marketing strategy, including podcasts and, to a lesser extent, flash briefings. As more immediate proof of concept for voice technology, as a component of a post-secondary marketing program, a recent graduate of SAIT produced a flash briefing for his employer. (Hale, 2021)

Opportunities

As outlined earlier, the Innovation and Design course, entering its fifth year of existence in Fall 2021, has evolved greatly both in over-arching learning objectives (more design thinking focussed) and the case subject on which to study and apply learning. One thing we have learned about technology adoption in the last three decades is something that consumers have been telling us for time immemorial. They will adopt what they want when they want it. Three years after the course lead of "Innovation and Design" decided to implement the "Alexa Project", the early hype for voice-first technology appears to have outstripped actual demand. Or perhaps it is still a technology a bit ahead of its time for mass adoption. Nevertheless, the "Innovation and Design" course will once again offer the "Alexa Project" as its core case-based learning tool in the short term while monitoring how smart-speaker usage, in general, is developing as a consumer product.

CONCLUSION

Through these three distinct and unique classroom applications, it is clear that WIL takes place in many formats. However, student learning was enhanced in each instance, and students reported feeling better prepared for the workplace. Whether it is creating flashing briefings for Alexa, learning a new approach to sales presentations, or working with client-based learning, students develop skills beyond the earned credit demonstrating the real value of WIL.

REFERENCES

Alberta 2030: Building skills for jobs strategy summary. (2021). *Government of Alberta*. https://open.alberta.ca/publications/alberta-2030-building-skills-for-jobs-strategy-summary

Baden, D., & Parkes, C. (2013). Experiential learning: Inspiring the business leaders of tomorrow. *Journal of Management Development, 32*(3), 295–308. doi:10.1108/02621711311318283

Business Higher Education Roundtable (BHER). (2016). *Taking the Pulse of Work-integrated Learning in Canada*. https://bher.ca/wp-content/uploads/2016/10/BHER-Academica-report-full.pdf

Dean, B., Eady, M. J., & Yanamandram, V. (2020). Editorial: Advancing Non-placement Work-integrated Learning Across the Degree. *Journal of University Teaching & Learning Practice*, *17*(4). Advance online publication. doi:10.53761/1.17.4.1

Kinsella, B. (2021). *Alexa skill counts surpass 80K in US, Spain adds the most skills, new skill rate falls globally*. https://voicebot.ai/2021/01/14/alexa-skill-counts-surpass-80k-in-us-spain-adds-the-most-skills-new-skill-introduction-rate-continues-to-fall-across-countries/

Kruger, E. (2020). *Evaluating in reality: Critical essay on innovation, design and voice tech*. Personal Communications - Interview with Dave Gaudet.

Lee, S. A. (2008). Increasing student learning: A comparison of students' perceptions of learning in the classroom environment and their industry-based experiential learning Assignments. *Journal of Teaching in Travel & Tourism*, *7*(4), 37–54. doi:10.1080/15313220802033310

Moffatt, R. (2020). *Evaluating in reality: Critical essay on innovation, design and voice tech*. Personal Communications - Interview with Dave Gaudet.

Mueller, P. A., & Oppenheimer, D. M. (2014). The pen is mightier than the keyboard: Advantages of longhand over laptop note taking. *Psychological Science*, *25*(6), 1–10. doi:10.1177/0956797614524581 PMID:24760141

O'Shea, A. (2014). Models of WIL. In S. Ferns (Ed.), Work integrated learning in the curriculum. Higher Education Research and Development Society of Australia guide (pp. 7-14). Hammondville: Higher Education Research and Development Society of Australasia.

QuirkLogic. (2020). *Presentation to SAIT marketing faculty* [unpublished].

Roseman, S. (2020). *The Forum for Innovation and Growth*. Harvard Business School. https://www.hbs.edu/forum-for-growth-and-innovation/blog/post/why-voice-is-the-next-disruptive-technology

SAIT. (2020). *Learner exit survey, work integrated learning 2018-19. Business Information and Analysis*. SAIT.

SAIT. (2021). *About us*. https://www.sait.ca/about-sait

Smart speaker market value worldwide 2014-2025. (2021). *Statista*. https://www.statista.com/statistics/1022823/worldwide-smart-speaker-market-revenue/

Stirling, A., Kerr, G., MacPherson, E., & Heron, A. (2016). *A practical guide for work-integrated learning: Effective practices to enhance the educational quality of structured work Experiences Offered through Colleges and Universities.* Higher Education Quality Council of Ontario.

RBC and Riipen expand experiential learning partnership for youth across Canada. Riipen. (2020, October 15). https://www.riipen.com/blog/rbc-and-riipen-expand-experiential-learning-partnership-for-youth-across-canada

The Innovative Work-Integrated Learning Initiative. (2020). *Government of Canada.* https://www.canada.ca/en/employment-social-development/programs/work-integrated-learning.html

Wood, Y. I., Zegwaard, K. E., & Fox-Turnbull, W. H. (2020). Conventional, remote, virtual, and simulated work-integrated learning: A meta-analysis of existing practice. *International Journal of Work Integrated Learning, 21*(4), 331–354.

Zegwaard, K., & Rowe, A. (2019). Research-informed curriculum and advancing innovative practices in work-integrated learning. *International Journal of Work-Integrated Learning, 20*(4), 323–334.

Chapter 9
Motivation in Online Learning

Şenol Orakcı
iD https://orcid.org/0000-0003-1534-1310
Faculty of Education, Aksaray University, Turkey

Yalçın Dilekli
Faculty of Education, Aksaray University, Turkey

EXECUTIVE SUMMARY

Online learning is accepted as an effective educational learning process that can respond to rapidly and constantly changing learner needs. Increasing the quality of online learning is an important point to be addressed. Within this context, motivation in online learning that affects what learners will learn, how they will learn, and when they will learn is one of the most important components because the motivation of learners has a very important place in terms of achieving desired goals in the learning and teaching process. It is not easy to continuously motivate learners in online learning process over a long period. Creating the motivation of everyone involved in the learning and teaching process is very important in terms of the efficiency and quality of the process. Within the context of a theoretical framework, "motivation," "motivation process," "types of motivation," "internal motivation," "extrinsic motivation," "the importance of motivation in education," and "motivation in online learning" were addressed in the present study.

INTRODUCTION

Similar to e-learning concepts, online learning can be expressed as the realization of learning by using networks regardless of time and place. Carliner (2004) expresses

DOI: 10.4018/978-1-7998-8310-4.ch009

online learning as accessing all kinds of resources that support learning and learning through a computer and network technology.

According to Watson, Murin, Vashaw, Gemin, and Rapp, (2013) online learning is a kind of learning, where faculty and students are geographically separated, a web-based education management software is used to provide a structured learning environment, and instructor-led training. It can take place simultaneously (communication where participants can interact in real time, such as online video) or separately (time separated communication such as e-mail, online discussion forums). It can be accessed from multiple settings (from school or outside of school).

In other words, online learning is a learning environment that removes barriers such as socio-economic status and enables individuals the opportunity to benefit from the superiority of lifelong education, where communication can be established with other learners and teachers simultaneously or asynchronously through the online learning environment, the internet or a computer network, and where interaction can be established in two ways with the visual and auditory abilities provided by computer technology.

Oblinger and Oblinger (2005) state that online learning should be completely synchronous, that is, with the teacher and the learner being in different places at the same time. Horton (2006) stated that online learning can be in four different types: instructor-led, student-led, synchronous and asynchronous. Instructor-led online learning is defined as a tutor conducting a lesson with a group of students online as in a normal lesson; Student-led online learning can be defined as online learning environments in which students can progress at their own pace. While synchronous online learning requires the instructor and the learner to be online at the same time and engage in educational activities at the same time, asynchronous online learning provides an environment where the instructors and learners can be online at different times or the learner can learn at his own pace without a tutorial. Today, learning management systems (LMS), which we can call an online learning tool and environment, can include all types of time and space as a standard (Horton, 2006).

LMS is defined as an online community that provides students with access to Internet-based resources and enables instructors and administrative staff to manage, monitor and access collective course and student information (Oliveira, Cunha, & Nakayama, 2016; Wilans & Seary, 2011). According to Lonn and Teasley (2009), "learning management systems are web-based systems that enable teachers and students to share materials, send assignments and grades, and communicate online" (p. 211). A learning management system includes various features that enable faculty members to share learning materials and interact with their students synchronously and asynchronously (Oliveira, Cunha, & Nakayama, 2016; Vovides, Sanchez-Alonso, Mitropoulou, & Nickmans, 2007). Learning management systems also construct learning on interaction, presenting information regularly, using more than one media together, bringing different languages and resources together and enabling alternative technologies (Oliveira, Cunha, & Nakayama, 2016). "LMS" that provides easy access to content is a way of, evaluating students, providing feedback, and establishing teacher-student and student-student communication online (Porter, 2013). "LMS" is also defined as institutional level and server-based software systems to provide, transmit and manage online learning asynchronously (Berking & Gallagher, 2011). In summary, "LMS" serves students, teachers, staff and parents by providing a way to share learning content, materials and student evaluations. In addition, "LMS" can provide communication between students, teachers and parents through tools such as discussion forums and e-mails (Berking & Gallagher, 2011; Oliveira, Cunha, & Nakayama, 2016). Learning management systems are preferred by many institutions in online learning and are widely used today due to their flexible features and ease of use (Naveh, Tubin, & Pliskin, 2012). The use of learning management systems is very common, especially at higher education level. A "LMS" has many useful features for tutorials today. At the university level, there are many popular "LMS" such as "Blackboard", "Desire2Learn", "Its learning", "Moodle", and "Sakai". Learning management systems have many features such as creating courses / courses, creating classes, event planning, preparing curriculum, making announcements, chatting tools, test - quiz tools, creating materials, uploading materials and distributing them to users. Apart from these, they can also host different tools such as social media integration ("Facebook", "Twitter" etc.) and "wiki" (Jamsri, 2015; Naveh, Tubin, & Pliskin, 2012).

Online learning is accepted as an effective educational learning process that can respond to rapidly and constantly changing learner needs. Learners' demand for online learning causes many institutions today to focus on this issue. Institutions open various programs in order to meet the needs of learners and to respond to the demands. In particular, online diploma programs, undergraduate and graduate programs offered by higher education institutions are examples of this situation. Thanks to increasing programs, online learning also attracts the attention of learners with the quality of the programs (Bağrıacık, 2015).

Rapidly developing technologies create differences in people's lifestyles and even these differentiations affect education life. Considering the reflections of developing new technologies on education, learners are getting acquainted with learning environments supported by new technologies, unlike classical learning environments. Online learning environments, which are seen as an alternative to traditional learning environments, can be considered as one of the reflections of new technologies in education. The motivation problems experienced in traditional learning environments should also be reviewed for online environments (Deimann & Bastiaens, 2010; Hoskins & Hooff, 2005). Because it can be said that academic motivation is important in increasing student success in online learning environments as well as in traditional learning environments.

Increasing use of technology in education increases the types of education that will support or provide an alternative to traditional teaching. However, it is not easy to continuously motivate learners in the education-training process over a long period (Deimann, & Bastiaens, 2010; Deimann, Weber, & Bastiaens, 2009; Keller, 2015; Keller, Deimann, & Liu, 2005; Keller, & Deimann, 2012; Keller, & Suzuki, 2004). In addition, new generation learners, although they seem technologically equipped, have difficulties in getting used to distance learning environments and may find these environments mixed and different (Keller, 1983; Keller, 1987; Keller, 2000; Keller, 2005a; Keller, 2006a; Keller, 2015). In this case, motivating learners becomes an important problem. However, this problem is even more complex, especially in learning environments where learners need self-discipline in online learning (Pittenger & Doering, 2010). In this section, the importance of motivation in online learning will be examined in the context of a theoretical framework.

MOTIVATION

Motivation is a broad topic that has very different meanings. Keller (1979) expressed motivation as "stimulating, directing and maintaining behavior". From this point of view, it is possible to define motivation as the power that moves a person towards a certain goal. The concept of motivation can also be defined as the most important source of power that determines the direction, intensity and determination of behavior. It is the intermediate variable used to define individuals in their efforts to achieve goals, or to define this process. Motivation in education is used as a concept related to the participation of learners in the education and training process and to increase their success and desire. Educational psychologists, on the other hand, define motivation as guiding the behavior of the learner voluntarily or through external methods (Acar, 2009). An inner force that forces the individual to act is the most well-known definition of the concept of motivation. Another one, which is accepted as one of the common definitions, is the individual's ideas, beliefs, demands, fears, etc. It is the process of activating the individual to achieve his / her own goals with the combination of emotions or the effect of any of them (Kahraman, 2017).

As in cases where the definitions for the concept of motivation intersect on a common denominator, it can also be the opposite. The common point of the people who define the concept of motivation is that it should be a force that mobilizes the individual and ensures the continuity of the movement. The point where they differ from each other is the complexity of the process.

Schunk (1992) defined motivation as orienting towards a behavioral process for a certain goal and continuing this orientation process. It is one of the most important factors in learning-teaching processes and a prerequisite for learning (Akbaba, 2006). Behavioral theory, cognitive theory, and constructivist theory have different views on motivation. Behavioral approach theorists state that the most effective approach to motivation is the careful use of rewards or reinforcements. Behaviorism supports the idea that students must master certain skills before progressing to the next level (Driscoll, 2000). Reinforcers should be used to ensure motivation (Bacanlı, 2003). From a cognitive-based perspective, information is symbolic, and in order to be processed, information must be submitted or delivered to permanent memory (Driscoll, 2000). Bandura (1977) states that motivation has more causes than external stimulation, and individual differences and readiness to learn are some of them. Bandura (1977) stated that learning will be difficult to achieve as a result of learning goals being unrealistic goals. Bandura (1977) states that goals or intentions play a central role in social cognitive theory, and that this is actually the discrepancy between the motivation that serves students' goals and their actual achievements. For these reasons, the expectation of an individual to achieve a goal and the value of that goal in the individual determine motivation. In a constructivist approach that focuses on the idea that knowledge is built by learners while trying to make sense of their experiences, students should be actively involved in determining what they will learn. Constructivist teaching methods are student-centered approaches that activate information sharing, inquiry and discussion, such as collaborative learning, active learning, and problem-based learning. Motivation for these approaches is one of the key concepts of deep learning (Driscoll, 2000). Students' motivation for learning is a psychological condition that is a prerequisite for achieving deep learning (Gee, 2003).

One of the most extensive studies on the structure of motivation is Pintrich's (1988) study, which aims to explore the dynamic interaction between motivation and cognition. Pintrich (1988) states that in order to fully understand the learning process, it is important to consider the cognitive components of student learning as well as motivation. Pintrich (1988) states that there is a positive correlation between motivation and cognitive factors, and cognitive commitment increases with the increase in the level of motivation. Pintrich (1989) argues that the relationship between motivation and cognition is not only dynamic but also synergistic. Pintrich (1989) also states that the effect of the interaction between motivation and cognition is more important than individual differences. The collaborative nature of the relationship between motivation and cognition is a crucial aspect of student learning (Pintrich, 1989). However, it is stated that there is a relationship between self-regulated learning and motivation, self-regulated learning imposes responsibility on the individual and provides a sense of competence, and these two factors are key components of intrinsic motivation (Corno & Rohrkemper, 1985; Corno, & Randi, 1999; Corno, & Kanfer, 1993). Zimmerman (1989) states that self-efficacy is also one of the variables affecting motivation and can be accepted as a structure within self-regulated learning. Pintrich, Smith, Garcia, and McKeachie (1993) argue that the general motivational structure consists of three main components; expectation, value and affect. "Expectation" can be stated as students' beliefs about completing a learning task, and the variables of self-efficacy and control belief constitute this component. "Value" tries to explain why students are attached to learning tasks, and this component consists of internal goal setting focusing on learning-specialization, external goal setting focusing on grades and acceptance by other individuals, task value beliefs that explain how interesting, necessary and useful the course learned for the student. "Affect" is a component that explains students' anxiety about exams (Pintrich, Smith, Garcia, & McKeachie, 1993). This structure is one of the structures that best explains learner motivation with its sub-components (Pintrich, Smith, Garcia, & McKeachie, 1991; Pintrich, Smith, Garcia, & McKeachie, 1993; Büyüköztürk, Akgün, Demirel, & Özkahveci, 2004). Since motivation is a very complex and comprehensive concept, it is associated with various variables in different fields. In this context, instinct, impulse, motivation process and types of motivation, which are among the motivation concepts in this study, are explained.

1. Instinct

Being consciously motivated to achieve a goal and to solve a problem is unique to humans. The motivation of an animal happens completely instinctively unconsciously. Instinct is defined as the innate tendency to behave in the same way in all living things and which cannot be learned. It occurs naturally by itself (Bacanlı, 2003; Kahraman, 2017).

2. Impulse

Motivation, which is one of the concepts of motivation can be defined as an effort to meet the physical needs of the individual. Drinking water when thirsty, sleeping, breathing, and eating are among the actions of a person as a result of urges. The impulse and the concept of motive are sometimes confused. The situation that separates the two concepts from each other is that most of the motives are learnable, but impulses are not learned (Ayhan, 2000; Erkuş, 1994).

3. Motive

Motive is defined as the internal power that leads the individual to a behavior in order to live and increase the quality of life, to satisfy the need consciously and regularly. Based on this definition, it is possible to say that the concept of motive includes impulse and need.

Primary motives are the innate motives that people try to feed in order to sustain their life and continue their bloodline. Eating, drinking, safety, sexuality, breathing, etc. can be given as examples for these motives. Learned motives, which consist of environmental, cultural and social factors, are defined as secondary motives. As an example of secondary motives, belonging, power, security, status, success can be given (Erkuş, 1994; Özbay, 2004).

MOTIVATION PROCESS

The motivation process starts with the needs of the individual. Motives that arise as a result of the needs create tension in people when they cannot reach the desired goal. This state of tension makes people act by forcing them to satisfy their motives. When a person reaches his/her goal, he/she gets rid of tension because he/she satisfies his/her motives adequately. As a result of the motivations that are satisfied, the person becomes happy.

TYPES OF MOTIVATION

When the literature is reviewed, motivation is discussed in two dimensions as the source that guides human behaviors. They are intrinsic and extrinsic motivation.

1. Intrinsic Motivation

The source of the person's behavior is within himself/herself. The individual decides how much effort he / she will achieve at the time that he / she wants to achieve. The needs of the individual are the main source of motivation. Therefore, since it depends on the fulfillment of individual needs, it is impossible for intrinsic motivation to occur when there is no need and expectation. Intrinsic motivation is also defined as motivation to learn (Başaran, 2000). In short, intrinsic motivation, unlike extrinsic motivation caused by external influences, exists within the individual and motivates a person's behavior by his/her interest in the nature of the task (Ryan & Deci, 2000a). Low intrinsic motivation to learn a subject is insufficient for learning, and this motivation quickly disappears. This type of intrinsic motivation only meets basic academic needs for remembering and understanding learning content (Ryan & Deci, 2000b). Intrinsic motivation is the desire to do something because it is interesting or enjoyable. Creating high-interest learning experiences involving the personalization of themes, objects, and characters contributes to better content learning and intrinsic motivation to maintain a task (Ryan & Deci, 2000a; Ryan & Deci, 2000b; Driscoll, 2000). Intrinsic factors create an intrinsic motivation that encourages students to participate in activities for their own sake, often as a result of the satisfaction experienced during commitment to learning activities. Awards and other external factors have no effect on how students feel about the activity (Ryan & Deci, 2000b; Ryan, Rigby, & Przybylski, 2006; Driscoll, 2000) should be changed as (Driscoll, 2000; Ryan & Deci, 2000b; Ryan, Rigby, & Przybylski, 2006).

2. Extrinsic Motivation

The source of the person's behavior is outside of himself / herself. It is stated that extrinsic motivation is not as effective as intrinsic motivation because it does not show continuity in achieving the goal of the individual. Because the continuation of the effort and desire of the person is possible with external effects. Reinforcers in Skinner's theory are related to extrinsic motivation. Reward, social support, punishment, and encouragement can be given as examples (Başaran, 2000). In short, extrinsic motivation is closely related to rewards and is to do a duty for one's own good. Extrinsic motivation includes rewards, recognition or directives. In a learning environment, extrinsic motivation has the potential to reconcile goals and direct focus to performance (Driscoll, 2000; Ryan & Deci, 2000b). A student who is motivated to do homework because of fear of the consequences of his/her parents is externally motivated. However, his/her autonomy is different from the student who is motivated to finish his/her homework because his/her fear will help him/her get better grades. Both individuals have an extrinsic motivation but have different levels of autonomy. Using extrinsic rewards is good when performance (or the product of a performance) is the goal, but learning is definitely not a performance-based process (Driscoll, 2000).

Chen and Jang (2010), emphasizing the importance of motivation for online learning environments, adapted a motivation scale developed by Vallerand, Pelletier, Briere, Senecal and Vallieres (1993) within the framework of self-determination theory to online learning environments. Researchers who used this questionnaire to determine the motivation levels of students for an online course revealed that the dimensions of intrinsic motivation, extrinsic motivation and lack of motivation in the self-determination theory are important factors in determining the level of motivation.

Self-determination theory can be summarized as the process of internalizing extrinsic motivation, which involves students who want to stay away from academic activities are directed to work in order to be rewarded or to avoid punishment. In this way, students who encounter extrinsic motivation elements feel a sense of self-regulation as they increase their success. Then, with the effect of positive social reinforcements such as praise and feedback, further increase in intrinsic motivation levels is achieved (Schunk, 2011, p.501).

THE IMPORTANCE OF MOTIVATION IN EDUCATION

Motivation of the individual in line with his/her goals is important. The existing motives of the individual cause the individual to behave in line with his/her goal. People focus on the goal as a result of motivation.

In the education and training process, the necessary environment should be prepared to meet the needs. Motivated teacher and learner take action towards doing the desired behavior. Due to this situation, motivation is an important factor for increasing efficiency in the education and training process. Motivation is required to activate or direct a behavior. The most effective weapon to direct human behavior is to provide motivation. This is also valid for the realization of education. Creating the motivation of everyone involved in the training process is very important in terms of the efficiency and quality of the process. If administrators, teachers and learners know each other well and act by knowing their needs, they can increase the efficiency of education by motivating each other (Dur, 2014).

Motivation is one of the most important factors affecting academic achievement (Cunningham, 2003; Matuga, 2009; Renchler, 1992; Zimmerman, 1990). When students' motivation levels increase, their interest, curiosity and desire towards their lessons increase, which makes it easier for them to learn and increases their success (Sansone, Fraughton, Zachary, Butner, & Heiner, 2011; Soydan et al., 2012). Francis et al. (2004) defines motivation as an important academic engagement that can affect the academic performance level of the student. In a study conducted by Uzbaş (2009), it was stated by the psychological counselor units working in primary and secondary schools that the reasons for students' failure were due to exam anxiety and lack of motivation. Identifying and resolving problems related to academic motivation is an effective factor in increasing student success (Karagüven, 2012). In this context, it can be said that motivation is an important factor that affects academic success.

Rapidly developing technologies create differences in people's lifestyles and even these differences affect education and training life. Considering the reflections of developing new technologies on education, day by day learners are introduced to learning environments supported by new technologies, different from classical learning environments. Online learning environments, seen as an alternative to traditional learning environments, can be considered as one of the reflections of new technologies on education. Academic achievement, cognitive load and motivation problems experienced in traditional learning environments should also be reviewed for online environments (Hoskins & Hooff, 2005). Because it can be said that academic motivation is important in increasing student success in online learning environments as well as in traditional learning environments.

MOTIVATION IN ONLINE LEARNING

The motivation of learners has a very important place in the learning and teaching process (Keller, 1979; Keller, 2010a; Keller, 2006b). However, the success or failure of learners in learning environments is explained by the phenomenon of motivation (Fryer & Bovee, 2016; Gabrielle, 2003; Giesbers, Rienties, Tempelaar, & Gijselaers, 2014; Keller, 2008a; Keller, 2008b). Motivation in online learning affects what learners will learn, how they will learn and when they will learn (Barak, Watted, & Haick, 2016; Deimann & Bastiaens, 2010; Hartnett, George, & Dron, 2011; Keller, 2010b; Keller, 2010c; Kumarawadu, 2001; Vallerand, & Bissonnette, 1992). Studies reveal that learners who have high motivation in learning environments reach achievement in difficult learning situations, like the learning process, realize deep learning, and are determined and creative (Knowles & Kerkman, 2007; Semmar, 2006; West, Hannafın, Hill, & Song, 2013).

Motivation has long been one of the important fields of study of educational theorists. Educational theorists have generally investigated the function and effect of motivation in the learning process with various theories they developed. Motivation is handled in different ways in terms of behavioral, cognitive, constructivist and sociocultural learning theories. Behaviorists believe that learning takes place in the context of stimulus-response and that learning is reinforced with external stimuli, that is, motivational elements. In this understanding, the result is important and the behaviors that are supported or rewarded are likely to be repeated in the future (Ertmer and Newby, 1993; Wighting, Liu, & Rovai, 2008).

In the context of the behavioral approach, human behavior is either supported or eliminated. In addition, in this understanding, the teacher is at the center of the learning environment and is also the giver of reward and punishment. In addition to this situation, learners are passive learners, that is, individuals who receive information. In this case, the moves made from outside affect the motivation of the learner (Snowman, McCown, & Biehler, 2012).

The counseling, guidance, support and praise of teachers in online learning environments are regarded as an external effect for learners (Jokelova, 2012; Jokelova,

2013). However, presenting the contents previously prepared by the instructor of the course to the learners in large learning environments where mass open online courses are conducted and making an evaluation based on these can be shown as an example of behavioral approach (Bonk & Khoo, 2014; Turner, & Patrick, 2008).

Researchers have put forward different perspectives as well as behavioral approach in making sense of learning processes and styles. At the end of the 1950s, a paradigm shift began in learning theory, and educators began to understand learning processes by emphasizing more complex cognitive structures such as thinking, problem solving, information processing, and language instead of observed behaviors (Ertmer & Newby, 1993). With the use of computers and tools in education and training with the cognitive approach, more complex structures related to learning have come to the fore. In this approach, learning is seen as the process of acquiring knowledge. The teacher is seen as a counselor who transfers information, provides meaningful learning, increases motivation and consequently facilitates learning. According to this approach, learners are active information seekers. In this way, in the long term, metacognitive competencies such as action competencies, self-regulation and self-planning skills, which are also included in the learners' motivation model, develop. Cognitive psychology in online learning environments facilitates the adaptation of teaching materials, motivation and learning strategies according to learners' learning styles (Bonk, 2002; Bonk & Khoo, 2014).

In the constructivist approach, learners make connections, discover, learn and create meaning based on their previous learning and experiences. In this approach, the learner rather than the teacher is in the center, and the role of the teacher is facilitating and guiding (Kawachi, 2003; Ertmer & Newby, 1993; Jokelova, 2012). In this case, it is extremely important for the teacher to support the learner using motivation strategies. In this context, social presence is extremely important in constructivist teaching approach for online learning environments. The closeness and instantness of the teacher increases the participation, satisfaction and all learning of the learners. For this, online promotions, support systems and giving feedback are important in terms of constructivist approach and instantness (Bonk & Khoo, 2014; Jokelova, 2012).

Motivation has an important place in the sociocultural approach. However, first of all, the role of the social environment in this approach is emphasized. People begin to learn from the people around them and their social worlds (Vygotsky, 1978). In addition, cognitive development is fueled by the interaction between human and culture. At this point, the sociocultural approach and motivational design model show significant similarities in terms of factors such as the importance of learner-teacher interaction, providing attention in the learning process and relating to learning goals. For an effective and efficient learning process in today's online learning environments. Efforts are made for learners to interact with the instructor, learner and learning materials. At this point, as the interaction increases, the roles of learner and teacher get closer to each other, and the teacher often assumes the role of counselor or facilitator. In the context of the approaches given above, there are many reasons that hinder motivation in online learning environments. Some of these reasons may be due to the learner, the tools used or the content. According to Litt and Moorei (2013), the factors that hinder or decrease the motivation of learners in online learning environments and thus delay their learning are listed as follows.

- "Technology",
- "Content",
- "Lack of communication and interaction",
- "Issues in everyday life",
- "Strickness of the lecturer",
- "Lack of personalization / differentiation in teaching".

Litt and Moorei (2013) state that if these factors are structured according to learners and teachers, motivation may increase and also learning can be realized more easily. In addition, the same researchers stated that when appropriate strategies and tactics are applied in the four areas given below, motivation will increase.

- Interactivity (Technology-based two-way communication) determining the type and level of interaction, course content, regular announcement, timely and personalized e-mail, participation in discussions, social presence),
- Feedback (Personalized and timely feedback),
- Diversity (Innovative, engaging course materials),
- Technological Tools (Ease of use, serving the purpose).

Strategies and tactics that can be applied in these four areas are discussed in many motivation models or approaches. Information on these models is given below.

In short, the concept of motivation has been studied in different ways in terms of behavioral, cognitive, constructivist and sociocultural theories. Behaviorists believe that learning takes place with the stimulus-response effect and the learning process is reinforced by extrinsic motivation. Since more counselors who teach in online learning are accepted as guiding persons, they are considered as external influences for learners. In the cognitive approach where learning is seen as the process of acquiring knowledge, the use of technology in the education process and the complex structures related to learning come to the fore. In the process, the learner is in the role of information seeker while the teacher is in the role of transferring the information and increasing the motivation. In this case, it causes the development of learners' metacognitive competencies. Cognitive psychology in distance education ensures that motivation and learning strategies are tailored to learners. The constructivist approach is learner-centered and guides the instructive learners to make connections with their previous learning and experiences. The level of social presence is a very important detail for the constructivist approach in online learning. The sincerity and closeness of the teacher increases the satisfaction and motivation of the learners' participation. In the sociocultural approach, the environment of learners' social environment is important. In addition, this approach places emphasis on the learner-teacher interaction in the learning process, the learning process and the relationship with what they learn. For a sociocultural approach in online learning, it is necessary to provide interaction between learner-instructor and teaching materials.

CONCLUSION AND DISCUSSION

The realization of education depends on many different variables. As in formal education processes, the quality, permanence and success rate of education are important in online learning. There are many studies on the purpose of increasing the quality of online learning. It is known that there are many factors affecting quality, permanence and success in line with the studies. Within the scope of this research, among these factors, motivation is one of the most important factors. Motivation, which affects all areas of our lives, is also very important in the education process. As emphasized in the present study, there are two types of motivation that help the learners to realize their learning. They are intrinsic motivation and extrinsic motivation. Intrinsic motivation comes from the inside of the person who does not allow any external intervention. Extrinsic motivation, on the other hand, is a situation of interfering with a person's motivation with various variables and factors. Increasing motivation and ensuring its continuity in online learning in order to promote efficient learning has proved to be very effective in the education process.

SUGGESTIONS

The researchers divide learning mindsets into three: "sense of belonging," "purpose and relevance," and "growth mindset." These three components are indispensable if we want to promote intrinsic motivation, because these components form ways to motivate students in the online education process. In this context, Kelleher and Hulleman's (2020) recommendations below are highly noteworthy.

1) "Creating a Feeling of Belonging"

- *"Make students feel understood":* Incorporate activities, topics, and examples that students can relate to in your lessons, so they see that they can come to class with their true identities every day. Do your best to eliminate threats to identities. Every student deserves to feel seen, heard, respected, and that their unique story is part of the big story of the class. For example, when starting your online classes, create a routine where everyone speaks and each student's name is spoken by someone else. Have "circle chats" in your online classes and encourage your students to talk "from their own perspective". Determine the classroom rules and norms with your students and post them on the home page of your "LMS". Visit and update this list periodically.

- *"Reduce barriers to connecting online":* Tell students that there is an easy way to communicate with you outside of the classroom—you can manage expectations by telling them how often you respond—and that they can do it with peace of mind. While setting clear expectations for the whole class, it's also important to be creative and proactive in identifying and addressing the emotional or academic challenges students face individually. For instance, alternate one-on-one phone and video calls with each child, or offer them the ability to reach you directly via text or call.

- *"Remind yourself that social time is just as important as academic time":* If you teach online, use some of your precious time for social connection. Start your lesson with a social ritual. For example, try a short "mental stretch" break; Before class starts, offer students chat time or form small groups for social interaction. This is not wasted class time. It is an investment that will help students stay motivated and engaged in the long run.

2) Working for Purpose and Relevance

- *"Try to state the purpose clearly":* Teachers often ignore the importance of purpose and interest in creating motivation and think that they have put enough effort in this direction. State the purpose of assignments and activities deliberately and regularly—especially when you are away from your students.

- *"Use online surveys to learn and use students' interests":* Ask students what their interests and passions are, and design activities that target topics that your students are personally interested in. These activities do not always have to be academic. To make deep connections in the distance learning process, you have to give up some of your traditional content – the goal should be to increase student long-term engagement throughout the year.

- *"Give students choice"*: Adding a well-chosen and limited number of options to the subject or setting is great for helping increase motivation during distance learning – students feel empowered while learning how to improve their choice skills. But remember that too many choices create "decision fatigue".

3) "Hard Work, Failure, and Growth Mindset"

- *"Explain how learning happens"*: Start by talking to your students. Say that studying is hard, but gets easier with time thanks to effective study strategies. Teach them neuroplasticity (the brain's ability to undergo structural or physiological changes) – this demanding practice helps restructure their brains.
- *"Share effective study strategies with them"*: Students prefer study strategies such as "paraphrasing key concepts", "active retrieval", and "spaced practice" rather than "rereading" and "highlighting" – do not forget to take the time to allow them to practice and develop these strategies. It is especially important to be persistent during distance learning because students are more often on their own and need different strategies for self-regulation.
- *"Help your students in difficult situations"*: Do not be afraid to tell students that sometimes they will have difficulties and will need various tactics to overcome them. "Have you created a classroom environment where children can seek help from their classmates and feel comfortable?", or "Have you considered setting up small study groups to communicate better?", "Have you provided easy ways for your students to contact you during office hours?", "Have you encouraged them to contact you when they had difficulties?", "Have you created a useful and easily accessible list of class resources on your LMS?"
- *"Use technology to create a low-risk environment"*: You can set up secondary-value quizzes or use technical tools like "Pear Deck", "Quizlet Live", and "Poll Everywhere" to conduct "gradeless retrieval practice" and "formative assessments". Reposition these "exams" as part of continuing learning and help students see them as useful tools to understand where they are, how well their study strategy is working, and what to do next. Finally, don't confuse low risk with easy. When students are challenged, they work harder and learn more deeply. Take time to make mistakes in your lessons and learn from those mistakes.
- *"Change your grading system and structure"*: Contrary to traditional belief in education, grades do not motivate students to do their best and do not lead to better learning or performance. Even if overall assessments are beyond

your control, consider organizing your midterm grades by assigning points and grades based on continually improving student work. Not only does this help struggling students, it also allows top-achieving students to demonstrate that they put in the effort to show clear improvement in their skill level.

- *"Be prepared to constantly update your teaching methods"*: Use your formative assessments to continually adjust your teaching methods, as it is difficult to "read the room" and determining what your students know in the virtual classroom. This is a great way to model the "the growth mindset" behaviors you want your students to adopt.

- *"Establish a digital record of competence"*: Motivation can also be increased when students notice their increased proficiency. Instead of leaving it to chance, create short activities to encourage it – for example, take an older work and do a "then and now" comparison, or create a simple online portfolio that can be revisited and updated regularly. Make sure students associate their competencies with hard work and the right strategies, not innate abilities.

REFERENCES

Acar, S. (2009). *Web tabanlı performans tabanlı öğrenmede ARCS motivasyon stratejilerinin öğrencilerin akademik başarılarına, öğrenmenin kalıcılığına, motivasyonlarına ve tutumlarına etkisi* (Unpublished doctoral dissertation). Gazi University.

Akbaba, S. (2006). Eğitimde motivasyon. *Kazım Karabekir Üniversitesi Eğitim Fakültesi Dergisi*, (13), 343–361.

Ayhan, A. (2000). *Gelişim ve Öğrenme Psikolojisi*. Alfa Yayınları.

Bacanlı, H. (2003). *Gelişim ve öğrenme*. Nobel Yayın Dağıtım.

Bağrıacık, A. (2015). *Çevrimiçi öğrenme ortamlarında ders alan öğrencilerin etkileşim algıları ile doyun düzeyleri arasındaki ilişki* (Unpublished Master's thesis). Gazi University, Eğitim Bilimleri Enstitüsü, Ankara.

Bandura, A. (1977). *Social learning theory*. Prentice-Hall.

Barak, M., Watted, A., & Haick, H. (2016). Motivation to learn in massive open online courses: Examining aspects of language and social engagement. *Computers & Education*, *94*, 49–60. doi:10.1016/j.compedu.2015.11.010

Başaran, İ. E. (2000). *Örgütsel Davranış*. Feryal Matbaası.

Berking, P., & Gallagher, S. (2011). Choosing a learning management system. *Choosing a Learning Management System, Advanced Distributed Learning (ADL) Co-Laboratories*, 40-62. https://qrisnetwork.org/sites/default/files/conference-session/resources/210ChoosingAnLMS.PDF

Bonk, C. J. (2002). *Online teaching in an online world*. http://publicationshare.com/docs/corp_survey.pdf

Bonk, C. J., & Khoo, E. (2014). *Adding some TEC-VARIETY: 100+ activities for motivating and retaining learners online*. Open World Books.

Büyüköztürk, Ş., Akgün, Ö. E., Kahveci, Ö., & Demirel, F. (2004). Güdülenme ve öğrenme stratejileri ölçeğinin Türkçe formunun geçerlik ve güvenirlik çalışması. *Kuram ve Uygulamada Eğitim Bilimleri*, *4*(2), 207–239.

Carliner, S. (2004). An overview of online learning. Armherst, MA: Human Resource Development Press

Corno, L., & Kanfer, R. (1993). The role of volition in learning and performance. *Review of Research in Education*, *19*, 301–341. doi:10.2307/1167345

Corno, L., & Randi, J. (1999). A design theory for classroom instruction in self-regulated learning. In Instructional-design theories and models, volume II: A new paradigm of instructional theory. Mahwah. NJ: Lawrence Erlbaum Assoc.

Corno, L., & Rohrkemper, M. (1985). The intrinsic motivation to learn in the classroom. In C. Ames & R. Ames (Eds.), *Research on motivation in education* (Vol. 2, pp. 53–90). Academic Press.

Cunningham, G. K. (2003). *Can education schools be saved?* American Enterprise Institute.

Deimann, M. (2006). *Towards the development of a volitional design model*. http://ifbm.fernuni-hagen.de/lehrgebiete/mediendidaktik/archiv1/Deimann_Jure2006.pdf

Deimann, M., & Bastiaens, T. (2010). The role of volition in distance education: An exploration of its capacities. *International Review of Research in Open and Distributed Learning*, *11*(1), 1. doi:10.19173/irrodl.v11i1.778

Deimann, M., Weber, B., & Bastiaens, T. (2009). Entwicklung und verbreitung eines tests zur analyse der willensstärke in schule und hochschule [Development of a test of volitional competence in schools and universities]. *Unterrichtswissenschaft*, *37*(4), 362–379.

Driscoll, M. (2000). *Psychology o f learning for instruction* (2nd ed.). Allyn and Bacon.

Dur, B. (2014). *Lise öğretmenlerinin motivasyon düzeyi ve motivasyon düzeyi ile okul kültürü arasındaki ilişki* (Unpublished Master's thesis). İstanbul Aydın University Sosyal Bilimler Enstitüsü, İstanbul.

Erkuş, A. (1994). Psikoloji Terimleri Sözlüğü. Doruk Yayınları.

Ertmer, P. A., & Newby, T. J. (1993). Behaviorism, cognitivism, constructivism: Comparing critical features from an instructional design perspective. *Performance Improvement Quarterly*, *6*(4), 50–72. doi:10.1111/j.1937-8327.1993.tb00605.x

Francis, A., Goheer, A., Haver-Dieter, R., Kaplan, A. D., Kerstetter, K., Kirk, A. L., & Yeh, T. (2004). *Promoting Academic Achiement and Motivation: A Discussion & Contemporary Issues Based Approach*. University of Maryland.

Fryer, L. K., & Bovee, H. N. (2016). Supporting students' motivation for e-learning: Teachers matter on and offline. *Intenet and Higher Education*, *30*, 21–29. doi:10.1016/j.iheduc.2016.03.003

Gabrielle, D. (2003). *The effects of technology-mediated instructional strategies on motivation, performance, and self-directed learning* (Unpublished doctoral dissertation). Florida Eyalet University.

Gee, J. P. (2003). What video games have to teach us about learning and literacy. *Computers in Entertainment*, *1*(1), 20–20. doi:10.1145/950566.950595

Giesbers, B., Rienties, B., Tempelaar, D., & Gijselaers, W. (2014). A dynamic analysis of the interplay between asynchronous and synchronous communication in online learning: The impact of motivation. *Journal of Computer Assisted Learning*, *30*(1), 30–50. doi:10.1111/jcal.12020

Hartnett, M., George, A. S., & Dron, J. (2011). Examining motivation in online distance learning environments: Complex, multifaceted and situation-dependent. *The International Review of Research in Open and Distributed Learning*, *12*(6), 20–38. doi:10.19173/irrodl.v12i6.1030

Horton, W. (2006). *E-learning by design*.

Hoskins, S. L., & Hooff, J. C. (2005). Motivation and ability: Which students use online learning and what influence does it have on their achievement? *British Journal of Educational Technology*, *36*(2), 177–192. doi:10.1111/j.1467-8535.2005.00451.x

Jamsri, P. (2015). *The integrating of teaching and learning through technology in high school: learning management systems (LMS) and alternatives* (Unpublished doctoral dissertation).

Jokelova, A. (2012). *Effects of Relevance-and Confidence-enhancing motivational strategies, suggested strategies, and statements on academic performance and course satisfaction in undergraduate students of a blended public speaking course* (Unpublished doctoral dissertation). South Alabama Üniversitesi.

Jokelova, A. (2013). ARCS motivational model: Theoretical concepts and its use in online courses. *Journal of Educational Psychology, 81*(3), 329.

Kahraman, Z. (2017). *Okul yöneticileri ile öğretmenlerin örgütsel adalet algıları ve motivasyon düzeyleri arasındaki ilişki* (Unpublished Master's thesis). Marmara University, İstanbul.

Karagüven, H. Ü. (2012). Akademik motivasyon ölçeğinin Türkçeye adaptasyonu. *Kuram ve Uygulamada Eğitim Bilimleri, 12*(4), 1599–2620.

Kawachi, P. (2003). Support for Collaborative e-Learning in Asia. *The Asian Society of Open and Distance Education, 1*(1), 46–59.

Kelleher, I., & Hulleman, C. (2020). *The Science of Keeping Kids Engaged— Even From Home.* Retrieved from https://www.edutopia.org/article/science-keeping-kids-engaged-even-home?fbclid=IwAR06vzRa4sblUUYizaqJ_mP2xyjvMrS1rthJOkGokWHwL2L8RR1vVzKXvrA

Keller, J. M. (1979). Motivation and instructional design: A theoretical perspective. *Journal of Instructional Development, 2*(4), 26–34. doi:10.1007/BF02904345

Keller, J. M. (1983). *Instructional design theories and models: An overview of their current status.* Lawrence Erlbaum.

Keller, J. M. (1987). Development and use of the ARCS model of motivational design. *Journal of Instructional Development, 10*(3), 2–10. doi:10.1007/BF02905780

Keller, J. M. (2000). *How to integrate learner motivation planning into lesson planning: The ARCS model approach.* Paper presented at VII Semanario, Santiago, Cuba.

Keller, J. M. (2005). Course interest course survey – Short form. Academic Press.

Keller, J. M. (2006a). What is motivational design? Florida State University.

Keller, J. M. (2006b). *Development of two measures of learner motivation.* Yayımlanmamış bildiri.

Keller, J. M. (2008a). First principles of motivation to learn and e-learning. *Distance Education, 29*(2), 175–185. doi:10.1080/01587910802154970

Keller, J. M. (2008b). An integrative theory of motivation, volition, and performance. *Technology, Instruction, Cognition, and Learning, 6*(2), 79–104.

Keller, J. M. (2010a). *Motivational design for learning and performance: The ARCS model approach.* Springer. doi:10.1007/978-1-4419-1250-3

Keller, J. M. (2010b). Five fundamental requirements for motivation and volition. *Revista Inter Ação, 35*(2), 305–322.

Keller, J. M. (2010c). Challenges in learner motivation: A holistic, integrative model for research and design on learner motivation. In *The 11th international conference on education research new educational paradigm for learning and instruction* (pp. 1-18). Academic Press.

Keller, J. M. (2015). *Integrating motivation into ADL. Applying the ARCS-V motivation model.* http://www.fels.dk/adlforum/index.php/confirmed-speaker-2015/

Keller, J. M., & Deimann, M. (2012). Motivation, volition, and performance. In R. A. Reiser & J. V. Dempsey (Eds.), *Trends and issues in instructional design and technology.* Pearson Education.

Keller, J. M., Deimann, M., & Liu, Z. (2005). Effects of integrated motivational and volitional tactics on study habits, attitudes, and performance. *2005 AECT Konferansı,* 234.

Keller, J. M., & Suzuki, K. (2004). Learner motivation and e-learning design: A multinationally validated process. *Journal of Educational Media, 29*(3), 231–239. doi:10.1080/1358165042000283084

Knowles, E., & Kerkman, D. (2007). An investigation of students attitude and motivation toward online learning. *Student Motivation, 2,* 70–80. doi:10.46504/02200708kn

Kumarawadu, P. (2001). Motivation of online learners: review of practices and emerging trends. Sri Lanka Institute of Information Technology.

Litt, S., & Moorei, A. (2013). *Motivating the distance learning student.* http://www.slideshare.net/fscjopen/motivating-the-distance-learningstudent? qid=a58d06b8-fcce-4771-b195cdae2821a05evev=defaultveb=vefrom_search=14

Lonn, S., & Teasley, S. D. (2009). Saving time or innovating practice: Investigating perceptions and uses of Learning Management Systems. *Computers & Education, 53*(3), 686–694. doi:10.1016/j.compedu.2009.04.008

Matuga, J. M. (2009). Self-regulation, goal orientation, and academic achievement of secondary students in online university courses. *Journal of Educational Technology & Society, 12*(3), 4–11.

Naveh, G., Tubin, D., & Pliskin, N. (2012). Student satisfaction with learning management systems: A lens of critical success factors. *Technology, Pedagogy and Education, 21*(3), 337–350. doi:10.1080/1475939X.2012.720413

Oblinger, D. G., & Oblinger, J. L. (2005). *Educating the net generation.* EDUCAUSE.

Oliveira, P. C. D., Cunha, C. J. C. D. A., & Nakayama, M. K. (2016). Learning Management Systems (LMS) and e-learning management: An integrative review and research agenda. *JISTEM-Journal of Information Systems and Technology Management, 13*(2), 157–180. doi:10.4301/S1807-17752016000200001

Özbay, Y. (2004). Gelişim ve Öğrenme Psikolojisi. Öğreti Yayınları.

Pintrich, P. R. (1988). A process-oriented view of student motivation and cognition. *New Directions for Institutional Research, 57*(57), 65–79. doi:10.1002/ir.37019885707

Pintrich, P. R. (1989). The dynamic interplay of student motivation and cognition in the college classroom. *Advances in Motivation and Achievement: a Research Annual, 6*, 117–160. doi:10.2224bp.2005.33.4.341

Pintrich, P. R., Smith, D. A., Garcia, T., & McKeachie, W. J. (1993). Reliability and predictive validity of the Motivated Strategies for Learning Questionnaire (MSLQ). *Educational and Psychological Measurement, 53*(3), 801–813. doi:10.1177/0013164493053003024

Pintrich, P. R., Smith, D. A. F., Garcia, T., & McKeachie, W. J. (1991). *A Manual for the use of the motivated strategies for learning.* School of Education Building, The University of Michigan.

Pittenger, A., & Doering, A. (2010). Influence of motivational design on completion rates in online self-study pharmacy-content courses. *Distance Education, 31*(3), 275–293. doi:10.1080/01587919.2010.513953

Porter, G. W. (2013). Free choice of learning management systems: Do student habits override inherent system quality? *Interactive Technology and Smart Education, 10*(2), 84–94. doi:10.1108/ITSE-07-2012-0019

Renchler, R. (1992). Student motivation, school culture, and academic achievement. *ERIC/CEM Trends and Issues Series, 7.*

Ryan, R. M., & Deci, E. L. (2000a). Intrinsic and extrinsic motivations: Classic definitions and new directions. *Contemporary Educational Psychology, 25*(1), 54–67. doi:10.1006/ceps.1999.1020 PMID:10620381

Ryan, R. M., & Deci, E. L. (2000b). Self-determination theory and the facilitation of intrinsic motivation, social development, and well-being. *The American Psychologist, 55*(1), 68–78. doi:10.1037/0003-066X.55.1.68 PMID:11392867

Ryan, R. M., Rigby, C. S., & Przybylski, A. (2006). The motivational pull of video games: A self-determination theory approach. *Motivation and Emotion, 30*(4), 344–360. doi:10.100711031-006-9051-8

Sansone, C., Fraughton, T., Zachary, J., Butner, J., & Heiner, C. (2011). Self-regulation of motivation when learning online: The importance of who, why and how. *Educational Technology Research and Development, 59*(2), 199–212. doi:10.100711423-011-9193-6

Schunk, D. H. (1992). Theory and research on student perceptions in the classroom. In Student perceptions in the classroom (pp. 3-23). Hillsdale, NJ: Erlbaum.

Schunk, D. H. (2011). Eğitimsel bir bakışla öğrenme teorileri [Learning theories and educational perspective]. Ankara: Nobel Akademik Yayıncılık.

Semmar, Y. (2006). Distance learners and academic achievement: The roles of selfefficacy, self-regulation and motivation. *Journal of Adult and Continuing Education, 12*(2), 244–256. doi:10.7227/JACE.12.2.9

Snowman, J., McCown, R., & Biehler, R. (2012). *Psychology applied to teaching* (13th ed.). Wadesworth, Cengage Learning.

Soydan, B., Büyükeken, G., Aktaş, H. İ., Özbak, H., Büyükeskil, M., Uykür, N., . . . Özkan, S. (2012). *Başarı algısı ile akademik başarı arasındaki ilişkinin incelenmesi.* Selçuklu rehberlik ve araştırma merkezi.

Turner, J. C., & Patrick, H. (2008). How does motivation develop and why does it change? Reframing motivation research. *Educational Psychologist, 43*(3), 119–131. doi:10.1080/00461520802178441

Uzbaş, A. (2009). Okul psikolojik danışmanlarının okulda saldırganlık ve şiddete yönelik görüşlerinin değerlendirilmesi. *Mehmet Akif Ersoy Üniversitesi Eğitim Fakültesi Dergisi*, (18), 90–110.

Vallerand, R. J., & Bissonnette, R. (1992). Intrinsic, extrinsic, and amotivational styles as predictors of behavior: A prospective study. *Journal of Personality*, *60*(3), 599–620. doi:10.1111/j.1467-6494.1992.tb00922.x

Vallerand, R. J., Pelletier, L. G., Blais, M. R., Briere, N. M., Senecal, C., & Vallieres, E. F. (1993). On the assessment of intrinsic, extrinsic, and amotivation in education: Evidence on the concurrent and construct validity of the academic motivation scalet. *Educational and Psychological Measurement*, *53*(1), 159–172. doi:10.1177/0013164493053001018

Vovides, Y., Sanchez-Alonso, S., Mitropoulou, V., & Nickmans, G. (2007). The use of e-learning course management systems to support learning strategies and to improve self-regulated learning. *Educational Research Review*, *2*(1), 64–74. doi:10.1016/j.edurev.2007.02.004

Vygotsky, L. S. (1978). *Mind in society: The development of higher psychological processes*. Harvard university press.

Watson, J., Murin, A., Vashaw, L., Gemin, B., & Rapp, C. (2010). *Keeping pace with K-12 online learning: An annual review of policy and practice*. Evergreen Education Group.

West, R. E., Hannafin, M. J., Hill, J. R., & Song, L. (2013). Cognitive Perspectives On Online Learning Environments. In Handbook of Distance Education. Routledge.

Wighting, M. J., Liu, J., & Rovai, A. P. (2008). Distinguishing sense of community and motivation characteristics between online and traditional college students. *Quarterly Review of Distance Education*, *9*(3), 285–295.

Wilans, J., & Seary, K. (2011). "I feel like I'm being hit from all directions": Enduring the bombardment as a mature-age learner returning to formal learning. *Australian Journal of Adult Learning*, *51*(1), 119–142.

Zimmerman, B. J. (1989). *A social cognitive view of self-regulated academic learning*. Academic Press.

Zimmerman, B. J. (1990). Self-Regulated Learning and Academic Achievement: An Overview. *Educational Psychologist*, *25*(1), 3–17. doi:10.120715326985ep2501_2

KEY TERMS AND DEFINITIONS

Extrinsic Motivation: It involves engaging in a behavior in order to earn external rewards or avoid punishment.

Intrinsic Motivation: It refers to behavior that is driven by internal rewards.

Motivation: The motive, emotion that drives a person towards a specific purpose.

Online Learning: It is a kind of learning that allows learners to easily access rich learning resources and actively participate in learning activities without time and space limits.

Chapter 10

Assessment of 21st Century Skills:
Use of Creative Story Writing for Assessing Graphs

Garima Basnal

ⓘ https://orcid.org/0000-0002-8853-1708
Australian Council for Educational Research, India

EXECUTIVE SUMMARY

This chapter describes an action research in which creative story writing was used to assess student understanding of graph construction. Students were encouraged to write stories involving motion and visually depict verbal descriptions of stories in the form of tables and line graphs. Student work revealed several misconceptions held by students vis-à-vis writing motion-based stories, tabulation of data, plotting of graphs, and establishing congruence between stories and graphs. This study suggests several feedback measures that can be used by teachers to rectify these misconceptions.

INTRODUCTION

Students cannot learn everything that they need to know in adult life during school years. They need to be lifelong learners who can keep on acquiring new knowledge and skills for themselves as per the needs of the ever changing world. Various international and national documents have consistently been reporting that present day education system based on the 'banking concept of education' (Friere, 2006)

DOI: 10.4018/978-1-7998-8310-4.ch010

is not equipping students to face real life problems (Partnership for 21st Century Skills, 2015, GOI, 2020). Consequently, such students face numerous challenges in adapting to the changing requirements of the world. All the more, even after amassing higher qualifications, such students fail to achieve good jobs as the present day job market requires a workforce which possess 21st century skills like critical thinking, collaboration, creativity, communication (OECD, 2022).

Recently, there has been an increasing recognition that creativity and creative thinking should be fostered as one of the 21st century skill (Adams et al., 2015; Griffin et al., 2012; Kereluik, Mishra, Fahnoe, & Terry, 2013; Partnership for 21st Century Skills, 2015, GOI, 2020). In many cases, this recognition is explicitly enshrined in school curricula. For example, Scotland's Curriculum for Excellence considers creativity fundamental to the development of a successful learner (Education Scotland, 2013). Similarly, in Australia, there has been an emphasis on developing "successful learners, confident and creative individuals, and active and informed citizens" (Ministerial Council on Education, Employment, Training and Youth Affairs, 2008). On similar lines, India's National Education Policy reinstates the importance of development of creativity among students so as to encourage logical decision-making and innovation by them (GOI, 2020). It categorically mentions:

Given the 21st century requirements, quality higher education must aim to develop good, thoughtful, well-rounded, and creative individuals. It must enable an individual to study one or more specialized areas of interest at a deep level, and also develop character, ethical and Constitutional values, intellectual curiosity, scientific temper, creativity, spirit of service, and 21st century capabilities across a range of disciplines including sciences, social sciences, arts, humanities, languages, as well as professional, technical, and vocational subjects (GOI, 2020, p. 34).

Drawing from the vision of new education policy, Indian education system is moving towards development of critical, innovative thinking, problem solving among its' students, thus, emphasising the development of creative potential of each individual. Of lately, there has been a significant thrust on skill development in Indian education. A dedicated government ministry—Ministry of Skill Development and Entrepreneurship has been created to foster 21st century skills among country's youth. It is aided by its functional arms – Directorate General of Training (DGT), National Skill Development Agency (NSDA), National Council for Vocational Education and Training (NCVET), National Skill Development Corporation (NSDC), National Skill Development Fund (NSDF) and 38 Sector Skill Councils (SSCs) as well as 33 National Skill Training Institutes (NSTIs/NSTI(w)), about 15000 Industrial Training Institutes (ITIs) under DGT and 187 training partners registered with NSDC. In addition, collaborations with international organizations, industry and NGOs have been initiated for multi-level engagement and impactful implementation of skill development efforts across the country.

Programme of International Student Assessment (PISA) framework on creative thinking suggests that it is crucial to foster and assess creative thinking among students as it "can have a positive influence on students' academic interest and achievement, identity and socio-emotional development by supporting the interpretation of experiences, actions and events in novel and personally meaningful ways" (https://www.oecd.org/pisa/innovation/creative-thinking/).

Creativity has often been related to the domain of arts and music. Specifically, there has been a constant neglect of creative thinking in mathematics classrooms (Meissner, 2005). One of the reasons could be teachers' ignorance of the fact that "the essence of mathematics is to think creatively, and not simply arrive at the correct answer" (Mann, 2006, p. 238). Researchers have long been urging the mathematics teachers' community to pursue the development of mathematical creative potential of each student considering it to be an essential goal of school mathematics (Leikin, 2009). Sriraman (2004) reinforced this idea by suggesting that to promote creativity in mathematics education it is imperative that teachers learn to present it as a surprising matter engaging students in solving authentic problems embedded in real contexts that incites imagination encouraging students to engage in trial and error methods of arriving at solutions of the problems. However, research simultaneously reports that teachers find it challenging in adopting, innovating, and designing appropriate pedagogic and assessment processes fostering creativity among their students (Meissner, 2005).

Keeping Pelczer and Rodriguez's (2011) argument in view, who categorically mention that creative thinking is present in all individuals and mathematics education can promote it among all students using tasks with adjusted structure, this study uses mathematics stories as a problem-posing and problem-solving task where students have the opportunity to use multiple pathways to arrive at the solution of the problem, to foster mathematical creativity.

Problem posing in mathematics education research has been used to refer both to the generation of new problems and to the reformulation of given problems (Silver, 1997). In line with Stoyanova & Ellerton (1996) work, this study considers mathematical problem posing as the process by which students are encouraged to construct personal interpretations of real-life situations and formulate them as meaningful mathematical problems. Bonotto (2009) suggests that problem posing provides an opportunity for interpretation and critical analysis of reality as students are engaged in segregation of significant data from non-significant data; discovering the relationship between various elements of the data; and investigating if the numerical data involved in problem-solving is contextually coherent.

Situated in the context of graph instruction in middle-school mathematics classrooms, this study presents a case of a teacher who used a problem posing approach in the context of story-writing as an assessment tool to uncover student misconceptions vis-à-vis graph construction. According to National Council of Teachers of Mathematics (NCTM, 2000), middle-school children should develop competencies in modelling and solving various contextualized problems using representations, such as, graphs, tables, equations, etc.

CREATIVITY AS A 21ST CENTURY SKILL

Creativity has been variably defined across research literature. Sternberg and Lubart (1999) define creativity as the ability of an individual to produce work that is both novel and appropriate. Plucker, Beghetto, and Dow (2004) understand creative potential as "the interaction among aptitude, process and environment by which an individual or group produces a perceptible product that is both novel and useful within a social context" (p.90). Australian Council for Educational Research defines creative thinking as "the capacity to generate many different kinds of ideas, manipulate ideas in unusual ways and make unconventional connections in order to outline novel possibilities that have the potential to elegantly meet a given purpose" (Ramalingam et al., 2020, p.2). While unpacking ACER's creative thinking construct, it consists of three strands, including seven aspects in total. These strands are as follows: generation of ideas, experimentation, and quality of ideas. Generation of ideas refers to the ability of an individual to produce range of diverse ideas that can be manipulated, combined, or synthesized in novel ways to produce useful solutions to problems or leading to the development of new products. Experimentation implies an individual's capacity to be flexible and see things from a wide range of perspectives i.e. seeing information that is already known, in new ways. This is often called as thinking outside the box. Furthermore, a creative individual portrays flexibility in thinking. They manipulate the elements of a task by combining, subverting, twisting or grafting elements together in unlikely ways to open up new possibilities. It is widely established in all the research frameworks that usefulness of the end product of creativity and creative thinking determines the quality of ideas generated during the process. If ideas are novel but not useful to the context, then they may not be qualified as creative.

Amabile's (2016) description of 'componential theory of creativity' outlines creativity as a multi-dimensional product. It suggests that for any individual to produce creative work following four components are essential: domain-relevant skills, creativity-relevant processes, task motivation, and a conducive environment. The model specifies that creative production fundamentally requires some base resources or raw materials (i.e. domain-specific skills, including knowledge and technical skills), a set of processes or skills for combining these base resources in innovative ways (i.e. creativity-relevant processes entailing appropriate cognitive styles supportive of creative engagement), and a driver (i.e. task motivation) fostering individual interaction with creative processes. In addition, environmental factors play a crucial role either acting as inhibitors or facilitators to an individual's creative engagement.

Mathematical Creativity as a 21st Century Skill

Mathematical creativity is defined as the production of novel and appropriate response, product, or solution to an open-ended task (Amabile, 2016). She further suggested that a creative idea must be different from what has been done before, however, the degree of difference may vary. In few cases, the idea can be absolutely unique leading to paradigm shifts whereas in other cases an idea can only be slightly different from the previous one. However, for any idea to be called as creative it is essential that they are useful and serve the goal.

Sriraman (2004) observed that mathematical creativity is rooted in the intellectual abilities and personality traits of each individual. In order to foster mathematical creativity among students, teachers need to engineer appropriate human and material environment that fosters creative performance of all individuals. Kontorovich et al. (2011) further suggests that to nurture mathematical creativity classroom environment should promote mastery of mathematical algorithms, procedures, rapidity, and simultaneously provide appropriate avenues to make conjectures, hypothesize, refute, adapt plans, and justify the processes students use during problem solving in the classrooms. On similar lines, Silver (1997) argued that problem-solving and problem-posing tasks serve as a bedrock for students to develop more creative approaches to mathematics. These tasks enable teachers to augment their students' capacity vis-à-vis core dimensions of creativity, namely, fluency, flexibility, and originality. In order to synthesize diverse ideas on creativity in mathematics education, Joklitschke, Rott, & Schindler (2021) have undertaken a systematic literature review of empirical studies published between 2006 and 2019. They have identified five predominant notions of creativity in mathematics education: fluency, flexibility, and/or other characteristics, (2) divergent thinking, (3) sequence of stages, (4) mathematical reasoning and (5) the person-, product-, process-, and/or behaviour-based notion of creativity.

Assessment of Creative Thinking

Assessment of creativity started in 1950's with the work of psychologist J.P. Guildford. He formulated the notion of divergent thinking, i.e., the ability to generate multiple solutions to an open-ended problem as a measure of creativity (Guilford, 1950). Eventually, measurement of divergent thinking became a popular mechanism for assessing creativity in the second half of the 20th century. For example, the Torrance Tests of Creative Thinking (TTCT) (Torrance, 1966) based on assessment of divergent thinking are widely used even today. Gradually, researchers began examining broader issues, such as the relationship of creativity to human intelligence and problem solving, (e.g., Sternberg & Lubart, 1999), the role of context (e.g., Amabile, 2016), and the role of domain knowledge in creativity (e.g., Haavold, Siraman, & Lee, 2020).

Plucker and Makel (2010) have classified predominant ways of assessing creativity: Assessments of divergent thinking; Assessments of creative personality: Activity checklists of experience associated with creative production; Attitudinal scales; Assessment of creative products. Recently, from a comprehensive review of 85 instruments that are being use for measuring creativity, Henriksen, Mishra, and Mehta (2015) observed that nearly half of the available tools are designed for use with adults, thus, leaving very few that could be within schools. Australian Council for Educational Research is working towards devising a learning progression of creativity that could serve as a useful tool for assessing creativity (Ramalingam et al., 2020).

Programme of International Student Assessment mentions that while assessing student's creative thinking, the tool should examine students' capacity to "engage productively in the generation, evaluation and improvement of ideas that can result in original and effective solutions, advances in knowledge, and impactful expressions of imagination" (OECD, 2022). This is in line with the studies conducted in the domain of mathematics education (e.g., Leikin, 2009; Mann, 2006) which unequivocally suggests that the students' productions of problem posing and problem solving can serve as a powerful tool for assessment of students' mathematical creativity.

Silver (1997) elaborates that problem-solving and problem-posing involves various sub-processes, such as, formulation of the problem, attempting to solve it, reformulating of the problem, and eventually leading to a feasible solution to the problem. He suggests that both the process and the products of this activity can be evaluated to define students' demonstration of mathematical creativity. Dindyal et al. (2014) used Practical Worksheet (PW) as a cognitive scaffold for assessing students' problem solving processes. It consists of scoring rubric for assessing their progress at various stages of the problem solving and a list of prompts that can support students to self-scaffold themselves while they are engaged in solving problems.

Leikin (2009) proposed three dimensions of creativity: fluency, flexibility and originality that can be taken into account for assessing problem-solving. Fluency refers to the number of issues raised that fit the requirements of the problem; flexibility refers to the number of responses presented that illustrate different ways of thinking about the problem; and originality refers to the number of unique or rare responses produced. Thus, problem solving is a privileged context for the study of creativity in mathematics classroom.

USING STORIES IN MATHEMATICS

Mann (2006) reminds us that in order for creativity to be recognized, appreciated and shared, it is necessary that the "development of mathematical communication skills" happens (p. 251). Schiro and Lawson (2004) observed that stories transform the abstract, objective, and deductive mathematical world into a subject surrounded by imagination, subjective meaning, and feelings. They pointed out that stories could be used to teach algorithms, concepts, problem solving, connections, and communication. Many educational researchers since then have used storytelling as a pedagogical tool in mathematics classrooms, specifically, in primary classrooms. Casey and colleagues (2008) used story texts in developing preschool children's geometry skills. Goral and Gnadinger (2006) used a fantasy story to deepen the concept of place value of grade one children in the USA. They observed that children get emotionally absorbed in solving problems of the characters in the story. This way they develop lasting impressions of the mathematical concepts. Lemonidis and Kaiafa (2019) explored the role of storytelling in the teaching of fractions to the third-grade students in Florina (Greece). They identified specific mathematical skills, such as, comparing fractions, finding equivalent fractions, creating representations, and problem solving best developed through storytelling pedagogy.

Though storytelling approach has been widely used in primary classrooms its powerful influence in teaching secondary school mathematics cannot be undermined. Balakrishnan (2008) presented nine unique stories to develop abstract mathematical concepts, such as, irrational numbers, Pythagoras theorem, exponents etc. among secondary school students. She observed that storytelling served as bedrock for facilitating dynamic interactions among teacher and students. They were able to see the big ideas and generalise the concept beyond the immediate story context.

Of lately, there is spurt in mathematics education researchers using digital storytelling as a pedagogical tool (Wu & Chen, 2020). Digital storytelling refers to the art of telling stories blending digital media, including text, pictures, recorded audio narration, music, and video using computer software (Robin, 2008). Albano and Pierri (2014) presented a part of their ongoing research project "Obiettivo 500" being carried out in Italy, where they used Raymond and Ohler's Storytelling Design Model. Their mathematical story focussed on *representation* as the fundamental mathematical capability. Situated in the life of a journalist who is expected to predict election result using different forms of graphs, the story encouraged graph interpretations skills among learners.

Research in mathematics education is not only restricted to storytelling but also extends to story writing. For example, Lacefield and Markert (2019) noted that creative writing supports students' understanding of mathematical concepts by providing them freedom to reformulate and review their mathematical thinking in their own ways. Creating problem stories enable students to develop literacy and numeracy competencies, metacognitive strategies, and creativity (Saradinha, Palhares, & Azevedo, 2014). In addition, these researchers suggested that creating stories provide an engaging platform to students with enhanced opportunities to reflect on the usability of their mathematical understandings.

THE CASE STUDY: GRAPH INSTRUCTION

Research indicates that contextualizing graph instruction in classrooms helps in activating learners' prior knowledge structures and enables them to apply the newly acquired knowledge of graph interpretation and construction to solve real world problems (Glazer 2011; Friel, Curcio, & Bright, 2001). Shah and Hoeffner (2002) compared viewers' interpretation of graphs that depicted familiar data (such as, number of car accidents, number of drunk drivers and traffic density) and unfamiliar relationships (e.g., ice-cream sales, fat content, etc.). His research suggested that in familiar contexts, viewers tended to describe general trends while in unfamiliar contexts, they only observed local maxima and minima. Thereby, clearly indicating that context familiarity is supportive in the development of graph interpretation skills.

This study extends the research from graph interpretation to graph construction using creative story writing as formative assessment tool. Formative Assessment is often planned as an integral component of teaching and is orientated to support progression in learning (Black & Wiliam, 1998). Wiliam and Thompson (2007) conceptualized the following as the key strategies of formative assessment: clarifying the learning intentions and criteria of success, engineering effective classroom discussions and other learning tasks, providing constructive feedback, activating students as instructional resources for one another, and activating students as the owners of their own learning. To this end, Heritage (2010) adds that co-constructing learning criteria of the assessment task with students helps them to internalize the notion of 'quality' work. Thereby, helping them to review their work while they are developing it with reference to the assessment criteria. Formative feedback provided to students focuses on quality of students' work rather than making comparisons with other students, helps them in identifying tasks that are hard and require extra attention, provide specific guidance on how to improve (Hattie & Timperley, 2007).

This study reports an action research carried out by the author herself on using creative story writing as a formative assessment strategy to support graph instruction of middle-school students. Data reported in this study is drawn from Bansal (2017).

Task Description

This task was conducted with grade 8 students in a cosmopolitan city in India. Average class strength was 40. It required 7-8 teaching periods of an hour each.

Sessions on graphs began with an initial brainstorming on the *estimation of distance and time*. On day one, using different prompts from their daily lives I engaged students' in dialogic interactions to strengthen their estimation skills (Bansal, 2018). Questions, such as, what is the distance between your table and chalkboard, distance between your house and school, time taken to reach from home to school while walking and while travelling by a car, and so on were used to engage them in distance-time estimation exercises.

On the second day, I introduced students to different *mathematical facts*, such as, axes, indexing, coordinate drawings, etc. The concept of scale was discussed with the help of various maps (e.g., the map of the city, country, and world drawn on an A4 size sheet), thereby, providing them experiences of different scales as students at this age develop multiplicative reasoning. I provided data sets to students and encouraged them to plot graphs for the data provided to them. I also discussed different *types of graphs*, namely, line graphs, bar graphs, picture graphs with them using graph samples drawn from their familiar contexts. Towards the end of the lesson, I asked students to collect a few samples of different forms of graphs that they see around them in magazines, textbooks, newspapers etc.

Following teacher instructions, students had brought different types of graphs to the classroom. Using the samples of graphs they had brought from magazines, textbooks, newspapers etc., I initiated *graph comprehension* exercises on day three. I divided students into groups. Each group having five students were assigned one graph. They were all asked to provide verbal interpretations to the graphs. All the student groups worked on their graphs for the entire class time. In the next class on day four, all the groups were requested to display their graphs and associated verbal interpretations. Students' description revealed their current levels of understanding, commonly held misconceptions, and their different problem solving strategies. I summarised their difficulties and addressed them in a whole-class discussion.

Friel, Curcio and Bright (2001) noted that along with developing graph comprehension among middle-school students, it is vital to make them "inventers of displays that convey their own messages about the meanings of the data they are using" (p. 150). Therefore, after conducting graph comprehension exercise on day four, I initiated *formative assessment* task with students on day five. Students were divided in groups. Each group had 4-5 students. This task–Graphing my story—was aimed at contextualizing graph instruction. It involved writing a story involving motion. Following story writing, the next step was to tabulate the mathematical data involved in the story and plot it in a distance-time line graph.

Heritage (2010) observed that clarity of assessment criteria encourages learners to keep a focus on learning, monitor their progress in relation to goals and develops a greater sense of intrinsic motivation. Assessment criteria for the task were co-constructed along with the students. It entailed:

Writing a story involving motions of two characters that could be plotted on a graph
Communication of the mathematical data related to motion of two characters in the story in a tabular format
Plotting of distance-time graph demonstrating visually motion of characters described in the story
Graph drawn should have an appropriate scale chosen corresponding to the data sets, names of the physical quantities represented by the axes along with units should be mentioned, co-ordinates should be marked accurately, index to distinguish between the motions of two different characters should be provided
Data plotted in the graph, table and the story should be in congruence

Students worked on this task for the entire class time. All the student groups presented their responses in the next class. Their responses elicited several misconceptions held by them. It is discussed in detail in the next section.

Misconceptions Revealed in Student Work

Interpreting assessment evidence in light of learning goals is an essential step of an effective formative assessment (Bansal, 2020). It enables the teacher to identify 'just the right gap' between students' existing levels of understanding and desired educational goals (Heritage, 2010). When a teacher fails to identify the learning gaps during interpretation of assessment evidence, evidence gathered from assessment tasks becomes dangling data, which cannot be used to further student learning.

Interpretation of student responses yielded several misconceptions held by the students. This section describes student-held misconceptions in the following categories: Writing the story, Tabulation of data, Plotting of distance-time graphs, and Establishing congruence between verbal and visual description.

Writing the Story

Students wrote a variety of stories. It ranged from folk stories describing a race between a rabbit and a tortoise, a thirsty crow, to their journey from their homes to school in bus, metro, cars, or science fiction etc. Learning goals of the task that were co-constructed along with the learners clearly articulated that student stories should involve motion of characters which could be described visually in the form of graph.

Students' work samples revealed that some of the students failed to pay attention to motion aspect of the story. They wrote imaginative stories without any reference to the mathematical data, thus making it impossible to be described by visual representations in graphs. In other cases, students' mathematical data pointed towards unrealistic data, further pointing towards misconceptions associated with estimation of distance and time. Some stories included only partial mathematical data i.e. either distance or time, thus rendering it insufficient for plotting distance-time graphs. Some samples of student work and the misconceptions revealed in their work in included in Table 1.

Table 1. Misconceptions in story writing

Tasks	Common misconceptions with illustrations
Story writing	Misconception: Partial mathematical data either of distance or time *Student work sample* I went to the market on my motorbike. For first half an hour, I drove at the speed of 100 km/h. It was a sunny winter afternoon, I was really enjoying my drive. Suddenly, I encountered a traffic jam on the road. I got off my bike to find out the possible reasons for the jam. When I asked people who were standing over there, I found a truck had hot a bike rider. There was police and ambulance. Bike rider was hit badly and was taken to the hospital. People were murmuring that bike riders drive recklessly causing such accidents. I realized that driving at 100km/h is not a good idea for me as well. Therefore, I drove at 25 km/h in the remaining part of my journey. *Specific misconceptions revealed in the work sample:* Data for speed is mentioned. Whereas to plot distance-time graph, data of distance and time is required.

Tabulating the Data

Zevenbergen, Shelley, and Wright (2004) observed that while plotting distance-time graphs it is important to tabulate distance and time as continuous variables. Analysis of student responses revealed that a few students represented physical quantities of time and distance as cardinal quantities, thus, presenting distance and time as discrete variables. Other errors entailed discrepancies between units of distance and time mentioned in the story and in the table, between the data described in the story and included in the table. A few students did not mention either the titles or units of the physical quantities being represented by the columns in the table. In other cases, few students did not represent the names of the characters whose data was being included in the table. While some of them communicated the data of only one of the characters in the table while they had included motion of two characters numerically in the story. Some samples of student work and the misconceptions revealed in their work in included in Table 2.

Table 2. Misconceptions in tabulating the data included in the story

Tasks	Common misconceptions with illustrations
Table	Misconceptions: Representation of distance or time as discrete variables

Student work sample

S.No	Distance (in km)	Time (in hour)
1	3	1
2	3	0.5
3	5	1
4	8	1.5
5	10	1.5
6	10	0.5

Specific misconceptions revealed in the work sample:
Time is represented as a cardinal quantity. A character can't go backward in time as is represented by decreasing value of time for the two positions at 3 km (represented by S.No. 1 and 2) or between distances 12km and 13km (represented by S.No. 7 and 8).

Plotting Graphs

Students' graphical representations revealed several procedural errors. It included student distance-time graphs without any mention of the titles of the axes, units of

Table 3. Misconceptions in plotting distance-time graphs

Tasks	Common misconceptions with illustrations
Plotting graphs	General misconceptions in students work Choice of appropriate scale with respect to the data set Problems in plotting of coordinates Choosing two different origin for representing distance and time Axes not labelled Index not provided Units of the two physical quantitates were missing *Student work sample (figure 1)* *Specific misconceptions revealed in the work sample:* Students did not mention titles of the axes, thus, no meaningful inference can be drawn out of the graph. Student had represented initial points of the axes differently. There are two "0s" of the two axes in the plot.

the quantities being measured. Some student graphs had two different origins for two quantities being represented the two axes. In a few cases, students forgot (were unaware of) to mention the index which is imperative to decipher whose motion is being represented by a particular plot line. Some samples of student work and the misconceptions revealed in their work in included in Table 3.

Correspondence between Verbal and Visual Descriptions

Student work samples revealed that there existed incongruity between verbal descriptions in the story, and its visual depiction in terms of table and graphs. This dissonance arose either due to use of different datasets as included in the stories and represented by tabular and graphical representations; or a mismatch between the units of physical quantities being described. Other errors included problems in choice of appropriate scale unit corresponding to their data sets, difficulties in plotting correct coordinates in graphs. Some students plotted hypothetical data which was not mentioned in stories. Table 4 presents commonly held student misconceptions that emerged from student work.

Lesson Wrap-up and Feedback

Feedback is an essential step to complete formative assessment loop. After interpretation of student misconceptions, I used several activities to develop the required mathematical understanding necessary to accomplish this task successfully. These misconceptions were discussed in the class and the student groups were encouraged to self-assess their work in light of the following prompt questions as provided in Table 5.

Figure 1. Student created distance-time graph

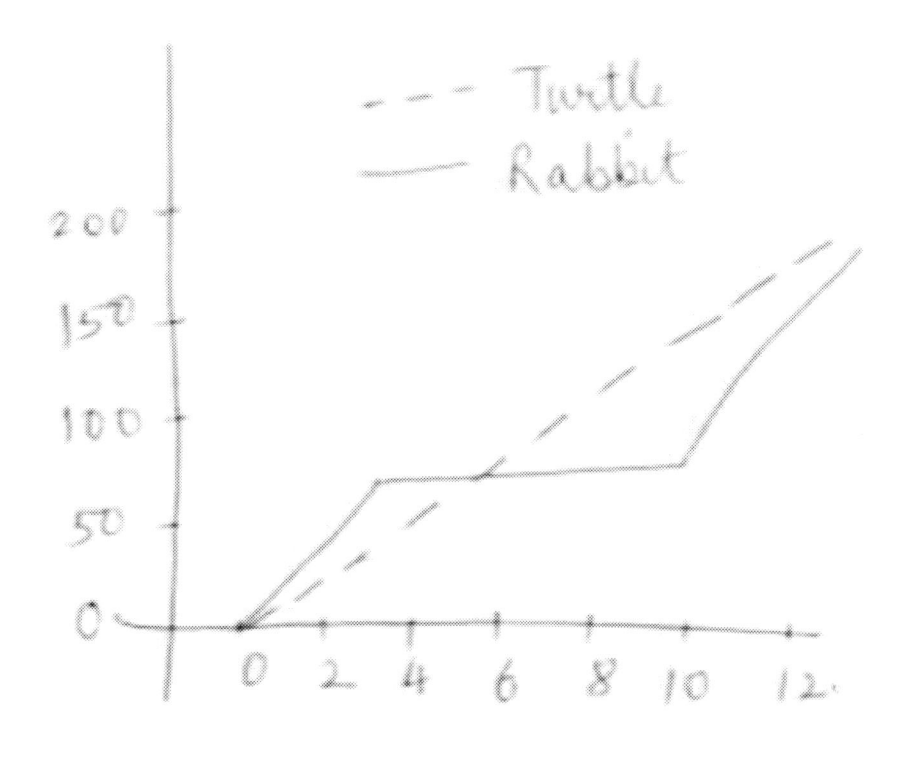

CONCLUSION

PISA framework on mathematical literacy observes that use of mathematics to solve problems set in real-world situations are influential in the development of various 21st century skills among students, such as, critical thinking, communication, creativity and problem-solving (OECD, 2022). When faced with real-world challenges, students are get an opportunity to apply their mathematical ideas, choose appropriate mathematical strategies and representations to arrive at creative solutions to problems. Research has also noted that creative writing in the mathematics classroom promotes transfer of mathematical ideas in the real world and encourages student engagement (Saradina et al., 2014).

Table 4. Misconceptions in establishing correspondence between story, tabular data, and graphical representations

Tasks	Common misconceptions with illustrations
Establishing correspondence between story, table, and graphs	General misconceptions in students work Data included in stories was different from data included in graphs Mismatch between the units of physical quantitates as included in stories and plotted in graphs Hypothetical data was plotted which was not included in the story *Student work sample* Once there was a girl named Sunidhi. She was very much interested in going for trekking to the mountains. So, her father planned a visit to their village in the summer vacations. Sunidhi was very excited to reach her hometown. When she reached her village, she asked her father to go for a walk with her. She wanted to see the beautiful flora and fauna over there. Next morning, both of them started their journey at 7 am. Initially, Sunidhi was very excited and walked very rapidly. On her way, she was very amazed to see many new birds, tall trees and variety of other animals and reptiles. By 8 am, they had covered 3 km distance but soon, Sunidhi got tired and asked her father to sit for a minute. Sunidhi's father knew that the next village was just a few meters ahead so, he carried her in his arms and reached the next village. There Sunidhi rested for half an hour and then, stood up to continue her journey. Then, they again walked for 2 kms in 1 hour. They reached a shop where Sunidhi bought two bottles of cold drinks and some snacks. From there, they covered 3 kms in 1.5 hours but again Sunidhi got tired. But since there was no village nearby, she was forced to walk for 2 km more which she covered in 1.5 hours. Meanwhile, she ate the snacks and drank one bottle of soft drink. Then Sunidhi and her father reached another village where again, she rested for half an hour. Seeing Sunidhi so tired, her father decided to go back to their village which was now only 3 km away from that place. As soon as he informed Sunidhi about his plan, she got happy and energetic. On her way back to their village, initially, she walked comparatively slowly. She could cover first 2 km in 1.5 hours but as soon as her father told her that only 1 km was left, she increased her walking speed and covered rest of the distance in only 30 minutes. On reaching her village, Sunidhi was very tired as well as happy. Her wish was fulfilled. She quickly told her mother about her experience and then, went to sleep. *Specific error revealed in the work sample* Student perceived time as a cardinal quantity as could be observed from the table. In the graph, student plotted time as a continuous variable. This shows dissonance between verbal description, tabulated data and the graphical representation.

This study used creative story writing for assessing student understanding of graphs. A scaffolding approach was adopted in which the need for various components of a graph emerged from a real-world problem context. The task encouraged students to write creative stories involving motion, and plot their verbal description visually in the forms of distance-time graphs. So to say, the task explicitly emphasized the connections between visual features demonstrated in graph and their meaning encoded in the verbal description. Like Dindyal et al. (2014), this study underscores the importance of assessing the process as well as product of problem-solving. In

Figure 2. Student created tabular description and graph

S.No	Distance (in km)	Time (in hour)
1	3	1
2	3	0.5
3	5	1
4	8	1.5
5	10	1.5
6	10	0.5
7	12	1.5
8	13	0.5

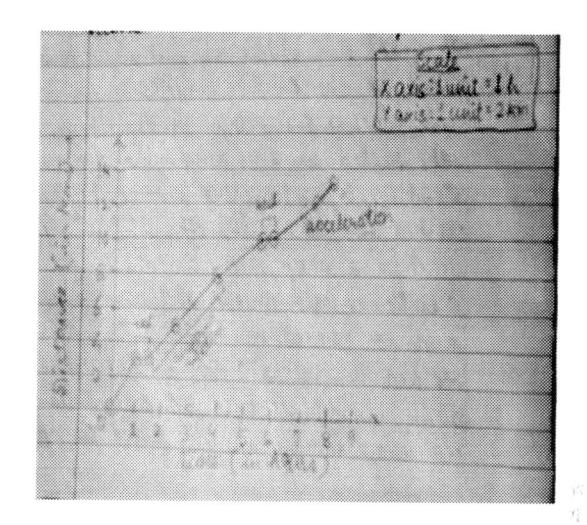

order to assess the process, assessment criteria of the task was co-constructed with the students. They were encouraged to self-assess their work in correspondence with the assessment criteria. Due to specific focus on the problem-solving process, several student-held misconceptions emerged during the execution of the task. This chapter provides an exhaustive list of students' misconceptions regarding graphs which are presented under the following categories: writing stories in line with the problem requirements, tabulating data involved in stories, plotting distance-time graphs, and establishing correspondence between stories, tables, and graphs.

Student-held misconceptions clearly demonstrate different ways in which students' process mathematical concepts. Therefore, this study suggests that teachers need to focus on the learning pathways adopted by students to plan differentiated instruction suitable to their respective teaching contexts. Furthermore, while assessing mathematical problem-solving, teachers should carefully consider intermediate strategies and specific steps undertaken by the students to arrive at the final products. The misconceptions elicited during the process can serve as a crucial resource for providing desired instructional correctives to students. This study also provides specific feedback measures for each of the student misconception elicited during the problem-solving process. Thereby, supporting the implementation of problem-solving tasks by teacher in their respective classrooms.

Table 5. Feedback activities

Tasks	Teacher prompts used for encouraging student self-assessment of their work
Story writing	What kind of mathematical data do you require for plotting a distance-time graph? Does your story include that data? How is distance being travelled by the key characters in your story changing with time? What data do you think is required for plotting your actor's motion graphically in a distance-time plot? Revisit your story to identify whether you have included that data mathematically in your story, What is the total distance covered by the character in your story? Is it realistic? Why or why not? What is the time taken by the character in your story for the total journey? Is it realistic? Why or why not?"
Tabulating the data	Can you suggest which character's motion is being described by your table? Would you like to check whether the data represented in your tabular description in included in your story and vice-versa? Would you like to check the correspondence of units in tabular data and in story? How would you explain decrease in time when the distance travelled by the character is increasing? Is it possible for somebody to go back in time? Think and elaborate.
Plotting the graphs	Whose motion is being represented by the line plot? What are the names of the physical quantities being represented by the two axes in the graph? What are the units of physical quantities in which the motion in graph was being described? What is the scale of graph? Is the scale chosen suitable for the mathematical data in your story? Why or why not? How can the viewer distinguish between the two line plots? Where is the origin of the axes? In your opinion, should both the axes have same or different origins? Why or why not? What does an origin represent?
Correspondence between verbal and visual description	Can you name the ordered pairs being represented by specific points in your graph? Can you locate these coordinates in your story and table? Can you provide information from the graph about how far a particular character has travelled in the story? Can you provide information about the time taken by a particular character in your story during different sections of his journey from your graph? These questions encouraged movement from visual to verbal description and vice-versa, thus, focusing specifically on connections between all the three aspects. In cases where students found it difficult to plot points from the table on graphs, or identify coordinates on graph, and/or choose scale, etc., teacher may choose to scaffold by focusing on mathematical requirements for plotting of graphs.

REFERENCES

Albano, G., & Pierri, A. (2014). Digital storytelling for improving mathematical literacy. In *Proceedings of Problem@Web International Conference* (pp. 23-34). Academic Press.

Balakrishnan, C. (2008). *Teaching secondary school mathematics through storytelling* (Unpublished thesis). Simon Fraser University.

Bansal, G. (2017). Teaching graphs: Using stories for uncovering students' misconceptions. *Mathematics in School*, 3-10. www.m-a.org.uk

Bansal, G. (2018). Teacher discursive moves: Conceptualising a schema of dialogic discourse in science classrooms. *International Journal of Science Education, 40*(15), 1891–1912. doi:10.1080/09500693.2018.1514543

Bansal, G. (2020). Understanding gaps in teacher interpretation of formative assessment evidence. *The School Science Review, 101*(377), 67–72.

Black, P., & Wiliam, D. (1998). Assessment and classroom learning. *Assessment in Education: Principles, Policy & Practice, 5*(1), 7–74. doi:10.1080/0969595980050102

Casey, B., Erkut, S., Ceder, I., & Young, J. M. (2008). Use of a storytelling context to improve girls' and boys' geometry skills in kindergarten. *Journal of Applied Developmental Psychology, 29*(1), 29–48. doi:10.1016/j.appdev.2007.10.005

Curcio, F. R. (1989). *Developing Graph Comprehension. Elementary and Middle School Activities.* National Council of Teachers of Mathematics.

Friel, S. N., Curcio, F. R., & Bright, G. W. (2001). Making Sense of Graphs: Critical Factors Influencing Comprehension and Instructional Implications. *Journal for Research in Mathematics Education, 32*(2), 124–158. doi:10.2307/749671

Glazer, N. (2011). Challenges with Graph Interpretation: A Review of the Literature. *Studies in Science Education, 47*(2), 183–210. doi:10.1080/03057267.2011.605307

Goral, M. B., & Gnadinger, C. M. (2006). Using storytelling to teach mathematical concepts. *Australian Primary Mathematics Classroom, 11*(1), 4–8.

Heritage, M. (2010). *Formative Assessment: Making It Happen in the Classroom.* Corwin.

Lacefield, W., & Markert, L. (2019). Creative Writing in the Mathematics Classroom. *Proceedings of the Annual Meeting of the Georgia Association of Mathematics Teacher Educators, 13*(1). 10.20429/gamte.2019.130106

Leikin, R. (2009). Exploring mathematical creativity using multiple solution tasks. In R. Leikin, A. Berman, & B. Koichu (Eds.), *Creativity in mathematics and the education of gifted students* (pp. 129–145). Sense Publishers. doi:10.1163/9789087909352_010

Lemonidis, C., & Kaiafa, I. (2019). The Effect of Using Storytelling Strategy on Students' Performance in Fractions. *Journal of Education and Learning, 8*(2), 165–175. doi:10.5539/jel.v8n2p165

Mathematics Assessment Resource Service (MARS), University of Nottingham and UC Berkeley. (2015). *Mathematics Assessment Project CLASSROOM CHALLENGES: A Formative Assessment Lesson.* Retrieved from http://map.mathshell.org/download. php?fileid=1680

National Council of Teachers of Mathematics (NCTM). (2000). *Principles and Standards for School Mathematics.* NCTM.

OECD. (2022). *PISA 2015 Draft Mathematics Framework.* OECD. Retrieved from https://pisa2022-maths.oecd.org/

Robin, B. R. (2008). Digital storytelling: A powerful technology tool for the 21st century classroom. *Theory into Practice, 47*(3), 220–228. doi:10.1080/00405840802153916

Robin, B. R. (2008). Digital storytelling: A powerful technology tool for the 21st century classroom. *Theory into Practice, 47*(3), 220–228. doi:10.1080/00405840802153916

Sadler, D. (1989). Formative Assessment and the design of instructional systems. *Instructional Science, 18*(2), 119–144. doi:10.1007/BF00117714

Schiro, M., & Lawson, D. (2004). *Oral storytelling and teaching mathematics: Pedagogical and multicultural perspectives.* Sage Publications.

Schiro, M. S., & Lawson, D. (2004). *Oral Storytelling and Teaching Mathematics: Pedagogical and Multicultural Perspectives.* SAGE Publications.

Shah, P., & Carpenter, P. A. (1995). Conceptual Limitations in Comprehending Line Graphs. *Journal of Experimental Psychology, 124*(1), 43–61. doi:10.1037/0096-3445.124.1.43

Shah, P., & Hoeffner, J. (2002). Review of Graph Comprehension Research: Implications for Practice. *Educational Psychology Review, 14*(1), 47–69. doi:10.1023/A:1013180410169

Wiliam, D., & Thompson, M. (2007). Integrating assessment with instruction: what will it take to make it work? In C. A. Dwyer (Ed.), *The Future of Assessment: Shaping Teaching and Learning* (pp. 53–82). Lawrence Erlbaum Associates.

Wu, J., & Chen, D. T. V. (2020). A systematic review of educational digital storytelling. *Computers & Education, 147*, 1–32. doi:10.1016/j.compedu.2019.103786

Zevenbergen, R., Dole, S., & Wright, R. J. (2004). *Teaching Mathematics in Primary Schools.* Allen & Unwin.

ENDNOTE

[1]   Idea for this formative assessment task emerged from the work of Mathematics Assessment Resource Service (MARS, 2015), a group of school teachers and academics, who have devised formative assessment tasks on graph interpretation.

Compilation of References

Abbagnano, N., & Visalberghi, A. (2019). History of pedagogy. Economic Culture Fund (FCE).

Aboagye, E., Yawson, J. A., & Appiah, K. N. (2020). COVID-19 and e-learning: The challenges of students in tertiary institutions. *Social Education Research*, *2*(1), 1–8. doi:10.37256er.122020422

ACAPT. (2020). *Classroom and Lab Considerations and Resources*. Version Two.

Acar, S. (2009). *Web tabanlı performans tabanlı öğrenmede ARCS motivasyon stratejilerinin öğrencilerin akademik başarılarına, öğrenmenin kalıcılığına, motivasyonlarına ve tutumlarına etkisi* (Unpublished doctoral dissertation). Gazi University.

Akbaba, S. (2006). Eğitimde motivasyon. *Kazım Karabekir Üniversitesi Eğitim Fakültesi Dergisi*, (13), 343–361.

Akour, A., Al-Tammemi, A. B., Barakat, M., Kanj, R., Fakhouri, H. N., Malkawi, A., & Musleh, G. (2020). The Impact of the COVID-19 Pandemic and Emergency Distance Teaching on the Psychological Status of University Teachers: A Cross-Sectional Study in Jordan. *The American Journal of Tropical Medicine and Hygiene*, *103*(6), 2391–2399. doi:10.4269/ajtmh.20-0877

Akulwar-Tajane, I., Parmar, K., Naik, P., & Shah, A. (2020). Rethinking Screen Time during COVID-19: Impact on Psychological Well-Being in Physiotherapy Students. *Int J Clin Exp Med Res*, *4*(4), 201–216.

Al Qasim, N., & Al Fadda, H. (2013). From CALL to MALL: The effectiveness of podcast on EFL higher education students' listening comprehension. *English Language Teaching*, *6*(9). Advance online publication. doi:10.5539/elt.v6n9p30

Albano, G., & Pierri, A. (2014). Digital storytelling for improving mathematical literacy. In *Proceedings of Problem@Web International Conference* (pp. 23-34). Academic Press.

Alberta 2030: Building skills for jobs strategy summary. (2021). *Government of Alberta*. https://open.alberta.ca/publications/alberta-2030-building-skills-for-jobs-strategy-summary

Aldhahi, M. I., Alqahtani, A. S., Baattaiah, B. A., & Al-Mohammed, H. I. (2021). Exploring the relationship between students' learning satisfaction and self-efficacy during the emergency transition to remote learning amid the coronavirus pandemic: A cross-sectional study. *Educ Inf Technol (Dordr)*, 1-18. http://www.ncbi.nlm.nih.gov/pubmed/34276239

Allen, S. (2016). Applying Adult Learning Principles to Online Course Design. *Dist Learn*, *13*(3), 25–32.

Altbach, P. G., Reisberg, L., & Rumbley, L. E. (2009). *Trends in global higher education: Tracking an academic revolution: A report prepared for the UNESCO 2009 World Conference on Higher Education.* Retrieved from https://unesdoc.unesco.org/images/0018/001832/183219e.pdf

American Physical Therapy Association. (2021). https://www.apta.org/

Andersen, A. K. (2020). Educating free citizens for the 21st century. *IUL Research*, *1*(1), 8–23.

Arnove, R. F. (2005). To what ends: Educational reform around the world. *Indiana Journal of Global Legal Studies*, *12*(1), 79–95. doi:10.2979/gls.2005.12.1.79

Arocena, R., & Sutz, J. (2001). *The Latin-American university of the future.* UDUAL.

Arvidsson, T. S., & Kuhn, D. (2021). Realizing the full potential of individualizing learning. *Contemporary Educational Psychology, 65*, 101960. Advance online publication. doi:10.1016/j.cedpsych.2021.101960

Asmoro, S. P., Suciati, S., & Prayitno, B. A. (2021). Empowering scientific thinking skills of students with different scientific activity types through guided inquiry. *International Journal of Instruction, 14*(1), 947–962. doi:10.29333/iji.2021.14156a

Ayhan, A. (2000). *Gelişim ve Öğrenme Psikolojisi.* Alfa Yayınları.

Bacanlı, H. (2003). *Gelişim ve öğrenme.* Nobel Yayın Dağıtım.

Baden, D., & Parkes, C. (2013). Experiential learning: Inspiring the business leaders of tomorrow. *Journal of Management Development, 32*(3), 295–308. doi:10.1108/02621711311318283

Bağrıacık, A. (2015). *Çevrimiçi öğrenme ortamlarında ders alan öğrencilerin etkileşim algıları ile doyun düzeyleri arasındaki ilişki* (Unpublished Master's thesis). Gazi University, Eğitim Bilimleri Enstitüsü, Ankara.

Balakrishnan, C. (2008). *Teaching secondary school mathematics through storytelling* (Unpublished thesis). Simon Fraser University.

Bamanger, E. M., & Alhassan, R. (2015). Exploring Podcasting in English as a Foreign Language Learners' Writing Performance. *Journal of Education and Practice.*

Bandura, A. (1977). *Social learning theory.* Prentice-Hall.

Bang, M., & Vossoughi, S. (2016). *Participatory design research and educational justice: Studying learning and relations within social change making.* Academic Press.

Bansal, G. (2017). Teaching graphs: Using stories for uncovering students' misconceptions. *Mathematics in School*, 3-10. www.m-a.org.uk

Bansal, G. (2018). Teacher discursive moves: Conceptualising a schema of dialogic discourse in science classrooms. *International Journal of Science Education, 40*(15), 1891–1912. doi:10.1080/09500693.2018.1514543

Bansal, G. (2020). Understanding gaps in teacher interpretation of formative assessment evidence. *The School Science Review, 101*(377), 67–72.

Barak, M., Watted, A., & Haick, H. (2016). Motivation to learn in massive open online courses: Examining aspects of language and social engagement. *Computers & Education, 94*, 49–60. doi:10.1016/j.compedu.2015.11.010

Barber, M., Donnelly, K., Rizvi, S., & Summers, L. (2013). *An avalanche is coming: Higher education and the revolution ahead.* The Institute of Public Policy Research.

Barsotti, S. (2020). The Transformation of Higher Education After the COVID Disruption: Emerging Challenges in an Online Learning Scenario. *Carnegie Mellon University News.* www.cmu.edu/news/stories/archives/2020/september/higher-education-covid-disruption.html

Başaran, İ. E. (2000). *Örgütsel Davranış.* Feryal Matbaası.

Bentz, V. M., & Shapiro, J. J. (1998). *Mindful inquiry in social research.* Sage.

Beristáin, H. (2010). *Rhetoric and Poetic dictionary.* Editorial Porrúa.

Berk, A., Berg, M.S., Mortimer, M.S., Walton, B., & Yeo, P. (2005). Measuring the Effectiveness of Faculty Mentoring Relationships. *Academic Medicine, 80*(1), 66-71.

Berking, P., & Gallagher, S. (2011). Choosing a learning management system. *Choosing a Learning Management System, Advanced Distributed Learning (ADL) Co-Laboratories*, 40-62. https://qrisnetwork.org/sites/default/files/conference-session/resources/210ChoosingAnLMS.PDF

Black, P., & Wiliam, D. (1998). Assessment and classroom learning. *Assessment in Education: Principles, Policy & Practice, 5*(1), 7–74. doi:10.1080/0969595980050102

Blackwell, J. E. (1989). Mentoring: An action strategy for increasing minority faculty. *Academe, 75*(5), 8–14. doi:10.2307/40249734

Blaschke, L. M., & Hase, S. (2016). Heutagogy: A holistic framework for creating twenty-first-century self-determined learners. In The future of ubiquitous learning: Learning designs for emerging pedagogies (pp.25-40). Springer. doi:10.1007/978-3-662-47724-3_2

Blaxter, L., Hughes, C., & Tight, M. (2010). Managing your project. In *How to research* (4th ed., pp. 134–154). Open University Press.

Bonk, C. J. (2002). *Online teaching in an online world.* http://publicationshare.com/docs/corp_survey.pdf

Bonk, C. J., & Khoo, E. (2014). *Adding some TEC-VARIETY: 100+ activities for motivating and retaining learners online.* Open World Books.

Bosak, M. M. (2019). China's Senkaku Islands ambition. *The Japan Times*. Retrieved from: https://www.japantimes.co.jp/opinion/2019/06/12/commentary/japan-commentary/chinas-senkaku-islands-ambition/#.XaoXlegzY2w

Botelho, N. (2021). Reflection in motion: An embodied approach to reflection on practice. *Reflective Practice*, 22(2), 147–158. doi:10.1080/14623943.2020.1860926

Bowen, J. (2018). *A History of Western Education: The Ancient World: Orient and Mediterranean 2000 BC–AD 1054*. Routledge. doi:10.4324/9781315016221

Braun, V., & Clarke, V. (2006). Using thematic analysis in psychology. *Qualitative Research in Psychology*, 3(2), 77–101. doi:10.1191/1478088706qp063oa

Brockbank, A., & McGill, I. (2007). *Aprendizaje reflexivo en la educación superior*. Morata.

Burgos, D., Tlili, A., & Tabacco, A. (2020). Education in a crisis context: Summary, insights and future. In Radical solutions for education in a crisis context: COVID-19 as an opportunity for global learning (pp. 3-9). Springer.

Business Higher Education Roundtable (BHER). (2016). *Taking the Pulse of Work-integrated Learning in Canada*. https://bher.ca/wp-content/uploads/2016/10/BHER-Academica-report-full.pdf

Büyüköztürk, Ş., Akgün, Ö. E., Kahveci, Ö., & Demirel, F. (2004). Güdülenme ve öğrenme stratejileri ölçeğinin Türkçe formunun geçerlik ve güvenirlik çalışması. *Kuram ve Uygulamada Eğitim Bilimleri*, 4(2), 207–239.

Byram, M., & Wagner, M. (2018). Language Teaching for Intercultural and International Dialogue. *Foreign Language Annals*, 51(1), 140–151. doi:10.1111/flan.12319

Cabrera, J. (2016). *Factors of Failure in National Education Systems Reforms*. https://www.academia.edu/27118771/Factors_of_Failure_in_National_Education_Systems_Reforms_2nd_Draft_

Carliner, S. (2004). An overview of online learning. Armherst, MA: Human Resource Development Press

Cartwright, L. (2020). Using thematic analysis in social work research. *Sage (Atlanta, Ga.)*.

Casey, B., Erkut, S., Ceder, I., & Young, J. M. (2008). Use of a storytelling context to improve girls' and boys' geometry skills in kindergarten. *Journal of Applied Developmental Psychology*, 29(1), 29–48. doi:10.1016/j.appdev.2007.10.005

Chan, S. (2010). Applications of Andragogy in Multi-Disciplined Teaching and Learning. *Journal of Adult Education*, 39(2), 25–35.

Chartered Society of Physiotherapy. (2020). *COVID-19 Guidance for Higher Education Institutions (Updated Oct 2020)*. https://www.csp.org.uk/system/files/documents/2020-10/COVID_19%20Guidance%20Oct%202020_0.pdf

Chartered Society of Physiotherapy. (2021). *Digital Physiotherapy.* https://www.csp.org.uk/professional-clinical/digital-physio

Chen, J. H., Li, Y., Wu, A. M. S., & Tong, K. K. (2020). The overlooked minority: Mental health of International students worldwide under the COVID-19 pandemic and beyond. *Asian Journal of Psychiatry, 54*, 102333. http://www.ncbi.nlm.nih.gov/pubmed/32795955

Choy, S. Ch., Dinham, J., Yim, J., & Williams, P. (2020). Comparing reflective practices of pre-service teachers in Malaysia and Australia: A mixed-methods approach. *Issues in Educational Research, 30*(4), 1264–1285.

Chun, D. M. (2011). Developing Intercultural Communicative Competence through Online Exchanges. *CALICO Journal, 28*(2), 392–419. doi:10.11139/cj.28.2.392-419

Chun, D., Kern, R., & Smith, B. (2016). Technology in Language Use, Language Teaching, and Language Learning. *Modern Language Journal, 100*(S1), 64–80. doi:10.1111/modl.12302

Cicha, K., Rizun, M., Rutecka, P., & Strzelecki, A. (2021). COVID-19 and Higher Education: First-Year Students' Expectations toward Distance Learning. *Sustainability, 13*(4), 1–19. doi:10.3390u13041889

Cleland, J., Tan, E. C. P., Tham, K. Y., & Low-Beer, N. (2020). How Covid-19 opened up questions of sociomateriality in healthcare education. *Advances in Health Sciences Education: Theory and Practice, 25*(2), 479–482. http://www.ncbi.nlm.nih.gov/pubmed/32378152

Copely, J. (2007). Audio and Video Podcasts of Lectures for Campus-based students: Production and Evaluation of Student Use. *Innovations in Education and Teaching International, 44*(4), 387–399. doi:10.1080/14703290701602805

Copi, I. M., & Cohen, C. (2011). *Introduction to logic.* LIMUSA.

Corno, L., & Randi, J. (1999). A design theory for classroom instruction in self-regulated learning. In Instructional-design theories and models, volume II: A new paradigm of instructional theory. Mahwah. NJ: Lawrence Erlbaum Assoc.

Corno, L., & Kanfer, R. (1993). The role of volition in learning and performance. *Review of Research in Education, 19*, 301–341. doi:10.2307/1167345

Corno, L., & Rohrkemper, M. (1985). The intrinsic motivation to learn in the classroom. In C. Ames & R. Ames (Eds.), *Research on motivation in education* (Vol. 2, pp. 53–90). Academic Press.

Crawford, J., Butler-Henderson, K., Rudolph, J., Malkawi, B., Glowatz, M., Burton, R., Magni, P., & Lam, S. (2020). COVID-19: 20 Countries' Higher Education Intra-Period Digital Pedagogy Responses. *J of Appl Learn and Teach, 3*(1), 9–28. https://doi.org/https://doi.org/10.37074/jalt.2020.3.1.7

Creswell, J. W. (2007). *Qualitative inquiry and research design: Choosing among five approaches* (2nd ed.). Sage.

Creswell, J. W. (2007). *Qualitative inquiry and research design: Choosing among five traditions* (2nd ed.). Sage.

Creswell, J. W. (2014). *Research design: Qualitative, quantitative and mixed methods approaches* (4th ed.). Sage.

Crotty, M. (1998). *The foundations of social research: Meaning and perspective in the research process.* Sage.

Cummings, W. K. (2010). How Educational Systems Form and Reform. In J. Zajda & M.A. Geo-JaJa (Eds.), The politics of education reforms (pp. 19-39). Springer. doi:10.1007/978-90-481-3218-8_2

Cunningham, G. K. (2003). *Can education schools be saved?* American Enterprise Institute.

Curcio, F. R. (1989). *Developing Graph Comprehension. Elementary and Middle School Activities.* National Council of Teachers of Mathematics.

Danowitz, M. A., & Tuitt, F. (2011). Enacting inclusivity through engaged pedagogy: A higher education perspective. *Equity & Excellence in Education, 44*(1), 40–56. Advance online publication. doi:10.1080/10665684.2011.539474

de la Fuente, J., Pachon-Basallo, M., Santos, F. H., Peralta-Sanchez, F. J., Gonzalez-Torres, M. C., Artuch-Garde, R., Paoloni, P. V., & Gaetha, M. L. (2021). How Has the COVID-19 Crisis Affected the Academic Stress of University Students? The Role of Teachers and Students. *Frontiers in Psychology, 12*, 626340. doi:10.3389/fpsyg.2021.626340

De Wit, H. (2011). Globalisation and internationalisation of higher education. *Internationalisation of Universities in the Network Society, 8*(2), 241-325.

Deakins, J. (2021, Mar. 9). The Riot at the University of Colorado Was Driven by Pandemic Fatigue and Pent-up Emotion. *Denver Post.*

Dean, B., Eady, M. J., & Yanamandram, V. (2020). Editorial: Advancing Non-placement Work-integrated Learning Across the Degree. *Journal of University Teaching & Learning Practice, 17*(4). Advance online publication. doi:10.53761/1.17.4.1

Deardorff, D. (2006). The Identification and Assessment of Intercultural Competence as a Student Outcome of Internationalization at Institutions of Higher Education in the United States. *Journal of Studies in International Education, 10*(3), 241–166. doi:10.1177/1028315306287002

Dede, C. J., & Richards, J. (Eds.). (2020). *The 60-Year Curriculum: New Models for Lifelong Learning in the Digital Economy.* Routledge. doi:10.4324/9781003013617

Deimann, M. (2006). *Towards the development of a volitional design model.* http://ifbm.fernuni-hagen.de/lehrgebiete/mediendidaktik/archiv1/Deimann_Jure2006.pdf

Deimann, M., & Bastiaens, T. (2010). The role of volition in distance education: An exploration of its capacities. *International Review of Research in Open and Distributed Learning, 11*(1), 1. doi:10.19173/irrodl.v11i1.778

Deimann, M., Weber, B., & Bastiaens, T. (2009). Entwicklung und verbreitung eines tests zur analyse der willensstärke in schule und hochschule [Development of a test of volitional competence in schools and universities]. *Unterrichtswissenschaft, 37*(4), 362–379.

Demirdag, S. (2019). Critical thinking as a predictor of self- esteem of university students. *The Alberta Journal of Educational Research, 65*(4), 305–319. https://journalhosting.ucalgary.ca/index.php/ajer/article/view/56587

Denzin, N. K., & Lincoln, Y. S. (1998). *Collecting and interpreting qualitative materials.* Sage.

Dickinson, H., Smith, C., Yates, S., & Bertuol, M. (2020). *Not even remotely fair: Experiences of students with disability during COVID-19.* Report prepared for Children and Young People with Disability Australia (CYDA).

Digital literacy and young people: Key findings and implications. (2018). Department of Internal Affairs.

Doherty, L. E. (Ed.). (2009). *Homer's Odyssey.* Oxford University Press.

Dörnyei, Z. (1998). Motivation in second and foreign language learning. *Language Teaching, 31*(3), 117–135. doi:10.1017/S026144480001315X

Douse, M., & Uys, P. (2018). Educational Planning in the Age of Digitisation. *Educational Planning, 25*(2), 7–23.

Driscoll, M. (2000). *Psychology of learning for instruction* (2nd ed.). Allyn and Bacon.

Dur, B. (2014). *Lise öğretmenlerinin motivasyon düzeyi ve motivasyon düzeyi ile okul kültürü arasındaki ilişki* (Unpublished Master's thesis). İstanbul Aydın University Sosyal Bilimler Enstitüsü, İstanbul.

Dziuban, C., Graham, C., Moskal, P., Norberg, A., & Sicilia, N. (2018). Blended Learning: The New Normal and Emerging Technologies. *Int J Educ Tech High Educ, 15*(3). Advance online publication. doi:10.118641239-017-0087-5

Edison Research. (2021). *The Infinite Dial, 2021.* https://www.edisonresearch.com/the-infinite-dial-2021-2/

Ekicia, M., & Erdemb, M. (2020). Developing Science Process Skills through Mobile Scientific Inquiry. *Thinking Skills and Creativity, 36,* 100658. Advance online publication. doi:10.1016/j.tsc.2020.100658

Elayyan, S. (2021). The future of education according to the fourth industrial revolution. *Journal of Educational Technology and Online Learning, 4*(1), 23–30.

Engelbertink, M., Colomer, J., Woudt- Mittendorff, K. M., Alsina, Á., Kelders, S. M., Ayllón, S., & Westerhof, G. J. (2021). The reflection leveland the construction of professional identity of university students. *Reflective Practice*, 22(1), 73–85. doi:10.1080/14623943.2020.1835632

Erkuş, A. (1994). Psikoloji Terimleri Sözlüğü. Doruk Yayınları.

Ertmer, P. A., & Newby, T. J. (1993). Behaviorism, cognitivism, constructivism: Comparing critical features from an instructional design perspective. *Performance Improvement Quarterly*, 6(4), 50–72. doi:10.1111/j.1937-8327.1993.tb00605.x

Fayolle, A., Lamine, W., Mian, S., & Phan, P. (2020). Effective models of science, technology and engineering entrepreneurship education: Current and future research. *The Journal of Technology Transfer*, 1–11.

Feliz, U. (2005). E-learning pedagogy in the third millennium: The need for combining social and cognitive constructivist approaches. ReCALL: The Journal of Eurocall, 17(1), 85-100.

Fereday, J., & Muir-Cochrane, E. (2006). Demonstrating rigor using thematic analysis: A hybrid approach of inductive and deductive coding and theme development. *International Journal of Qualitative Methods*, 5(1), 80–92. doi:10.1177/160940690600500107

Fisher, P. B., & McAdams, E. (2015). Gaps in sustainability education. *International Journal of Sustainability in Higher Education*, 16(4), 407–423. doi:10.1108/IJSHE-08-2013-0106

Flynn, W. J., & Vredevoogd, J. (2010). The future of learning: 12 views on emerging trends in higher education. *Planning for Higher Education*, 38(2), 5.

Francis, A., Goheer, A., Haver-Dieter, R., Kaplan, A. D., Kerstetter, K., Kirk, A. L., & Yeh, T. (2004). *Promoting Academic Achiement and Motivation: A Discussion & Contemporary Issues Based Approach*. University of Maryland.

Freire, P. (1970). *Pedagogy of the Oppressed*. Continuum.

Friedman, T. L. (2005). *The World is Flat: A Brief History of the Twenty-First Century*. Farrar, Straus and Giroux.

Friel, S. N., Curcio, F. R., & Bright, G. W. (2001). Making Sense of Graphs: Critical Factors Influencing Comprehension and Instructional Implications. *Journal for Research in Mathematics Education*, 32(2), 124–158. doi:10.2307/749671

Frisk, E., & Larson, K. (2011). Educating for Sustainability: Competencies & Practices for Transformative Action. *Journal of Sustainability Education*, 2. http://www.jsedimensions.org/wordpress/wp-content/uploads/2011/03/FriskLarson2011.pdf

Fryer, L. K., & Bovee, H. N. (2016). Supporting students' motivation for e-learning: Teachers matter on and offline. *Intenet and Higher Education*, 30, 21–29. doi:10.1016/j.iheduc.2016.03.003

Fuller, K., & Stevenson, H. (2019). Global education reform: Understanding the movement. *Educational Review*, 71(1), 1–4. doi:10.1080/00131911.2019.1532718

Gabrielle, D. (2003). *The effects of technology-mediated instructional strategies on motivation, performance, and self-directed learning* (Unpublished doctoral dissertation). Florida Eyalet University.

Gadamer, H.G. (2007). *Truth and method*. Follow Me Editions.

Gadamer, H.-G. (1988). *Truth and Method*. Sheed and Ward.

Gagnon, K., Young, B., Bachman, T., Longbottom, T., Severin, R., & Walker, M. J. (2020). Doctor of Physical Therapy Education in a Hybrid Learning Environment: Reimagining the Possibilities and Navigating a "New Normal". *Physical Therapy*, *100*(8), 1268–1277. http://www.ncbi.nlm.nih.gov/pubmed/32424417

Galle, F., Sabella, E. A., Ferracuti, S., De Giglio, O., Caggiano, G., Protano, C., Valeriani, F., Parisi, E. A., Valerio, G., Liguori, G., Montagna, M. T., Romano Spica, V., Da Molin, G., Orsi, G. B., & Napoli, C. (2020). Sedentary Behaviors and Physical Activity of Italian Undergraduate Students during Lockdown at the Time of CoViD-19 Pandemic. *International Journal of Environmental Research and Public Health*, *17*(17). http://www.ncbi.nlm.nih.gov/pubmed/32854414

García-Morales, V. J. (2021, February). The Transformation of Higher Education After the COVID Disruption: Emerging Challenges in an Online Learning Scenario. *Frontiers in Psychology*, *11*. www.frontiersin.org/articles/10.3389/fpsyg.2021.616059/full

Gardner, R. C. (1985). *Social Psychology and Second Language Learning: The Role of Attitudes and Motivation*. Edward Arnold.

Gee, J. P. (2003). What video games have to teach us about learning and literacy. *Computers in Entertainment*, *1*(1), 20–20. doi:10.1145/950566.950595

Gencheva, N., & Gencheva-Vassileva, A. (2020). A Study on Some Aspects of Distance Learning for Physiotherapy Students during a Pandemic. *Pedagogy*, *92*(7s), 280–290.

Ghaffarzadegan, N., Larson, R., & Hawley, J. (2017). Education as a complex system. *Systems Research and Behavioral Science*, *34*(3), 211–215. doi:10.1002res.2405 PMID:28522920

Giesbers, B., Rienties, B., Tempelaar, D., & Gijselaers, W. (2014). A dynamic analysis of the interplay between asynchronous and synchronous communication in online learning: The impact of motivation. *Journal of Computer Assisted Learning*, *30*(1), 30–50. doi:10.1111/jcal.12020

Glazer, N. (2011). Challenges with Graph Interpretation: A Review of the Literature. *Studies in Science Education*, *47*(2), 183–210. doi:10.1080/03057267.2011.605307

Gómez Flores, A. M. (2018). *Expression and communication*. IC Editorial.

Goodson, I. (2007). All the lonely people: The struggle for private meaning and public purpose in education. *Critical Studies in Education*, *48*(1), 131–148. doi:10.1080/17508480601120954

Goral, M. B., & Gnadinger, C. M. (2006). Using storytelling to teach mathematical concepts. *Australian Primary Mathematics Classroom*, *11*(1), 4–8.

Gravetter, F. J., & Forzano, L. B. (2019). *Research Methods for the Behavioral Sciences*. Cengage Learning.

Green, J. K., Burrow, M. S., & Carvalho, L. (2020). Designing for transition: Supporting teachers and students cope with emergency remote education. *Postdigital Science and Education*, *2*(3), 906–922. doi:10.100742438-020-00185-6

Green, M. F., Marmolejo, F., & Egron-Polak, E. (2012). The internationalization of higher education: Future prospects. In D. K. Deardorff, H. de Wit, J. D. Heyl, & T. Adams (Eds.), *The SAGE handbook of international higher education*. Sage. doi:10.4135/9781452218397.n24

Grundstein, M. J., Fisher, C., Titmuss, M., & Cioppa-Mosca, J. (2021). The Role of Virtual Physical Therapy in a Post-Pandemic World: Pearls, Pitfalls, Challenges, and Adaptations. *Physical Therapy*, *101*(9). http://www.ncbi.nlm.nih.gov/pubmed/34106273

Gutiérrez, K. D., & Jurow, A. S. (2016). Social design experiments: Toward equity by design. *Journal of the Learning Sciences*, *25*(4), 565–598. doi:10.1080/10508406.2016.1204548

Haoran, C., Shupei, Y., & Sixiao, L. (2021). Call them COVIDiots: Exploring the effects of aggressive communication style and psychological distance in the communication of COVID-19. *Public Understanding of Science (Bristol, England)*, *30*(3), 240–257. doi:10.1177/0963662521989191 PMID:33517854

Harrison, N., & Luckett, K. (2019). Experts, knowledge and criticality in the age of 'alternative facts': Re-examining the contribution of higher education. *Teaching in Higher Education*, *24*(3), 259–271. doi:10.1080/13562517.2019.1578577

Hartnett, M., George, A. S., & Dron, J. (2011). Examining motivation in online distance learning environments: Complex, multifaceted and situation-dependent. *The International Review of Research in Open and Distributed Learning*, *12*(6), 20–38. doi:10.19173/irrodl.v12i6.1030

Hasan, M., & Hoon, T. (2013). Podcast Applications in Language Learning: A Review of Recent Studies. *English Language Teaching*, *6*(2), 128–135.

Hava, K. (2021). The effects of the flipped classroom on deep learning strategies and engagement at the undergraduate level. *Participatory Educational Research*, *8*(1), 379–394. doi:10.17275/per.21.22.8.1

Hendrich, S., Licklider, B., Thompson, K., Thompson, J., Haynes, C., & Wiersema, J. (2018). Development of scientific thinking facilitated by reflective self-assessment in a communication-intensive food science and human nutrition course. *Journal of Food Science Education*, *17*(1), 8–13. doi:10.1111/1541-4329.12127

Henrickson, M. (2020). Kiwis and COVID-19: The Aotearoa New Zealand response to the global pandemic. *The International Journal of Community and Social Development*, *2*(2), 121–133. doi:10.1177/2516602620932558

Herda, E. A. (1999). *Research Conversations and Narrative: a Critical Hermeneutic Orientation in Participatory Inquiry*. Praeger.

Heritage, M. (2010). *Formative Assessment: Making It Happen in the Classroom*. Corwin.

Hockly, N. (2012). Digital literacies. *ELT Journal, 66*(1), 108–112. doi:10.1093/elt/ccr077

Holdsworth, S., Turner, M., & Scott Young, C. M. (2018). Not drowning, waving. Resilience and university: A student perspective. *Studies in Higher Education, 43*(11), 1837–1853. doi:10.1080/03075079.2017.1284193

Holzer, J., Lüftenegger, M., Korlat, S., Pelikan, E., Salmela-Aro, K., Spiel, C., & Schober, B. (2021). Higher education in times of COVID-19: University students' basic need satisfaction, self-regulated learning, and well-being. *AERA Open, 7*(1), 1–13. doi:10.1177/23328584211003164 PMID:34192126

Honig, M. I. (2004). Where's the "up" in bottom-up reform? *Educational Policy, 18*(4), 527–561. doi:10.1177/0895904804266640

Horton, W. (2006). *E-learning by design*.

Hoskins, S. L., & Hooff, J. C. (2005). Motivation and ability: Which students use online learning and what influence does it have on their achievement? *British Journal of Educational Technology, 36*(2), 177–192. doi:10.1111/j.1467-8535.2005.00451.x

Hoven, C. (2020). National College COVID-19 Study. In *Will U.S. College Students' Lives Be Forever Transformed by COVID-19?* Columbia University Press. dc.alumni.columbia.edu/covidcollegestudy

Hung, A. (2016). Enhancing Feedback Provision through Multimodal Video Technology. *Computers & Education, 98*, 90–101. doi:10.1016/j.compedu.2016.03.009

Ibili, E. (2020). Examination of Health Science University Students' Level of Readiness for E-Learning. *International Online Journal of Education & Teaching, 7*(3), 1010–1030.

Ikram, F., & Rabbani, M. A. (2021). Academic Integrity in Traditional Vs Online Undergraduate Medical Education Amidst COVID-19 Pandemic. *Cureus, 13*(3), e13911. doi:10.7759/cureus.13911

Iyengar, R. (2020). Education as the path to a sustainable recovery from COVID-19. *Prospects: Comparative Journal of Curriculum, Learning, and Assessment, 49*(1–2), 77–80. doi:10.100711125-020-09488-9 PMID:32836429

Jacobi, M. (1991). Mentoring and undergraduate academic success: A literature review. *Review of Educational Research, 61*(4), 505–532. doi:10.3102/00346543061004505

Jaeger, W. (2019). Paideia: The ideals of Greek culture. Economic Culture Fund (FCE).

Jain, S. (2019). *Research methodology in arts, science and humanities*. Society Publishing.

Jamsri, P. (2015). *The integrating of teaching and learning through technology in high school: learning management systems (LMS) and alternatives* (Unpublished doctoral dissertation).

Jirout, J. J. (2020). Supporting early scientific thinking through curiosity. *Frontiers in Psychology, 11*, 1717. Advance online publication. doi:10.3389/fpsyg.2020.01717 PMID:32849029

Jokelova, A. (2012). *Effects of Relevance-and Confidence-enhancing motivational strategies, suggested strategies, and statements on academic performance and course satisfaction in undergraduate students of a blended public speaking course* (Unpublished doctoral dissertation). South Alabama Üniversitesi.

Jokelova, A. (2013). ARCS motivational model: Theoretical concepts and its use in online courses. *Journal of Educational Psychology, 81*(3), 329.

Jonker, H., März, V., & Voogt, J. (2020). Curriculum flexibility in a blended curriculum. *Australasian Journal of Educational Technology*.

Kabat-Zinn, J. (2021). This Loving-Kindness Meditation Is a Radical Act of Love. *Mindful: Healthy Mind, Healthy Life*. www.mindful.org/this-loving-kindness-meditation-is-a-radical-act-of-love/

Kahraman, Z. (2017). *Okul yöneticileri ile öğretmenlerin örgütsel adalet algıları ve motivasyon düzeyleri arasındaki ilişki* (Unpublished Master's thesis). Marmara University, İstanbul.

Karagüven, H. Ü. (2012). Akademik motivasyon ölçeğinin Türkçeye adaptasyonu. *Kuram ve Uygulamada Eğitim Bilimleri, 12*(4), 1599–2620.

Kavaliauskiene, G., & Anusiene, L. (2009). English for Specific Purposes: Podcasts for Listening Skills. *Filologija. Edukologija, 17*(2), 28–37. doi:10.3846/1822-430X.2009.17.2.28-37

Kawachi, P. (2003). Support for Collaborative e-Learning in Asia. *The Asian Society of Open and Distance Education, 1*(1), 46–59.

Kay, R. H. (2012). Exploring the use of video podcasts in education: A comprehensive review of the literature. *Computers in Human Behavior, 28*(3), 820–831. doi:10.1016/j.chb.2012.01.011

Kelleher, I., & Hulleman, C. (2020). *The Science of Keeping Kids Engaged—Even From Home.* Retrieved from https://www.edutopia.org/article/science-keeping-kids-engaged-even-home?fbc lid=IwAR06vzRa4sblUUYizaqJ_mP2xyjvMrS1rthJOkGokWHwL2L8RR1vVzKXvrA

Keller, J. M. (2000). *How to integrate learner motivation planning into lesson planning: The ARCS model approach.* Paper presented at VII Semanario, Santiago, Cuba.

Keller, J. M. (2005). Course interest course survey – Short form. Academic Press.

Keller, J. M. (2006a). What is motivational design? Florida State University.

Keller, J. M. (2006b). *Development of two measures of learner motivation.* Yayımlanmamış bildiri.

Keller, J. M. (2010c). Challenges in learner motivation: A holistic, integrative model for research and design on learner motivation. In *The 11th international conference on education research new educational paradigm for learning and instruction* (pp. 1-18). Academic Press.

Keller, J. M. (2015). *Integrating motivation into ADL. Applying the ARCS-V motivation model.* http://www.fels.dk/adlforum/index.php/confirmed-speaker-2015/

Keller, J. M., Deimann, M., & Liu, Z. (2005). Effects of integrated motivational and volitional tactics on study habits, attitudes, and performance. *2005 AECT Konferansı, 234.*

Keller, J. M. (1979). Motivation and instructional design: A theoretical perspective. *Journal of Instructional Development, 2*(4), 26–34. doi:10.1007/BF02904345

Keller, J. M. (1983). *Instructional design theories and models: An overview of their current status.* Lawrence Erlbaum.

Keller, J. M. (1987). Development and use of the ARCS model of motivational design. *Journal of Instructional Development, 10*(3), 2–10. doi:10.1007/BF02905780

Keller, J. M. (2008a). First principles of motivation to learn and e-learning. *Distance Education, 29*(2), 175–185. doi:10.1080/01587910802154970

Keller, J. M. (2008b). An integrative theory of motivation, volition, and performance. *Technology, Instruction, Cognition, and Learning, 6*(2), 79–104.

Keller, J. M. (2010a). *Motivational design for learning and performance: The ARCS model approach.* Springer. doi:10.1007/978-1-4419-1250-3

Keller, J. M. (2010b). Five fundamental requirements for motivation and volition. *Revista Inter Ação, 35*(2), 305–322.

Keller, J. M., & Deimann, M. (2012). Motivation, volition, and performance. In R. A. Reiser & J. V. Dempsey (Eds.), *Trends and issues in instructional design and technology.* Pearson Education.

Keller, J. M., & Suzuki, K. (2004). Learner motivation and e-learning design: A multinationally validated process. *Journal of Educational Media, 29*(3), 231–239. doi:10.1080/1358165042000283084

Kijima, R., & Lipscy, P. Y. (2020). International assessments and education policy: Evidence from an elite survey. In J. Kelley & B. Simmons (Eds.), *The Power of global performance indicators* (pp. 174–202). Cambridge University Press. doi:10.1017/9781108763493.007

Kikuchi, K., & Sakai, H. (2009). Japanese learners' demotivation to study English: A survey study. *JALT Journal, 31*(2), 183–204.

Kim, S., Raza, M., & Seidman, E. (2019). Improving 21st-century teaching skills: The key to effective 21st-century learners. *Research in Comparative and International Education, 14*(1), 99–117.

Kimura, Y., Nakata, Y., & Okumura, T. (2001). Language Learning Motivation of EFL Learners in Japan—A Cross-Sectional Analysis of Various Learning Milieus. *JALT Journal, 23*(1), 47–68. doi:10.37546/JALTJJ23.1-3

Kinsella, B. (2021). *Alexa skill counts surpass 80K in US, Spain adds the most skills, new skill rate falls globally.* https://voicebot.ai/2021/01/14/alexa-skill-counts-surpass-80k-in-us-spain-adds-the-most-skills-new-skill-introduction-rate-continues-to-fall-across-countries/

Knowles, E., & Kerkman, D. (2007). An investigation of students attitude and motivation toward online learning. *Student Motivation, 2,* 70–80. doi:10.46504/02200708kn

Kramsch, C., & Aden, J. (2012). *ELT and intercultural/transcultural learning* [Approche culturelle en didactique des langues: hommage à Albane Cain]. Retrieved from https://www.academia.edu/4280731/ELT_AND_INTERCULTURAL_TRANSCULTURAL_LEARNING

Kristof, N. (2021). If You Would Go Out on a Limb for Us, It Might Just Save Our Lives. *New York Times.* www.nytimes.com/2021/05/29/opinion/sunday/covid-impact-us.html

Kruger, E. (2020). *Evaluating in reality: Critical essay on innovation, design and voice tech.* Personal Communications - Interview with Dave Gaudet.

Kumarawadu, P. (2001). Motivation of online learners: review of practices and emerging trends. Sri Lanka Institute of Information Technology.

Lacefield, W., & Markert, L. (2019). Creative Writing in the Mathematics Classroom. *Proceedings of the Annual Meeting of the Georgia Association of Mathematics Teacher Educators, 13*(1). 10.20429/gamte.2019.130106

Larsen, T. S. D. (2008). *Surviving the Arctic; Narrative Identity of Foreign Women in Norway.* University of San Francisco Press.

Lee, S. A. (2008). Increasing student learning: A comparison of students' perceptions of learning in the classroom environment and their industry-based experiential learning Assignments. *Journal of Teaching in Travel & Tourism, 7*(4), 37–54. doi:10.1080/15313220802033310

Leikin, R. (2009). Exploring mathematical creativity using multiple solution tasks. In R. Leikin, A. Berman, & B. Koichu (Eds.), *Creativity in mathematics and the education of gifted students* (pp. 129–145). Sense Publishers. doi:10.1163/9789087909352_010

Lemonidis, C., & Kaiafa, I. (2019). The Effect of Using Storytelling Strategy on Students' Performance in Fractions. *Journal of Education and Learning, 8*(2), 165–175. doi:10.5539/jel.v8n2p165

Levin, B. (2004). *Reforming education: From origins to outcomes.* Routledge. doi:10.4324/9780203482193

Litt, S., & Moorei, A. (2013). *Motivating the distance learning student.* http://www.slideshare.net/fscjopen/motivating-the-distance-learningstudent? qid=a58d06b8-fcce-4771-b195cdae282 1a05evev=defaultveb=vefrom_search=14

Lonn, S., & Teasley, S. D. (2009). Saving time or innovating practice: Investigating perceptions and uses of Learning Management Systems. *Computers & Education, 53*(3), 686–694. doi:10.1016/j.compedu.2009.04.008

López Gómez, E. (Coord.). (2016). General didactics and teacher training. International University of La Rioja, S.A.

Lord, G. (2008). Podcasting communities and second language pronunciation. *Foreign Language Annals, 41*(2), 364–379. Advance online publication. doi:10.1111/j.1944-9720.2008.tb03297.x

Lozada, O. P., Beltrán, O. M., Vargas, F. A., Martin, D. A., Hincapié, B. S., Herrera, M., & Pérez, B. A. (2013). *Humanization of university teaching practice.* doi:10.14742/ajet.4926

Malik, R. S. (2018). Educational challenges in 21st century and sustainable development. *Journal of Sustainable Development Education and Research, 2*(1), 9–20.

Manalo, E. (Ed.). (2019). *Deeper learning, dialogic learning, and critical thinking: Research-based strategies for the classroom* (1st ed.). Routledge. doi:10.4324/9780429323058

Marginson, S., & van der Wende, M. (2007). *Globalisation and higher education* (OECD Education Working Papers No. 8). Retrieved from http://atoz.ebsco.com.ezproxy.liv.ac.uk/Customization/Tab/11404?tabId=8817

Mathematics Assessment Resource Service (MARS), University of Nottingham and UC Berkeley. (2015). *Mathematics Assessment Project CLASSROOM CHALLENGES: A Formative Assessment Lesson.* Retrieved from http://map.mathshell.org/download. php?fileid=1680

Matuga, J. M. (2009). Self-regulation, goal orientation, and academic achievement of secondary students in online university courses. *Journal of Educational Technology & Society, 12*(3), 4–11.

Mayfield, B. (2019). *The purpose of education: a talk on teaching our students how to think* [Unpublished thesis]. Ball State University, Muncie, IN, United States.

McAndrews, C., & Hansberry, J. (2018). Facilitation and dialogue as methods of reflective practice in professional education. *Planning Practice and Research, 33*(1), 86–95. doi:10.1080/02697459.2017.1419653

McLeod, S. (2020). Maslow's Hierarchy of Needs. *Simply Psychology.* www.simplypsychology.org/maslow.html

McMurtrie, B. (2021, April). Teaching: After the Pandemic, What Innovations Are Worth Keeping? *The Chronicle of Higher Education, 1.* www.chronicle.com/newsletter/teaching/2021-04-01

Meleo-Erwin, Z., Kollia, B., Fera, J., Jahren, A., & Basch, C. (2021). Online support information for students with disabilities in colleges and universities during the COVID-19 pandemic. *Disability and Health Journal, 14*(1), 101013. http://www.ncbi.nlm.nih.gov/pubmed/33082111

Merkel, W. (2020). "What I Mean Is...": The role of dialogic interactions in developing a statement of teaching philosophy. *Journal of Second Language Writing, 48,* 100702. Advance online publication. doi:10.1016/j.jslw.2019.100702

Meza Salcedo, G., Rubio Rodríguez, G., Mesa, L., & Blandón, A. (2020). Formative and pedagogical nature of the literature review in research. *Technological Information, 31*(5), 153-162. doi:10.4067/S0718-07642020000500153

Middleton, A. (2009). Beyond podcasting: Creative approaches to designing educational audio. *ALT-J Research in Learning Technology, 17*(2), 143–155. doi:10.1080/09687760903033082

Miller, G. E. (1990). The assessment of clinical skills/competence/performance. *Academic Medicine, 65*(9, Suppl), S63–S67. doi:10.1097/00001888-199009000-00045

Milne, A. (2017). *Colouring in the white spaces: Reclaiming cultural identity in whitestream schools.* Peter Lang. doi:10.3726/b10459

Ministry of Education. (2021). *The Statement of National Education and Learning Priorities (NELP) and the Tertiary Education Strategy (TES).* Retrieved from https://education.govt.nz/our-work/overall-strategies-and-policies/the-statement-of-national-education-and-learning-priorities-nelp-and-the-tertiary-education-strategy-tes

Moeller, A. J., & Nugent, K. (2014). Building intercultural competence in the language classroom. In S. Dhonau (Ed.), *2014 report of the Central States Conference on the Teaching of Foreign Languages* (pp. 1–18). Richmond, VA: Robert M. Terry.

Moffett, J., Hammond, J., Murphy, P., & Pawlikowska, T. (2021). The ubiquity of uncertainty: A scoping review on how undergraduate health professions' students engage with uncertainty. *Advances in Health Sciences Education: Theory and Practice, 26*(3), 913–958. http://www.ncbi.nlm.nih.gov/pubmed/33646469

Moore, K., & Shemberger, M. (2019). Mass Communication Andragogy for Teaching Online Adult Learners. *Teach Journal Mass Commun, 9*(1), 35–40.

Mueller, P. A., & Oppenheimer, D. M. (2014). The pen is mightier than the keyboard: Advantages of longhand over laptop note taking. *Psychological Science, 25*(6), 1–10. doi:10.1177/0956797614524581 PMID:24760141

Muilenburg, L. Y., & Berge, Z. L. (2005). Student barriers to online learning: A factor analytic study. *Distance Education, 26*(1), 29–48. doi:10.1080/01587910500081269

Muñoz, C. (2007). CLIL: Some Thoughts on its Psycholinguistic Principles. *Revista Española de Lingüística Aplicada, 1*, 17-26. Retrieved from https://dialnet.unirioja.es/servlet/articulo?codigo=2575488

Murphy, B. G. (2017). *Inside our schools: Teachers on the failure and future of education reform.* Harvard Education Press.

National Council of Teachers of Mathematics (NCTM). (2000). *Principles and Standards for School Mathematics.* NCTM.

Naveh, G., Tubin, D., & Pliskin, N. (2012). Student satisfaction with learning management systems: A lens of critical success factors. *Technology, Pedagogy and Education, 21*(3), 337–350. doi:1 0.1080/1475939X.2012.720413

Nikitina, L., & Furuoka, F. (2019). Language learners' mental images of Korea: Insights for the teaching of culture in the language classroom. *Journal of Multilingual and Multicultural Development, 40*(9), 774–786. Advance online publication. doi:10.1080/01434632.2018.1561704

Nind, M., Holmes, M., Insenga, M., Lewthwaite, S., & Sutton, C. (2020). Student perspectives on learning research methods in the social sciences. *Teaching in Higher Education, 25*(7), 797–811. doi:10.1080/13562517.2019.1592150

Nursalam, N. (2020). Glocal Vision to Deconstruct Internationalization in Indonesian Higher Education. *Journal of Social Studies Education Research, 11*(1), 137–152.

O'Dowd, R. (2012). Intercultural communicative competence through telecollaboration. In J. Jackson (Ed.), The Routledge Handbook of Language and Intercultural Communication (pp. 340–356). Academic Press.

O'Shea, A. (2014). Models of WIL. In S. Ferns (Ed.), Work integrated learning in the curriculum. Higher Education Research and Development Society of Australia guide (pp. 7-14). Hammondville: Higher Education Research and Development Society of Australasia.

Oblinger, D. G., & Oblinger, J. L. (2005). *Educating the net generation*. EDUCAUSE.

Odegaard, N. B., Myrhaug, H. T., Dahl-Michelsen, T., & Roe, Y. (2021). Digital learning designs in physiotherapy education: A systematic review and meta-analysis. *BMC Medical Education, 21*(1), 48. http://www.ncbi.nlm.nih.gov/pubmed/33441140

OECD. (2022). *PISA 2015 Draft Mathematics Framework*. OECD. Retrieved from https://pisa2022-maths.oecd.org/

Olave Encina, K., Moni, K., & Renshaw, P. (2020). Exploring the emotions of international students about their feedback experiences. *Higher Education Research & Development, 39*(2), 200–2014. doi:10.1080/07294360.2020.1786020

Oliveira, P. C. D., Cunha, C. J. C. D. A., & Nakayama, M. K. (2016). Learning Management Systems (LMS) and e-learning management: An integrative review and research agenda. *JISTEM-Journal of Information Systems and Technology Management, 13*(2), 157–180. doi:10.4301/S1807-17752016000200001

Olivier, B., Verdonck, M., & Caseleijn, D. (2020). Digital technologies in undergraduate and postgraduate education in occupational therapy and physiotherapy: a scoping review. *JBI Evid Synth, 18*(5), 863-892. http://www.ncbi.nlm.nih.gov/pubmed/32813350

Organisation for Economic Co-operation and Development & PISA. (2010). *What Students Know and Can Do: Student Performance in Reading, Mathematics and Science*. OECD.

Ossiannilsson, E. (2020). Some challenges for universities in a post crisis, as COVID-19. In Radical solutions for education in a crisis context: COVID-19 as an opportunity for global learning (pp. 99-112). Springer.

Owens, T. L. (2017). Higher education in the sustainable development goals framework. *European Journal of Education, 52*(4), 414–420. doi:10.1111/ejed.12237

Özbay, Y. (2004). Gelişim ve Öğrenme Psikolojisi. Öğreti Yayınları.

Ozuah, P. (2005). First, There was Pedagogy and Then Came Andragogy. *The Einstein Journal of Biology and Medicine; EJBM, 21*, 83–87.

Parsons, M. (2021). Podcasting Technology for Student Engagement and English Language Learning in the Japanese Context. In D. Ktoridou, E. Doukanari, & N. Eteokleous (Eds.), *Fostering Meaningful Learning Experiences Through Student Engagement* (pp. 245–265). IGI Global. doi:10.4018/978-1-7998-4658-1.ch013

Parsons, M., Garant, M., & Shikova, E. (in press). Video-Exchange Telecollaboration: Towards Developing Interculturality in EFL Environments. In S. M. Hilliker (Ed.), *Second Language Teaching and Learning through Virtual Exchange*. De Gruyter Mouton.

Pasek, J. (2018). It's not my consensus: Motivated reasoning and the sources of scientific illiteracy. *Public Understanding of Science (Bristol, England), 27*(7), 787–806. doi:10.1177/0963662517733681 PMID:28942728

Pérez, B.C., Vigil, M.G., Georgíeva, D., Níkleva, Jiménez, Á.J., MaríaTeresa, L., Molina, Ó., Morales, F.F. & Rodríguez, L. S. (2011). The Esepod Project: Improving Listening Skills Through Mobile Learning. *Proceedings of the 4th International ICT for Language Learning.* https://www.researchgate.net/publication/259009828_The_Esepod_Project_Improving_Listening_Skills_Through_Mobile_Learning

Pérez, S., Saritas, O., Pook, K., & Warden, C. (2011). Ready for the future? Universities' capabilities to strategically manage their intellectual capital. *Foresight, 13*(2), 31–48. doi:10.1108/14636681111126238

Perry, S. L., Baker, J. O., & Grubbs, J. B. (2021). Ignorance or culture war? Christian nationalism and scientific illiteracy. *Public Understanding of Science (Bristol, England), 30*(8), 1–17. doi:10.1177/09636625211006271 PMID:33855921

Philip, A. V., & Zakkariya, K. A. (2020). Effective Engagement of Digital Natives in the Ever-Transforming Digital World. In Digital Transformation in Business and Society (pp. 113-125). Palgrave Macmillan. doi:10.1007/978-3-030-08277-2_7

Pintrich, P. R. (1988). A process-oriented view of student motivation and cognition. *New Directions for Institutional Research, 57*(57), 65–79. doi:10.1002/ir.37019885707

Pintrich, P. R. (1989). The dynamic interplay of student motivation and cognition in the college classroom. *Advances in Motivation and Achievement: a Research Annual, 6*, 117–160. doi:10.2224bp.2005.33.4.341

Pintrich, P. R., Smith, D. A. F., Garcia, T., & McKeachie, W. J. (1991). *A Manual for the use of the motivated strategies for learning*. School of Education Building, The University of Michigan.

Pintrich, P. R., Smith, D. A., Garcia, T., & McKeachie, W. J. (1993). Reliability and predictive validity of the Motivated Strategies for Learning Questionnaire (MSLQ). *Educational and Psychological Measurement, 53*(3), 801–813. doi:10.1177/0013164493053003024

Pittenger, A., & Doering, A. (2010). Influence of motivational design on completion rates in online self-study pharmacy-content courses. *Distance Education, 31*(3), 275–293. doi:10.1080 /01587919.2010.513953

Porter, G. W. (2013). Free choice of learning management systems: Do student habits override inherent system quality? *Interactive Technology and Smart Education, 10*(2), 84–94. doi:10.1108/ ITSE-07-2012-0019

Priestley, M., & Drew, V. (2016, September). *Teachers as agents of curriculum change: closing the gap between purpose and practice* [Paper Presentation]. *The European Conference for Educational Research*, Dublin, Ireland.

Qiang, R., Han, Q., Guo, Y., Bai, J., & Karwowski, M. (2018). Critical thinking disposition and scientific creativity: The mediating role of creative self-efficacy. *The Journal of Creative Behavior, 54*(1), 90–99. doi:10.1002/jocb.347

Quintiliani, L., Sisto, A., Vicinanza, F., Curcio, G., & Tambone, V. (2021). Resilience and psychological impact on Italian university students during COVID-19 pandemic. Distance learning and health. *Psychology Health and Medicine*, 1–12. doi:10.1080/13548506.2021.1891266

QuirkLogic. (2020). *Presentation to SAIT marketing faculty* [unpublished].

Ramsay-Jordan, N. (2020). Preparation and The Real World of Education: How Prospective Teachers Grapple with Using Culturally Responsive Teaching Practices in the Age of Standardized Testing. *International Journal of Educational Reform, 29*(1), 3–24. doi:10.1177/1056787919877142

Ranganathan, H., Singh, D. K. A., Kumar, S., Sharma, S., Chua, S. K., Ahmad, N. B., & Harikrishnan, K. (2021). Readiness towards online learning among physiotherapy undergraduates. *BMC Medical Education, 21*(1), 376. http://www.ncbi.nlm.nih.gov/pubmed/34246264

Rasmussen, P., Muir-Cochrane, E., & Henderson, A. (2012). Document analysis using an aggregate and iterative process. *International Journal of Evidence-Based Healthcare, 10*(2), 142–145. doi:10.1111/j.1744-1609.2012.00262.x PMID:22672603

RBC and Riipen expand experiential learning partnership for youth across Canada. Riipen. (2020, October 15). https://www.riipen.com/blog/rbc-and-riipen-expand-experiential-learning-partnership-for-youth-across-canada

Renchler, R. (1992). Student motivation, school culture, and academic achievement. *ERIC/CEM Trends and Issues Series, 7*.

Ren, J. (2020). Cultivation of Humanistic Qualities in the Blended Teaching Model of College English. *In International Conference on Education Studies: Experience and Innovation* (pp. 602-604). Atlantis Press. 10.2991/assehr.k.201128.112

Rentner, D., Kober, N., & Frizzell, M. (2016). *Listen to us: Teacher views and voices.* Retrieved from Centre on Education Policy website: http://www.cepc.org/displayDocument. cfm?DocumentID=1456

Ricoeur, P. (1981). *Hermeneutics and the Human Sciences.* Cambridge University Press. doi:10.1017/CBO9781316534984

Robin, B. R. (2008). Digital storytelling: A powerful technology tool for the 21st century classroom. *Theory into Practice, 47*(3), 220–228. doi:10.1080/00405840802153916

Robinson, K., & Aronica, L. (2014). *The element: how finding your passion changes everything.* Penguin Books. http://rbdigital.oneclickdigital.com

Roessger, K. M. (2020). Assessment strategies for reflective learning in the workplace. A pragmatic approach. *Adult Learning, 31*(4), 175–184. Advance online publication. doi:10.1177/1045159520941947

Roe, Y., Rowe, M., Odegaard, N. B., Sylliaas, H., & Dahl-Michelsen, T. (2019). Learning with technology in physiotherapy education: Design, implementation and evaluation of a flipped classroom teaching approach. *BMC Medical Education, 19*(1), 291. http://www.ncbi.nlm.nih. gov/pubmed/31366351

Romero-Blanco, C., Rodriguez-Almagro, J., Onieva-Zafra, M. D., Parra-Fernandez, M. L., Prado-Laguna, M. D. C., & Hernandez-Martinez, A. (2020a). Physical Activity and Sedentary Lifestyle in University Students: Changes during Confinement Due to the COVID-19 Pandemic. *International Journal of Environmental Research and Public Health, 17*(18). http://www.ncbi. nlm.nih.gov/pubmed/32916972

Romero-Blanco, C., Rodriguez-Almagro, J., Onieva-Zafra, M. D., Parra-Fernandez, M. L., Prado-Laguna, M. D. C., & Hernandez-Martinez, A. (2020b). Sleep Pattern Changes in Nursing Students during the COVID-19 Lockdown. *International Journal of Environmental Research and Public Health, 17*(14). http://www.ncbi.nlm.nih.gov/pubmed/32698343

Roseman, S. (2020). *The Forum for Innovation and Growth.* Harvard Business School. https://www. hbs.edu/forum-for-growth-and-innovation/blog/post/why-voice-is-the-next-disruptive-technology

Russow, L. C. (2003). Digitization of education: A panacea? *Journal of Teaching in International Business, 14*(2-3), 1–11. doi:10.1300/J066v14n02_01

Ryan, R. M., & Deci, E. L. (2000a). Intrinsic and extrinsic motivations: Classic definitions and new directions. *Contemporary Educational Psychology, 25*(1), 54–67. doi:10.1006/ceps.1999.1020 PMID:10620381

Ryan, R. M., & Deci, E. L. (2000b). Self-determination theory and the facilitation of intrinsic motivation, social development, and well-being. *The American Psychologist, 55*(1), 68–78. doi:10.1037/0003-066X.55.1.68 PMID:11392867

Ryan, R. M., Rigby, C. S., & Przybylski, A. (2006). The motivational pull of video games: A self-determination theory approach. *Motivation and Emotion, 30*(4), 344–360. doi:10.100711031-006-9051-8

Saavedra, E. (2018). *The effects of mobile devices on student learning in a New Zealand- based university preparation course: A case study* (Doctoral thesis). University of Southern Queensland, Australia.

Saavedra, E., & Sanders, L. (2016). Building on identifiable common student experiences to enable success. *FABENZ: Accessibility, flexibility, equity.* Retrieved from http://fabenz.org.nz/wp-content/uploads/2016/12/Saavedra-and-Sanders.pdf

Sadler, D. (1989). Formative Assessment and the design of instructional systems. *Instructional Science, 18*(2), 119–144. doi:10.1007/BF00117714

Sahlberg, P. (2006). Education reform for raising economic competitiveness. *Journal of Educational Change, 7*(4), 259–287. doi:10.100710833-005-4884-6

Saida, R., & Yusubovna, K. G. (2020). Humanization of education as the basis of pedagogical communication. *European Journal of Research and Reflection in Educational Sciences, 8*(2).

SAIT. (2020). *Learner exit survey, work integrated learning 2018-19. Business Information and Analysis.* SAIT.

SAIT. (2021). *About us.* https://www.sait.ca/about-sait

Salazar, A., Palomo-Osuna, J., de Sola, H., Moral-Munoz, J. A., Duenas, M., & Failde, I. (2021). Psychological Impact of the Lockdown Due to the COVID-19 Pandemic in University Workers: Factors Related to Stress, Anxiety, and Depression. *International Journal of Environmental Research and Public Health, 18*(8). http://www.ncbi.nlm.nih.gov/pubmed/33924133

Sanchiz, M., Amadieu, F., & Chevalier, A. (2020). An evolving perspective to capture individual differences related to fluid and crystallized abilities in information searching with a search engine. In *Understanding and Improving Information Search* (pp. 71–96). Springer. doi:10.1007/978-3-030-38825-6_5

Sansone, C., Fraughton, T., Zachary, J., Butner, J., & Heiner, C. (2011). Self-regulation of motivation when learning online: The importance of who, why and how. *Educational Technology Research and Development, 59*(2), 199–212. doi:10.100711423-011-9193-6

Schiro, M. S., & Lawson, D. (2004). *Oral Storytelling and Teaching Mathematics: Pedagogical and Multicultural Perspectives.* SAGE Publications.

Schiro, M., & Lawson, D. (2004). *Oral storytelling and teaching mathematics: Pedagogical and multicultural perspectives.* Sage Publications.

Schunk, D. H. (1992). Theory and research on student perceptions in the classroom. In Student perceptions in the classroom (pp. 3-23). Hillsdale, NJ: Erlbaum.

Schunk, D. H. (2011). Eğitimsel bir bakışla öğrenme teorileri [Learning theories and educational perspective]. Ankara: Nobel Akademik Yayıncılık.

Scutter, S., Stupans, I., Sawyer, T., & King, S. (2010). How do students use podcasts to support learning? *Australasian Journal of Educational Technology, 26*(2). Advance online publication. doi:10.14742/ajet.1089

Selwyn, N. (2019). *Should robots replace teachers? AI and the future of education.* John Wiley & Sons.

Semmar, Y. (2006). Distance learners and academic achievement: The roles of selfefficacy, self-regulation and motivation. *Journal of Adult and Continuing Education, 12*(2), 244–256. doi:10.7227/JACE.12.2.9

Shah, P., & Carpenter, P. A. (1995). Conceptual Limitations in Comprehending Line Graphs. *Journal of Experimental Psychology, 124*(1), 43–61. doi:10.1037/0096-3445.124.1.43

Shah, P., & Hoeffner, J. (2002). Review of Graph Comprehension Research: Implications for Practice. *Educational Psychology Review, 14*(1), 47–69. doi:10.1023/A:1013180410169

Shaked, H., & Schechter, C. (2019). School middle leaders' sense making of a generally outlined education reform. *Leadership and Policy in Schools, 18*(3), 412–432. doi:10.1080/15700763.2018.1450513

Sharifian, F. (208). Learning Intercultural Competence. In A. In Burns & J. C. Richards (Eds.), The Cambridge Guide to Learning English as a Second Language. Academic Press.

Smart speaker market value worldwide 2014-2025. (2021). *Statista.* https://www.statista.com/statistics/1022823/worldwide-smart-speaker-market-revenue/

Smith, S. (2012). Why Japan, South Korea, and China Are So Riled Up Over a Few Tiny Islands. *The Atlantic.* Retrieved from: https://www.theatlantic.com/international/archive/2012/08/why-japan-south-korea-and-china-are-so-riled-up-over-a-few-tiny-islands/261224/

Smith, M. D. (2020, July). Are Universities Going the Way of CDs and Cable TV? *Atlantic, 22.* www.theatlantic.com/ideas/archive/2020/06/university-like-cd-streaming-age/613291/

Snowman, J., McCown, R., & Biehler, R. (2012). *Psychology applied to teaching* (13th ed.). Wadesworth, Cengage Learning.

Soydan, B., Büyükeken, G., Aktaş, H. İ., Özbak, H., Büyükeskil, M., Uykür, N., . . . Özkan, S. (2012). *Başarı algısı ile akademik başarı arasındaki ilişkinin incelenmesi.* Selçuklu rehberlik ve araştırma merkezi.

Stawicki, S. P., Jeanmonod, R., Miller, A. C., Paladino, L., Gaieski, D. F., Yaffee, A. Q., De Wulf, A., Grover, J., Papadimos, T. J., Bloem, C., Galwankar, S. C., Chauhan, V., Firstenberg, M. S., Di Somma, S., Jeanmonod, D., Garg, S. M., Tucci, V., Anderson, H. L., Fatimah, L., ... Garg, M. (2020). The 2019-2020 Novel Coronavirus (Severe Acute Respiratory Syndrome Coronavirus 2) Pandemic: A Joint American College of Academic International Medicine-World Academic Council of Emergency Medicine Multidisciplinary COVID-19 Working Group Consensus Paper. *Journal of Global Infectious Diseases*, *12*(2), 47–93. http://www.ncbi.nlm.nih.gov/pubmed/32773996

Stirling, A., Kerr, G., MacPherson, E., & Heron, A. (2016). *A practical guide for work-integrated learning: Effective practices to enhance the educational quality of structured work Experiences Offered through Colleges and Universities.* Higher Education Quality Council of Ontario.

Suhail, M., Sharath, C., & Mathew, A. (2020). Contemporary Learning or E-Learning in Physiotherapy, Pre and Post COVID-19: Short Communication. *J Nov Physiother Rehabil, 4*(1), 9-10.

Sullivan, W. (1972, Mar. 29). The Einstein Papers. A Man of Many Parts. *New York Times*.

Syahrin, A., Dawud, Suwignyo, H., & Priyatni, E. T. (2019). Creative Thinking Patterns In Student's Scientific Works. *Eurasian Journal of Educational Research*, *19*(81), 21–36. doi:10.14689/ejer.2019.81.2

Tae Woo, K., Duhachek, A., Briñol, P., & Petty, R. (2020). How posting online reviews can influence the poster's evaluations. *Personality and Social Psychology Bulletin*, 1–13. doi:10.1177/0146167220976449 PMID:33267745

Takeuchi, M. A., Sengupta, P., Shanahan, M. C., Adams, J. D., & Hachem, M. (2020). Transdisciplinarity in STEM education: A critical review. *Studies in Science Education*, *56*(2), 213–253. doi:10.1080/03057267.2020.1755802

Taras, H. (2006). *How Health Affects a Child's School Performance*. University of San Diego Press. health.ucsd.edu/news/2006/Pages/04_07_Taras.aspx

Tenforde, A. S., Borgstrom, H., Polich, G., Steere, H., Davis, I. S., Cotton, K., O'Donnell, M., & Silver, J. K. (2020). Outpatient Physical, Occupational, and Speech Therapy Synchronous Telemedicine: A Survey Study of Patient Satisfaction with Virtual Visits During the COVID-19 Pandemic. *American Journal of Physical Medicine & Rehabilitation*, *99*(11), 977–981. http://www.ncbi.nlm.nih.gov/pubmed/32804713

Teo, P. (2020). Teaching for the 21st century: A case for dialogic pedagogy. *Learning, Culture and Social Interaction*, *21*, 170–178. doi:10.1016/j.lcsi.2019.03.009

Tertiary Education Commission. (2020). *The Tertiary Education Strategy*. Retrieved from https://www.tec.govt.nz/focus/our-focus/tes/

The Innovative Work-Integrated Learning Initiative. (2020). *Government of Canada*. https://www.canada.ca/en/employment-social-development/programs/work-integrated-learning.html

The Sustainable Development Goals Report 2017. (2017). https://unstats.un. org/sdgs/files/report/2017/TheSustainableDevelopmentGoalsReport2017.pdf

Toraman, Ç., Özdemir, H. F., Koşan, A. M. A., & Orakcı, Ş. (2020). Relationships between Cognitive Flexibility, Perceived Quality of Faculty Life, Learning Approaches, and Academic Achievement. *International Journal of Instruction*, *13*(1).

Turner, J. C., & Patrick, H. (2008). How does motivation develop and why does it change? Reframing motivation research. *Educational Psychologist*, *43*(3), 119–131. doi:10.1080/00461520802178441

Umar, M. (2020). Humanistic Approaches in Learning Processes Package C Equity Program (Case Study of the Setia Mandiri Community Learning Center). In *1st International Conference on Lifelong Learning and Education for Sustainability* (pp. 206-211). Atlantis Press.

UN. (n.d.). *The Sustainable Development Agenda.* https://www.un.org/sustainabledevelopment/development-agenda/

UNESCO. (2015). *Education 2030 Framework for Action: Towards inclusive and equitable quality education and lifelong learning for all.* http://www.unesco.org/new/fileadmin/MULTIMEDIA/HQ/ED/ED_new/pdf/FFA-ENG-27Oct15.pdf

UNESCO. (2016). *Education for people and planet: Creating sustainable futures for all.* https://en.unesco.org/gem-report/report/2016/education-people-and-planet-creating-sustainable-futures-all

UNESCO. (2016a). Education for people and planet: Creating sustainable futures for all (Global Education Monitoring Report 2016). Paris: Author.

UNESCO. (2016b). *Evaluation of UNESCO's regional conventions on the recognition of qualifications in higher education.* Author.

UNESCO. (2017). *Education for Sustainable Development Goals: Learning objectives.* https://unesdoc.unesco.org/ark:/48223/pf0000247444.page=21

UNESCO. (2018a). *Policy brief, education for sustainable development and SDGs.* https://en.unesco.org/sites/default/files/gap_pn1_-_esd_and_the_sdgs_policy_brief_6_page_version.pdf

UNESCO. (2019). *Meeting commitments: Are countries on track to achieve the SDG4?* http://uis.unesco.org/sites/default/files/documents/meeting-commitments-are-countries-on-track-achieve-sdg4.pdf

UNESCO. (2020). *Education: From disruption to recovery.* https://en.unesco.org/covid19/educationresponse

UNESCO. (2020a). *COVID-19 education response.* https://en.unesco.org/covid19/educationresponse

UNESCO. (2020b). *Nine ideas for public action—New publication from the International Commission on the Futures of Education.* Paris: UNESCO. https://en.unesco.org/futuresofeducation/news/nine-ideas-for-public-action

UNESCO. (2020c). *Nurturing the social and emotional wellbeing of children and young people during crises. UNESCO COVID-19 education response.* https://unesdoc.unesco.org/ark:/48223/pf0000373271

Unge, J., Lundh, P., Gummesson, C., & Amner, G. (2018). Learning Spaces for Health Sciences – What is the Role of e-Learning in Physiotherapy and Occupational Therapy Education? A Literature Review. *The Physical Therapy Review, 23*(1). Advance online publication. doi:10.1080/10833196.2018.1447423

United Nations. (2012). *Higher Education Sustainability Initiative.* Retrieved 20 October 2021 from https://sustainabledevelopment.un.org/sdinaction/hesi

United Nations. (2015). *Resolution adopted by the General Assembly on 25 September 2015: Transforming our world: The 2030 Agenda for Sustainable Development A/RES/70/1.* Retrieved from https://www.un.org/ga/search/view_doc.asp?symbol=A/RES/70/1&Lang=E

United Nations. (2015). *Transforming Our World: The 2030 Agenda for Sustainable Development.* United Nations.

United Nations. (2016). *The Sustainable Development Goals Report 2016.* http://www.un.org.lb/Library/Assets/The-Sustainable-Development-Goals-Report-2016- Global.pdf

United Nations. (2017a). *Statistical Commission. Report on the forty-eighth session.* https://unstats.un.org/unsd/statcom/48th-session/documents/Report-on-the-48th-Session-ofthe-Statistical-Commission-E.pdf

Uzbaş, A. (2009). Okul psikolojik danışmanlarının okulda saldırganlık ve şiddete yönelik görüşlerinin değerlendirilmesi. *Mehmet Akif Ersoy Üniversitesi Eğitim Fakültesi Dergisi,* (18), 90–110.

Vallerand, R. J., & Bissonnette, R. (1992). Intrinsic, extrinsic, and amotivational styles as predictors of behavior: A prospective study. *Journal of Personality, 60*(3), 599–620. doi:10.1111/j.1467-6494.1992.tb00922.x

Vallerand, R. J., Pelletier, L. G., Blais, M. R., Briere, N. M., Senecal, C., & Vallieres, E. F. (1993). On the assessment of intrinsic, extrinsic, and amotivation in education: Evidence on the concurrent and construct validity of the academic motivation scalet. *Educational and Psychological Measurement, 53*(1), 159–172. doi:10.1177/0013164493053001018

Vovides, Y., Sanchez-Alonso, S., Mitropoulou, V., & Nickmans, G. (2007). The use of e-learning course management systems to support learning strategies and to improve self-regulated learning. *Educational Research Review, 2*(1), 64–74. doi:10.1016/j.edurev.2007.02.004

Vygotsky, L. S. (1978). *Mind in society: The development of higher psychological processes.* Harvard university press.

Waller, R. E., Lemoine, P. A., Mense, E. G., & Richardson, M. D. (2019). Higher education in search of competitive advantage: Globalization, technology and e-learning. *International Journal of Advanced Research and Publications*, *3*(8), 184–190.

Walpola, R., & Lucas, Ch. (2021). Reflective practice: The essential competency for health systems and healthcare practitioners during the COVID-19 pandemic. *Reflective Practice*, *22*(2), 143–146. doi:10.1080/14623943.2020.1860925

Ware, P., & O'Dowd, R. (2008). Peer Feedback on Language Form in Telecollaboration. *Language Learning & Technology*, *12*(1), 43–63.

Watson, J., Murin, A., Vashaw, L., Gemin, B., & Rapp, C. (2010). *Keeping pace with K-12 online learning: An annual review of policy and practice*. Evergreen Education Group.

Wattal, A. M., & Singh, C. (2021, June 8). An era of new-age school assessments. *Hindustan Times*. https://www.hindustantimes.com/analysis/an-era-of-new-age-school-assessments-101622990312580.html

Weitz, N., Carlsen, H., Nilsson, M., & Skånberg, K. (2018). Towards systemic and contextual priority setting for implementing the 2030 Agenda. *Sustainability Science*, *13*(2), 531–548.

West, R. E., Hannafin, M. J., Hill, J. R., & Song, L. (2013). Cognitive Perspectives On Online Learning Environments. In Handbook of Distance Education. Routledge.

Wighting, M. J., Liu, J., & Rovai, A. P. (2008). Distinguishing sense of community and motivation characteristics between online and traditional college students. *Quarterly Review of Distance Education*, *9*(3), 285–295.

Wilans, J., & Seary, K. (2011). "I feel like I'm being hit from all directions": Enduring the bombardment as a mature-age learner returning to formal learning. *Australian Journal of Adult Learning*, *51*(1), 119–142.

Wilcha, R. J. (2020). Effectiveness of Virtual Medical Teaching During the COVID-19 Crisis: Systematic Review. *JMIR Medical Education*, *6*(2), e20963. http://www.ncbi.nlm.nih.gov/pubmed/33106227

Wiliam, D., & Thompson, M. (2007). Integrating assessment with instruction: what will it take to make it work? In C. A. Dwyer (Ed.), *The Future of Assessment: Shaping Teaching and Learning* (pp. 53–82). Lawrence Erlbaum Associates.

Wilson, C. (2014). Semi-structured interviews. *Interview techniques for UX Practitioners: A user-centred design method*, 23-41.

Wood, Y. I., Zegwaard, K. E., & Fox-Turnbull, W. H. (2020). Conventional, remote, virtual, and simulated work-integrated learning: A meta-analysis of existing practice. *International Journal of Work Integrated Learning*, *21*(4), 331–354.

World Health Organization. (2020a). *Rehabilitation Competency Framework*. Geneva: World Health Organization. https://apps.who.int/iris/handle/10665/338782

World Health Organization. (2020b). *Using a Contextualized Competency Framework to Develop Rehabilitation Programmes and their Curricula: A Stepwise Guide for Programme and Curriculum Developers, Version for Field Testing.* World Health Organization. https://apps.who.int/iris/handle/10665/339205

World Health Organization. (2021). *Coronavirus disease (COVID-19) outbreak.* Retrieved from https://www.who.int/es/emergencies/diseases/novel-coronavirus-2019

World Physiotherapy. (2019). *Description of Physical Therapy: Policy Statement.* https://world.physio/policy/ps-descriptionPT

World Physiotherapy. (2020). *WCPT Response to COVID-19 Briefing Paper 1: Immediate Impact on the Higher Education Sector and Response to Delivering Physiotherapy Entry Level Education.* https://www.wcpt.org/sites/wcpt.org/files/files/wcptnews/images/Education-Briefing-1-HEI-A4.pdf

Wrightsman, L. (1981). *Research methodologies for Assessing mentoring.* Paper presented at the Conference of the American Psychological Association, Los Angeles, CA.

Wu, J., & Chen, D. T. V. (2020). A systematic review of educational digital storytelling. *Computers & Education, 147*, 1–32. doi:10.1016/j.compedu.2019.103786

Wu, Y.-C. J., & Shen, J.-P. (2016). Higher education for sustainable development: A systematic review. *International Journal of Sustainability in Higher Education, 17*(5), 633–651. doi:10.1108/IJSHE-01-2015-0004

Xavier, M., & Meneses, J. (2020). *Dropout in Online Higher Education: A scoping review from 2014 to 2018.* eLearn Center, Universitat Oberta de Catalunya.

Yaacob, A., Mohd Asraf, R., Hussain, R. M. R., & Ismail, S. N. (2021). Empowering Learners' Reflective Thinking through Collaborative Reflective Learning. *International Journal of Instruction, 14*(1), 709–726. doi:10.29333/iji.2021.14143a

Yang, L., & McCall, B. (2014). World education finance policies and higher education access: A statistical analysis of World Development Indicators for 86 countries. *International Journal of Educational Development, 35*, 25–36. doi:10.1016/j.ijedudev.2012.11.002

Yeung, P. (2017). Why can't Chinese graduates speak good English? Blame the teaching methods. *South China Morning Post.* Retrieved from: https://www.scmp.com/comment/insight-opinion/article/2110113/why-cant-chinese-graduates-speak-good-english-blame-teaching

Yin, R. K. (2003). *Case study research: Design and methods* (3rd ed.). Sage.

Youde, A. (2020). I don't need peer support: Effective tutoring in blended learning environments for part-time, adult learners. *Higher Education Research & Development, 39*(5), 1040–1054. doi:10.1080/07294360.2019.1704692

Youth plan 2020-2022. (2020). *Turning voice into action: Rebuilding and recovering.* Ministry of Youth Development. https://www.myd.govt.nz/young-people/youth-plan/youth-plan.html

Compilation of References

Zawacki Richter, O. (2021). The current state and impact of Covid-19 on digital higher education in Germany. *Human Behavior and Emerging Technologies, 3*(1), 218–226. doi:10.1002/hbe2.238 PMID:33363276

Zegwaard, K., & Rowe, A. (2019). Research-informed curriculum and advancing innovative practices in work-integrated learning. *International Journal of Work-Integrated Learning, 20*(4), 323–334.

Zevenbergen, R., Dole, S., & Wright, R. J. (2004). *Teaching Mathematics in Primary Schools.* Allen & Unwin.

Zimmerman, B. J. (1989). *A social cognitive view of self-regulated academic learning.* Academic Press.

Zimmerman, B. J. (1990). Self-Regulated Learning and Academic Achievement: An Overview. *Educational Psychologist, 25*(1), 3–17. doi:10.120715326985ep2501_2

Zotzmann, K. (2015). The Impossibility of Defining and Measuring Intercultural Competencies. In D. J. Rivers (Ed.), *Resistance to the Known.* Palgrave Macmillan. doi:10.1057/9781137345196_8

Related References

To continue our tradition of advancing academic research, we have compiled a list of recommended IGI Global readings. These references will provide additional information and guidance to further enrich your knowledge and assist you with your own research and future publications.

Aburezeq, I. M., & Dweikat, F. F. (2017). Cloud Applications in Language Teaching: Examining Pre-Service Teachers' Expertise, Perceptions and Integration. *International Journal of Distance Education Technologies, 15*(4), 39–60. doi:10.4018/IJDET.2017100103

Adera, B. (2017). Supporting Language and Literacy Development for English Language Learners. In J. Keengwe (Ed.), *Handbook of Research on Promoting Cross-Cultural Competence and Social Justice in Teacher Education* (pp. 339–354). Hershey, PA: IGI Global. doi:10.4018/978-1-5225-0897-7.ch018

Ahamer, G. (2011). How Technologies Can Localize Learners in Multicultural Space: A Newly Developed "Global Studies" Curriculum. *International Journal of Technology and Educational Marketing, 1*(2), 1–24. doi:10.4018/ijtem.2011070101

Ahamer, G. (2015). Conclusions from Social Dynamics in Collaborative Environmental Didactics. *International Journal of Technology and Educational Marketing, 5*(2), 68–92. doi:10.4018/IJTEM.2015070105

Ahamer, G. (2015). Designing and Analyzing Social Dynamics for Collaborative: Environmental Didactics. *International Journal of Technology and Educational Marketing, 5*(2), 46–67. doi:10.4018/IJTEM.2015070104

Ahamer, G. (2017). Quality Assurance for a Developmental "Global Studies" (GS) Curriculum. In I. Management Association (Ed.), Educational Leadership and Administration: Concepts, Methodologies, Tools, and Applications (pp. 438-477). Hershey, PA: IGI Global. doi:10.4018/978-1-5225-1624-8.ch023

Ahamer, G. (2017). Quality Assurance for a Developmental "Global Studies" (GS) Curriculum. In I. Management Association (Ed.), Educational Leadership and Administration: Concepts, Methodologies, Tools, and Applications (pp. 438-477). Hershey, PA: IGI Global. doi:10.4018/978-1-5225-1624-8.ch023

Alegre de la Rosa, O. M., & Angulo, L. M. (2017). Social Inclusion and Intercultural Values in a School of Education. In S. Mukerji & P. Tripathi (Eds.), *Handbook of Research on Administration, Policy, and Leadership in Higher Education* (pp. 518–531). Hershey, PA: IGI Global. doi:10.4018/978-1-5225-0672-0.ch020

Ambikairajah, E., Sethu, V., Eaton, R., & Sheng, M. (2014). Evolving Use of Educational Technologies: Enhancing Lectures. In F. Alam (Ed.), *Using Technology Tools to Innovate Assessment, Reporting, and Teaching Practices in Engineering Education* (pp. 241–258). Hershey, PA: IGI Global. doi:10.4018/978-1-4666-5011-4.ch018

Anderson, K. M. (2017). Preparing Teachers in the Age of Equity and Inclusion. In I. Management Association (Ed.), Medical Education and Ethics: Concepts, Methodologies, Tools, and Applications (pp. 1532-1554). Hershey, PA: IGI Global. doi:10.4018/978-1-5225-0978-3.ch069

Awdziej, M. (2017). Case Study as a Teaching Method in Marketing. In D. Latusek (Ed.), *Case Studies as a Teaching Tool in Management Education* (pp. 244–263). Hershey, PA: IGI Global. doi:10.4018/978-1-5225-0770-3.ch013

Bain, B. (2014). Exploring Assessment of Critical Thinking Learning Outcomes in Online Higher Education. In V. Wang (Ed.), *Handbook of Research on Education and Technology in a Changing Society* (pp. 1191–1202). Hershey, PA: IGI Global. doi:10.4018/978-1-4666-6046-5.ch089

Banas, J. R., & York, C. S. (2017). Pre-Service Teachers' Motivation to Use Technology and the Impact of Authentic Learning Exercises. In L. Tomei (Ed.), *Exploring the New Era of Technology-Infused Education* (pp. 121–140). Hershey, PA: IGI Global. doi:10.4018/978-1-5225-1709-2.ch008

Bariso, E. U. (2015). Educational Policy Analysis Debates and New Learning Technologies in England. In M. Khosrow-Pour (Ed.), *Encyclopedia of Information Science and Technology* (3rd ed.; pp. 2371–2378). Hershey, PA: IGI Global. doi:10.4018/978-1-4666-5888-2.ch230

Beycioglu, K., & Wildy, H. (2015). Principal Preparation: The Case of Novice Principals in Turkey. In K. Beycioglu & P. Pashiardis (Eds.), *Multidimensional Perspectives on Principal Leadership Effectiveness* (pp. 1–17). Hershey, PA: IGI Global. doi:10.4018/978-1-4666-6591-0.ch001

Beycioglu, K., & Wildy, H. (2017). Principal Preparation: The Case of Novice Principals in Turkey. In I. Management Association (Ed.), Educational Leadership and Administration: Concepts, Methodologies, Tools, and Applications (pp. 1152-1169). Hershey, PA: IGI Global. doi:10.4018/978-1-5225-1624-8.ch054

Bharwani, S., & Musunuri, D. (2018). Reflection as a Process From Theory to Practice. In M. Khosrow-Pour, D.B.A. (Ed.), Encyclopedia of Information Science and Technology, Fourth Edition (pp. 1529-1539). Hershey, PA: IGI Global. doi:10.4018/978-1-5225-2255-3.ch132

Bisschoff, T., & Rhodes, C. (2011). Transformation through Marketing: A Case of a Secondary School in South Africa. In P. Tripathi & S. Mukerji (Eds.), *Cases on Innovations in Educational Marketing: Transnational and Technological Strategies* (pp. 263–272). Hershey, PA: IGI Global. doi:10.4018/978-1-60960-599-5.ch016

Bodomo, A. B. (2010). Educational Technologies (WebCT): Creating Constructivist and Interactive Learning Communities. In A. Bodomo (Ed.), *Computer-Mediated Communication for Linguistics and Literacy: Technology and Natural Language Education* (pp. 252–290). Hershey, PA: IGI Global. doi:10.4018/978-1-60566-868-0.ch010

Bohjanen, S. L., Cameron-Standerford, A., & Meidl, T. D. (2018). Capacity Building Pedagogy for Diverse Learners. In J. Keengwe (Ed.), *Handbook of Research on Pedagogical Models for Next-Generation Teaching and Learning* (pp. 195–212). Hershey, PA: IGI Global. doi:10.4018/978-1-5225-3873-8.ch011

Brewer, J. C. (2018). Measuring Text Readability Using Reading Level. In M. Khosrow-Pour, D.B.A. (Ed.), Encyclopedia of Information Science and Technology, Fourth Edition (pp. 1499-1507). Hershey, PA: IGI Global. doi:10.4018/978-1-5225-2255-3.ch129

Brown, S. L. (2017). A Case Study of Strategic Leadership and Research in Practice: Principal Preparation Programs that Work – An Educational Administration Perspective of Best Practices for Master's Degree Programs for Principal Preparation. In V. Wang (Ed.), *Encyclopedia of Strategic Leadership and Management* (pp. 1226–1244). Hershey, PA: IGI Global. doi:10.4018/978-1-5225-1049-9.ch086

Brzozowski, M., & Ferster, I. (2017). Educational Management Leadership: High School Principal's Management Style and Parental Involvement in School Management in Israel. In V. Potocan, M. Üngan, & Z. Nedelko (Eds.), *Handbook of Research on Managerial Solutions in Non-Profit Organizations* (pp. 55–74). Hershey, PA: IGI Global. doi:10.4018/978-1-5225-0731-4.ch003

Cannaday, J. (2017). The Masking Effect: Hidden Gifts and Disabilities of 2e Students. In P. Dickenson, P. Keough, & J. Courduff (Eds.), *Preparing Pre-Service Teachers for the Inclusive Classroom* (pp. 220–231). Hershey, PA: IGI Global. doi:10.4018/978-1-5225-1753-5.ch011

Capobianco, B. M., & Lehman, J. D. (2010). Fostering Educational Technology Integration in Science Teacher Education: Issues of Teacher Identity Development. In J. Yamamoto, J. Kush, R. Lombard, & C. Hertzog (Eds.), *Technology Implementation and Teacher Education: Reflective Models* (pp. 245–257). Hershey, PA: IGI Global. doi:10.4018/978-1-61520-897-5.ch014

Chao, G. H., Hsu, M. K., & Scovotti, C. (2013). Predicting Donations from a Cohort Group of Donors to Charities: A Direct Marketing Case Study. In J. Wang (Ed.), *Optimizing, Innovating, and Capitalizing on Information Systems for Operations* (pp. 196–214). Hershey, PA: IGI Global. doi:10.4018/978-1-4666-2925-7.ch010

Chauhan, A. (2015). Beyond the Phenomenon: Assessment in Massive Open Online Courses (MOOCs). In E. McKay & J. Lenarcic (Eds.), *Macro-Level Learning through Massive Open Online Courses (MOOCs): Strategies and Predictions for the Future* (pp. 119–140). Hershey, PA: IGI Global. doi:10.4018/978-1-4666-8324-2.ch007

Coffman, T. L., & Klinger, M. B. (2013). Managing Quality in Online Education. In G. Kurubacak & T. Yuzer (Eds.), *Project Management Approaches for Online Learning Design* (pp. 220–233). Hershey, PA: IGI Global. doi:10.4018/978-1-4666-2830-4.ch011

Contreras, E. C., & Contreras, I. I. (2018). Development of Communication Skills through Auditory Training Software in Special Education. In M. Khosrow-Pour, D.B.A. (Ed.), Encyclopedia of Information Science and Technology, Fourth Edition (pp. 2431-2441). Hershey, PA: IGI Global. doi:10.4018/978-1-5225-2255-3.ch212

Cook, R. G. (2011). Educational Marketing: Coming Down from the Cloud Using Landing Gear. In U. Demiray & S. Sever (Eds.), *Marketing Online Education Programs: Frameworks for Promotion and Communication* (pp. 26–31). Hershey, PA: IGI Global. doi:10.4018/978-1-60960-074-7.ch003

Cook, R. G., & Ley, K. (2015). Past, Future and Presents: Meeting New Online Challenges with Primal Marketing Solutions. *International Journal of Technology and Educational Marketing, 5*(2), 19–33. doi:10.4018/IJTEM.2015070102

Cooley, D., & Whitten, E. (2017). Special Education Leadership and the Implementation of Response to Intervention. In F. Topor (Ed.), *Handbook of Research on Individualism and Identity in the Globalized Digital Age* (pp. 265–286). Hershey, PA: IGI Global. doi:10.4018/978-1-5225-0522-8.ch012

Cosner, S., Tozer, S., & Zavitkovsky, P. (2017). Enacting a Cycle of Inquiry Capstone Research Project in Doctoral-Level Leadership Preparation. In I. Management Association (Ed.), Educational Leadership and Administration: Concepts, Methodologies, Tools, and Applications (pp. 1460-1481). Hershey, PA: IGI Global. doi:10.4018/978-1-5225-1624-8.ch067

Crawford, C. M. (2018). Instructional Real World Community Engagement. In M. Khosrow-Pour, D.B.A. (Ed.), Encyclopedia of Information Science and Technology, Fourth Edition (pp. 1474-1486). Hershey, PA: IGI Global. doi:10.4018/978-1-5225-2255-3.ch127

Crosby-Cooper, T., & Pacis, D. (2017). Implementing Effective Student Support Teams. In P. Dickenson, P. Keough, & J. Courduff (Eds.), *Preparing Pre-Service Teachers for the Inclusive Classroom* (pp. 248–262). Hershey, PA: IGI Global. doi:10.4018/978-1-5225-1753-5.ch013

Curran, C. M., & Hawbaker, B. W. (2017). Cultivating Communities of Inclusive Practice: Professional Development for Educators – Research and Practice. In C. Curran & A. Petersen (Eds.), *Handbook of Research on Classroom Diversity and Inclusive Education Practice* (pp. 120–153). Hershey, PA: IGI Global. doi:10.4018/978-1-5225-2520-2.ch006

Dass, S., & Dabbagh, N. (2018). Faculty Adoption of 3D Avatar-Based Virtual World Learning Environments: An Exploratory Case Study. In I. Management Association (Ed.), Technology Adoption and Social Issues: Concepts, Methodologies, Tools, and Applications (pp. 1000-1033). Hershey, PA: IGI Global. doi:10.4018/978-1-5225-5201-7.ch045

Davison, A. M., & Scholl, K. G. (2017). Inclusive Recreation as Part of the IEP Process. In C. Curran & A. Petersen (Eds.), *Handbook of Research on Classroom Diversity and Inclusive Education Practice* (pp. 311–330). Hershey, PA: IGI Global. doi:10.4018/978-1-5225-2520-2.ch013

DeCoito, I. (2018). Addressing Digital Competencies, Curriculum Development, and Instructional Design in Science Teacher Education. In M. Khosrow-Pour, D.B.A. (Ed.), Encyclopedia of Information Science and Technology, Fourth Edition (pp. 1420-1431). Hershey, PA: IGI Global. doi:10.4018/978-1-5225-2255-3.ch122

DeCoito, I., & Richardson, T. (2017). Beyond Angry Birds™: Using Web-Based Tools to Engage Learners and Promote Inquiry in STEM Learning. In I. Levin & D. Tsybulsky (Eds.), *Digital Tools and Solutions for Inquiry-Based STEM Learning* (pp. 166–196). Hershey, PA: IGI Global. doi:10.4018/978-1-5225-2525-7.ch007

Delmas, P. M. (2017). Research-Based Leadership for Next-Generation Leaders. In R. Styron Jr & J. Styron (Eds.), *Comprehensive Problem-Solving and Skill Development for Next-Generation Leaders* (pp. 1–39). Hershey, PA: IGI Global. doi:10.4018/978-1-5225-1968-3.ch001

Demiray, U., & Ekren, G. (2018). Administrative-Related Evaluation for Distance Education Institutions in Turkey. In K. Buyuk, S. Kocdar, & A. Bozkurt (Eds.), *Administrative Leadership in Open and Distance Learning Programs* (pp. 263–288). Hershey, PA: IGI Global. doi:10.4018/978-1-5225-2645-2.ch011

Dickenson, P. (2017). What do we Know and Where Can We Grow?: Teachers Preparation for the Inclusive Classroom. In P. Dickenson, P. Keough, & J. Courduff (Eds.), *Preparing Pre-Service Teachers for the Inclusive Classroom* (pp. 1–22). Hershey, PA: IGI Global. doi:10.4018/978-1-5225-1753-5.ch001

Dickerson, J., & Coleman, H. V. (2012). Technology, E-Leadership and Educational Administration in Schools: Integrating Standards with Context and Guiding Questions. In V. Wang (Ed.), *Encyclopedia of E-Leadership, Counseling and Training* (pp. 408–422). Hershey, PA: IGI Global. doi:10.4018/978-1-61350-068-2.ch030

Dickerson, J., Coleman, H. V., & Geer, G. (2012). Thinking like a School Technology Leader. In V. Wang (Ed.), *Technology and Its Impact on Educational Leadership: Innovation and Change* (pp. 53–63). Hershey, PA: IGI Global. doi:10.4018/978-1-4666-0062-1.ch005

Donne, V., & Hansen, M. (2017). Teachers' Use of Assistive Technologies in Education. In L. Tomei (Ed.), *Exploring the New Era of Technology-Infused Education* (pp. 86–101). Hershey, PA: IGI Global. doi:10.4018/978-1-5225-1709-2.ch006

Donne, V., & Hansen, M. A. (2018). Business and Technology Educators: Practices for Inclusion. In I. Management Association (Ed.), Business Education and Ethics: Concepts, Methodologies, Tools, and Applications (pp. 471-484). Hershey, PA: IGI Global. doi:10.4018/978-1-5225-3153-1.ch026

Dreon, O., Shettel, J., & Bower, K. M. (2017). Preparing Next Generation Elementary Teachers for the Tools of Tomorrow. In M. Grassetti & S. Brookby (Eds.), *Advancing Next-Generation Teacher Education through Digital Tools and Applications* (pp. 143–159). Hershey, PA: IGI Global. doi:10.4018/978-1-5225-0965-3.ch008

Drinka, D., Voge, K., & Yen, M. Y. (2005). From Principles to Practice: Analyzing a Student Learning Outcomes Assessment System. *Journal of Cases on Information Technology*, 7(3), 37–56. doi:10.4018/jcit.2005070103

Durak, H. Y., & Güyer, T. (2018). Design and Development of an Instructional Program for Teaching Programming Processes to Gifted Students Using Scratch. In J. Cannaday (Ed.), *Curriculum Development for Gifted Education Programs* (pp. 61–99). Hershey, PA: IGI Global. doi:10.4018/978-1-5225-3041-1.ch004

Egorkina, E., Ivanov, M., & Valyavskiy, A. Y. (2018). Students' Research Competence Formation of the Quality of Open and Distance Learning. In V. Mkrttchian & L. Belyanina (Eds.), *Handbook of Research on Students' Research Competence in Modern Educational Contexts* (pp. 364–384). Hershey, PA: IGI Global. doi:10.4018/978-1-5225-3485-3.ch019

Ekren, G., Karataş, S., & Demiray, U. (2017). Understanding of Leadership in Distance Education Management. In I. Management Association (Ed.), Educational Leadership and Administration: Concepts, Methodologies, Tools, and Applications (pp. 34-50). Hershey, PA: IGI Global. doi:10.4018/978-1-5225-1624-8.ch003

Elmore, W. M., Young, J. K., Harris, S., & Mason, D. (2017). The Relationship between Individual Student Attributes and Online Course Completion. In K. Shelton & K. Pedersen (Eds.), *Handbook of Research on Building, Growing, and Sustaining Quality E-Learning Programs* (pp. 151–173). Hershey, PA: IGI Global. doi:10.4018/978-1-5225-0877-9.ch008

Ercegovac, I. R., Alfirević, N., & Koludrović, M. (2017). School Principals' Communication and Co-Operation Assessment: The Croatian Experience. In I. Management Association (Ed.), Educational Leadership and Administration: Concepts, Methodologies, Tools, and Applications (pp. 1568-1589). Hershey, PA: IGI Global. doi:10.4018/978-1-5225-1624-8.ch072

Everhart, D., & Seymour, D. M. (2017). Challenges and Opportunities in the Currency of Higher Education. In K. Rasmussen, P. Northrup, & R. Colson (Eds.), *Handbook of Research on Competency-Based Education in University Settings* (pp. 41–65). Hershey, PA: IGI Global. doi:10.4018/978-1-5225-0932-5.ch003

Farmer, L. S. (2017). Managing Portable Technologies for Special Education. In V. Wang (Ed.), *Encyclopedia of Strategic Leadership and Management* (pp. 977–987). Hershey, PA: IGI Global. doi:10.4018/978-1-5225-1049-9.ch068

Farmer, L. S. (2018). Optimizing OERs for Optimal ICT Literacy in Higher Education. In J. Keengwe (Ed.), *Handbook of Research on Mobile Technology, Constructivism, and Meaningful Learning* (pp. 366–390). Hershey, PA: IGI Global. doi:10.4018/978-1-5225-3949-0.ch020

Fındık, L. Y. (2017). Self-Assessment of Principals Based on Leadership in Complexity. In I. Management Association (Ed.), Educational Leadership and Administration: Concepts, Methodologies, Tools, and Applications (pp. 978-991). Hershey, PA: IGI Global. doi:10.4018/978-1-5225-1624-8.ch047

Flor, A. G., & Gonzalez-Flor, B. (2018). Dysfunctional Digital Demeanors: Tales From (and Policy Implications of) eLearning's Dark Side. In I. Management Association (Ed.), The Dark Web: Breakthroughs in Research and Practice (pp. 37-50). Hershey, PA: IGI Global. doi:10.4018/978-1-5225-3163-0.ch003

Floyd, K. K., & Shambaugh, N. (2017). Instructional Design for Simulations in Special Education Virtual Learning Spaces. In T. Kidd & L. Morris Jr., (Eds.), *Handbook of Research on Instructional Systems and Educational Technology* (pp. 202–215). Hershey, PA: IGI Global. doi:10.4018/978-1-5225-2399-4.ch018

Giovannini, J. M. (2017). Technology Integration in Preservice Teacher Education Programs: Research-based Recommendations. In M. Grassetti & S. Brookby (Eds.), *Advancing Next-Generation Teacher Education through Digital Tools and Applications* (pp. 82–102). Hershey, PA: IGI Global. doi:10.4018/978-1-5225-0965-3.ch005

Good, S., & Clarke, V. B. (2017). An Integral Analysis of One Urban School System's Efforts to Support Student-Centered Teaching. In J. Keengwe & G. Onchwari (Eds.), *Handbook of Research on Learner-Centered Pedagogy in Teacher Education and Professional Development* (pp. 45–68). Hershey, PA: IGI Global. doi:10.4018/978-1-5225-0892-2.ch003

Grobler, B. (2015). The Relationship between Emotional Competence and Instructional Leadership and Their Association with Learner Achievement. In K. Beycioglu & P. Pashiardis (Eds.), *Multidimensional Perspectives on Principal Leadership Effectiveness* (pp. 373–407). Hershey, PA: IGI Global. doi:10.4018/978-1-4666-6591-0.ch017

Hamidi, F., Owuor, P. M., Hynie, M., Baljko, M., & McGrath, S. (2017). Potentials of Digital Assistive Technology and Special Education in Kenya. In C. Ayo & V. Mbarika (Eds.), *Sustainable ICT Adoption and Integration for Socio-Economic Development* (pp. 125–151). Hershey, PA: IGI Global. doi:10.4018/978-1-5225-2565-3.ch006

Heavin, C., & Neville, K. (2015). Addressing the Learning Needs of Future IS Security Professionals through Social Media Technology. In M. Khosrow-Pour (Ed.), *Encyclopedia of Information Science and Technology* (3rd ed.; pp. 4766–4775). Hershey, PA: IGI Global. doi:10.4018/978-1-4666-5888-2.ch468

Henderson, L. K. (2017). Meltdown at Fukushima: Global Catastrophic Events, Visual Literacy, and Art Education. In R. Shin (Ed.), *Convergence of Contemporary Art, Visual Culture, and Global Civic Engagement* (pp. 80–99). Hershey, PA: IGI Global. doi:10.4018/978-1-5225-1665-1.ch005

Hismanoglu, M. (2012). Important Issues in Online Education: E-Pedagogy and Marketing. In I. Management Association (Ed.), E-Marketing: Concepts, Methodologies, Tools, and Applications (pp. 676-701). Hershey, PA: IGI Global. doi:10.4018/978-1-4666-1598-4.ch041

Howard, B. C. (2008). Common Features and Design Principles Found in Exemplary Educational Technologies. *International Journal of Information and Communication Technology Education*, *4*(4), 31–52. doi:10.4018/jicte.2008100104

Howard, B. C., & Tomei, L. A. (2008). The Classroom of the Future and Emerging Educational Technologies: Introduction to the Special Issue. *International Journal of Information and Communication Technology Education*, *4*(4), 1–8. doi:10.4018/jicte.2008100101

Hudgins, T., & Holland, J. L. (2018). Digital Badges: Tracking Knowledge Acquisition Within an Innovation Framework. In I. Management Association (Ed.), Wearable Technologies: Concepts, Methodologies, Tools, and Applications (pp. 1118-1132). Hershey, PA: IGI Global. doi:10.4018/978-1-5225-5484-4.ch051

Ion, G., Tomàs, M., Castro, D., & Salat, E. (2015). Analysis of the Tasks of School Principals in Secondary Education in Catalonia: Case Study. In K. Beycioglu & P. Pashiardis (Eds.), *Multidimensional Perspectives on Principal Leadership Effectiveness* (pp. 39–58). Hershey, PA: IGI Global. doi:10.4018/978-1-4666-6591-0.ch003

Janus, M., & Siddiqua, A. (2018). Challenges for Children With Special Health Needs at the Time of Transition to School. In I. Management Association (Ed.), Autism Spectrum Disorders: Breakthroughs in Research and Practice (pp. 339-371). Hershey, PA: IGI Global. doi:10.4018/978-1-5225-3827-1.ch018

Jesus, R. A. (2018). Screencasts and Learning Styles. In M. Khosrow-Pour, D.B.A. (Ed.), Encyclopedia of Information Science and Technology, Fourth Edition (pp. 1548-1558). Hershey, PA: IGI Global. doi:10.4018/978-1-5225-2255-3.ch134

Kaplan-Rakowski, R., & Rakowski, D. (2011). Educational Technologies for the Neomillennial Generation. In E. Dunkels, G. Franberg, & C. Hallgren (Eds.), *Interactive Media Use and Youth: Learning, Knowledge Exchange and Behavior* (pp. 12–31). Hershey, PA: IGI Global. doi:10.4018/978-1-60960-206-2.ch002

Karpinski, A. C., D'Agostino, J. V., Williams, A. K., Highland, S. A., & Mellott, J. A. (2018). The Relationship Between Online Formative Assessment and State Test Scores Using Multilevel Modeling. In M. Khosrow-Pour, D.B.A. (Ed.), Encyclopedia of Information Science and Technology, Fourth Edition (pp. 5183-5192). Hershey, PA: IGI Global. doi:10.4018/978-1-5225-2255-3.ch450

Kats, Y. (2017). Educational Leadership and Integrated Support for Students with Autism Spectrum Disorders. In I. Management Association (Ed.), *Educational Leadership and Administration: Concepts, Methodologies, Tools, and Applications* (pp. 101-114). Hershey, PA: IGI Global. doi:10.4018/978-1-5225-1624-8.ch007

Kaya, G., & Altun, A. (2018). Educational Ontology Development. In M. Khosrow-Pour, D.B.A. (Ed.), Encyclopedia of Information Science and Technology, Fourth Edition (pp. 1441-1450). Hershey, PA: IGI Global. doi:10.4018/978-1-5225-2255-3.ch124

Keough, P. D., & Pacis, D. (2017). Best Practices Implementing Special Education Curriculum and Common Core State Standards using UDL. In P. Dickenson, P. Keough, & J. Courduff (Eds.), *Preparing Pre-Service Teachers for the Inclusive Classroom* (pp. 107–123). Hershey, PA: IGI Global. doi:10.4018/978-1-5225-1753-5.ch006

Kilburn, M., Henckell, M., & Starrett, D. (2018). Factors Contributing to the Effectiveness of Online Students and Instructors. In M. Khosrow-Pour, D.B.A. (Ed.), Encyclopedia of Information Science and Technology, Fourth Edition (pp. 1451-1462). Hershey, PA: IGI Global. doi:10.4018/978-1-5225-2255-3.ch125

Konecny, L. T. (2017). Hybrid, Online, and Flipped Classrooms in Health Science: Enhanced Learning Environments. In I. Management Association (Ed.), *Flipped Instruction: Breakthroughs in Research and Practice* (pp. 355-370). Hershey, PA: IGI Global. doi:10.4018/978-1-5225-1803-7.ch020

Kowch, E. G. (2013). Towards Leading Diverse, Smarter and More Adaptable Organizations that Learn. In J. Lewis, A. Green, & D. Surry (Eds.), *Technology as a Tool for Diversity Leadership: Implementation and Future Implications* (pp. 11–34). Hershey, PA: IGI Global. doi:10.4018/978-1-4666-2668-3.ch002

Krezmien, M., Powell, W., Bosch, C., Hall, T., & Nieswandt, M. (2017). The Use of Tablet Technology to Support Inquiry Science for Students Incarcerated in Juvenile Justice Settings. In I. Levin & D. Tsybulsky (Eds.), *Optimizing STEM Education With Advanced ICTs and Simulations* (pp. 267–295). Hershey, PA: IGI Global. doi:10.4018/978-1-5225-2528-8.ch011

Leach, L. F., Winn, P., Erwin, S., & Benedict, L. P. (2015). What 21st Century Students Want: Factors that Influence Student Selection of Educational Leadership Graduate Programs. *International Journal of Technology and Educational Marketing*, 5(1), 15–28. doi:10.4018/ijtem.2015010102

Leng, H. K. (2014). An Update on the Use of Facebook as a Marketing Tool by Private Educational Institutions in Singapore. In I. Lee (Ed.), *Trends in E-Business, E-Services, and E-Commerce: Impact of Technology on Goods, Services, and Business Transactions* (pp. 191–205). Hershey, PA: IGI Global. doi:10.4018/978-1-4666-4510-3.ch011

Leone, S. (2018). An Open Learning Format for Lifelong Learners' Empowerment. In M. Khosrow-Pour, D.B.A. (Ed.), *Encyclopedia of Information Science and Technology, Fourth Edition* (pp. 1517-1528). Hershey, PA: IGI Global. doi:10.4018/978-1-5225-2255-3.ch131

Ley, K., & Gannon-Cook, R. (2010). Marketing a Blended University Program: An Action Research Case Study. In S. Mukerji & P. Tripathi (Eds.), *Cases on Technology Enhanced Learning through Collaborative Opportunities* (pp. 73–90). Hershey, PA: IGI Global. doi:10.4018/978-1-61520-751-0.ch005

Loose, W., & Marcos, T. (2016). Instructional Design for Millennials: Instructor Efficiency in Streamlining Content, Assignments, and Assessments. In P. Dickenson & J. Jaurez (Eds.), *Increasing Productivity and Efficiency in Online Teaching* (pp. 1–25). Hershey, PA: IGI Global. doi:10.4018/978-1-5225-0347-7.ch001

Lovell, K. L. (2017). Development and Evaluation of Neuroscience Computer-Based Modules for Medical Students: Instructional Design Principles and Effectiveness. In J. Stefaniak (Ed.), *Advancing Medical Education Through Strategic Instructional Design* (pp. 262–276). Hershey, PA: IGI Global. doi:10.4018/978-1-5225-2098-6.ch013

Manuel, N. N. (2016). Angolan Higher Education, Policy, and Leadership: Towards Transformative Leadership for Social Justice. In N. Ololube (Ed.), *Handbook of Research on Organizational Justice and Culture in Higher Education Institutions* (pp. 164–188). Hershey, PA: IGI Global. doi:10.4018/978-1-4666-9850-5.ch007

Marouchou, D. V. (2015). The Impact of Academic Beliefs on Student Learning. In M. Khosrow-Pour (Ed.), *Encyclopedia of Information Science and Technology* (3rd ed.; pp. 4796–4804). Hershey, PA: IGI Global. doi:10.4018/978-1-4666-5888-2.ch471

McCormack, V. F., Stauffer, M., Fishley, K., Hohenbrink, J., Mascazine, J. R., & Zigler, T. (2018). Designing a Dual Licensure Path for Middle Childhood and Special Education Teacher Candidates. In D. Polly, M. Putman, T. Petty, & A. Good (Eds.), *Innovative Practices in Teacher Preparation and Graduate-Level Teacher Education Programs* (pp. 21–36). Hershey, PA: IGI Global. doi:10.4018/978-1-5225-3068-8.ch002

McDaniel, R. (2017). Strategic Leadership in Instructional Design: Applying the Principles of Instructional Design through the Lens of Strategic Leadership to Distance Education. In V. Wang (Ed.), *Encyclopedia of Strategic Leadership and Management* (pp. 1570–1584). Hershey, PA: IGI Global. doi:10.4018/978-1-5225-1049-9.ch109

Memon, R. N., Ahmad, R., & Salim, S. S. (2018). Critical Issues in Requirements Engineering Education. In I. Management Association (Ed.), Computer Systems and Software Engineering: Concepts, Methodologies, Tools, and Applications (pp. 1953-1976). Hershey, PA: IGI Global. doi:10.4018/978-1-5225-3923-0.ch081

Mendenhall, R. (2017). Western Governors University: CBE Innovator and National Model. In K. Rasmussen, P. Northrup, & R. Colson (Eds.), *Handbook of Research on Competency-Based Education in University Settings* (pp. 379–400). Hershey, PA: IGI Global. doi:10.4018/978-1-5225-0932-5.ch019

Mense, E. G., Griggs, D. M., & Shanks, J. N. (2018). School Leaders in a Time of Accountability and Data Use: Preparing Our Future School Leaders in Leadership Preparation Programs. In E. Mense & M. Crain-Dorough (Eds.), *Data Leadership for K-12 Schools in a Time of Accountability* (pp. 235–259). Hershey, PA: IGI Global. doi:10.4018/978-1-5225-3188-3.ch012

Mense, E. G., Griggs, D. M., & Shanks, J. N. (2018). School Leaders in a Time of Accountability and Data Use: Preparing Our Future School Leaders in Leadership Preparation Programs. In E. Mense & M. Crain-Dorough (Eds.), *Data Leadership for K-12 Schools in a Time of Accountability* (pp. 235–259). Hershey, PA: IGI Global. doi:10.4018/978-1-5225-3188-3.ch012

Mestry, R., & Naicker, S. R. (2017). Exploring Distributive Leadership in South African Public Primary Schools in the Soweto Region. In I. Management Association (Ed.), Educational Leadership and Administration: Concepts, Methodologies, Tools, and Applications (pp. 1041-1064). Hershey, PA: IGI Global. doi:10.4018/978-1-5225-1624-8.ch050

Monaghan, C. H., & Boboc, M. (2017). (Re)Defining Leadership in Higher Education in the U.S. In V. Wang (Ed.), *Encyclopedia of Strategic Leadership and Management* (pp. 567–579). Hershey, PA: IGI Global. doi:10.4018/978-1-5225-1049-9.ch040

Muthee, J. M., & Murungi, C. G. (2018). Relationship Among Intelligence, Achievement Motivation, Type of School, and Academic Performance of Kenyan Urban Primary School Pupils. In M. Khosrow-Pour, D.B.A. (Ed.), Encyclopedia of Information Science and Technology, Fourth Edition (pp. 1540-1547). Hershey, PA: IGI Global. doi:10.4018/978-1-5225-2255-3.ch133

Naranjo, J. (2018). Meeting the Need for Inclusive Educators Online: Teacher Education in Inclusive Special Education and Dual-Certification. In D. Polly, M. Putman, T. Petty, & A. Good (Eds.), *Innovative Practices in Teacher Preparation and Graduate-Level Teacher Education Programs* (pp. 106–122). Hershey, PA: IGI Global. doi:10.4018/978-1-5225-3068-8.ch007

Nkabinde, Z. P. (2017). Multiculturalism in Special Education: Perspectives of Minority Children in Urban Schools. In J. Keengwe (Ed.), *Handbook of Research on Promoting Cross-Cultural Competence and Social Justice in Teacher Education* (pp. 382–397). Hershey, PA: IGI Global. doi:10.4018/978-1-5225-0897-7.ch020

Nkabinde, Z. P. (2018). Online Instruction: Is the Quality the Same as Face-to-Face Instruction? In J. Keengwe (Ed.), *Handbook of Research on Digital Content, Mobile Learning, and Technology Integration Models in Teacher Education* (pp. 300–314). Hershey, PA: IGI Global. doi:10.4018/978-1-5225-2953-8.ch016

O'Connor, J. R. Jr., & Jackson, K. N. (2017). The Use of iPad® Devices and "Apps" for ASD Students in Special Education and Speech Therapy. In Y. Kats (Ed.), *Supporting the Education of Children with Autism Spectrum Disorders* (pp. 267–283). Hershey, PA: IGI Global. doi:10.4018/978-1-5225-0816-8.ch014

Okolie, U. C., & Yasin, A. M. (2017). TVET in Developing Nations and Human Development. In U. Okolie & A. Yasin (Eds.), *Technical Education and Vocational Training in Developing Nations* (pp. 1–25). Hershey, PA: IGI Global. doi:10.4018/978-1-5225-1811-2.ch001

Paciga, K. A., & Hoffman, J. L. (2015). Realizing the Potential of e-Books in Early Education. In M. Khosrow-Pour (Ed.), *Encyclopedia of Information Science and Technology* (3rd ed.; pp. 4787–4795). Hershey, PA: IGI Global. doi:10.4018/978-1-4666-5888-2.ch470

Paulson, E. N. (2017). Adapting and Advocating for an Online EdD Program in Changing Times and "Sacred" Cultures. In I. Management Association (Ed.), Educational Leadership and Administration: Concepts, Methodologies, Tools, and Applications (pp. 1849-1876). Hershey, PA: IGI Global. doi:10.4018/978-1-5225-1624-8.ch085

Petersen, A. J., Elser, C. F., Al Nassir, M. N., Stakey, J., & Everson, K. (2017). The Year of Teaching Inclusively: Building an Elementary Classroom for All Students. In C. Curran & A. Petersen (Eds.), *Handbook of Research on Classroom Diversity and Inclusive Education Practice* (pp. 332–348). Hershey, PA: IGI Global. doi:10.4018/978-1-5225-2520-2.ch014

Pfannenstiel, K. H., & Sanders, J. (2017). Characteristics and Instructional Strategies for Students With Mathematical Difficulties: In the Inclusive Classroom. In C. Curran & A. Petersen (Eds.), *Handbook of Research on Classroom Diversity and Inclusive Education Practice* (pp. 250–281). Hershey, PA: IGI Global. doi:10.4018/978-1-5225-2520-2.ch011

Preast, J. L., Bowman, N., & Rose, C. A. (2017). Creating Inclusive Classroom Communities Through Social and Emotional Learning to Reduce Social Marginalization Among Students. In C. Curran & A. Petersen (Eds.), *Handbook of Research on Classroom Diversity and Inclusive Education Practice* (pp. 183–200). Hershey, PA: IGI Global. doi:10.4018/978-1-5225-2520-2.ch008

Randolph, K. M., & Brady, M. P. (2018). Evolution of Covert Coaching as an Evidence-Based Practice in Professional Development and Preparation of Teachers. In V. Bryan, A. Musgrove, & J. Powers (Eds.), *Handbook of Research on Human Development in the Digital Age* (pp. 281–299). Hershey, PA: IGI Global. doi:10.4018/978-1-5225-2838-8.ch013

Rawlins, P., & Kehrwald, B. (2010). Education Technology in Teacher Education: Overcoming Challenges, Realizing Opportunities. In R. Luppicini & A. Haghi (Eds.), *Cases on Digital Technologies in Higher Education: Issues and Challenges* (pp. 50–63). Hershey, PA: IGI Global. doi:10.4018/978-1-61520-869-2.ch004

Rell, A. B., Puig, R. A., Roll, F., Valles, V., Espinoza, M., & Duque, A. L. (2017). Addressing Cultural Diversity and Global Competence: The Dual Language Framework. In L. Leavitt, S. Wisdom, & K. Leavitt (Eds.), *Cultural Awareness and Competency Development in Higher Education* (pp. 111–131). Hershey, PA: IGI Global. doi:10.4018/978-1-5225-2145-7.ch007

Riel, J., Lawless, K. A., & Brown, S. W. (2017). Defining and Designing Responsive Online Professional Development (ROPD): A Framework to Support Curriculum Implementation. In T. Kidd & L. Morris Jr., (Eds.), *Handbook of Research on Instructional Systems and Educational Technology* (pp. 104–115). Hershey, PA: IGI Global. doi:10.4018/978-1-5225-2399-4.ch010

Roberts, C. (2017). Advancing Women Leaders in Academe: Creating a Culture of Inclusion. In S. Mukerji & P. Tripathi (Eds.), *Handbook of Research on Administration, Policy, and Leadership in Higher Education* (pp. 256–273). Hershey, PA: IGI Global. doi:10.4018/978-1-5225-0672-0.ch012

Rodgers, W. J., Kennedy, M. J., Alves, K. D., & Romig, J. E. (2017). A Multimedia Tool for Teacher Education and Professional Development. In C. Martin & D. Polly (Eds.), *Handbook of Research on Teacher Education and Professional Development* (pp. 285–296). Hershey, PA: IGI Global. doi:10.4018/978-1-5225-1067-3.ch015

Romanowski, M. H. (2017). Qatar's Educational Reform: Critical Issues Facing Principals. In I. Management Association (Ed.), *Educational Leadership and Administration: Concepts, Methodologies, Tools, and Applications* (pp. 1758-1773). Hershey, PA: IGI Global. doi:10.4018/978-1-5225-1624-8.ch080

Ruffin, T. R., Hawkins, D. P., & Lee, D. I. (2018). Increasing Student Engagement and Participation Through Course Methodology. In M. Khosrow-Pour, D.B.A. (Ed.), *Encyclopedia of Information Science and Technology, Fourth Edition* (pp. 1463-1473). Hershey, PA: IGI Global. doi:10.4018/978-1-5225-2255-3.ch126

Rutaisire, J. (2011). Innovations in Technology for Educational Marketing: Stakeholder Perceptions and Implications for Examinations System in Rwanda. In P. Tripathi & S. Mukerji (Eds.), *Cases on Innovations in Educational Marketing: Transnational and Technological Strategies* (pp. 214–233). Hershey, PA: IGI Global. doi:10.4018/978-1-60960-599-5.ch013

Sabina, L. L., Curry, K. A., Harris, E. L., Krumm, B. L., & Vencill, V. (2017). Assessing the Performance of a Cohort-Based Model Using Domestic and International Practices. In I. Management Association (Ed.), Educational Leadership and Administration: Concepts, Methodologies, Tools, and Applications(pp. 913-929). Hershey, PA: IGI Global. doi:10.4018/978-1-5225-1624-8.ch044

Santamaría, A. P., Webber, M., & Santamaría, L. J. (2017). Effective School Leadership for Māori Achievement: Building Capacity through Indigenous, National, and International Cross-Cultural Collaboration. In I. Management Association (Ed.), Educational Leadership and Administration: Concepts, Methodologies, Tools, and Applications (pp. 1547-1567). Hershey, PA: IGI Global. doi:10.4018/978-1-5225-1624-8.ch071

Santamaría, L. J. (2017). Culturally Responsive Educational Leadership in Cross-Cultural International Contexts. In I. Management Association (Ed.), Educational Leadership and Administration: Concepts, Methodologies, Tools, and Applications (pp. 1380-1400). Hershey, PA: IGI Global. doi:10.4018/978-1-5225-1624-8.ch064

Sarafidou, J., & Xafakos, E. (2015). Transformational Leadership and Principals' Innovativeness: Are They the "Keys" for the Research and Innovation Oriented School? In K. Beycioglu & P. Pashiardis (Eds.), *Multidimensional Perspectives on Principal Leadership Effectiveness* (pp. 324–348). Hershey, PA: IGI Global. doi:10.4018/978-1-4666-6591-0.ch015

Segredo, M. R., Cistone, P. J., & Reio, T. G. (2017). Relationships Between Emotional Intelligence, Leadership Style, and School Culture. *International Journal of Adult Vocational Education and Technology, 8*(3), 25–43. doi:10.4018/IJAVET.2017070103

Shaik, N., & Ritter, S. (2012). Social Media Based Relationship Marketing. In I. Management Association (Ed.), E-Marketing: Concepts, Methodologies, Tools, and Applications (pp. 88-110). Hershey, PA: IGI Global. doi:10.4018/978-1-4666-1598-4.ch006

Shalev, N. (2017). Empathy and Leadership From the Organizational Perspective. In Z. Nedelko & M. Brzozowski (Eds.), *Exploring the Influence of Personal Values and Cultures in the Workplace* (pp. 348–363). Hershey, PA: IGI Global. doi:10.4018/978-1-5225-2480-9.ch018

Siamak, M., Fathi, S., & Isfandyari-Moghaddam, A. (2018). Assessment and Measurement of Education Programs of Information Literacy. In R. Bhardwaj (Ed.), *Digitizing the Modern Library and the Transition From Print to Electronic* (pp. 164–192). Hershey, PA: IGI Global. doi:10.4018/978-1-5225-2119-8.ch007

Siozos, P. D., & Palaigeorgiou, G. E. (2008). Educational Technologies and the Emergence of E-Learning 2.0. In D. Politis (Ed.), *E-Learning Methodologies and Computer Applications in Archaeology* (pp. 1–17). Hershey, PA: IGI Global. doi:10.4018/978-1-59904-759-1.ch001

Siu, K. W., & García, G. J. (2017). Disruptive Technologies and Education: Is There Any Disruption After All? In I. Management Association (Ed.), Educational Leadership and Administration: Concepts, Methodologies, Tools, and Applications (pp. 757-778). Hershey, PA: IGI Global. doi:10.4018/978-1-5225-1624-8.ch037

Skibba, K., Moore, D., & Herman, J. H. (2013). Pedagogical and Technological Considerations Designing Collaborative Learning Using Educational Technologies. In J. Keengwe (Ed.), *Research Perspectives and Best Practices in Educational Technology Integration* (pp. 1–27). Hershey, PA: IGI Global. doi:10.4018/978-1-4666-2988-2.ch001

Slagter van Tryon, P. J. (2017). The Nurse Educator's Role in Designing Instruction and Instructional Strategies for Academic and Clinical Settings. In J. Stefaniak (Ed.), *Advancing Medical Education Through Strategic Instructional Design* (pp. 133–149). Hershey, PA: IGI Global. doi:10.4018/978-1-5225-2098-6.ch006

Slattery, C. A. (2018). Literacy Intervention and the Differentiated Plan of Instruction. In *Developing Effective Literacy Intervention Strategies: Emerging Research and Opportunities* (pp. 41–62). Hershey, PA: IGI Global. doi:10.4018/978-1-5225-5007-5.ch003

Smith, A. R. (2017). Ensuring Quality: The Faculty Role in Online Higher Education. In K. Shelton & K. Pedersen (Eds.), *Handbook of Research on Building, Growing, and Sustaining Quality E-Learning Programs* (pp. 210–231). Hershey, PA: IGI Global. doi:10.4018/978-1-5225-0877-9.ch011

Souders, T. M. (2017). Understanding Your Learner: Conducting a Learner Analysis. In J. Stefaniak (Ed.), *Advancing Medical Education Through Strategic Instructional Design* (pp. 1–29). Hershey, PA: IGI Global. doi:10.4018/978-1-5225-2098-6.ch001

Spring, K. J., Graham, C. R., & Ikahihifo, T. B. (2018). Learner Engagement in Blended Learning. In M. Khosrow-Pour, D.B.A. (Ed.), Encyclopedia of Information Science and Technology, Fourth Edition (pp. 1487-1498). Hershey, PA: IGI Global. doi:10.4018/978-1-5225-2255-3.ch128

Stocklin, S. (2015). Building Capacity by Managing a Mission. In J. Feng, S. Stocklin, & W. Wang (Eds.), *Educational Strategies for the Next Generation Leaders in Hotel Management* (pp. 115–139). Hershey, PA: IGI Global. doi:10.4018/978-1-4666-8565-9.ch005

Storey, V. A., Anthony, A. K., & Wahid, P. (2017). Gender-Based Leadership Barriers: Advancement of Female Faculty to Leadership Positions in Higher Education. In V. Wang (Ed.), *Encyclopedia of Strategic Leadership and Management* (pp. 244–258). Hershey, PA: IGI Global. doi:10.4018/978-1-5225-1049-9.ch018

Stottlemyer, D. (2018). Develop a Teaching Model Plan for a Differentiated Learning Approach. In *Differentiated Instructional Design for Multicultural Environments: Emerging Research and Opportunities* (pp. 106–130). Hershey, PA: IGI Global. doi:10.4018/978-1-5225-5106-5.ch005

Stottlemyer, D. (2018). Developing a Multicultural Environment. In *Differentiated Instructional Design for Multicultural Environments: Emerging Research and Opportunities* (pp. 1–27). Hershey, PA: IGI Global. doi:10.4018/978-1-5225-5106-5.ch001

Swami, B. N., Gobona, T., & Tsimako, J. J. (2017). Academic Leadership: A Case Study of the University of Botswana. In N. Baporikar (Ed.), *Innovation and Shifting Perspectives in Management Education* (pp. 1–32). Hershey, PA: IGI Global. doi:10.4018/978-1-5225-1019-2.ch001

Swanson, K. W., & Collins, G. (2018). Designing Engaging Instruction for the Adult Learners. In M. Khosrow-Pour, D.B.A. (Ed.), Encyclopedia of Information Science and Technology, Fourth Edition (pp. 1432-1440). Hershey, PA: IGI Global. doi:10.4018/978-1-5225-2255-3.ch123

Swartz, B. A., Lynch, J. M., & Lynch, S. D. (2018). Embedding Elementary Teacher Education Coursework in Local Classrooms: Examples in Mathematics and Special Education. In D. Polly, M. Putman, T. Petty, & A. Good (Eds.), *Innovative Practices in Teacher Preparation and Graduate-Level Teacher Education Programs* (pp. 262–292). Hershey, PA: IGI Global. doi:10.4018/978-1-5225-3068-8.ch015

Taliadorou, N., & Pashiardis, P. (2015). Emotional Intelligence and Political Skill Really Matter in Educational Leadership. In K. Beycioglu & P. Pashiardis (Eds.), *Multidimensional Perspectives on Principal Leadership Effectiveness* (pp. 228–256). Hershey, PA: IGI Global. doi:10.4018/978-1-4666-6591-0.ch011

Taliadorou, N., & Pashiardis, P. (2017). Emotional Intelligence and Political Skill Really Matter in Educational Leadership. In I. Management Association (Ed.), Educational Leadership and Administration: Concepts, Methodologies, Tools, and Applications (pp. 1274-1303). Hershey, PA: IGI Global. doi:10.4018/978-1-5225-1624-8.ch060

Tam, F. W., & Kwan, P. Y. (2011). School Images, School Identity, and How Parents Select Schools for Their Children: The Case of Hong Kong. In P. Tripathi & S. Mukerji (Eds.), *Cases on Innovations in Educational Marketing: Transnational and Technological Strategies* (pp. 87–103). Hershey, PA: IGI Global. doi:10.4018/978-1-60960-599-5.ch005

Tandoh, K. A., & Ebe-Arthur, J. E. (2018). Effective Educational Leadership in the Digital Age: An Examination of Professional Qualities and Best Practices. In J. Keengwe (Ed.), *Handbook of Research on Digital Content, Mobile Learning, and Technology Integration Models in Teacher Education* (pp. 244–265). Hershey, PA: IGI Global. doi:10.4018/978-1-5225-2953-8.ch013

Tinoca, L., Pereira, A., & Oliveira, I. (2014). A Conceptual Framework for E-Assessment in Higher Education: Authenticity, Consistency, Transparency, and Practicability. In S. Mukerji & P. Tripathi (Eds.), *Handbook of Research on Transnational Higher Education* (pp. 652–673). Hershey, PA: IGI Global. doi:10.4018/978-1-4666-4458-8.ch033

Tobin, M. T. (2018). Multimodal Literacy. In M. Khosrow-Pour, D.B.A. (Ed.), Encyclopedia of Information Science and Technology, Fourth Edition (pp. 1508-1516). Hershey, PA: IGI Global. doi:10.4018/978-1-5225-2255-3.ch130

Torres, M. L., & Ramos, V. J. (2018). Music Therapy: A Pedagogical Alternative for ASD and ID Students in Regular Classrooms. In P. Epler (Ed.), *Instructional Strategies in General Education and Putting the Individuals With Disabilities Act (IDEA) Into Practice* (pp. 222–244). Hershey, PA: IGI Global. doi:10.4018/978-1-5225-3111-1.ch008

Toulassi, B. (2017). Educational Administration and Leadership in Francophone Africa: 5 Dynamics to Change Education. In S. Mukerji & P. Tripathi (Eds.), *Handbook of Research on Administration, Policy, and Leadership in Higher Education* (pp. 20–45). Hershey, PA: IGI Global. doi:10.4018/978-1-5225-0672-0.ch002

Umair, S., & Sharif, M. M. (2018). Predicting Students Grades Using Artificial Neural Networks and Support Vector Machine. In M. Khosrow-Pour, D.B.A. (Ed.), Encyclopedia of Information Science and Technology, Fourth Edition (pp. 5169-5182). Hershey, PA: IGI Global. doi:10.4018/978-1-5225-2255-3.ch449

Usman, L. M. (2011). Adult Education and Sustainable Learning Outcome of Rural Widows of Central Northern Nigeria. *International Journal of Adult Vocational Education and Technology*, 2(2), 25–41. doi:10.4018/javet.2011040103

Vettraino, L., Castello, V., Guspini, M., & Guglielman, E. (2018). Self-Awareness and Motivation Contrasting ESL and NEET Using the SAVE System. In M. Khosrow-Pour, D.B.A. (Ed.), Encyclopedia of Information Science and Technology, Fourth Edition (pp. 1559-1568). Hershey, PA: IGI Global. doi:10.4018/978-1-5225-2255-3.ch135

Wang, V. C. (2013). Marketing Educational Programs through Technology and the Right Philosophies. In P. Tripathi & S. Mukerji (Eds.), *Marketing Strategies for Higher Education Institutions: Technological Considerations and Practices* (pp. 15–24). Hershey, PA: IGI Global. doi:10.4018/978-1-4666-4014-6.ch002

Wiemelt, J. (2017). Critical Bilingual Leadership for Emergent Bilingual Students. In I. Management Association (Ed.), Educational Leadership and Administration: Concepts, Methodologies, Tools, and Applications (pp. 1606-1631). Hershey, PA: IGI Global. doi:10.4018/978-1-5225-1624-8.ch074

Williams, D. D. (2006). Measurement and Assessment Supporting Evaluation in Online Settings. In D. Williams, M. Hricko, & S. Howell (Eds.), *Online Assessment, Measurement and Evaluation: Emerging Practices* (pp. 1–9). Hershey, PA: IGI Global. doi:10.4018/978-1-59140-747-8.ch001

Wolf, F., Seyfarth, F. C., & Pflaum, E. (2018). Scalable Capacity-Building for Geographically Dispersed Learners: Designing the MOOC "Sustainable Energy in Small Island Developing States (SIDS)". In U. Pandey & V. Indrakanti (Eds.), *Open and Distance Learning Initiatives for Sustainable Development* (pp. 58–83). Hershey, PA: IGI Global. doi:10.4018/978-1-5225-2621-6.ch003

Woodley, X. M., Mucundanyi, G., & Lockard, M. (2017). Designing Counter-Narratives: Constructing Culturally Responsive Curriculum Online. *International Journal of Online Pedagogy and Course Design, 7*(1), 43–56. doi:10.4018/IJOPCD.2017010104

Woods, P. A., & Woods, G. J. (2011). Lighting the Fires of Entrepreneurialism?: Constructions of Meaning in an English Inner City Academy. *International Journal of Technology and Educational Marketing, 1*(1), 1–24. doi:10.4018/ijtem.2011010101

Yell, M. L., & Christle, C. A. (2017). The Foundation of Inclusion in Federal Legislation and Litigation. In C. Curran & A. Petersen (Eds.), *Handbook of Research on Classroom Diversity and Inclusive Education Practice* (pp. 27–52). Hershey, PA: IGI Global. doi:10.4018/978-1-5225-2520-2.ch002

Zhao, J. (2011). China Special Education: The Perspective of Information Technologies. In P. Ordóñez de Pablos, J. Zhao, & R. Tennyson (Eds.), *Technology Enhanced Learning for People with Disabilities: Approaches and Applications* (pp. 34–43). Hershey, PA: IGI Global. doi:10.4018/978-1-61520-923-1.ch003

Zinger, D. (2016). Developing Instructional Leadership and Communication Skills through Online Professional Development: Focusing on Rural and Urban Principals. In A. Normore, L. Long, & M. Javidi (Eds.), *Handbook of Research on Effective Communication, Leadership, and Conflict Resolution* (pp. 354–370). Hershey, PA: IGI Global. doi:10.4018/978-1-4666-9970-0.ch019

Zutshi, A., Pogrebnaya, M., & Fermelis, J. (2014). Wellness Programs in Higher Education: An Australian Case. In N. Baporikar (Ed.), *Handbook of Research on Higher Education in the MENA Region: Policy and Practice* (pp. 391–419). Hershey, PA: IGI Global. doi:10.4018/978-1-4666-6198-1.ch017

About the Contributors

Sriya Chakravarti is a pedagogical pioneer who has worked with several educational strategy boards and committees to bring innovation into education through curriculum design, program establishment and policymaking. She believes in quality education for all and retains a strong leadership and community development perspective. Dr Chakravarti is fascinated with the role and place of technology in the future of education. Her research explores how education can help us create a better future and if technology infused education can truly deliver equality of opportunity and skills. Dr Chakravarti is a Fellow of the Royal Society of Arts (FRSA, UK) and a Principal Fellow of the Higher Education Academy (PFHEA, UK). She has worked on various educational projects for the United Nations fraternity. Her expertise revolves around hybrid learning, blending learning, gamification in learning and creating microlearning modules. She has researched, developed, taught, and led educational initiatives in the USA, UAE, UK, India, Germany, Malaysia, Mexico, Thailand, Vietnam, Laos, and Cambodia.

* * *

Yalçın Dilekli is an associated professor in the department of curriculum and instruction in the Aksaray Universtiy, Faculty of Education. After 14 years of teaching experience in middle and high schools, he took a PhD degree in curriculum and instruction from Balıkesir University. His research interests are curriculum development, teaching thinking skills, higher ordering thinking skills and teaching-learning process.

Rob Eirich is an educator with over 10 years of teaching experience in mainly business, marketing and digital marketing. His main areas of expertise as an industry practitioner include professional selling, lead generation, customer journey management and marketing analytics.

Mikel Garant is Professor of Applied Linguistics at The College of Global Talent, Beijing Institute of Technology, Zhuhai (BITZH). Dr. Garant's academic interests include multimodality, translation and English language education, and intercultural communication.

Julie Gathercole is a passionate educator who has taught a variety of marketing and business courses at the Southern Alberta Institute of Technology, Mount Royal University, and the University of Victoria. Prior to teaching full-time, Julie spent over fifteen years in marketing and communication leadership roles with numerous well-known organizations such as United Way, TD Bank, Molson Coors, the Government of British Columbia, and the BC Olympic Games Secretariat. When not teaching, Julie volunteers her time with motionball, which engages young professionals and raises funds for Special Olympics Canada, loves to travel and rescues senior dogs. Julie holds a Bachelor of Public Relations from Mount Saint Vincent University and an MBA from Royal Roads.

Sandra Gudino Paredes has a degree in Administration, Master in Educational Technology and a PhD in Educational Innovation from the School of Education and Humanities of the Tecnológico de Monterrey. She currently serves as a teacher and director of the Master of Education, she is certified in Positive Discipline by the PDA Association of the United Kingdom. Member of the Mexican Association of Comparative Education, Association for Moral Education, American Education Research Association (AERA), and the Mexican Council for Educational Research.

Felipe Jasso Pena is coordinator of training and attention to users of the Digital Education Postgraduate programs Tecnologico de Monterrey. Ph.D. with emphasis on Education, Studies master's degrees in education, library and information science, higher education, and public administration. His main work activities are related to teaching and library work.

Mahati Kopparla is a Postdoctoral fellow at the Werklund School of Education, University of Calgary, Canada. Dr. Kopparla's research focusses on bridging the gap between children's experiences in the classroom and their daily life. Specifically, Dr. Kopparla is interested in exploring the scope of STEM education in raising awareness and action towards local and global concerns of social and environmental justice.

Tamar Larsen is a cultural anthropologist and professor of Nordic Studies exploring the intersections of gender, policy, leadership, business, and ethics. She is Director of the Norway Global Seminar at the University of Colorado at Boulder. Tamar has taught at the Haas School of Business at U.C. Berkeley, coached ministry department heads of the African Union in Addis Ababa, Ethiopia, and performed as an artist with the Metropolitan Opera. She finds great mystery in cross-cultural issues surrounding language, identity, and values. She continues to work globally to build bridges between communities, using music, dance, food, and culture to further authentic care of "others". She is a native of Berkeley, California, USA.

Maha Mohammad is an associate professor at the Department of Physiotherapy in the School of Rehabilitation Sciences at The University of Jordan. She obtained her B.Sc. in Physiotherapy from The University of Jordan and M.Sc. and Ph.D. from University of Pittsburgh in the United States. She teaches the neurology courses in the B.Sc. and M.Sc. programs. Dr. Mohammad currently serves as the head of the department.

Şenol Orakcı is an assistant professor in the Department of Curriculum and Instruction at Aksaray University in Turkey. His scholarship focuses on teacher education, curriculum studies, and international education. He has published several books, book chapters, articles and conference papers in the field of Curriculum and Instruction.

Martin Parsons is a Professor at Hannan University in Osaka Japan. His research interests include multimodality, CALL, CLIL and English language education in Japan.

Aditi Pathak has over 15 years of experience in the field of education and is currently working with UNESCO MGIEP as a National Programme Officer.

Dania Qutishat is an Associate Professor at the Department of Physiotherapy in the School of Rehabilitation Sciences at The University of Jordan. She obtained her B.Sc. in Physiotherapy from The University of Jordan and M.Sc. and Ph.D. from Sheffield Hallam University in the UK. Research interests include physiotherapy higher education, ethics in rehabilitation and physical activity. She is the course leader of different courses in the B.Sc. and M.Sc. programs especially those related to management in physiotherapy and exercise prescription.

Emily Saavedra is a Senior Lecturer at Massey University, Aotearoa New Zealand, and a Senior Fellow of the Higher Education Academy. She is currently the Academic Coordinator for Foundation Education at Massey University based in Auckland. Prior to joining Massey University, she has taught in a variety of contexts across South America, Asia, the Middle East, and New Zealand. Her current interests include blended learning, curriculum design, inter-cultural intelligence, and supporting students to achieve their potential within an academic context. She holds a Doctor of Education from the University of Southern Queensland, Australia.

Leonard Sanders has a PhD in English and Cultural Studies from Massey University. He is currently teaching critical academic literacies, core competencies, and Foundation Humanities and Social Sciences at Massey University, Auckland, Aotearoa New Zealand. Leonard's teaching career includes over twenty years in tertiary institutions in Japan, mostly at Komazawa University, Tokyo. He has experience in various roles within the tertiary context and is especially interested in cross-cultural interactions, media studies, and blended learning.

Index

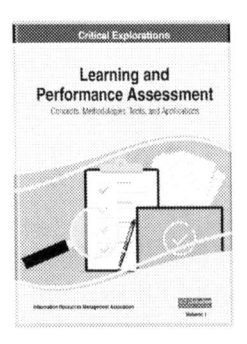

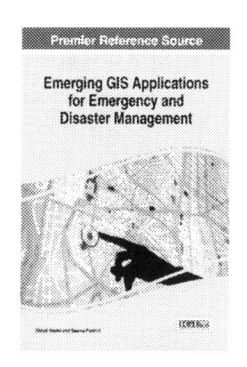

IGI Global Author Services

Providing a high-quality, affordable, and expeditious service, IGI Global's Author Services enable authors to streamline their publishing process, increase chance of acceptance, and adhere to IGI Global's publication standards.

Benefits of Author Services:

- **Professional Service:** All our editors, designers, and translators are experts in their field with years of experience and professional certifications.
- **Quality Guarantee & Certificate:** Each order is returned with a quality guarantee and certificate of professional completion.
- **Timeliness:** All editorial orders have a guaranteed return timeframe of 3-5 business days and translation orders are guaranteed in 7-10 business days.
- **Affordable Pricing:** IGI Global Author Services are competitively priced compared to other industry service providers.
- **APC Reimbursement:** IGI Global authors publishing Open Access (OA) will be able to deduct the cost of editing and other IGI Global author services from their OA APC publishing fee.

Author Services Offered:

English Language Copy Editing
Professional, native English language copy editors improve your manuscript's grammar, spelling, punctuation, terminology, semantics, consistency, flow, formatting, and more.

Scientific & Scholarly Editing
A Ph.D. level review for qualities such as originality and significance, interest to researchers, level of methodology and analysis, coverage of literature, organization, quality of writing, and strengths and weaknesses.

Figure, Table, Chart & Equation Conversions
Work with IGI Global's graphic designers before submission to enhance and design all figures and charts to IGI Global's specific standards for clarity.

Translation
Providing 70 language options, including Simplified and Traditional Chinese, Spanish, Arabic, German, French, and more.

Hear What the Experts Are Saying About IGI Global's Author Services

"Publishing with IGI Global has been *an amazing experience* for me for sharing my research. The *strong academic production* support ensures quality and timely completion." – **Prof. Margaret Niess, Oregon State University, USA**

"The service was *very fast, very thorough, and very helpful* in ensuring our chapter meets the criteria and requirements of the book's editors. I was *quite impressed and happy* with your service." – **Prof. Tom Brinthaupt, Middle Tennessee State University, USA**

Learn More or Get Started Here: For Questions, Contact IGI Global's Customer Service Team at cust@igi-global.com or 717-533-8845

IGI Global
PUBLISHER of TIMELY KNOWLEDGE
www.igi-global.com